Human–Computer Interface Design

A. G. Sutcliffe

Professor of Systems Engineering
School of Informatics
City University, London

SECOND EDITON

MACMILLAN

First edition 1988
Second edition 1995

Published by
MACMILLAN PRESS LTD
Houndmills, Basingstoke, Hampshire RG21 2XS
and London
Companies and representatives
throughout the world

ISBN 0–333–59499–1

A catalogue record for this book is available from the British Library.

Typeset by Richard Powell Editorial and Production Services, Basingstoke, Hampshire RG22 4TX

Printed in Great Britain by Antony Rowe Ltd, Chippenham, Wiltshire

10 9 8 7 6 5 4 3 2 1
04 03 02 01 00 99 98 97 96 95

Contents

Preface

The motivation for this book started when I introduced a course on Human–Computer Interaction in the BSc Computation degree at UMIST and looked for a course textbook. At the time (1984) there were few books on the subject as a whole and no really suitable textbooks for undergraduate courses. Although that situation has now changed, I find my motivation undiluted for another reason. Increasingly, human–computer interaction has become part of software development which practitioners in industry and academics recognise as important, yet the subject is taught in very few computer science courses. Even when it is, HCI is often treated as an 'add on' rather than as an integral part of software engineering. Unless we educate the system developers who are being trained now, there is little chance of changing the current practice of poor interface design.

The primary aim of this book is to give knowledge of the theory, models and methods relevant to human–computer interaction, and skills for designing better human–computer interfaces. As computer scientists are the major creators of software and, hence, human–computer interfaces, it is vital that they acquire knowledge and good practices of interface design. If this part of their education is neglected, poor interfaces will continue to be foisted on users, making systems frustrating or unbearable, even though the internal software might be a perfect example of good software engineering practices. I have attempted to place interface design into a framework of software development by drawing on methods from systems analysis and design as well as ideas in human–computer interaction. Accordingly, I place HCI and its components within the systems design life cycle.

User interface design concerns designing for people. It seems commonsense for designers to be knowledgeable about the subject of their designs, in this case people. Therefore, some appreciation of human psychology is important to human–computer interaction; principally, perception and cognition, which cover how we see, hear, think, learn and remember. It was not my intention to turn computer scientists into psychologists, so the treatment of psychological material has to be brief and is presented without extensive reference to background research.

In addition to providing psychological background to the subject, this book aims to teach a methodical approach and practical skills in user interface design. The material is organised in four sections. Chapters 1 and 2 introduce the nature of HCI as an engineering-based discipline and cover the psychological background, establishing general principles of human–computer interaction. Chapter 3 introduces task analysis and the method of interface design which continues in Chapter 6 (dialogue) and 7 (presentation) as a method thread. Chapter 8 supplements this thread by considering information systems user interfaces in more detail. Chapters 4 and 5 investigate the artefacts/architectures side of HCI, so the tools for building interfaces are interleaved with how to design interfaces in Chapters 3 to 8. Quality assurance, usability and evaluation methods are described in Chapter 9 to complete the method thread. Chapter 10 is more specialised in that it covers more advanced material such as intelligent user interfaces and explanation. Chapter 11 concludes with an examination of Computer Supported Co-operative Work, alternative approaches to design, and a brief survey of current research topics in the subject.

Human–computer interaction is a large field of endeavour with ill-defined edges. An undergraduate text covering the whole field would be impossible; I have therefore been selective in the topics for study. Many issues which are more hardware-oriented are not treated in depth; also, system environment issues, social consequences of computer systems, and experimental design in the psychological tradition receive little space. These topics are more than capably investigated by others whose works are cited in the references.

It is a pleasure to acknowledge the help and stimulation I have received from members of the Centre for HCI Design at City, who have contributed many research and teaching ideas in this book. Also, I am indebted to Gillian Martin's painstaking work in checking and proofreading the text. Any inaccuracies which remain are of my own making. Finally, my last motivation for taking up the author's pen was self-interest. The first edition of this book was prepared on a variety of word processing software with inadequate interfaces. Advances in the usability of word processing software has made the second edition easier to prepare, although text–image integration is still not as easy as it should be and some software is showing dangerous signs of actually becoming worse, as more icons crowd menu bars in each successive release. Even though HCI has made great advances we need to be on our guard. The quest to stamp out user vicious software will be with us for many years to come.

Centre for HCI Design, City University, January 1995 AGS

Acknowledgements

The author and publishers wish to thank the following for permission to use copyright material:

G. H. Fisher for illustrations of a duck/rabbit series from 'Materials for Experimental Studies of Ambiguous and Embedded Figures', *Research Bulletin of the Department of Psychology*, University of Newcastle upon Tyne, No. 4 (Figure 2.4, part).

Oxford University Press for the illustration of a hawk/goose from N. Tinbergen, *The Study of Instinct*, The Clarendon Press, 1951; and part of an illustration of mach bands from John P. Frisby, *Seeing: Illusion, Brain and Mind*, 1979 (Figures 2.3 and 2.4, part).

Academic Press, Inc. for an illustration of a speech spectogram by Peter Bailey in *Fundamentals of Human Computer Interaction*, edited by A. Monk, 1985, Figure 12.3 (Figure 2.7).

Harcourt Brace and Company for the illustration of the Hermann Grid from Peter H. Lindsay and Donald A. Norman, *Human Information Processing: An Introduction*, 2nd edn (Figure 1.38, p. 39), © 1977 by Harcourt Brace and Company.

Jakob Nielsen for Figures 5.8 and 5.9.

Every effort has been made to trace all of the copyright holders, but if any has been inadvertently overlooked, the publishers will be pleased to make the necessary arrangements at the first opportunity.

1 Introduction

This chapter sets the scene for interface design by first placing the human–computer interface within the context of human factors, software engineering and related subjects, and then exploring some justifications for why it is necessary to spend time and money designing human–computer interfaces. The chapter then reviews the debate within the Human–Computer Interaction (HCI) community about scientific and engineering approaches to the subject.

1.1 What is Human–Computer Interface Design?

Design of the human–computer interface is part of a wider subject area of Human–Computer Interaction. This, generally, but not exclusively, fits within Computer Science and is becoming an established part of the curriculum. However, HCI is an evolving subject and its boundaries are far from clear. I shall start, therefore, by drawing some boundaries around HCI and discussing its relationship with other subjects.

Some history

HCI has formed from a coalescence of interests and knowledge drawn from computer science and psychology, although it has also drawn upon linguistics, sociology, applied psychology, ergonomics and management science. Historically it started life as the Man–Machine Interface, in the early 1970s; see, for instance, James Martin's book on dialogue design (Martin, 1973). The Man–Machine Interface (MMI) was recognised in the UK's Alvey research programme as a sector alongside software engineering, intelligent knowledge-based systems and hardware. Further interest was stimulated by recognition in the EC's Esprit research initiative and the Japanese fifth-generation project. As a result MMI became an established area of research endeavour and was renamed, to the politically more correct 'Human–Computer Interaction'. The track record in industrial practice has been less encouraging. Most industrial structured development methods make little reference to HCI, although more recent versions (e.g. SSADM version 4, Object oriented analysis; Coad and Yourdon, 1991) do have sections on the human–computer interface, and some reference is made to graphical user interface design. The uptake of HCI methods in software design has been negligible. The success story, however, lies in the now all-pervasive technology of graphical user interfaces (GUIs). GUIs, originally pioneered by Xerox in the 1970s, were developed into a market winning product by Apple. The market success of Apple computers, rising from a small personal computer manufacturer to a dominant multibillion dollar corporation, is a testament to the importance of good interface design.

Interface design and HCI

Human–Computer Interface design, in the sense used in this book, is the engineering process of designing interactive computer systems so that they are efficient, pleasing, easy to use and do what people want. Interface design is related to the software engineering part of computer science. However, the human–computer interface covers more than software and hardware design; it is also concerned with the system environment and human organisations. Although software is the main component of interface design, design of the people part of systems, e.g. user procedures, manuals, etc., cannot be ignored. This book is focused on interactive system design, but it also covers a broader range of topics to give an introduction to the subject of HCI as a whole.

HCI research covers a broad field ranging from the environment in which the interactive system is situated, the effect of the interface on people, both individuals and groups, to techniques, methods and tools to help designers build interactive systems. HCI design subdivides into background theory and knowledge upon which design is based; issues related to the design process such as methods, principles and techniques; tool support for the design process; and, finally, quality assurance of the product. Hence, the core issues are:

- Understanding the essential properties of people which affects their interaction with computers.
- Analysing what people do with computer systems and their interfaces; understanding users' tasks and requirements.
- Specifying how the interface should function, how it should respond to the user, and its appearance.
- Designing interfaces so that users' needs are fulfilled and the system matches users' characteristics.
- Development of tools to help designers build better interfaces.
- Evaluating the properties of human–computer interfaces and their effect on people to ensure good quality.

Many of these topics would fit in a book on software engineering if references to people were deleted and interfaces substituted with systems. Indeed, interface design can be seen as user-centred system design and a further parallel can be drawn with software engineering:

- HCI in the small (programming in the small) deals with detail of interaction such as interactive devices, widgets, or formal specification of restricted dialogue sequences. This addresses how to design the detail of

interaction.
- HCI in the large is concerned with what to design and how an application should help people achieve a job of work. This perspective has a common motivation with subjects such as systems analysis and requirements engineering.

This book deals with both perspectives. Although the emphasis is primarily on the design process, the wider aspects of HCI will also be covered, e.g.

- Theories and models of interaction, the branch of HCI which attempts to understand what 'interaction' means in fundamental terms.
- Interactive artefacts; these are products of HCI which are becoming subjects almost in their own right, such as Hypertext, Multimedia, and more recently, Virtual Reality.
- Computer Supported Co-operative Work (CSCW), HCI at the group level of interaction.

1.2 Why Design Interfaces?

Before investing time, money and effort in any endeavour the prudent will always ask whether it is worth the investment. This section aims to convince you that it is.

First of all there is the penalty of designing applications with poor interfaces. People have complained for a long time that computer systems are difficult to use, jargon-ridden and obtuse. For many years they had to put up with this state of affairs because most systems were on large mainframe computers, had to be used as part of someone's job and were written by programmers in data processing departments who rarely met a user. Even when user complaints were received, most were ignored. The advent of the personal computer changed the situation. Users had direct control of systems, many could program their own applications, and computers came out of the office and into people's homes. Users would no longer tolerate user-vicious interfaces. Good interface design has become vital because of:

- Market choice in off-the-shelf software: people buy a product because they like its appearance, and what they see and try out is the interface.
- User resistance to poor interfaces: as standards are set by the market, people are less tolerant of bad interfaces in the bespoke designed system they use in their work environment.
- Poor interfaces can lead to system failure or inefficient usage. A good interface can rescue an otherwise poor software design; however, a bad interface will cause rejection of a system even though it may have excellent internal software design.

A further motivation is that HCI is rapidly becoming regulated by standards. ISO (International Standards Organization), which develops standards in association with national organisations such as BSI (UK), ANSI (USA) and DIN (Germany), is in the process of agreeing a raft of standards for HCI design under ISO 9241 (Stewart, 1991). Some parts of this standard are already official international standards (9421 parts 1–3, General Introduction, Guidance on Task Requirements, and Visual Display Requirements). Many other parts will be agreed soon. This means that good HCI products can be certified for an interface 'kite mark' (the badge of approval of the British Standards Institute), and hence gain competitive advantage. On the other hand, poor designs may be legally actionable under UK and European law. ISO VDU standards have already ensured that employers protect workers from eyesight problems which may be caused by prolonged usage. In the near future designers could be sued for poor design.

Interface design is important whether a system is to be sold as a product or developed as an in-house application. Computer systems are becoming increasingly interactive. As they do so the amount of code written for input and output (i.e. the interface) has increased. In most commercial information systems about 50% of the code is devoted to interface handling, so the interface is not only the most critical part of the system but also the largest and most expensive part of many projects.

The economic justification for good interface design is not hard to argue, although statistics to back up the arguments are hard to find, as is the case for software reliability and application of formal software engineering methods. However, several case studies have been reported. A small sample of these to make the case for good HCI are:

- A major computer company saved $41 700 in one day by making sign-on faster in a security application. This was achieved by iterative design (Karat, 1990).
- Improvements in the flight deck interface allowed the Boeing 757 to be flown by two pilots instead of three (Harris, 1984).
- A telephone company achieved a saving of $41 700 in a single day by reducing the time spent on enquiries by operators. Even though good design only delivered a small time saving per enquiry, the cumulative effect over millions of enquiries was enormous.

Poor interface design can have the following consequences:

- Increased frequency of errors in system operation and data entry. Mistakes cost time and money to rectify and errors which are not corrected can have damaging consequences if decisions are taken on inaccurate data.
- Poor system performance. The system may not handle the transaction volume it was designed for, or the accuracy of output may not achieve

targets, because the system is cumbersome to use and difficult to learn.

- System failure because of user rejection. This may be an extreme case considering users' tolerance of appalling software interfaces, but it happens. The US Department of Defense attributes its worst system failures to a combination of poor interface design and inadequate requirements analysis. Poor interface design can lead to market failure of off-the-shelf packages.
- User frustration, which may be manifest in low productivity, under-utilisation of the system, employee stress and, in extreme cases, sabotage of the system. All these consequences cost money and some may result in court cases under standards legislation.

Good interface design is essential for effective systems. This includes HCI in the large as well as the small. The system must help users to achieve their goals and carry out work more effectively. Furthermore, interactive systems should go beyond current practice and empower users so they can carry out work in new and more creative ways. Word processing is a good example of this. Most people can now write and format documents in ways which were difficult if not impossible with typewriters. Finally, systems should be pleasing to use and even fun. The enormous growth of the computer games sector shows the power of attractive stimulating interfaces in the market place.

In the past people have tolerated a variety of poor interactive systems. This is unlikely to be so in the future. Most people have been exposed to personal computer software with graphical user interfaces. While these interfaces are far from perfect, they are a quantum leap from the old-style command prompt systems such as CP/M and DOS. Good interface design is rapidly becoming the norm which cannot be ignored.

1.3 Approaches to HCI

Design is not an intuitive process. True, some designers have a flair for good, innovative design, but most people do not. Design is a process which has to be taught. It is a matter of applying knowledge to a problem and systematically working through a set of issues which, if addressed successfully, will lead to a good design. The knowledge may be guidelines, principles and techniques bound together by a method which shows designers how to proceed. As experience and design practice mature, more formal procedures and specification may be introduced. Currently the state of knowledge of HCI is largely at the stage of guidelines and principles. These are now widely available (e.g. Smith and Mosier, 1986; Brown, 1988; Mayhew, 1992; ISO 9421 draft standard parts 10–16) giving advice on a wide range of HCI issues. These can be supplemented by style guides (e.g. Apple, 1987; IBM, 1991) which advise about HCI in the small, such as how menus, command lines, windows and sliders, etc., should appear and be used in a design. The aim is to give a consistent 'look and feel' to all interfaces designed with the style. Style guides are offered with user interface development tool kits so the guides come with a set of interface building blocks which the designer can use to construct an application. These components, usually called 'widgets', implement menu panels, dialogue boxes, buttons, sliders, etc. Some of the more common style guides and look and feel environments are:

- *OSF/Motif.* Based on the Unix operating system and provides a UI development kit incorporating X-Windows, which is a lower-level UI widget set.
- *Apple MacApp.* The Apple development environment which is now evolving into a new multimedia version called Bedrock.
- *IBM CUA.* The Common User Access interface from IBM was intended to be a standard across all IBM operating systems, although it has been more influential on the PS/2, and IBM version of Unix.
- *Microsoft Windows.* This GUI environment was built on top of DOS as an answer to Apple. Microsoft Windows is probably the most widespread UI development environment.
- *Hewlett Packard's New Wave.* HP's version of the development environment also based on the Unix operating system.

Styles guides and development environments will be covered in more depth in Chapter 4. Although these environments and their associated guidelines can have improved interface design, they do not guarantee a usable interface. For that systematic methods, knowledge and experience are required.

Theories, models and craft

Different approaches can be adopted to the design problem. Long and Dowell (1989) proposed a three-level model to summarise how HCI design is and may be practised:

- *Craft level.* Design is by intuition and based on experience. The guarantee of getting a good design is limited by the talent and experience of individual designers. Much interface design today is still practised at the craft level. This situation is clearly unsatisfactory, as no one learns from the practice. There is no way of generalising lessons from one design to another.
- *Engineering.* Design is practised according to a set of systematic principles and methods. The guarantee of getting a good design is substantially improved as principles and methods can be taught. Poor designers will become better and even good designers may improve. The better examples of current HCI practice may be at the entry point on this level, but there is

still a long way to go. Engineering has to get its principles from somewhere. This leads to the next level, applied science.

- *Applied science*. Design is directly informed by the results from scientific investigation; in HCI this will be applied psychology. Unfortunately this leads to a dilemma. Psychology can prove facts about the world by experimentation, but it does so slowly. Each experiment takes time and usually only proves one or two facts. Interactive systems are composed of thousands of potentially uncertain facts, which psychology cannot prove to be true or false. Even worse, many of these facts influence each other, so it is hard to design experiments which prove general qualities of interfaces. This leads to the pessimistic conclusion that applied science may not be able to help.

However, some approaches have been proposed to solve the Engineering v. Science debate in the three levels of HCI. These are bridging models which try to link cognitive science to models more applicable to HCI design, while task artefact theory takes a more radical approach of focusing on products.

Bridging models

If experimental psychology cannot help HCI directly, then it may be able to do so indirectly. Cognitive psychology has proposed a series of models which describe and predict various aspects of human reasoning, memory and learning. Principles may be derived from these models to inform HCI design. Furthermore, such models may be used as 'tools for thought' by HCI designers. However, general cognitive models rarely have the ability to predict what users may do in a specific context. The influence of task and domain knowledge is usually vital for understanding a design problem.

To answer this challenge bridging models have been proposed (Barnard, 1991). These intermediate models are based on basic cognitive models but also include task and domain knowledge, thus enabling more specific predictions to be made. However, constructing such models so the predictions use cognitive theory as well as contextual information is not easy. Furthermore, building such models can be very time consuming; consequently, this approach has not solved the problem so far. Nevertheless, bridging models have their uses and a simple one will be introduced in Chapter 2.

HCI artefacts

This approach concentrates on the product rather than the design process. The idea is that well-engineered HCI products should incorporate good ideas. These ideas if described and formalised can be seen as theories of HCI, i.e. they explain and predict properties of good design within the scope or purpose for which an artefact was designed. Thus, HCI could progress by understanding how to design classes of artefacts rather than using universal models or principles. This has been developed as the task–artefact cycle (Carroll, 1989; Carroll *et al.*, 1991). Development and understanding proceed hand in hand (see Figure 1.1). The artefact or product is evaluated and more generalisable truths are extracted by 'claims analysis'. These truths are then fed back into the pool of HCI knowledge. New artefacts are designed by first understanding their purpose through a task analysis. Theory and principles may be imported from cognitive psychology to inform design. The artefact is then built and evaluated going through a cycle of iterative improvement. One problem with this approach is defining the scope of an artefact and how generalisable the claims can be. For instance, hypertext (see Chapter 7) can be seen as a good and successful HCI artefact. Claims can be extracted about why this should be so, but how far these claims can be applied to the design of related artefacts (e.g. information retrieval products) is unclear.

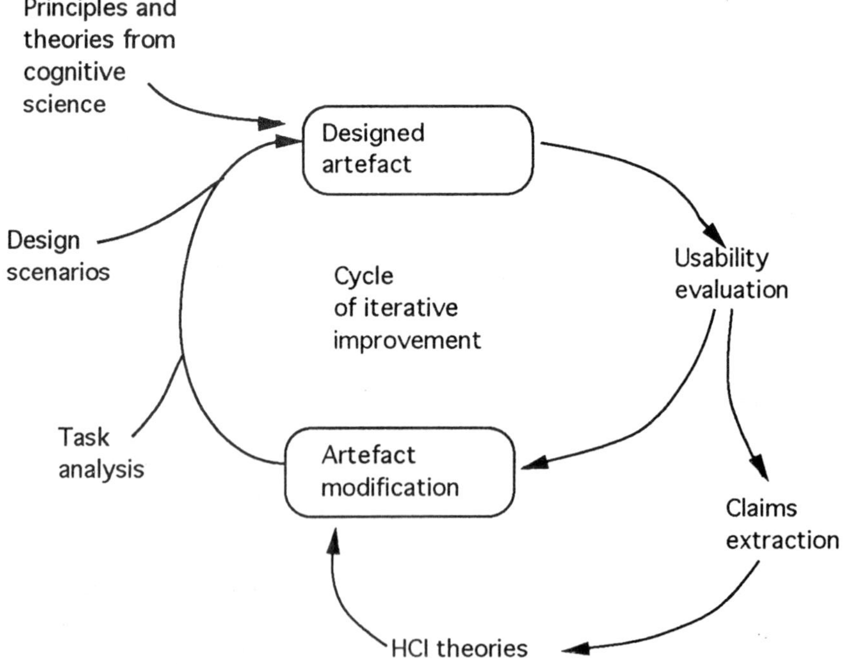

Figure 1.1 Task–artefact cycle (after Carroll, 1989).

Engineering principles

These follow the concept of civil and mechanical engineering design. If principles and rules can be devised, then designers should have predictive guidance for certain problem situations. For instance, bridge designers know how certain classes of bridge design are good for specific problems and how materials in bridge pillars will react to stress and load. Could HCI designs be amenable to similar treatment? Unfortunately, HCI is itself still dependent on an underlying science, psychology, which is far from complete. It is hard to derive design rules from rival theories of cognition. Worse still, computer systems are built in a bewildering variety of domains, so it is difficult to specify a problem class. Nevertheless, design principles can help, especially if they are given with scoping rules and caveats to explain when they may and may not apply. The engineering approach also advocates methods which bind principles and guidelines together into an agenda of issues which must be attended to. The engineering approach is the main theme followed in this book, although successful design will probably require all three, so I shall pick and mix these approaches where they complement each other.

1.4 HCI and Other Disciplines

One particular discipline, *ergonomics*, has made a considerable contribution to human–computer interaction. Ergonomics, also called human factors in the USA, is a branch of applied psychology which aims to improve the design of machines for people. Many of the recommendations from ergonomics can be applied to computers, in terms of both hardware, e.g. how VDU terminals should be constructed and positioned, and software, e.g. how the appearance of VDU displays is controlled. While several ergonomic issues will be described, constraints of space mean that many hardware and environmental issues, such as ergonomics of office design, lighting, seating, etc., will not be covered. Such detail could be found in Galer (1987).

Another important influence on HCI has been *cognitive psychology*. This is a branch of psychology which deals with theories, models and experimental investigations on mental phenomena such as memory, reasoning, problem solving and perception. Cognitive science uses computers extensively and shares many of the same motivations as Artificial Intelligence (AI), i.e. understanding how people and machines can think and learn. HCI draws upon cognitive psychology for models and theories of human–computer interaction. Psychology is an important parent science for HCI, as it supplies knowledge about people. Designing computer systems for people needs to take human cognitive abilities and limitations into account. *Linguistics* and *computational linguistics* share an interest in communication with HCI. Natural-language dialogues draw upon work in computational linguistics, while other influences come from discourse models of human–human communication .

Sociology also contributes knowledge to HCI, although so far its influence has been less important than psychology. Computer-supported co-operative work (CSCW) is a sub-area of HCI concerned with group work and computer tools to support such activity. Sociology contributes theories of group action and communication to help CSCW design, although, as with cognitive models, the influence of theory on design is often hard to find. Sociology has also contributed to the methodology of HCI in the large and requirements engineering by hermeneutics or ethnomethodology. Whether such methods and approaches become part of HCI or mainstream software engineering remains to be seen.

HCI and computer science

HCI permeates many parts of computer science. Its closest relatives are software engineering and subjects concerned with software design, e.g. systems analysis, specification and design. It is also related to artificial intelligence (AI) and knowledge-based systems, as many advanced interfaces require intelligent processes. Natural language, for instance, is a means of human–computer communication which requires AI.

The methodological part of HCI addresses many issues also found in software engineering. Requirements analysis is a common concern, while task analysis and systems analysis show many similarities. Both analyse functions and data structures, and object orientation influences both subjects. Specification is also an area of convergence, as software engineering formalisms have been used to specify the behaviour of interactive dialogues. Interactive software is as amenable to formal design as is any other software module, and a branch of HCI has applied formalisation to develop principles for design, specification techniques, and to a limited extent proof of designs against criteria for good interactivity. It is essential that HCI become an integral part of software engineering, in its formal context and in pragmatic methods for industrial systems development such as SSADM (Structured Systems Analysis and Design Methodology). To meet this aim, most of the design method presented in this book is placed within the context of SSADM, which, while not perfect, can claim to be the market leading method for commercial systems development in the UK.

Artificial intelligence shares HCI's interest in cognitive psychology. Both disciplines construct models of reasoning, memory and problem solving, although their approaches and perspective differ. AI is motivated towards building machines which can exhibit human-like qualities in language, vision, reasoning and learning, whereas HCI's interest is in using knowledge-based systems to help interaction. This happens in natural-language interfaces, intelligent dialogue management, adaptable user interfaces and intelligent agents.

HCI also shares interests with software architectures in computer science. Methods, techniques and guidelines will not be effective unless they are embedded with computerised support tools. HCI so far has had little influence on the CASE (Computer-Aided Software Engineering) community. In the future HCI will become a standard component of such tools as much as software engineering methods and principles. Interfaces are rapidly becoming more sophisticated and the construction of user interface design environments and UI management systems is becoming a subject in its own right. This theme is returned to in Chapter 9.

In conclusion, HCI is a core component of the computer science curriculum. It is an essential complement to software engineering and systems analysis/ design, and shares much with artificial intelligence.

1.5 Summary

This chapter has introduced the subject matter of HCI. A case for the importance of HCI in computer systems design has been made from the economic penalties of poor design practice. Poor interfaces increase errors and stress. Systems with poor interfaces will be underused or rejected; furthermore, designers will soon become liable for bad interfaces under standards legislation.

An outline of the subject matter of HCI is given. Approaches to theory and concepts of HCI start with the three-layer model of craft, engineering and applied science. Other variations such as bridging models, the influence of psychology on design and task artefact theory give different perspectives. HCI is an engineering type of discipline but it also embraces theoretical study and computer architectures for user interfaces. For more details on this debate see Carroll (1991).

The relationship of HCI to psychology and sociology is reviewed along with its place within computer science. HCI draws theory from psychology and to a lesser extent sociology. It is a core part of computer science and with software engineering constitutes the study of software design. HCI also shares many issues with artificial intelligence and uses knowledge-based systems in intelligent interfaces.

2 User Psychology

This chapter gives an overview of cognitive psychology which is relevant to human–computer interaction. It starts with how we perceive information from the environment with the senses of sight and hearing and then progresses to understanding the information we receive. Memory is then investigated; how information is coded and possibly stored, with the limitations of human memory. This leads on to mental activity and how we reason and solve problems. The control of mental activity as attention is reviewed with more general topics of stress and fatigue. The chapter concludes with a summary of principles of interaction based on knowledge of human psychology.

2.1 Understanding Users

Throughout this chapter a metaphor of a human–computer will be used, with the objective, I hope, of making human reasoning easier to understand. Please note that this view is just a model of how things may operate in the human mind based on psychological study; it is by no means a definitive statement of how the human brain is structured or how it operates. Such topics are still active areas of psychological research. Viewing the brain in terms of processors, memories and messages is a convenient analogy, nothing more.

Basic anatomy of the human processor

The human brain is composed of a vast number of nerve cells, estimates varying around 15 billion. Nerve cells are the basic elements of human information processing and memory. Nerve cells communicate by electrical signals, although this is not the same as in electrical circuits; instead it is electrochemical communication. This means that the human brain is not strictly digital like computers; rather, it works by a mixture of digital and analogue computing. Nerve cells can send signals to each other to indicate a state change, thus creating the digital 1/0 states necessary for computation. Nerve signals (called *impulses*) travel along nerve cells but to transfer to the next cell they must cross an intercell gap. This gap is very small (2–5 microns) but so is the electrical voltage, which means it cannot jump the gap. Inter-cell transmission is by chemical means. This electrochemical activity means that the speed of nerve messages is slow compared with speeds of electrical signals in computers.

Electrical signals from nerve cells usually come as a series of bursts, each signal being a transient 010 state change. The effect they have on receiving cells is to either increase or decrease the tendency of a receiving nerve to fire, giving a graded analogue effect. Inter-nerve cell connections can therefore be *inhibitory* and damp down a cell's activity, or *excitatory* and stimulate it. As most nerve cells in the brain have an average of 150 connections, this composite influence can be very complex and is capable of much more complex coding than in digital electronics. A recent branch of computer science, *neural computing*, has developed to build artificial versions of nervous processors.

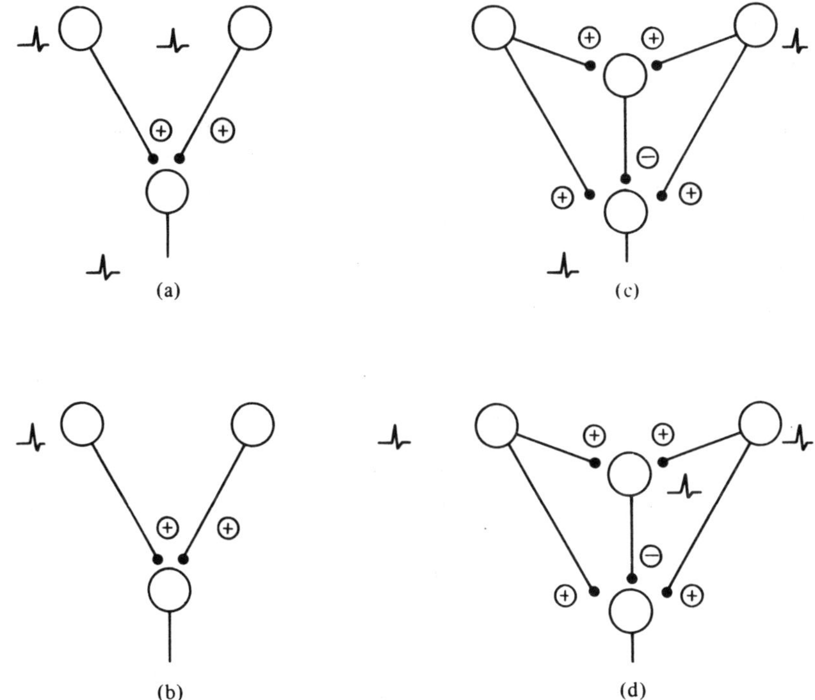

Figure 2.1 Connections between nerve cells to form a human logic circuit. The effect on the receiving cell depends on both the frequency of the impulses received from sending cells and the type of connection, which may be excitatory or inhibitory.

Neural AND is shown in (a) and (b). The upper cells both have excitatory connections to the lower, but both must fire as in (a) to make the lower cell fire. If one alone fires as in (b), the lower cell does not reach its threshold to fire.

An OR gate is shown in (c) and (d). Here a third cell is introduced in the middle which has excitatory connections from the upper ones but has an inhibitory connection to the lower one. One upper cell will trigger the lower but not the middle cell (OR); however, both upper cells fire the middle cell, which then inhibits the lower one from firing (the AND condition).

Nerve cells and their artificial equivalents in neural nets are organised in complex lattices and networks. The effect the cells have on one another is determined not only by the quantity of impulses they receive from other nerve cells but also by the sensitivity of their reaction. Some cells require many impulses to excite them sufficiently to fire, while others are tuned to hair-trigger levels. Tuning and different inhibitory or excitatory connections can imitate AND/OR logic gates and other familiar computer logic components, as illustrated in Figure 2.1. The use of feedback connections allows nerve cells to alter their connections according to patterns of input. This property allows the network to learn as new connections can be made and old ones suppressed.

Nerve cells in the brain are highly interconnected in a very complex network. The human wiring diagram is infinitely more complex and subtle than the most advanced micro processor and is still poorly understood. Attempts to follow the real architecture of the brain at lower levels at present are unrewarding; therefore to further our understanding of the human machine we shall use an abstract model, that is an interpretation of how the logical processing units in the brain may work.

Cognitive models

These models have been devised by psychologists to explain human mental activity by an analogy with computer processing. It is important to remember that models are only an abstraction; the final story of how the human machine works will be much more complex. Cognitive models, however, are useful because they illustrate the advantages and limitations of the human machine. In interface design we shall need to take these qualities into account. In the following sections perception and cognition will be explored using an information processing model based on research at Xerox by Card *et al.* (1983).

Another more recent model, Interactive Cognitive Sub-systems (Barnard *et al.*, 1988) will also be used to explain human information processing from a different viewpoint. All models require input from the outside world. This concerns *perception*, the process of receiving information from the outside world, while *cognition* is the mental activity we describe in everyday terms, as reasoning, problem solving, thinking and learning. The boundary between the two is blurred because, as we receive information, we also interpret it. We shall look at the receptive processes first.

2.2 Vision

Vision is the dominant sense we use when interacting with computers, which has implications for VDU screen design and other display devices.

Visual perception poses three problems:

- Receiving an external stimulus, in this case the electromagnetic radiation as light.

- Translating the stimulus into nerve impulses in a manner faithful to the stimulus.
- Attaching meaning to the stimulus.

To resolve the first problem nerve cells have to be sensitive to light. Light is a form of electromagnetic radiation with a wavelength between 400 and 700 nanometres (nm). Other forms of radiation have longer wavelengths, e.g. infrared radiation or heat, 1000 nm; or shorter wavelengths, such as X-rays. Within visible light, colour subdivisions are defined by wavelength; at the longer wavelengths (650–700 nm) is red light, progressing through the colours of the spectrum to blue light at short wavelengths (300 nm). Our ability to see varies according to the spectrum; generally, we have better acuity in the mid-range of our visible spectrum (i.e. yellow). For that reason yellow is a useful colour for warning, e.g. yellow is used on the front of trains, as it stands out. However, blue and red colours are not so easy to see; red should not be used for detail on VDU screens, as it is particularly hard to see when there is background light. Colour sensitivity varies between individuals and between colours. Most people can see yellows better than reds and blues; however, colour blindness should also be considered. Approximately 9% of the male population have some colour blindness, and the inability to discriminate reds and greens is most common.

The other physical property of light is its intensity, a measure of how much energy it contains. Unfortunately, human perception of light rarely bears a close relationship to the actual physical properties. Consequently, brightness of light in our everyday opinion is not just its physical intensity but is also conditioned by the difference between light intensities in an image.

Light has two objective measures, luminance and contrast, and one subjective measure, brightness.

Luminance is a measure of the light reflected from a surface. Generally, dark surfaces absorb more light and light ones absorb less light, so white objects appear to be brighter. Luminance, as measured by photographic light meters, is expressed in candelas per square metre (cd/m).

Contrast measures the difference in luminance between two surfaces and is expressed as a ratio:

$$\text{Contrast} = \frac{L_{max} - L_{min}}{L_{max} + L_{min}} \quad \text{or} \quad \frac{\{L(\text{object}) - L(\text{background})\}}{L(\text{background})}$$

The L_{max}/L_{min} formula gives a measure between 0 and 1 for low to high contrast. Hence, to make an object stand out in an image, a high overall luminance is desirable (L_{max}) and a large difference between the object and background. This matches with our intuitive feeling of high contrast of dark shadows in bright sunlight. On VDU screens displayed characters should have a high contrast with the background. Modern black-on-white displays ensure better visibility.

Brightness, on the other hand, is a subjective measure; although it may have a relationship to luminance, this is not always reliable. Brightness is measured by discrimination tests on thresholds or just noticeable differences. The limit of discrimination for human vision can be summarised by a ratio:

$$\frac{\mathrm{d}L}{L} = k$$

where $\mathrm{d}L$ = threshold luminance
L = background luminance
k = a constant, roughly 0.01 to 0.02 for VDU displays.

This gives a background/foreground ratio between 1:100 and 1:50, so, as the background luminance is increased, objects become increasingly difficult to see. Hence, VDU displays in bright sunlight can give problems, as users of lap-top computers with LCD (Liquid Crystal Displays) will notice. Our visual acuity, however, is not just dependent on luminance and contrast; other factors such as background lighting and image composition are important.

Visual acuity and sensitivity

Visual acuity is influenced by several factors. There is the complexity of the image itself, the intensity of the light, and image colour. Low light intensity makes images difficult to resolve. Absolute human visual sensitivity is remarkable, as the human eye can see in almost complete darkness, although the threshold of vision, i.e. the smallest quantity of light that can be seen, decreases with age. Even though people can see light at low intensities, they can resolve little detail and for normal working good illumination is required. This has implications for VDU displays. The advantages of good luminance in VDU displays are:

- Acuity increases with better luminance and with increased foreground/ background contrast.
- Better luminance means a smaller aperture in the eye, which increases the depth of field. In the eye, aperture is controlled by the iris; the effect is the same as reducing the camera stop from F5.6 to F8, which gives a better depth of focus.

On the minus side, increased luminance makes VDU flicker more obvious and direct glare may become uncomfortable. Visual flicker is caused by the eye discriminating changes in an image in a short time period. VDU flickers depend on the refresh rate, that is the number of times a second the screen is scanned and the image redrawn. If the change happens quickly enough, the eye assumes a continuous state and does not differentiate between each image. This quality, called the flicker fusion frequency, happens at approximately 32 images/s, and the continuous state illusion is exploited in motion picture photography. Usually VDU monitors use rates around 50 Hz (scans per second), which avoids flicker in most circumstances except for high luminance displays.

Human visual acuity is quite remarkable but individually very variable. Most people can resolve gaps of 2 mm at a distance of 2 m but this tells us little about how people see meaningful shapes. More important for interface design is resolution of more complex shapes and letters. The optician's test measures optimal visual ability as resolving letters 20 mm high on the bottom row at 6 m even though average ability is only capable of resolving 40 mm letters. Few people have perfect vision, so display design should accommodate average human abilities. One design implication is for the size of text characters.

The size of printed letters is measured in points, a point being roughly $\frac{1}{72}$ of an inch; thus, 10 point type has letters with an approximate height of $\frac{10}{72}$ or 0.14 of an inch. Printed text usually ranges between 18 and 8 point; anything smaller than 8 point is difficult to read for a long period of time. Most text on VDU displays, where the reading distance is 0.5 m, needs to be 12 point; however, text for overhead projector foils, when the reading distance is 2–5 m, should be 18–24 point.

Visual processing

Our eyes are sensitive to light because of photosensitive nerve cells. The receptive cells are specialised into receptors for black and white and for colour. These have an irregular distribution in the retina (see Figure 2.2), with black and white receptors being concentrated around the periphery, while colour receptors are more concentrated at the centre, with the maximum cell density in the fovea, which is the natural point of focus on the retina. This leads to central and peripheral vision. We can see quite a large area in front of us about 60 degrees either side of our nose, but we can only see detail in a small area we are focusing on. This is where the fovea or central area of the eye has been positioned. Peripheral vision is more like a monitor, good at detecting movement and change but poor at detail. This has implications for design of displays, for instance:

- In windows, do not expect people to attend to detail in two separate windows at once.
- In multimedia systems only one image should be presented at once, e.g. users can not attend to a still image and a video at the same time.
- For any interface, use of movement is a highly effective means of alerting the peripheral vision and drawing the user's attention.

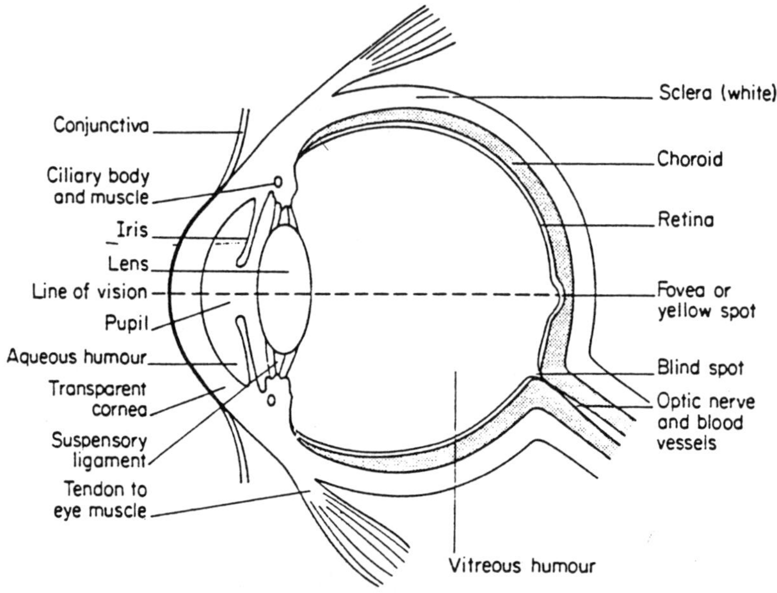

Figure 2.2 Anatomy of the eye showing the receptive surface (retina) and fovea, the part of the retina with the highest concentration of rods and cones.

Before images are transmitted to the brain the eye does a considerable amount of image enhancement. The human visual system is much better at dealing with variation in light intensity than even the most sophisticated camera This is because the eye has an automatic intensity adjustment device which turns the nerve cell sensitivity up in dark conditions and down in bright light. Another example of preprocessing is in the treatment of boundaries. The retina has feedback circuits which enhance boundary detection. The consequence is that our eyes pick up edges and especially moving edges very well indeed. This has implications for screen design, making moving stimuli very noticeable, and for icon design, in which clear boundaries become important. More abstraction of image qualities is carried out in the next stage, image interpretation. The main point of image reception is that it is not just a photographic process; even at this early stage certain qualities of the physical image are being abstracted.

Image interpretation

Nerve impulses are transmitted from the eyes to a specialised area of the brain, the optic cortex, where the received images are translated into what we see. The whole process is still not completely understood; however, the basic principles have been well investigated. Receptor cells have specialised roles responding to different primitive components within the image such as edges, corners, bars and gaps.

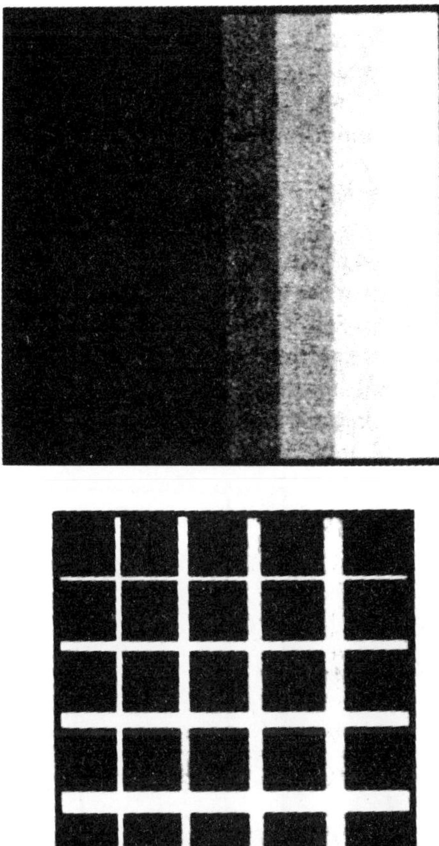

Figure 2.3 Perceptual illusions in contrast: Mach bands and the Hermann grid. The bands do not have the sharp change in brightness which we see, and the shadows in the grid intersections do not really exist.

Depending on the pattern of nerve impulses coming from the retina cell group, one particular receptor cell will fire, transmitting the message that this part of the visual field has a particular shape (bar, edge, etc.) in it. By combination of the many thousands of cells an image can be built up as a composite of primitive features which define shapes and complex pictures that we see. Artificial neural nets have been constructed as 'perceptrons' which can learn to recognise shapes and letters. Interestingly, these nets also show ability to recognise degraded images, just as we can see a smudged letter.

The optic cortex receives a mass of information encoding different qualities of the image. The cortex then has to create visual meaning, the image we see, out of this information. It does so by referring to past records in memory, using an object-property matching process and reasoning about the objects within the

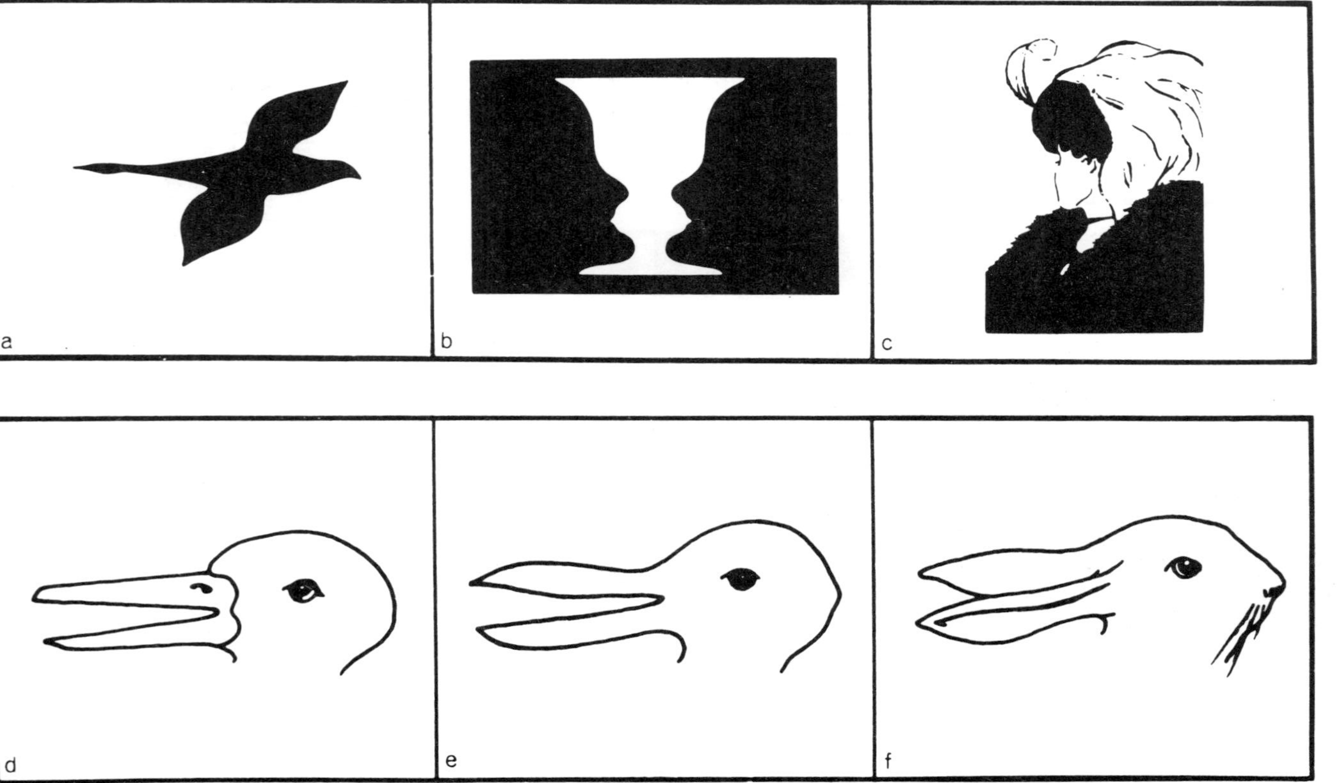

Figure 2.4 Ambiguity illusions. (a) hawk goose, (b) vase/faces, (c) young lady/mother-in-law and (bottom row) duck/rabbit series.

image. Marr (1982) demonstrated that we understand images by a series of processing steps: first, objects are identified in terms of basic shapes; then additional features are added, including depth and perspective in the image to give a 2.5D sketch; further processing may then follow for a true 3D perspective by comparing differences between the images in both eyes, i.e. stereoscopic vision.

Object identification usually works very well but sometimes the result is that what we see is not what is there, but rather our interpretation of what is there based on memory. Occasionally the process makes a mistake and we see a visual illusion. Visual illusions use two tricks to fool the eye and brain: ambiguity and suggestion. Ambiguous images are ones which are open to two or more interpretations; different people will see different images because they have attached their own meaning to the picture. Some well-known ambiguity illusions can be found in Figures 2.3 and 2.4. Suggestion fools the eye by giving it a false clue in an image. We then supply the missing information from memory to fit the clue, and create an illusion of what is there. Only on closer examination does a contradiction become apparent. Suggestion can also work by supplying insufficient information in an image and then giving an extra clue verbally. People instantly see something in an image which beforehand they couldn't see, as illustrated in the Dalmatian illusion (Figure 2.5). The implication of visual interpretation is that images are open to misinterpretation, because each person attaches their own meaning to what they see. As we shall see, icons, too, are open to many interpretations by different people. Correct interpretation of an iconic image can only be assured by testing its meaning.

2.3 Hearing and Speech

While vision is the dominant sense for human–computer communication at present, it is probable that hearing will assume at least equal importance in the future. Speech is the natural human communication medium and it would seem to be an appropriate method for computer control. Indeed, products such as DECTalk and Apple's Voice Navigator allow spoken commands to control computers and the IBM Dragon system is a speech-driven word processor. Speech is closely linked to problems of natural-language interfaces. Currently, abilities of computer speech systems depend on the recognition qualities and whether the system has to deal with different speakers or not, e.g.:

- Continuous speech versus isolated word recognition. The latter is much easier but artificial, and most systems now aim at continuous speech.
- Speaker dependent compared with speaker independent recognition. The former is easier, as the computer has to recognise only one person's

pronunciation, while the latter requires recognition of any voice. Speech differs considerably between males and females, voice tone and with dialect.

Figure 2.5 The power of suggestion on interpretation. When prompted, most people see a Dalmatian dog in the picture. Some, however, insist it is a cow.

Hearing involves the same set of problems as vision: reception of the stimulus, translating its properties into nerve impulses and then attaching meaning to the nerve messages. Sound is transmitted to us as a series of pressure waves in air. Sound waves have properties of frequency and intensity. Frequency is a measure of how close the sound waves are together and is recorded as the number of waves arriving at a point per second, expressed as thousands of cycles per second, called kilohertz. Sound frequency is usually described by people as *pitch*; the higher the frequency the higher the pitch of a sound.

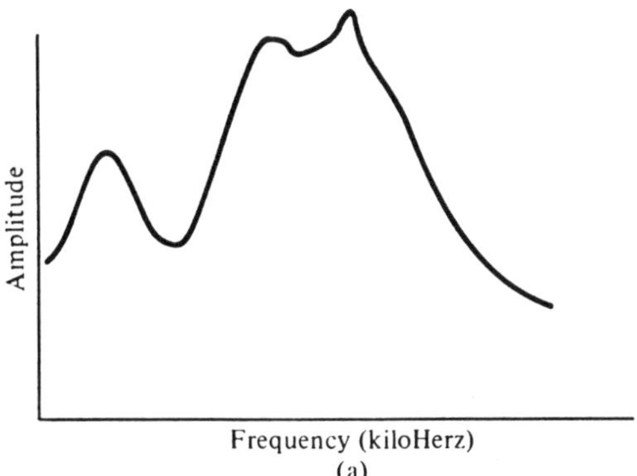

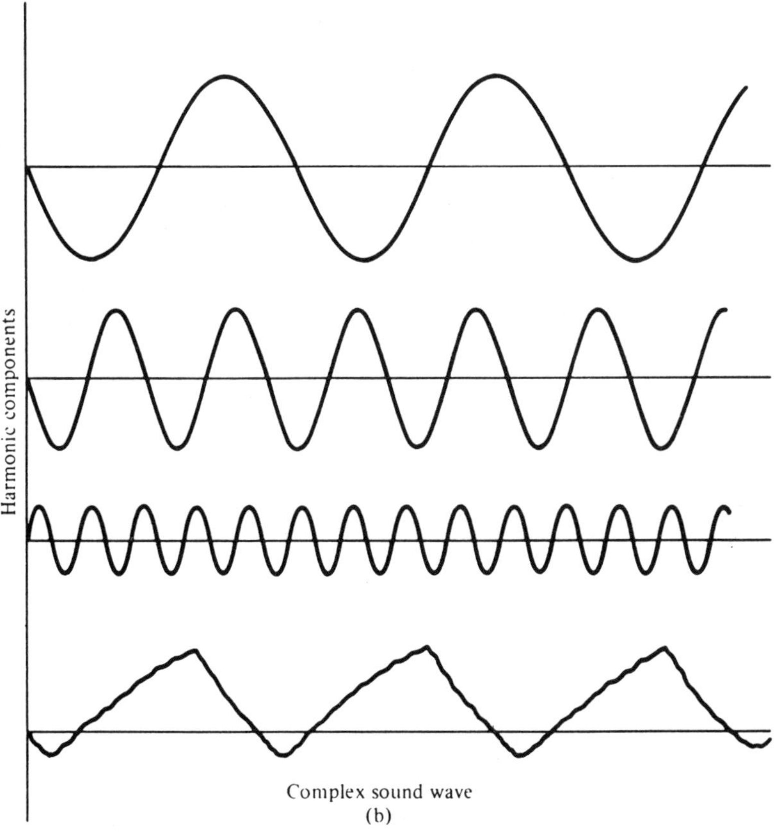

Figure 2.6 The frequency and amplitude of sound waves. (a) A simple sound wave showing the change of amplitude with frequency. (b) The dismembering of one complex frequency pattern into many simple frequency waves by the principle of Fourier analysis.

Sound intensity is a measure of the energy in the sound waves. Intensity is related to the amplitude, which is a measure of the sound wave energy at a particular frequency: see Figure 2.6. We refer to intensity as loudness of a sound but, as with vision, what we hear does not always correlate with the physical measurements. Lower-frequency sound transmits more energy and is therefore technically louder. People, however, will reliably describe a high-pitch but physically low-intensity sound as being louder than a low-pitch high-energy sound.

Most sounds are a composite of waves at many different frequencies. Even a simple sound produced by a tuning fork has a main frequency and a series of extra, higher frequencies called *harmonics*. The tone of a sound, in the musical sense of the word, is produced by complex combinations of these harmonic frequencies. As with the reception of light, considerable preprocessing occurs with hearing. The human ear is adapted to analyse complex sounds, and, in particular speech. Speech is such a complex combination of sound waves that a graphical representation in a spectrogram recording (see Figure 2.7) looks like a complete blur. The ear has to detect all the separate frequency and amplitude components in such a sound.

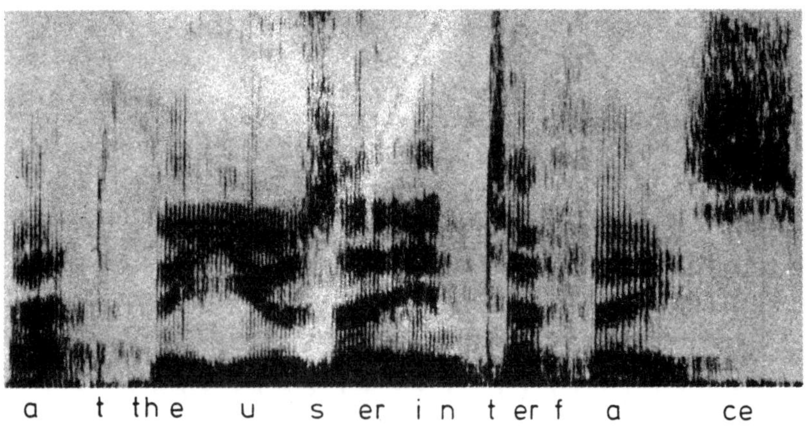

Figure 2.7 Sound spectogram of continuous speech. Note that there are no convenient gaps between the words.

Auditory preprocessing

Receptors in the inner ear show a similar specialisation to the optical system; some are tuned to activate for particular frequencies of sound, while others respond to the amplitude at a particular frequency. A sound composed of many frequencies is converted into a pattern of nerve impulses representing its various features. The frequency range for deciphering speech is from 260 Hz to

5600 Hz; however, the region of 2–3 kHz is most important. Telephones only transmit from 300 to 3000 Hz yet we can hear speech quite adequately. Our overall auditory acuity is in the range of 200–20,000 Hz, but the range decreases with age and individual abilities differ considerably.

The receptors have narrower bandwidths at lower frequencies with progressively wider bandwidths at higher frequencies; hence, the ear is tuned to extract more information from lower-frequency sound. The ear has to extract certain sounds mixed in with background noise. The relationship of sounds to background noise is expressed as decibels (dB), a logarithmic ratio of the power of the sound:background noise, usually referred to as the *signal/noise ratio.* So not only does the ear have to be sensitive to the overall frequency range but it also has to resolve small frequency components within a possibly noisy input. The key factors of auditory processing are:

- Frequency range for speech interpretation 260–5600 Hz, overall hearing range 200–10 000 Hz, although this is individually variable.
- Resolution is capable of telling frequency components 1/4 octave apart.
- Temporal resolution of sounds separated by 5–15 milliseconds (ms).
- Amplitude resolution of 1 dB in peaks of sound.

The design implications of this are that only part of the auditory range is necessary for speech. People will tolerate poor sound communications unless quality is vital, such as high-fidelity music in multimedia systems. Other implications are that background noise should be reduced for effective communication, although the human ear is good at suppressing superfluous noise. Finally, use of sound is very effective as a means of alerting and warning. Sound is an environmental change we are tuned to pick up. However, sound is a broadcast medium, so beware of annoying other users by overuse of warning sounds; and high-pitch sounds tend to be uncomfortable for most people.

Interpretation of sound

The most important aspect of sound from a human point of view is speech and language. Interpretation of speech is integrally linked with language understanding. To interpret sound the auditory system has to classify the input into three categories: noise and unimportant sounds which can be ignored; significant noise, that is sounds which are important and have meaning attached to them such as a dog's bark; and meaningful utterances composing language. The hearing system, like vision, makes use of past experience when interpreting input. Spoken language is full of mispronounced words, unfinished sentences and interruptions; furthermore, it happens quickly, so the interpretation mechanism has to keep pace with the input. Speech rates are in the range of 160–220 words per minute, so interpretation has to be rapid.

Language recognition from speech has to start by discovering the basic sound units of language, called *phonemes*. These sounds can then be matched to the basic units of written language, called *morphemes*, which correspond approximately to syllables, suffixes, prefixes, etc., and thereby words. Phonemes describe all the possible sounds in a language. These may differ considerably from the written language as in English plural nouns, which, although written with an 's' suffix, have two different sounds, 'z' as in hens, fens and 's' as in books, locks. Interpretation, however, does not use phonemes alone; it is a layered and integrated approach in which the brain makes use of language syntax (the grammar), semantics (the meaning of words and sentences), and pragmatics (knowledge of the context of communication), to decipher communication.

Speech does not appear as a sequence of conveniently separated phoneme sounds but as a continuous band of sound throughout a phrase or sentence. Simple template matching of sound spectrograms to phonemes is unsatisfactory because of the problem of finding word boundaries; in addition, a wide variety of physical sounds can be generated for one phoneme by different speeds of speech, different dialects and speech inaccuracies. Speech recognition systems use complex algorithms to detect the pattern changes in sound frequencies combined with phoneme templates.

People supply a significant amount of what they hear on the basis of expectancy. This can be demonstrated by experiments asking people to identify a sound masked by a cough in the middle of a sentence. Evidence of verbal suggestion is demonstrated by an experiment in which one word, 'eel', was heard as four different words depending on the sentence context:

- It was found that the eel was on the axle.
- It was found that the eel was on the shoe.
- It was found that the eel was on the table.
- It was found that the eel was on the orange.

The sound 'eel' was heard as wheel, heel, eel and peel, respectively, in the four sentences (Warren and Warren, 1970). Speech recognition suffers from illusions in a similar manner to the visual system, but the timing of perception is more critical and as a result the tolerance of speech interpretation mistakes is higher; consequently, illusions in speech are not referred to as such.

Memory plays a crucial role in both vision and hearing; consequently, the role of perception in the sense of receiving information and cognition in the sense of understanding and using external information can not be meaningfully separated. This leads to investigation of how memory works and how it is used in the processes of understanding and reasoning.

2.4 Learning and Memory

Human memory comes in two varieties: short-term working memory and long-term permanent storage. The information processing model will be used to place memory in the perspective of perception and cognition.

Model human processor

According to the model, each perceptual sense has a processor and associated short-term memory (STM). These memories form the input and output buffers of the human system, storing abstract images in visual short-term memory and sounds in auditory short-term memory. Each memory is associated with a sensory processor. The sensory processors analyse the contents of their memories and pass the resulting information to the cognitive processor for identification of the sensory input. The overall schema of the model human information processor is illustrated in Figure 2.8.

The capacity of sensory short memory is not clear but for vision it must be at least the contents of one visual field, i.e. what we can see at any one point in time. The contents decay rapidly in about 100 ms and are continually over-written by new input; so, when you close your eyes, the visual image vanishes quickly, although any transient 'afterimage' is your visual STM. The visual input buffer has to be overwritten because the quantity of data in an image is vast and images change continually; consequently, storing even a few images would take a vast amount of memory. This has implications for graphical user interfaces and multimedia; for instance, if images are not held on screen long enough, we shall not be able to extract much information from them. A consequence for multimedia using video or film is that we remember the gist of what happens but rarely any detail within individual scenes. The auditory input buffer, also referred to as echoic memory, may contain several phonemes' worth of sound because no one millisecond of sound contains enough information for correct language identification. The contents of echoic memory probably last for up to 1 s before they are lost.

The contents of visual and auditory STMs are in an abstract form after sensory processing, although no meaning has been attached to the input at this stage. Meaning is generated when information in the input short-term memories is passed on to the central cognitive short-term memory for interpretation. The cognitive processor is thought to be responsible for object identification. This is effected by matching the incoming information with past experience and then attaching semantic meaning to the image or sound. To complete the model, the cognitive processor has an associated STM which is used for storing temporary working information. The collection of short-term memories is often referred to as 'working memory'. The information may have come from the sensory processors or may have been retrieved from long-term memory.

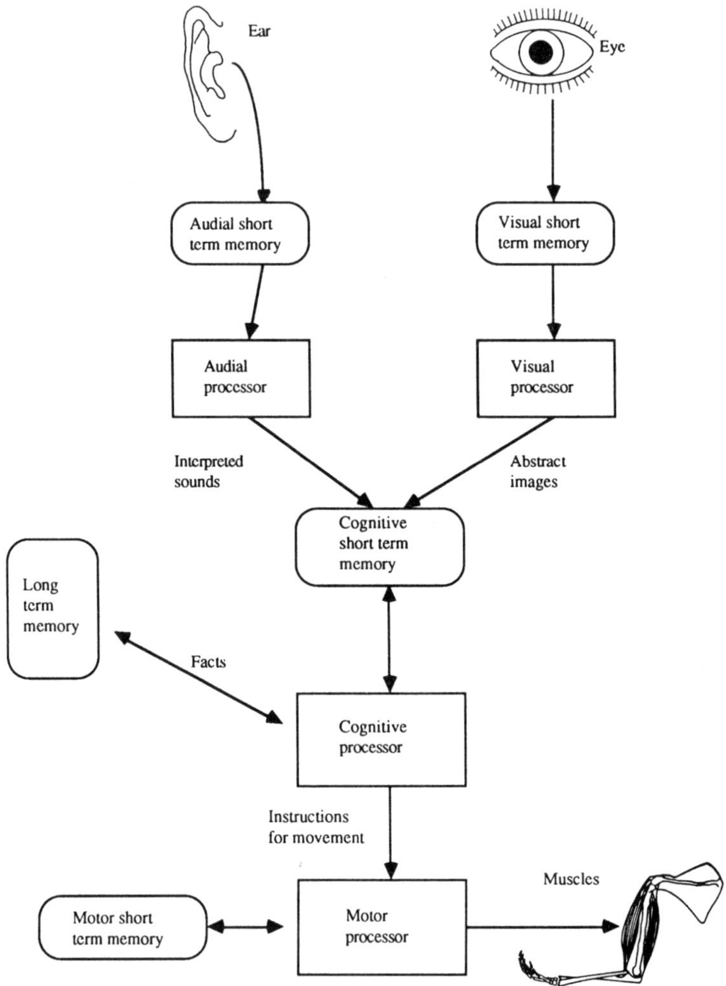

Figure 2.8 Information processing model of human perception and cognition (after Card et al., 1983).

The cognitive processor performs most of the actions which are considered in everyday language to be thinking. The results of thinking are either placed back in short-term memory, or may be stored in long-term memory, or may be passed on to the motor processor to elicit behaviour. The motor processor is responsible for controlling actions by muscle movements to create human behaviour, e.g. running, talking, pointing, etc., Its output is sent down the peripheral nervous system, which forms the body's data communications network, to the muscles. Speech output is a special case which requires a separate output processor and buffer of its own. Evidence indicates that approximately 2 s worth of speech can be held in the buffer, which allows words to be assembled in a sequence for rapid output. One problem with the model human processor is that it emphasises sequential processing, whereas much human reasoning and memorisation may use parallel processing. A more complex and flexible model of human mental activity is Interactive Cognitive Sub-systems (Barnard, 1988), which accounts for concurrency by envisaging a co-operative network of parallel processors.

Interactive Cognitive Sub-systems

This model (ICS) uses a bus architecture to connect a series of processors which have specialised tasks. The three-level view of perception, cognition and motor processors is replaced with a specialised division of functions:

- The visual sub-system is a preprocessor for image input and analyses the structure and content of visual input into a semantically processable form.
- The acoustic sub-system fulfils the same function for sound input. These sub-systems then transfer analysed sensory input across the data network for further cognitive processing.
- The morpholexical sub-system takes in low-level linguistic input (i.e. recognised linguistic sounds) and transforms it into words and parts of speech.
- The propositional sub-system deals with analysis of meaning in linguistic and other input. Linguistic processing of syntax and semantics is carried out here.
- The implication sub-system is the highest level of processing which transforms semantically analysed input into higher-level abstractions. This creates concepts and complex knowledge structures from input and long-term memory.
- The object sub-system is specialised for processing of visuo-spatial information and attaches meaning to images. This works in parallel with other sub-systems, so we can analyse the contents of a picture while understanding a verbal commentary about its contents.
- The articulatory sub-system is responsible for speech output.
- The limb sub-system is responsible for all other motor output.

Unlike the model human processor, ICS allows for considerable concurrency. Input flows into the system via the preprocessors and then through the cognitive processors (object, morpholexical → propositional → implication), and then back down again to be processed for output to the limb and articulatory sub-systems. The model (see Figure 2.9) provides operations for copying image records carrying the data between sub-systems and transformation of data within each processor. The control of communication is assumed to be a contention-based network, so many messages may be present related to several inputs at different levels of processing.

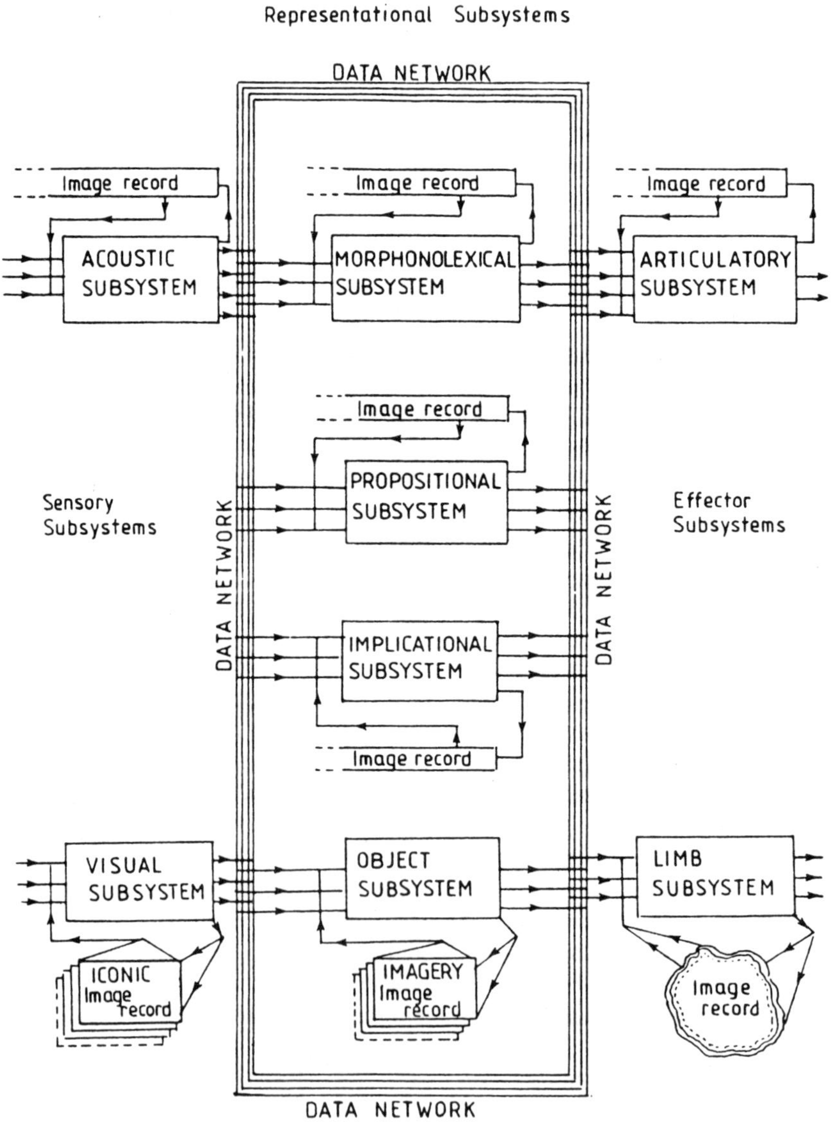

Figure 2.9 Interactive Cognitive Sub-Systems model (after Barnard et al., *1988). MPL = morphonolexical sub-system/records; PROP = propositional sub-system/records; IMPLIC = implicational sub-system/records.*

Within each sub-system, processing is sequential and limited, so messages have to queue for processing. In this way ICS can be used to analyse the demands made upon cognitive resources and predict problems in human–computer interaction. For instance, if different messages were given in separate media (e.g. text-based instruction on general editing given concurrently with graphical animation of the cut-and-paste commands in a word processing system), then both the morpholexical and the object system would fight for the resources of the propositional sub-system. However, the model needs considerable interpretation to decide the exact processing carried out by each sub-system and the necessary message passing. ICS has been used with an expert system extension giving processing rules within the sub-systems, to predict difficulties in human–computer interaction.

Both information processing models provide an outline description of the cognitive apparatus, although the whole system is known to be more complex. From here we shall examine the roles of short- and long-term memory

2.4.1 Short-term Memory

Short-term memory (STM) is the human equivalent of computer RAM, in other words the working memory of the central processor. In contrast to computers, human short-term memory is small and loses its contents unless it is refreshed every 200 ms. However, the read/write access time, about 70 ms, is quite quick, so information can be held in STM by continual rewriting.

According to the information processing model, short-term memory has to store information from many sources; hence, it may seem strange that experimental evidence indicates that it has a very limited capacity. In an influential paper, Miller (1956) summarised experiments which placed a limit on short-term memory of 7 items ± 2. Items were not stored as in computer memory 'bytes' but in 'chunks' of information. These can vary from simple characters and numerals to complex abstract concepts and images. The secret of expanding the limited storage in STM is to abstract qualities from the basic information and store the abstraction instead.

This concept is best understood by example. Telephone codes may be given in an unordered fashion, e.g. 01612363311; such large numbers are difficult to assimilate and remember, but break the number up into smaller units and memorisation is easier e.g. 0161–236 3311. The effect is to suggest a chunking strategy to the reader. Instead of storing ten separate digits, the number groups can be stored as whole chunks, reducing the storage required from ten chunks to three. The more order which can be imposed on the raw data the better the chunking. To convince yourself of the point try to quickly memorise the following:

832751984221 – accurate recall would be unusual
83-275-1984-221 – should present no problems, but what rules did you use to 'chunk' the numbers?

246
357
81012
91113

should also be recalled without error once the pattern has been seen. The second and third number sequences have order within them that promotes chunking. What has been stored is some quality of the data which can be used to reconstruct it, in the last case the algorithm of even/odd triplets in an ascending numeric series.

Subsequent research has shown that the human information processing model is a little simplistic (see Hitch, 1987). STM has at least two sub-systems; one deals with language-based data, the other with visuo-spatial information. The linguistic sub-system functions as a list but access is like a hybrid LIFO (last in, first out) queue. We tend to remember the last and first few items in the list and forget the middle. Storage and retrieval are generally sequential. The output memory for speech is like a loop in which words are placed to compose sentences. When we lose the thread of what we are saying, we place words in the wrong part of the loop. The whole short-term system, called *working memory*, is controlled by an executive, similar in concept to the cognitive processor. This more elaborate model helps explain differences in temporary memory for visual and textual information and how interference during memorisation impairs retention of information. In the latter case the executive appears to be distracted during the process of storing and refreshing the contents of working memory.

Some key features of working memory are:

- Rapid read/write access time – 70 ms.
- Memory decays quickly – 200 ms unless refreshed.
- Capacity is limited to 7 ± 2 chunks, but may be larger for image detail.
- Storage capacity can be increased by abstracting qualities of raw information.
- Distraction causes forgetting of recently learned material. Even a small number of simple chunks of information are lost if there is distraction during input.
- Other inputs impair recall. Supplying irrelevant material during input to working memory makes recall worse.
- Very similar inputs impair recall. Supplying closely related items during memorisation makes recall worse.
- Immediate memory for details in complex images is poor.

- Recall of items is better if both the word for, and a picture of, the item are presented together, compared with the image or word in isolation.
- People remember in the short-term (<30 s) by scanning back along the input, thus last in first out.

Working memory is one of the key limitations in human information processing. It has many consequences for interface design and these can be expressed in some general design guidelines:

- Minimise distraction during tasks and memorisation.
- Beware of overloading working memory, in terms of both quantity of information and time span of retention.
- Structuring (chunking) information helps memorisation.
- Images are helpful but need to be accompanied by text.

The central role working memory plays within computer interface operation will become apparent in Chapter 3 on task design. It limits our ability to process information during tasks. Its counterpart, long-term memory, is important in storing the knowledge which we use to help us understand and perform tasks.

2.4.2 Long-term Memory

Long-term memory is the main file store of the human system. It has a near infinite capacity, as no one has been able to demonstrate an upper limit on what we can remember. Memory failure appears to be a problem of not retrieving what is already inside our memory.

Retrieval of facts from memory can be remarkably fast, especially for frequently used items and procedures. Retrieval time for less frequently used information varies; it can be quick, but may be slow, especially for older people. Retrieval according to the information processing model is a function of the cognitive processor, but in reality the process must be more complex. Often, remembering a fact is not instantaneous; instead it comes back some minutes after the original effort to retrieve it. During the intervening time, attention will have been devoted to other matters; hence, it appears that a background memory processor must be invoked to effect difficult long-term memory searches. Memory appears to be activated by use, so frequently or recently used items are easier to recall. Memory also appears to be a two-phase process, as you can often have a fact on the tip of your tongue but can't quite remember it. This is consequence of:

- Recognition: the initial activation of a memory trace by cues.
- Recall: the actual retrieval of the information itself.

In frequently used memory both recognition and recall are so quick that no difference is noticed. However, it appears that memories are found by a process of activating a search process. There is also evidence of 'spreading activation', as remembering one fact often helps the recall of other related items. It is rather like a large net of interconnected facts which becomes sensitised by use.

Memory mechanisms

How memory works in the physical dimension is still a subject of considerable research. Computer simulations of learning, which may be regarded as a form of making new memories, have shown that human learning can be mimicked by complex algorithms which control how associations are formed between nodes in a neural net. The algorithms form new network pathways from inputs to outputs by altering weights on connections. One such algorithm is Hebb association, which states that if two adjacent nodes are activated together, then the weights should be changed to increase their association. This creates associative learning, as illustrated in Figure 2.10.

The models work by iterative cycling of activation around the network until a stable pattern of associations emerges. In some cases new meaningful associations can be generated. For example, in a network with inputs representing royal family trees in a parent–children format the network created new outputs which described kings and queens in terms of brother and sister relationships. This research, called *parallel distributed processing* (Rumelhart and McClelland, 1987), may form a credible model of human memory, as there is some evidence that human nerve cell networks change their connective properties during learning. So memorisation and learning may be by formation of complex pathways in neural networks. Forgetting, on the other hand, happens when the links decay with age or were poorly formed in the first place.

Memorisation is usually an effortful process. There are various methods of memorisation, the simplest being rote learning, in which information is committed to memory as a list with few associations between individual items. An example of rote learning is learning tables of numbers by heart. However, most learning is by association, in which facts are linked together to provide an access path. There is experimental evidence that the greater the number of separate access paths, or the more often an access path is used, the easier a fact is to remember. Depth of encoding means better recall. This is helped by reasoning carried out during memorisation, which creates more links and, hence, helps recall in the future.

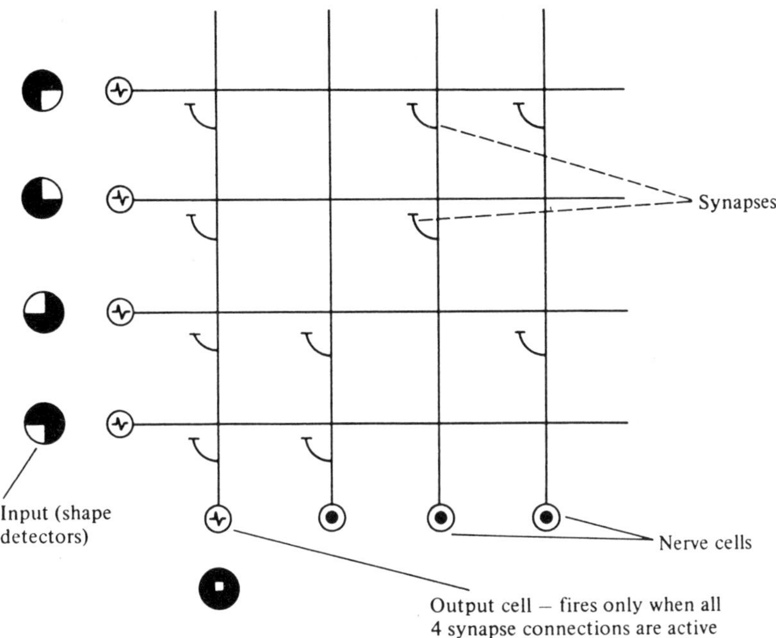

Figure 2.10 Memory schema: possible neural organisation in visual perception. The input comes from edge detectors; connections in the matrix can then detect different firing patterns among the input nerve cells. In the example the cell connected to all four inputs fires when a square is found. Firing in adjacent cells could make the synaptic contacts with output cells stronger.

Organisation of memory

The basic organisation of long-term memory is thought to be semantic, that is data are stored in terms of linguistically based concepts linked together in a highly developed network. One analogy is to consider long-term memory as a sophisticated network type of database with access paths as a chain of pointers to the information. As we become experts in any subject, we form rich interconnected models to describe the subject and help us solve problems. These models or memory schema help expert chess players plan moves, expert software engineers design systems, etc. Schemas, or semantic network models, as depicted in Figure 2.11(a), are not the whole story. Memory also has categories which contain many related items, and the network may act as a link to these categories. However, there may be two types of access, one chain of semantic pointers and a more direct access mechanism via image-related data. This gives rise to the possibility of two types of human memory, associative and analogue, the former storing concepts, while the latter stores abstractions of physical objects as found in images and sounds. The organisation of human memory is far from clear, although most evidence favours the view that all storage is finally of the semantic associative kind, with several different organisations.

(a) Semantic network model of memory. Objects are associated in a network of classification and attributes. The image of the object is not stored in a photographic form, rather a representation is generated from the network of interconnected labels which describe it.

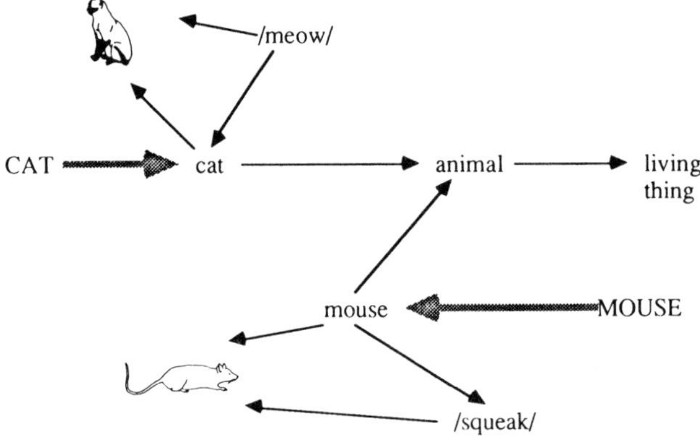

(b) Category model. Objects are held within categories which have descriptive tags for recall. Individual objects are not directly addressable, instead they are recalled by list searching the category contents.

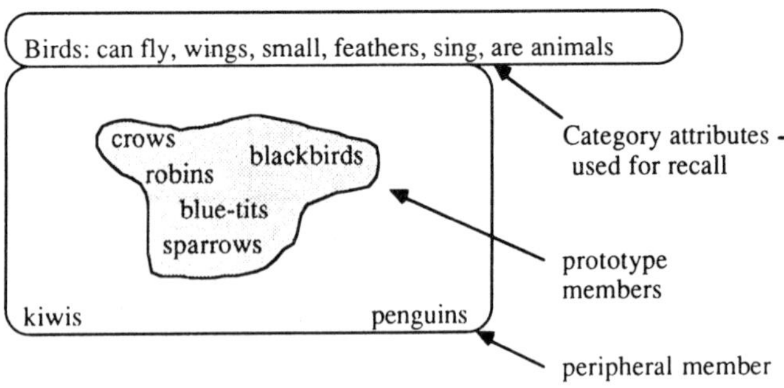

Figure 2.11 Organisation of memory: semantic network and category models.

Categorial memory This is memory of objects and their groupings or associations. There is evidence that we organise the world not into discrete non-overlapping categories but in a more fuzzy manner, with core and peripheral members. To illustrate the idea, most people have an idealised concept of a bird. A robin fits this core or prototypical image by having the properties: round, feathered, sings, lays eggs, etc. In contrast a penguin is a more peripheral member of birds because it does not share all the attributes of the prototype image and it has additional non-standard attributes, e.g. swims, can't fly. The concept is illustrated in Figure 2.11(b). Retrieval is more rapid and accurate for core items in categories and slower for peripheral items. Categorial memory probably has a three-level hierarchical classification, so we tend to organise our view of the world into superordinate categories (e.g. animals), categories (e.g. birds) and then sub-categories (e.g. birds of prey). This theory works well for concrete, physical objects, although the situation for more abstract concepts (e.g. religions) is less clear.

Procedural memory This is knowledge of actions and how to do things. It is held in two different forms: declarative or rule-based knowledge and procedural knowledge. When we start out knowing little about a subject, we acquire fragments of declarative knowledge as rules and mini-procedures. This knowledge, however, is not organised, so to carry out a task we have to reason with declarative knowledge fragments and compose them into a plan of action. This process, often described as 'figuring it out', involves considerable effort. This implicates memory in problem solving and indeed memory, learning and problem solving are all closely linked. Levels of reasoning and their associated organisation of memory were described in an influential three-level model by Rasmussen (1986):

- Knowledge level: problem solving uses heuristics and general knowledge. Little domain-specific knowledge exists in memory, so people have to solve problems from first principles. This level of reasoning requires conscious attention and is often difficult.
- Rule level: some knowledge of the domain or current problem exists but this knowledge is fragmented as isolated facts and rules in declarative (If..then..action) type format. Reasoning at this level is effortful and conscious. Fragments of domain knowledge have to be assembled with more general heuristics to solve the problem.
- Skill level: considerable domain knowledge exists in a highly structured form of memory. In this case the problem has essentially already been solved and the solution stored in memory as a procedure. The procedure is a method of doing something to achieve a goal, so skill level processing only requires recognising and retrieving the correct procedure. As we shall see in Section 2.6, this can cause errors.

As people become more familiar with a task, fragments of declarative knowledge become compiled into procedures that can then be run automatically. Hence, when we know how to do a task, we simply call the procedural knowledge of how to perform it automatically. This is easy because the working memory load has been avoided.

Script-based memory Scripts (Schank, 1982) are a form of procedural memory but also share characteristics with event-based memory. Scripts encode a sequence of events and their context which we have learned from experience. They represent prototypical 'stories' of what we expect to go on in a particular context. To take the classical example, when we enter a restaurant the usual sequence of events is to receive the menu, order a meal, eat it, pay for it and leave. These events are associated with a precondition of feeling hungry, objects such as the waiter, table, knife, fork, etc. Scripts are a hybrid artificial intelligence/cognitive model which describe how knowledge can be represented in computers as well as how it may be held in human memory. This type of memory shares the concept of prototypicality with categorial memory, as certain actions may be more representative than others in a class of related scripts.

Episodic or event memory In this, memory associations between an event and objects are made as a context. This type of memory may require less effort: for example, we remember objects on a desk that provides the context which are associated with the occurrence of an event such as writing a memo. Episodic memory is a powerful means of recall, especially when visual cues can be given. A related memory form is analogical or metaphoric memory.

Analogical memory In this case a set of facts and their associations are linked in a context; but there is more abstraction involved (see Gentner and Stevens, 1983). Analogical memory links two sets of domain knowledge which on first sight are unrelated. When the knowledge has been used in reasoning, further abstract links are created in memory to store the relationships. The concept is best explained by example. Take two domains, astronomy and chemistry, and their respective knowledge structures representing the relationships between the sun, planets, gravity and orbits on one hand, and atoms, nuclei, electrons, electromagnetic forces and orbits on the other. The linking analogy is the abstraction of satellites revolving around a central node on orbits determined by forces. Analogy is a useful way of exploiting existing memory by transferring it to new situations. This is the essence of metaphor design for graphical user interfaces; we recognise the link between two situations and transfer knowledge from one to another, although recognising analogies in the first place is not always easy. The icon-based desktop metaphor of graphical user interfaces uses metaphor memory to help us remember and understand the system as objects on a desktop.

Storing information in long-term memory is often linked to understanding facts. This is demonstrated by the way people reconstruct information from memory. Storage of data on every object of interest would swamp even the large capacity of human memory; consequently, associations are stored with a limited amount of basic data. To illustrate the point, try to find out in which compass direction you are facing while you read this book. This may be an easy task if you know your room faces a particular direction; a more likely scenario is that you will establish the direction either by reasoning based on where the sun rises and sets or by using geographic knowledge of landmarks which you can see. You can synthesise knowledge from associations between memorised facts rather than storing each fact individually. By storing links between facts we can memorise a large number of facts and reconstruct even more information by processing those links in new situations. The reasoning process also increases the depth of encoding and consequently often improves recall.

Memorisation techniques

Formation of access paths can be helped by memorisation techniques. Perhaps the most famous of these was invented by Solomides, an ancient Greek poet. His technique was to associate information with spatial features of a house; so the first part of a speech was linked with the entrance hall, the middle part with the living room, and the end with a bedroom, etc. This technique formed more associative links during memorisation and possibly exploited the visual access path to memory. This idea has been successfully applied as the rooms metaphor in the Xerox Notecards system. The screen appears as a set of rooms with different backgrounds linked by doors. Rooms store information in different parts of a database. The appearance and position of the room helps recall of the associated information.

Other memorisation techniques involve adding extra semantic cues by learning additional associations with the object to be retrieved. Examples are keywords, peg words, mnemonics, similes and acronyms.

Memorisation fails because an access path either decays through lack of use or was poorly constructed in the first place. Similar facts can interfere with recall, so well-recognised access paths which are sufficiently distinct from others are helpful in preventing recall errors. Distractions during the memorisation process also cause recall errors, as the access path is liable to be incomplete. So if attention is diverted during memorisation, for instance by a noisy environment, memory performance will suffer.

Sometimes we do not remember all at once but have the 'tip of the tongue' feeling that you know what is required but cannot exactly remember it. Partial recall is 'gist' memory when you retrieve related facts or approximations to what is required. Gist and partial recall are probably caused by spreading activation as the cue starts the search process through the network which stores the memory. If the network is not well formed or the cues are weak, then the activated search only progresses to a limited depth, hence finding general facts not the specific. Sometimes only recognition of familiarity is the result; this may be followed by 'gist' recall and full retrieval of the required item.

Memory is one of the critical limiting factors of human information processing which affects interface design in many ways. Interface design should strive to reduce the amount which has to be learned; but as learning is often unavoidable, memorisation should be helped by structuring information, and recall should be helped by memory cues. We deal with the complexity of the world by ordering and classifying it. The interface designer should support this process by imposing structure on a design, one of the basic HCI principles. We understand and memorise complex information by breaking the complexity down into simpler components using a hierarchical approach. Complex objects are remembered and, hence, understood, by storing facts which compose and describe objects in various categories, in combination with the access path of associations by which we analysed and understood the object in the first place. The more structure and categorisation we can put into a body of information the easier it is to learn.

Although building many cues into memory helps, the disadvantage comes when the cues are similar. This leads to interference when the wrong item is recalled because the cues are similar. This can be a considerable problem when versions of software change the interface; your memory for the old version is fine but the update is slightly different. Relearning the new version can be difficult unless interference can be avoided. Unfortunately, similarity also helps learning, so interference is a penalty which has to be anticipated in interface design to emphasise the similar for consistency and the dissimilar to avoid interference.

A second HCI principle which is important for memorisation and learning is consistency. The more consistent something is the easier it is to perceive patterns within it and, hence, to learn its structure and characteristics. Memory is always helped by recency and frequency; the more often we recall and use a piece of information the easier it is to learn it. Likewise, if we have used some information in the near past, recall is easier. Humans are good at pattern recognition and association; anything which helps to establish a pattern will help to reduce the learning burden. A summary of the important features of long-term memory is:

- Effectiveness of recall is correlated with the depth of processing on input, i.e. the effort put into memorisation.
- Recall is helped by unique cues and the distinctiveness of the item in memory in relation to other items stored with the same context/cues. Beware cue overloading with too many facts.
- Recall is hindered if distracting and irrelevant material is presented during memorisation.
- Recall suffers if one cue is used for many different objects (cue overload).
- Recall is better for pictorially presented material and for text presented with pictures than for text alone.

- Recall is better if the context of remembering fits the context of memorisation (episodic match).
- Similar items are more likely to be grouped in categories.
- Within categories prototypical items are easy to memorise and recall.

General guidelines can be derived to help memorisation and recall; however, as with short-term memory, care must be exercised in applying these guidelines. General advice does not always fit into specific contexts.

- Memorisation can be helped by enriching the information during learning. Reasoning and understanding what is being remembered helps.
- Structuring information can help categorial memory and creates extra links to retrieve items.
- Techniques can be used to add extra recall cues, e.g. keywords, spatial memorisation, etc.
- Visual presentation with text helps learning and recall.
- Consistency of associations creates better contexts for memorisation and recall.

2.5 Thinking and Problem Solving

Thinking, reasoning and problem solving are all human mental activities which process data derived from our senses and long-term memory. Problem solving is something we do every day of our lives when we come up against the unexpected. It may be defined as 'the combination of existing ideas to form new ideas'. An alternative view focuses on the cause. Problems arise when there is a discrepancy between a desired state of affairs and the current state of affairs and there is no obvious method to change the state. Problem solving progresses through several stages. The names of stages vary between authorities on the subject, so the following scheme is a generalisation:

1. Preparation or formulation: the goal state is defined and necessary information for a solution is gathered.
2. Incubation or searching: anticipated solutions are developed, tested and possibly rejected, leading to more information gathering and development of alternative hypotheses.
3. Inspiration: the correct solution is realised.
4. Verification: the solution is checked out to ensure it meets the goals and is consistent with the information available.

To illustrate how problem solving may work, another model will be employed. The Goals Operators Methods Selection rules (GOMS) model of Card *et al.* (1983) owes its heritage to the General Problem Solver model of Newell and Simon (1972).

Problem-solving models

The GOMS model is composed of a set of goals and sub-goals organised in a conceptual problem container, called the problem space. During the problem searching phase, goals are broken down into a sub-goal network; searching then proceeds by traversing the network and testing hypotheses at each node. At each sub-goal node data are read into short-term memory, evaluated and then stored back into long-term memory as searching progresses to the next sub-goal. Eventually, if the search network has been well constructed and all the facts are available to be evaluated, and the sub-goals pass the tests, the final node is reached resulting in the problem solution. This operation is the familiar reasoning strategy of problem solving by steps, viz. if X is A, then Y is probably B, which means that Z must be true, etc. It uses top down decomposition of the problem, a technique also adopted by structured analysis. However, not all problems can be approached in such a sequential manner.

Other components of the model are operators which describe the actions necessary to reach the goal and methods which group actions to give the strategy or approach to the problem. Actions ultimately are low-level cognitive primitives defined as perceptual, mental and motor in the extension of GOMS called the keystroke level model (Card *et al.*, 1983). This allows the time for simple 'unit tasks', e.g. deleting a word to be calculated from the sequence of perceptual, mental and motor actions, as these have set times of 70–100 ms. However, this low-level usage of GOMS can only predict error-free performance and getting the detailed sequence of actions right is difficult and time consuming.

Methods are controlled by selection rules, for choosing which strategy to follow. Facts are evaluated to give results either proving or disproving a sub-goal. According to the results the goal network may be reorganised as new hypotheses are introduced and old ones discarded. Methods describe how the network is formulated and traversed; essentially they are the problem-solving strategy. Humans use a variety of strategies, some of which they can articulate, but some appear to be unconscious, as in solutions which 'come in a flash'. This leads to difficulties when analysing human problem solving. The accepted method is protocol analysis (Ericsson and Simon, 1985), basically thinking out loud, by asking the subject to verbalise the problem-solving steps and procedures. Unfortunately, humans are often unaware of their own procedures in detail; consequently, steps can be omitted. Analysis of reasoning, therefore, poses problems for knowledge acquisition and problem solving in expert systems.

Reasoning strategies

People use a wide variety of problem-solving strategies, some of which have been incorporated into the semantics of databases, e.g. aggregation of properties to define an object, inheritance of properties in a classification scheme of objects, i.e. lower-level objects automatically assume the characteristics of their higher-level parents. Success in problem solving can often depend on using novel strategies, such as visualising the problem in spatial terms or treating it mathematically, as shown in Figure 2.12. People are naturally conservative in their approach to problem solving, and adopt the methods they are used to.

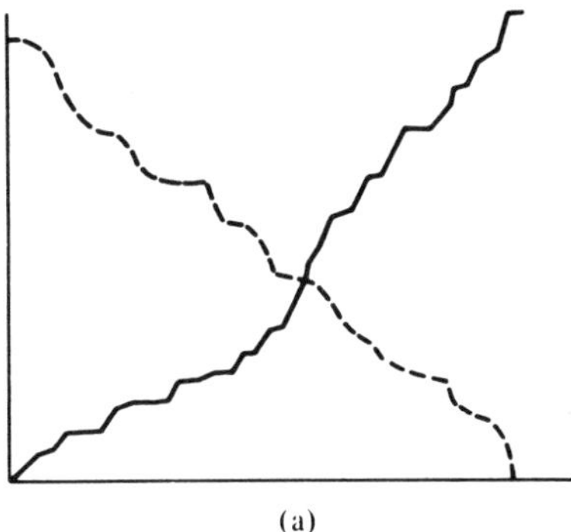

(a)

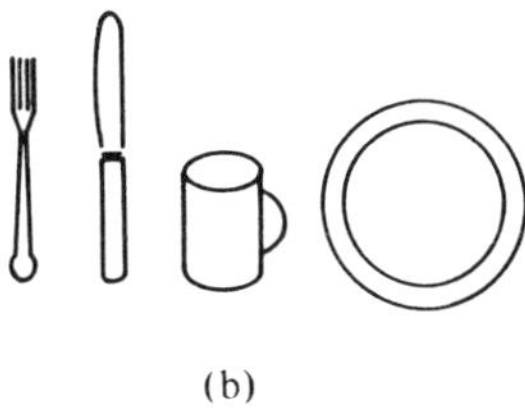

(b)

Figure 2.12 Two methods of problem solving. (a) Visualisation of the Buddhist monk problem. The problem is: a monk climbs a mountain path starting at dawn, stopping for rests on the way up and arriving just before sunset. The next day he descends by the same path, again stopping for rests but going faster than on the way up. Demonstrate that there is a point on the path which the monk will occupy at exactly the same time of day on both the up and down journeys. (b) Visual mental model of the problem to order 'the fork is on the left of the knife, the plate is to the right of the cup, and the knife and plate are not adjacent'.

One common problem-solving method is *inductive reasoning*. This is similar to classification; by observation of facts we conclude a new fact which describes the initial observations. Faced with a menagerie full of cows, lions, giraffes and bears, the observation may be made that they all have four legs, leading to the conclusion that animals are quadrupedal. This case is then generalised to other situations where it may apply. Abductive, or hypothesis-based, reasoning infers how a set of facts can be explained according to a causal model. It starts with an observation and reasons back to the action or event which caused it. So, if a computer screen goes blank, we may infer that the disk has crashed or the system has hung, based on our hypothesis about what happens when there is no feedback, and on the observed events. Our conclusion may be true, but, on the other hand, the blank screen could be the consequence of a long response time.

Another common reasoning strategy is *deduction*. Deductive reasoning starts with assertions and discovers new facts by logically examining the relationships or properties which the assertions describe. This is associative, or syllogistic reasoning, illustrated as follows:

All animals with wings can fly Bats are animals Bats have wings	} propositions or known facts
Therefore bats can fly	a new conclusion based on the propositions

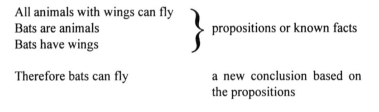

The procedure is to pattern match items and the truth conditions attached to them, from which new combinations of facts can be made. Logicians have formalised this process as propositional calculus and its more sophisticated brother, predicate calculus. Humans, however, do not normally obey these formalisms. While we reason well in terms of positive association, when negative terms are introduced our reasoning becomes illogical. Take the following problem, which is a classic in psychology:

> You are given four cards; on each card there is a number on one side and on the other a letter. A rule states that if there is a vowel on one side, then there must be an even number on the other. Which two cards should be turned over to prove the rule true or false?
>
> E K 4 7
>
> Most people go for cards E and 4. Logically this is not correct, because the rule states a vowel–even number link and not the converse. Finding a consonant on the reverse of 4 proves nothing. The correct answer is E and 7, because if 7 happens to have an even number, then the rule is wrong, but the rule says nothing about consonants (K) and nothing about even numbers always having vowels on the opposite side.

Only too often we tend to look for confirmatory evidence rather than ways of disproving our beliefs. This 'confirmation bias' can lead to many errors because, so long as the evidence confirms our course of action, we do not go looking for evidence to disprove our beliefs. Worse still, we often ignore contradictory evidence when it is available.

It appears that the content and context of a problem are more important than underlying logical structure and that reasoning in abstract terms is more difficult than with concrete examples. The important consequence is that we transfer our knowledge about context and content between problems rather than the underlying logical structure. This has implications for task design, because unfortunately, knowing one task does not help learning of another task with the same underlying logical structure. Instead context influences our decisions, which may result in the wrong method being applied to a problem because superficially it appears to be similar to a previous one.

Mental models

Human reasoning uses logic loosely but it is efficient in discovering associations, and problem solving by testing knowledge structures, i.e. a set of interconnected facts about the objects in the problem. To illustrate the point consider the assertions:

Some animals with wings can fly
Birds have wings
Therefore birds can fly

The conclusion may be regarded as valid but it is not logical, because the assertion does not state that all animals with wings can fly. We may also refute the argument from our knowledge that penguins have wings but cannot fly. We appear to construct mental models of things in terms of propositions. These truths are then used in reasoning rather than logical examination of the problem in detail. The explanation of cognitive processes by mental models has been advocated by Johnson-Laird (1983) and this work has had a wide influence on cognitive psychology. Mental models help explain observable phenomena about human mental abilities such as our inability to reason logically in some situations. Human ability to reason logically may be limited by working memory because to solve problems several associations have to be held in working memory. Consider whether other relationships are possible in the following:

Some Artists are Brokers
All Brokers are Consultants

We can form a model of the propositions symbolically:

A = B B = C	where A, B, C are individuals,
A = B B = C	() denotes an independent existence,
(A) (B) B = C	= is a link equating individual objects

Reasoning then proceeds by substitution to create

A = B
(A) (B)
A = C
(A) (C)

We conclude that some artists are also consultants.

This is an easy example, as the number of concepts does not exceed working memory limits, but when the number of terms increases, more than one mental model can be constructed for a set of propositions, and the relationships to be held in working memory increase. Furthermore, when negative terms are added, this militates against the positive pattern matching process. Not surprisingly, we reason poorly with complex logical relationships involving negation. Try to find other possible relationships in the following to prove the point:

No Brokers are Artists
Some Brokers are Consultants

More than one conclusion appears to be possible because more than one mental model can be constructed. In the case of No A are B and No B are C; there are two conclusions:

There are three disjunct sets: A, B and C. Set A and C may, however, be related, even though A, B and B, C are not.

Mental models may be either physical or conceptual. Physical models describe the relationships of objects in the real world in terms of spatial distribution of events in time. Physical models may be visualised, especially if the problem involves spatial reasoning, e.g. the fork is on the left of the knife; the plate is on the right-hand side of the knife. Conceptual models come in different manifestations. There is the surface linguistic expression, and an internal mental language which, although linguistically based, represents a further abstraction. Conceptual models are a type of internal mental language representing truth values about objects and their relationships. The form of mental models differs between people and depends on individual cognitive styles. Mental models are important in creating human–computer interfaces; for instance, a graphical metaphor should help the user acquire the correct mental model of the system. Another example is decision support systems with simulation interfaces. The mental model of how something works is portrayed by a graphical representation. This theme is revisited in Chapter 3. The main point to note is that mental models are based on people's experience, i.e. the truths which they may be expected to hold.

Skills and errors

The influential model of problem solving proposed by Rasmussen (1986) has three modes of reasoning according to experience of the domain. If we know little about the problem, previous knowledge and general rules of thumb or heuristics are used. After some experience, partial problem solutions are stored in memory as rules or declarative knowledge. Reasoning still requires some effort, as rules have to be organised in the correct order to solve the problem. Finally, after further experience has been gained, rules become organised in memory as procedures, i.e. runnable programmes which automatically solve the problem. Recognition of the correct calling conditions then invokes the automatic procedures (or skills) which consume less effort. People tend to minimise mental effort whenever possible, so there is a natural tendency to use skills and to automate new procedures with practice. This is the human equivalent of programming and compiling knowledge.

Acquisition of skill is by learning, the process of acquiring new memories for behavioural sequences and mental procedures of problem solving. Skill learning is subject to a law of diminishing returns known as the power law of practice, which, represented as the time taken to complete a task plotted against the practice time, forms a straight line on a log-log plot. The effect is that more practice yields an increasing small improvement in eventual performance. The power law can be formalised:

$$T = c + a(P + d)^{-b}$$

where c = near maximum speed (asymptotic)
T = task completion time
a = initial speed
P = practice time
d = possible number of trials before measurement
b = number of trials

Acquisition of skill is influenced by the same factors as memorisation. Frequent, regular learning sessions help skill acquisition, whereas gaps without practice help forgetting; positive feedback during task performance helps automation, as does presenting a clear model of the task and making the task steps easily recognisable. Redundant feedback only confuses. Skill learning is improved by use of context dependent learning; this is also important in binding activation of the skilled procedure in the correct circumstances (see also episodic memory).

Skill and automatic processing are important because they enable parallel processing to occur and reduce the need to attend to external stimuli and the load on working memory. The penalty we pay is that sometimes automatic procedures are triggered in the wrong circumstances, in the face of environmental cues which obviously contradict the course of action. Use of automatic behaviour presents a dilemma in matching calling conditions to the correct procedures. In such situations we make mistakes. Errors in problem solving tasks can be classified as 'slips', which are failures in carrying out a correct sequence of actions, and 'mistakes', when the plan of action was misconceived in the first place. Slips are probably caused by a distraction or failure in attention, so a step is missed out or not completed. True mistakes, however, are either a failure in matching the correct procedure to the problem or incorrect reasoning at the rule-based level. People are generally good at heuristic reasoning and this ability marks us apart from even the most sophisticated artificial intelligence machine. Ironically, when we are under pressure, this ability often deserts us, and we revert to automatic procedures which may well be inappropriate. When under stress or overtired, people tend to use the most frequent or recent procedures they have, even if the match to the triggering conditions is good. This frequency gambling is a penalty of activation of procedural memory and can lead to unfortunate consequences, some of which have been manifest in accidents in nuclear power stations (Reason, 1990).

The implications for interface designers are that tasks should be structured to help users solve problems. This can be done by constructing a clear mental model for the user which invokes appropriate parts of the user's experience. The GOMS model may be used as a framework for design, by breaking the problem down into goals, providing operators to test the goals and a method for approaching a solution. However, an over-rigid definition of problems in system design may be counter-productive. People use many different methods to solve problems and, in spite of good analysis, the designer may not choose the correct one. Hence, in decision support tasks, it is advisable to make the goals and operators explicit, while choice of the method may be left to the user. In co-operative expert systems, the user is left with the parts of the problem which are less predictable while the more 'logical' or deterministic reasoning is automated. Before moving on to the implications of human problem solving for human–computer interaction, it is worth summarising the salient features of reasoning, mental models and skill:

- We reason by applying procedures to memorised facts and environmental information.
- Problems are formulated as mental models which are a collection of facts and their relationships held in working memory.
- Human reasoning is not strictly logical; instead it tests propositions and compares facts which make up a mental model.

- Reasoning is heuristic in situations when little is known about the problem. Heuristic reasoning requires considerable effort.
- Experience leads to the results of reasoning being stored, first as declarative, rule-based knowledge and then as automatic procedures.
- Automatic procedures, or skills, have calling conditions. Mismatch of calling conditions and procedures can cause mistakes.

So far, data storage and processing, i.e. memory and reasoning, have been examined. The next element of human information processing is control: how the conflicting demands of problem solving, memorisation and recall, and sensory input are resolved. In computer terms this is a scheduling problem, the human equivalent is attention.

2.6 Control of Human Information Processing

The information processing model gives a picture of a sequential machine with a bottleneck at the cognitive processor and short-term memory. Even though we may be sequential to an extent in our reasoning, the human machine is capable of considerable multitasking. The control of activity is partly automatic and therefore unconscious, although some control is in the realm of our conscious. This we refer to as paying attention.

2.6.1 Attention

From the information processing model it should be apparent that there are several input/output channels competing for the resources of the cognitive processor and its short-term memory. Inputs from the visual and auditory systems compete with other senses which have not been reviewed, e.g. touch, smell, pain. In addition, the cognitive processor has to find time to access memory and control output to the motor processor and speech buffer.

The fact that we are basically sequential machines should be apparent from our poor ability to do two or more mental tasks concurrently. Try reading a newspaper and listening to the radio at the same time: either the radio or the newsprint will be remembered but not both. Attention is selective: the best we can do is to time slice between channels so we remember part of what the radio announcer said and a few things from the newspaper article. In spite of our sequential attention, we do have considerable capacity for concurrent processing. We have already encountered background memory tasks and parallel processing of input; in addition, we also do certain skills automatically, for instance driving a car while holding a conversation.

To complete all its tasks, the human machine must have more than one processor running concurrently. When driving a car and talking, the motor processor will be controlling the leg and arm muscles for steering and braking; the speech processor will be controlling the larynx to form speech; while the cognitive processor divides its attention between monitoring the senses for road traffic and listening to what has been said. Such complexity appears to strain the resources of the information processing model to its limits. Attention in the form of a system monitor plays a key role.

Although parallel processing undoubtedly occurs as demonstrated in the ICS model, there is a limiting sequential bottleneck in cognitive processing. Resource rationing has to occur and, as with a computer, this is controlled by scheduling with interrupts for important events. If little of interest is happening in the environment, we pay little attention to sensory input, as may happen when we are lost deep in thought. The instant something unexpected happens, for example a loud noise, our attention is immediately switched to the sensory input. The visual or auditory processors effectively put an interrupt on the cognitive processor. The input processors are continually competing for the cognitive processors' attention in this manner. In this battle our attentional apparatus is finely tuned to ignore constant states and pick up changes in the environment.

The human ability to ignore the steady state in the environment can lead to poor performance in monitoring tasks. If we have to concentrate on input with little variation, there is a natural tendency to ignore changes and for attention to wander as the cognitive processor polls other channels. Even worse, in long monitoring tasks fatigue may set in, with the result that we miss significant events in the environment. Distractions are very effective at diverting attention, particularly if the information is irrelevant to the task at hand. This probably occurs because the attention controller naturally polls all input, while task-enforced attention tries to over-ride this mechanism, with the undesirable effect of making people more sensitive to distracting signals.

Attention is influenced by the difficulty of the task, by distraction in the environment, and by motivation of the individual. More difficult tasks hold attention better than mundane boring ones, which explains why most people will read a good book without degraded attention but watching a blip on a radar screen soon becomes boring and performance suffers. Motivation is the internal will of an individual to do something, which can be influenced by physiological factors (e.g. hunger), psychological factors (fear, sleepiness) and sociological matters such as companionship and responsibility. Motivation is important in task design, when the designers should try to motivate users by giving them the appropriate level of interest, responsibility and reward for performance. Motivation is a study in its own right which cannot be dealt with here; for further study the reader is referred to Maslow (1987).

In interface and dialogue design, attention has to be directed to important messages and instructions. Care has to be exercised that the design does not produce too many competing demands for attention at once, thereby over-loading the cognitive processors' ability to deal with events. This can have important consequences in multimedia interaction. Attention tends to be diverted by change; hence, temporal media such as film, animation and sound will dominate over static media such as pictures and text. If too much information is presented at once, the attention scheduler cannot cope, leading to information overloading. Too much information arrives in a short space of time, exceeding the capacity of our cognitive resources. This leads to malfunction and breakdown of the human information processing, the symptoms of which are manifest in stress and task failure. While cognitive overload is not the only cause of stress, it is important to avoid it by good interface design.

2.6.2 Stress and Fatigue

Fatigue may result from continuous mental activity in overlong, mundane tasks and from intense concentration in tasks demanding difficult mental reasoning. In either case rest is required for the human mental system to readjust itself. Fatigue can be caused by repetitive tasks containing no break points. Interface design should therefore ensure that long continuous tasks are broken up by rest periods in which the user is allowed to do a mental reset. These break points, called 'closure events', should be placed at natural intervals during a task. These intervals could be at the end of an operational sequence, such as entering a transaction record, or a search and replace operation in a word processor. The more complex a task the more demanding and potentially more fatiguing it may be. Break points should be planned with task complexity in mind, with more frequent break points provided to counter increased risk of fatigue.

Task complexity, however, does not always lead to increased fatigue. People find stimulating but demanding tasks interesting. Complexity may hold their attention and delay the onset of fatigue for some considerable time, although highly demanding continuous activity should be avoided because users may be unaware of their tiredness and make mistakes. Mundane, non-stimulating tasks are liable to cause fatigue precisely because they do not stimulate interest and, hence, hold attention. Such tasks should best be avoided, but if they are necessary, a high frequency of break points helps to combat the strain of enforced attention to an uninteresting task.

Fatigue can also be caused by sensory factors. Strong stimuli, such as bright colours, intense light and loud noises, all cause sensory overloading as they bombard the perceptual system and demand attention. If exposure to such stimuli continues for a long time, the cognitive system will try to ignore the steady state in the environment; however, such strong signals are not easily ignored. This sets up a conflict in the attentional process which can become fatiguing. Excessive stimuli such as strong light can cause eye- and headaches, and loud noises may result in temporary deafness. Interface designers should avoid using too many strong stimuli, e.g. frequent use of sound warnings and too many bright colours at once.

2.7 Models of Interaction

So far this chapter has been considering human information processing. However, interface design concerns computer software as well as wider issues of the computer system environment. Therefore a model of interaction is necessary to help focus design issues. Norman's (1986, 1988) model has been one of the most influential models of people interacting with computers. It is simple, yet it encapsulates the key points about human–computer interaction. The essence, as shown in Figure 2.13, is that interaction occurs in cycles of user and system actions. These create the dialogue between the user and the computer. Between the two, as Norman points out, there are two gulfs which have to be bridged by the interface:

- The gulf of execution, when the user is faced with the question of what to do next. To help bridge this gulf the interface has to suggest and prompt the user about possible actions.
- The gulf of evaluation: this occurs after a user action and the consequent system response when the user has to figure out what has happened. Design here has to help by making the effects of user action explicit and giving a clear representation of the system state.

Interaction continues in a cycle of deciding what to do (formulate goal), user action, system reaction, and so on. However, things are a bit more complex than Norman's model suggests. First, how we plan what to do varies. Plans may come from procedural memory: we just retrieve the appropriate procedure and run it as a series of actions. Alternatively we may decide what to do according to the state of the environment we perceive. This is 'situated action', in which mini-plans are executed according to the input triggers from the environment. Interaction with graphical user interfaces may well be situated according to the interface display. There is still much debate about how plan or environmentally driven we are; the truth is probably that we are individually different, some people liking to do things in a well-determined manner, while others act more 'on the spur of the moment'.

Bridging the gulfs of execution and evaluation can be helped by use of analogical memory. This gives a context for interpretation in the interface metaphor. Design can also help by guiding users' attention to key messages. There are a set of issues which map to the basic cycle of interaction; for instance, for execution of a user action, design of prompts is important,and for evaluation feedback messages are necessary. To help the user to plan future goals, overviews and summaries are required. This leads into consideration of principles for HCI design.

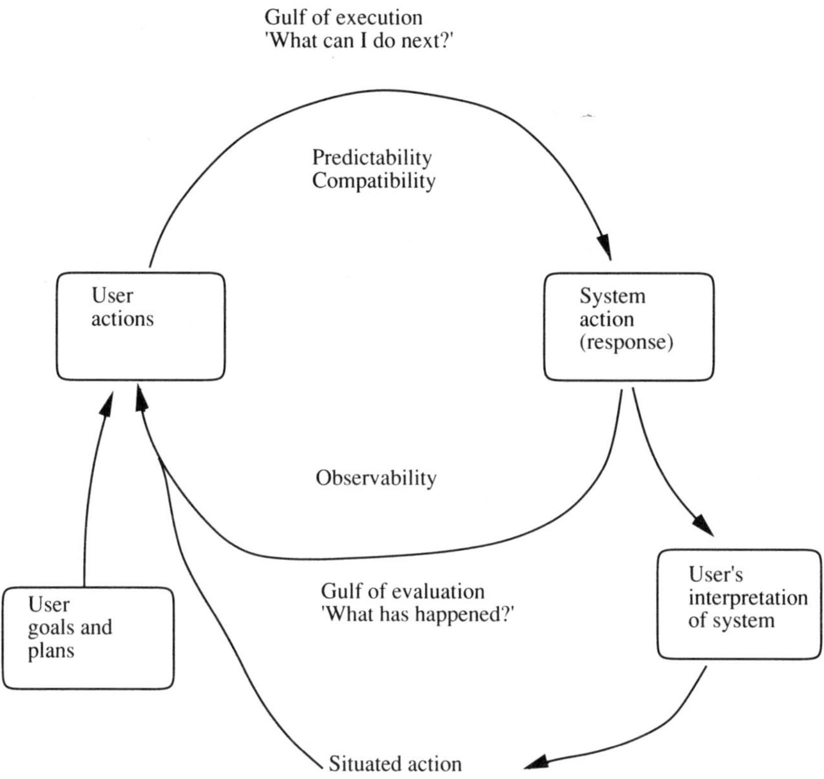

Figure 2.13 Cycle of human–computer interaction (after Norman, 1986).

2.8 Principles of Human–Computer Interaction

Models of human information processing and knowledge of cognitive psychology allow a set of tentative principles to be drawn up, although care has to be taken in applying principles in practice, because the context of design has a strong effect on the validity of generalisations drawn from psychology. Unfortunately, psychology does not lend itself to such a venture, as many explanations of human behaviour are still models and hypotheses, and in some areas little definite proof exists. However, some principles can be derived in spite of this limitation, although they have to be supplemented by justifications to substantiate them based on interpretation in a context, as well as empirical evidence of usability.

Seven basic principles are proposed:

Consistency This is similarity of patterns which may be perceived in tasks, in presentation of information and other facets of an interface design. Consistency reduces the human learning load and increases recognition by presenting a familiar pattern. As we are pattern recognition machines, the more consistent patterns are, the less we have to learn, and the easier an interface will be to use.

Compatibility This is the goodness of fit between the user's expectation and the reality of an interface design. This principle follows on from consistency to state that new designs should be compatible with, and therefore based upon, the user's previous experience. If this is followed, once again recognition is enhanced, learning is reduced and the interface should be easier to use. Compatibility relates to the concept of users' models; the essential concordance is between the user's mental model of the task and the task model embedded in software by the designer.

Predictability The interface should always suggest to the user what action is possible. This may be by messages, prompts, etc., or information may be contained in metaphors and icons in graphical user interfaces. Predictability has a sub-principle of observability which states that the current state of the system should be made explicit to the user. Only by having information about what can be done and the current state can users plan what to do next. An example would be highlighting a graphical object with 'handles' showing that it has been selected.

Adaptability Interfaces should adapt to the user in several ways. The user and not the computer should be in control; so the interface adapts to the user's speed of work and does not enforce continuous attention. Also, the interface should adapt to individual user characteristics, skill levels, etc., as to do otherwise would offend the compatibility principle. Adaptability, however, must not be overdone, otherwise the consistency of the interface is reduced.

Economy and error prevention This principle is based more on common sense than psychology. Interface designs should be economic in the sense that they achieve an operation in the minimum number of steps necessary and save users work whenever possible. Short cuts in dialogues and setting defaults are examples of this principle in design. Error prevention is the inverse, trying to save the user work by recovering from errors. Whenever possible, an interface should not allow the user to get into states causing damaging errors, e.g. deleting all files without backups.

User control The interface should function at the user's pace according to their commands and should not attempt to control the user. This principle is related to predictability, as users should be able to forecast what to do next from a system's current state. It has a sub-component: reversibility. This states that users should be able to backtrack at will when mistakes are made. Reversibility is manifest in 'undo' commands.

Structure Interface designs should be structured to reduce complexity, because humans process information by classifying and structuring it within a framework of understanding. We deal with complexity in the environment by imposing order on it and trying to automate solutions to problems. Classification, structuring of information, and skills are consequences of this propensity to organise and automate. Structuring should be compatible with the user's organisation of knowledge and not overburden memory. This leads to a sub-component of simplicity and relevance: information should be organised so only relevant information is presented to the user in a simple manner.

Principles are intended for overall guidance during design and as a set of criteria against which interfaces may be evaluated. To apply principles in the design process, they have to be translated into guidelines which pertain to different aspects of a human–computer interface. Guidelines, in turn, are modulated by the context of a particular application into design rules. Unfortunately, systems and people are complex and to issue a simple set of guidelines for all situations may be appealing but in reality would only be misleading.

A key point of user-centred design is to prevent overloading of human information processing facilities, in particular short-term memory. People deal with vast quantities of data from the environment by filtering them and abstracting interesting qualities from basic data. Hence, principles which help memory and human reasoning abilities are important. Designs need to be considered in terms of the objectives of creating good human–computer interfaces, which raises the question of assessment. The effectiveness of interface designs is measured in terms of usability, utility, efficiency and ultimately user satisfaction. There are three basic concerns about the quality of an interface design:

- How well does it fulfil the users' objectives?
- How easy is it to learn and use?
- How effective is it in helping users carrying out some work?

A design should aim to provide users with what they require in order to fulfil their objectives. This concept is common to systems analysis and HCI design, i.e. the matching of user requirements to the facilities provided in the system. In HCI terms this is called task fit, providing the appropriate tool to carry out a required task. A system may be easy to use and learn, but if it does not do what the user wants, it will be useless. Task fit is a consequence of the compatibility principle, memory and mental models, the users' expectation of reality and what they get.

Effectiveness is how well a computer system helps users achieve work at an acceptable cost. Cost can be incurred both on the computer side in programming and on the user side by mental effort, stress and operation time. Good design is about minimising human costs within the available budget of computer development costs. A major component of effectiveness is efficiency. This is often measured in terms of how easy an interface is to learn and use, combined with the inverse measure of how many mistakes are made. Generally it may be thought that there is a trade-off between ease of use and ease of learning, but evidence points the other way: interfaces should be easy to learn and easy to use. Efficiency is a consequence of the economy, consistency and compatibility principles. Utility and satisfaction with an interface depend on how it helps us. This is partly a consequence of compatibility but it also relates to the creative side of task support design. A computer system should empower people, or, put more simply, help them to do their work more creatively and enjoyably.

The concern for how much of an interface, and, hence, a system, is used is often ignored. There is a natural tendency for many computer products to add extra features with each successive release. A product which starts out life as a simple application can gradually evolve into a monster of considerable complexity. This imposes a learning penalty for new users in particular, who may only want a fraction of the overall functionality provided. Usability is also concerned with problems caused by excessive functionality. However, there are other reasons why many functions are never used, including poor task fit, poor training and poor interface design. Users may be ignorant of or can't be bothered to use a facility, even though it may fulfil their task very well.

Ideally a system should be sufficient for users' needs and compatible with their experience. This will be based on previous experience of computer and non-computer systems. It is the analyst's task to capture that knowledge and build the new system to be as compatible as possible with the users' expectations. Full compatibility may be technically impossible because of improvements to the logical design of the new system. Also, user models differ according to variation in individual experience; one single model cannot be completely compatible with each individual's view. The final design has to be a compromise with inter-individual variation.

2.9 Summary

Perception is the process of seeing and hearing. Images and sounds are received and coded in an abstract form as properties of the stimulus. Interpretation is effected by comparing the input with long-term memory. Memory may supply a considerable amount of what we see and hear, which creates illusions in some circumstances. Human information processing is composed of sensory, cognitive and motor processors with associated short-term and long-term memories. Short-term memory has limited capacity which may be expanded by increasing the level of abstraction of information. Information in short-term memory is held in chunk form and has to be refreshed frequently. Long-term memory has an infinite capacity and can be thought of as a highly networked database. Memory is essentially semantic, and has several different forms of organisation, e.g. procedural, categorial, analogical and script-event-based memory.

Problem solving involves steps of formulating, searching and verifying problem solutions. The GOMS model of problem solving consists of a network of goal sub-steps, each of which has tests associated with it. The network is traversed by a strategy called a method. Various methods are used by people to solve problems. Human reasoning is not strictly logical: instead we form mental models of problems and reason by association. Problem solutions are stored as skills and automatic processes which are called by a context. Mismatch of calling context and automatic behaviour can cause errors.

Human information processing is essentially sequential, although considerable concurrent processing occurs. Sequential scheduling is controlled by attention, which directs the resources of the cognitive processor. Attention has important consequences for task design. Fatigue affects attention and sensory processes and should be considered in task design.

From knowledge of psychology seven general principles of interface design can be drawn: consistency, compatibility, adaptability, predictability, economy, user control and structure. These principles should increase the effectiveness of interface design, which may be measured in terms of efficiency, task fit and usability.

Further Reading

For general texts on cognition, Glass *et al.* (1979) or Lindsay and Norman (1977) give comprehensive coverage of the field. Norman's (1988) book on the *Psychology of Everyday Things* is an excellent survey of cognition related to design in general as well as interface design. For more detail on perception Frisby (1979) gives a well illustrated description of vision, and Fry (1977) is a good general introduction to speech and hearing. A very readable account of memory, both working and long-term, can be found in Baddeley (1979). For more advanced study Christie and Gardiner (1987) contains chapters on most relevant topics in which authors summarise research in their field and give guideline summaries. Reason (1990) contains more on human error and memory, while Rasmussen (1986) deals with applied cognition in process control and human co-operation. Card *et al.* (1983), besides being the source of the GOMS model, makes instructive reading, although it does view cognition in a narrow perspective.

Questions and Exercises

1. Consider a task which involves diagnostic reasoning; figuring out why a computer or printer doesn't work is a typical example. Describe the steps you would go through to solve this sort of problem. Try describing the problem solving using goals and the GOMS concepts.

2. Using the same example of a diagnostic task, list the types of knowledge required to complete the diagnosis, e.g. knowledge about procedures, objects, concepts. List the sources of the knowledge. How should a computer system supply the knowledge which you did not already have?

3. How do skill and automated behaviour affect human–computer interaction? Discuss the problems skilled behaviour may cause when transferring between two similar word processors.

4. How can the HCI principle of 'consistency' be interpreted in terms of learning and memory? What different types of consistency are there and how do these help memorisation and recall?

5. Discuss the role of analogy in design of graphical user interfaces. Illustrate your answer with an example of how analogy or metaphor works in helping users predict what an interface should do.

3 Interface Analysis and Specification

This chapter covers the analysis phase of interface design in which information is gathered about users and the jobs they do. This work should be carried out and integrated with mainstream systems analysis, e.g. tasks in SSADM (Longworth and Nicholls, 1987). The steps involved are analysis of user characteristics; analysis of the user's job (called task analysis); and domain analysis, which investigates the system environment and the users' perceptions of it as they relate to their task. This information is then synthesised to design the user interface which supports the users' task.

The steps involved in interface analysis are summarised in Figure 3.1. The approach uses data flow diagrams as a notation from structured systems analysis and design (SA/SD), although other methods which have been developed within the field of human–computer interaction are also covered, to show where their ideas and concepts can be applied.

Interface design takes a task specification and requirements generated by traditional systems analysis and transforms them into an interactive system. Interface design is therefore an extension of standard software design, the main difference being one of emphasis on the user. HCI is primarily concerned with creating applications which help people. This may be viewed at two levels:

HCI in the large Specification and design of system functionality with particular attention to designing interactive software to co-operate with users in achieving a job of work

HCI in the small Design of the detail of interaction, i.e. the user–system dialogue and interface displays.

The two levels are, of course, linked. First, the system requirements have to be defined. For this stakeholder analysis is used to discover what needs to be investigated and what the overall goals of the system should be, before more detailed task analsyis is carried out. Task analysis continues by refining analysis of issues related to HCI in the large. This is followed by task design, which expands the ambit of design to include not only the technical (computer) system but also the socio- (people) system. Design involves not only construction of the software–user interface but also operational procedures for the human system of work, job descriptions and the system support environment, i.e. parts of the system to help the user, in terms of user manuals, training programmes, etc. (see Harker and Eason, 1989).

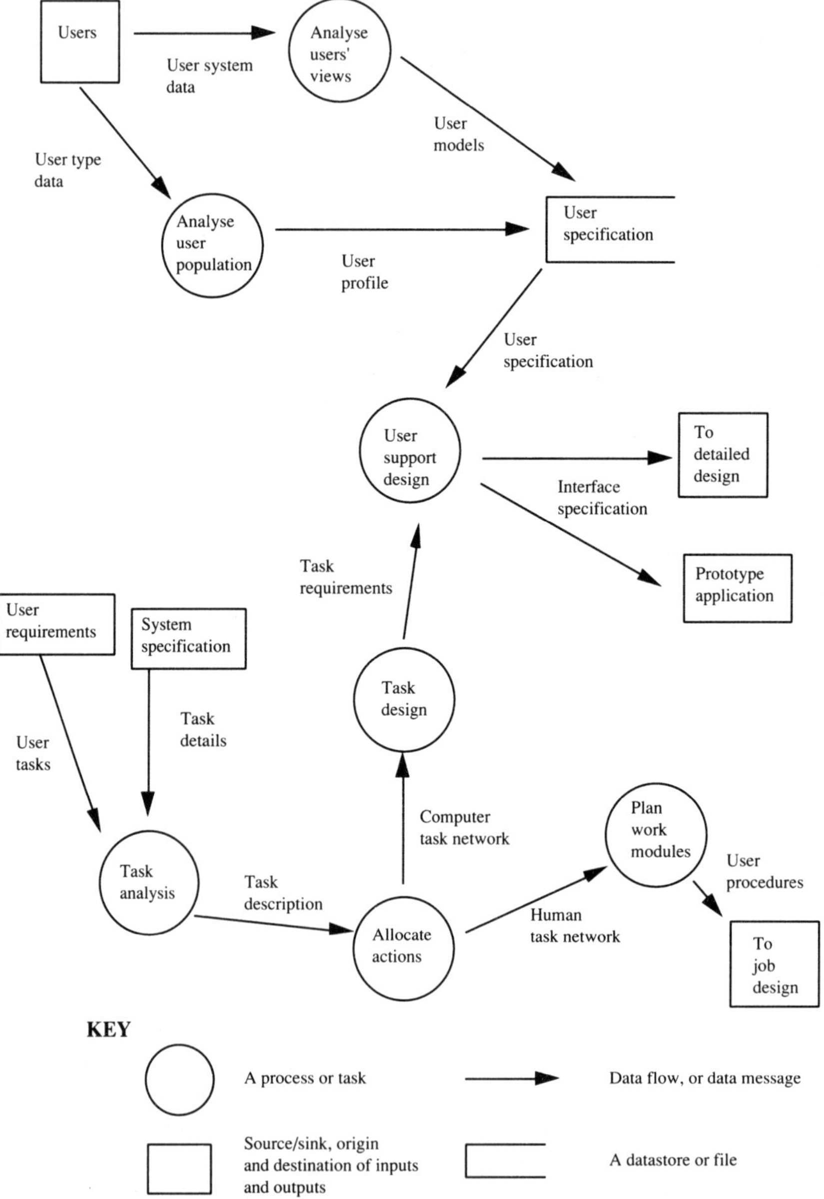

Figure 3.1 Data flow diagram showing steps in interface design.

3.1 Stakeholder Analysis

Stakeholders are users who have an interest in the system. The technique is to focus on the utility of the proposed application and how it might affect different people. Distinctions are drawn between the immediate users and others who may be influenced by the system. Primary users are the direct system operators, whereas secondary users may use the output of the system but do not operate the system itself (e.g. managers who use the information). Tertiary users may be influenced by the system output even though they do not directly use it, as in senior managers who use information from a system for planning and decision making. Stakeholder analysis looks at users' jobs and assesses the likely prospects for the introduction of technology. In this way it can be used as a means of validating the proposed functionality, and discovering new requirements. The overall effect should be to improve the task fit and hence utility of the delivered system.

The method gathers data on the users' profiles and projected system use. Some typical measures are:

- The target users' characteristics are recorded. This stage describes the profile of the prospective user groups (primary to tertiary), who they are, whether they work for the company or are general public, the age and sex range, culture and so on.
- The users' job profiles are described in terms of tasks. The number of user tasks affected by the new system is described according to primary or secondary use.
- The likely impact of the new system on the user's job is assessed. The technology may enhance work, make it easier but not improve it or in some cases make it more difficult by introducing controls. Impact analysis has two parts: first, the product developer's assessment of how the job will be changed; and second, how the user's attitude may be shaped by the new system. Users may see the introduction of technology as a threat to their jobs, or it may be seen as an improvement.
- The frequency of use is estimated and the mandatory or discretionary nature of use is noted.

Stakeholder analysis is best carried out in workshops involving users and the design teams. The teams should have a facilitator or moderator who is a member of neither community to act as a referee if necessary and a chairman other wise. This allows data to be captured directly, including rapid feedback so the design teams can respond by modifying their ideas. User involvement can be promoted so that the users start to define the functionality. Techniques such as idea writing and establishing group consensus can be used to generate lists of desired functionality. Each user writes their own selected wish list for the new system. The lists are then circulated to others to annotate with comments, supporting or otherwise. After this circulation the moderator assimilates the individual wish lists into a common one and this is then circulated for voting. Each user ranks their top ten desired functions, and the ranks are collated to give a group consensus. This stage increases the users' commitment to the system's success.

Functionalities

	Diary management	Electronic mail	Spreadsheets	Database	Calculator
Primary users (secretaries)	+++	+++	+++	+	-
Secondary users (junior managers)	++	++	+	++	+
Tertiary users (senior managers)	--	--	--	+	+

+++ = very favourable reaction

--- = very unfavourable reaction

Figure 3.2 Stakeholder analysis matrix showing categories of users with results of an analysis for an office information system.

User profiles can be used to estimate commitment of stakeholders. Questionnaires are used to get feedback on the impact of the proposed changes, and then the proposed functionality can be viewed in the light of its rating in improving people's jobs and their attitude to it. Quantitative techniques from questionnaire data allow the functionality to be ranked according to metrics and, hence, the system is defined by a systematic forecast of its future utility. The output from the method is a series of matrix tables which allow trade-off decisions and comparisons to be made (see Figure 3.2).

Further complexity can be introduced by adding more stakeholder groups to reflect the sociology of the organisation. For instance, tertiary stakeholders, senior management, may not use the system or the information it produces directly, although they will be interested in the system if it improves their ability to manage the business. In many organisations this is interpreted as simply improving control, but in more enlightened companies the creative improvement of work and the impact of the system on the quality of products are factors of interest to tertiary users. Stakeholder analysis can progress towards discovery of how to use technology for competitive advantage. If stakeholders are partitioned not only horizontally within the company but also laterally to model stakeholders in other companies, then a three-dimensional model of competitors, collaborator organisations and customers is created.

Stakeholder techniques are practical and in current practice. One of the better-known examples is the User Skills Task Match method (Fowler *et al.* (1988). The output from this technique is a list of requirements for the new system and functions for further investigation. Requirements can be divided into functional goals which the system must achieve, and non-functional goals related to performance criteria. Examples of the latter may be throughput volumes to be processed, desired response times, and usability criteria such as learning times, error tolerances, etc. They will reappear in Chapter 8, when they become usability goals. Functional goals feed directly into the next analysis step by defining what task should be investigated.

3.2 Task Analysis

Task analysis is the decomposition of the activities within the system. It is a similar activity to requirements analysis as practised in systems analysis and design, with the added proviso that in task analysis all the system tasks, including human-related actions, are described and not just the functions to be computerised.

3.2.1 HCI Methods for Task Analysis

Several methods of task analysis in human–computer interaction have been defined which address different issues. Unfortunately, their track record of use in industry is not good (Bellotti, 1988), so we shall examine these methods and transfer their recommendations into methods which are practised, e.g. SSADM. This is a viable approach, as the systems analysis and task analysis share many similarities in their concepts and approaches.

Hierarchical Task Analysis (HTA)

This is the grandfather of most methods (Annett *et al.*, 1971). It uses a top-down approach of functional decomposition by progressively dividing an area of activity into goals, sub-goals, and so on. When decomposition reaches a low level, the sub-goal is split into actions which are then ordered in a sequence. HTA can specify procedures using the familiar control constructs of Sequence, Selection and Iteration.

The method itself does not have a rigorous definition. Actions are considered to be primitives of the task model (i.e. they cannot be decomposed further). Little attention is paid to objects or data structures. The result of analysis is a task model represented as a hierarchy diagram composed of goals, sub-goals and actions.

Task Knowledge Structures

This is one of the most sophisticated task analysis and modelling methods. It consists of a modelling language for representing task knowledge, Task Knowledge Structures (TKS); and a set of analysis techniques to guide knowledge/fact gathering for task modelling, Knowledge Analysis for Tasks (KAT; Johnson, 1992). The method grew out of TAKD, Task Analysis for Knowledge Description. This modelled actions and objects in procedures and then generalised specific actions to generic actions and objects which could be used in design.

TKS originally aimed to model the knowledge necessary for a person to carry out a task. This is different from modelling activity directly, as it also covers knowledge held in memory. TKS is based on a theory of procedural memory (see Section 2.4). Tasks are organised in hierarchies of goals and sub-goals. Lower-level goals are decomposed into procedures which in turn model the sequence of actions necessary for the task. The modelling constructs provided by TKS are:

- Goals, which are the purpose or intent of a task. These describe what has to be achieved. Goals in turn are decomposed into sub-goals in a tree of arbitrary depth.
- Plans, organise goals in a tree, so a plan represents a hierarchical decomposition of goals and sub-goals which achieve a task.
- Procedures, model the activity carried out to satisfy a sub-goal. Each procedure is composed of actions and objects, and has preconditions and post-conditions. The latter model the permissible states when entering and exiting from the procedure.
- Actions, are primitive components of procedures. These are non-decomposable units of activity which act upon objects. Actions can be organised in procedures using control constructs of Sequence, Selection and Iteration.

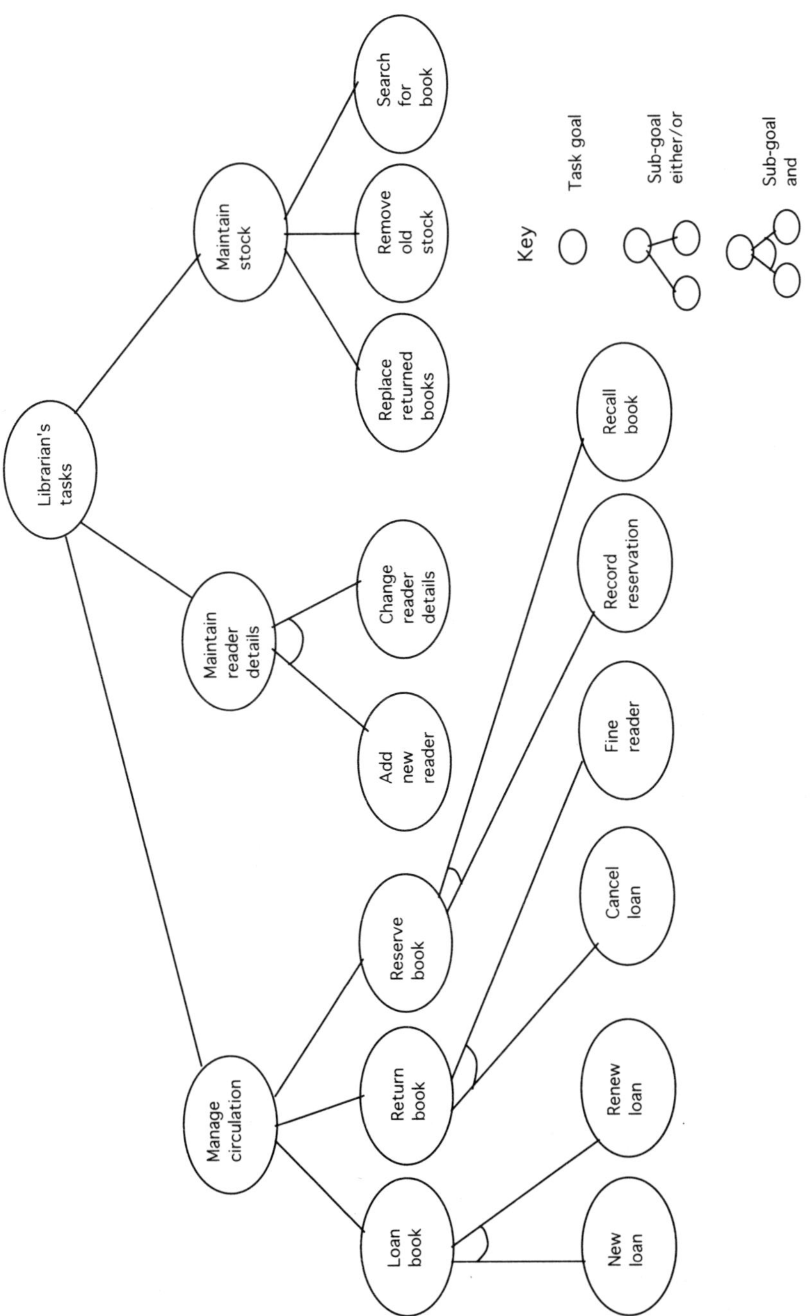

Figure 3.3 TKS goal tree of librarian's task.

- Objects are things which exist or data structures changed by actions.

An example TKS model is shown in Figure 3.3. Overall, a TKS analysis may consist of several such trees, one per task. The task sub-structure describes the activity in a domain and several task trees may be necessary fully to describe complex activity. A separate taxonomic sub-structure models the object hierarchy. This describes the domain objects and their classes. Certain actions may be considered to be key actions or vital to completion of the task. Weightings can be attached to actions to express their 'centrality' or how vital they are for a particular procedure from the user's point of view. The notion of centrality and much of the structure of TKS is based on models of categorial memory (see Chapter 2). Finally, TKS includes roles which allow links to be made between different parts of a task model according to different types of user, or user roles. Hence, TKS can describe different forms of the same task which match variations in activity.

The analytic method which accompanies TKS, Knowledge Analysis of Tasks, uses techniques drawn from knowledge elicitation, such as card sorting, protocol analysis and structured interviews. For further details of the method and TKS itself, the source to consult is Johnson (1992).

TKS has many concepts in common with software engineering approaches to systems analysis. Hierarchical decomposition and several modelling primitives are shared, such as actions, objects, composed into procedures, which in turn achieve goals. We shall use many of these concepts within the context of structured systems analysis.

Task and systems analysis

In view of the close relationship between task analysis and systems analysis, many concepts borrowed from HCI can be employed directly in SSADM. Task analysis maps to the functional decomposition part of SSADM, which was itself developed from earlier techniques of Structured Analysis as described by De Marco (1978) and Gane and Sarson (1979). The approach is to decompose the system into smaller units called functions; these are discrete pieces of work which achieve one goal. Functions may be directly equated with task-goals. Each function takes data in, does something to it (transforms the data) and then passes it to the next function. When a series of functions are linked together, they form a description of how the system operates. By linking functions with the data connections, called data flows, a map of the system activity can be built up as a data flow diagram (see Figure 3.4). This approach, called functional decomposition by systems analysts, is the essence of task analysis.

By successive refinement an increasingly detailed view of the system is obtained, first at the sub-system level, then at sub-sub-system level, and so on. When the units are reasonably small, their contents can be described as actions in a procedural sequence. Procedure consists of actions which achieve a purpose, as they do in task analysis. Procedures may model part of a person's job within the system or, possibly, an automated activity. Activity may be either physical (e.g. return book in a library system) or mental (e.g. choose supplier in sales order processing). Task analysis has the effect of widening the scope of systems analysis in two ways:

- Modelling the activity of people, even if this is unlikely or impossible to automate.
- Modelling the mental activity or reasoning carried out by people as well as the physical and logical activity normally covered by systems analysis.

Actions, described by verbs, are the primitive building blocks of tasks which cannot be decomposed further without losing meaning. For example, in an order-processing task, actions could be Check-Customer-Credit-Limit, Calculate-Order-Lead-Time, Determine-Discount. However, although Check-Invoice-Payment, Allocate-Stock are actions, Check-Days-Not>31 in Estimate-Order-Date is probably too low-level to be an action in its own right. Although the level of decomposition is a matter for the analyst's judgement, further decomposition would specify the logical operators of the comparison or mathematics for a calculation and this renders the description as a whole meaningless for interface design.

When to stop subdividing functions is a matter of judgement and experience, but one heuristic is to subdivide until each function achieves a single purpose and is at the stage when the procedural detail of how it works can be described in roughly half a page of concise English (e.g. 6–12 steps). For mental reasoning activities a higher level of granularity may be advisable (e.g. in foreign exchange dealing, actions may be 'obtain quotes, evaluate risks, select quotation') because lower-level detail on mental activity may be difficult if not impossible to elicit. Furthermore, low-level detail will not be needed unless an expert system is contemplated to automate some or all of the human reasoning.

The detail of procedures can be described in narrative or more formally as a sequence of actions in Structured English. Structured English is a constrained sub-set of English composed of a set of reserved words for expressing sequence control (If, Then, Else, Repeat, etc.), verbs which describe actions, nouns to describe data, and conjunctions/conditionals (And, Or, Not = >, etc.); see Figure 3.5. It describes how a task is carried out in terms of sequences of actions, alternatives and repetitions. The reserved word set combined with indentation of the text shows the scope of control. The procedure shows the sequence in which actions are performed and any exceptions to that sequence.

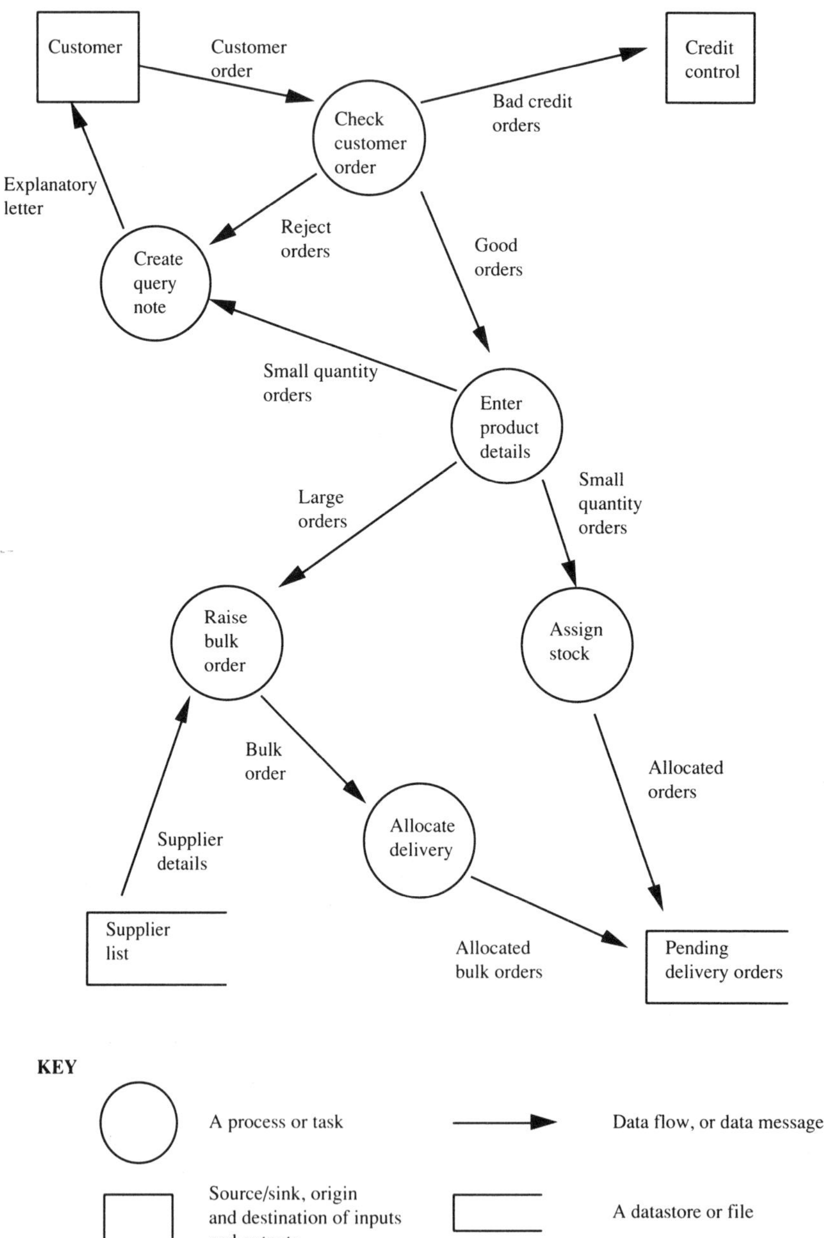

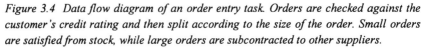

Figure 3.4 Data flow diagram of an order entry task. Orders are checked against the customer's credit rating and then split according to the size of the order. Small orders are satisfied from stock, while large orders are subcontracted to other suppliers.

H: = allocated to human operator
C: = allocated to computer

Function: Check Customer Order

Repeat while orders
- H: Enter customer number
- C: Check customer number
- C: If no number assume new customer & Pass to accounts
- C: Check customer against credit-control-list
- C: If customer on list Send to credit control
- H: Check order value against customer order credit limit
- C: If over limit Send to credit control

Function: Enter Product Details

Repeat for products ordered
- H: Enter product code
- C: Check product code
- C: If in stock Tick ex-stock column
- C: If not a stock item Tick direct column
- C: Check product quantity
- C: If less than minimum quantity Raise query note
- H: If over delivery limit and not a stock item Raise bulk order

Function: Raise Bulk Order

Repeat for high quantity products ordered
- H: Enter stock category against product code
- H: Create list of suppliers who have appropriate stock categories
- H&C: Find minimal number of suppliers who can deliver all the categories ordered
- H: Find suppliers who have quickest delivery dates for ordered categories
- C: Write out bulk order to suppliers

Function: Calculate Delivery Details

- H: Enter estimated delivery date
- C: Check delivery details present
- C: If absent Raise query note
- H: Stamp to authorise order

Figure 3.5 Task allocation in structured English.

Once a task has been described, the next step is to allocate all or parts of it to either people or computers. Task and action allocation is the first step of task design and is dealt with in Section 3.6.1.

3.3 Analysing User Characteristics

Human–computer interfaces should be built to suit the needs of people; consequently, it is important to discover what types of people will be using the interface. Groups of users vary in their knowledge of computers, general abilities and a variety of factors which affect their ability to deal with an interface. Therefore, the objective of user analysis is to obtain a thorough knowledge of the skills and experience of all users in order to be able to predict how they will react to different designs. This enables sound judgements to be made when matching the sophistication of the interface to users' abilities.

3.3.1 User Categories

Users have been categorised by many authors in a variety of schemas intended to describe user classes which have important implications for interface design. Four main categories of user are generally distinguished:

- *Naive*: users who have not previously encountered computer systems. They may show fear of computers, will be unfamiliar with their operation, and will have little or no knowledge about the system. Completely *naive* users are becoming rarer as computerisation spreads, but this user class will still be encountered when introducing computers into a non-automated environment.
- *Novice*: users with some experience of computers, although they may be unfamiliar with a new system. They will probably have little knowledge or experience with the system and are liable to make many mistakes; consequently, they need considerable support. Most users of new systems start as novices and progress with experience to becoming skilled, although, if usage frequency varies, they may regress to novice status after a period of inactivity.
- *Skilled*: users who have gained considerable experience with a system and are proficient operators. Most frequent users become skilled with time and require more economic, rapid-to-use interfaces with less support than novices. Skilled users, however, do not have much knowledge of the system structure, so they are unable to repair unexpected errors or extend the system capabilities. Instead they are skilled at operating one or more system tasks.
- *Expert*: experts or 'power users' are distinguished from skilled users by their knowledge of the internal system structure. Experts generally have some computer software expertise, good knowledge of how the system operates, and an ability to maintain and modify the basic system. Experts need a sophisticated interface so they can modify and extend the capabilities of the system.

Although the above categories provide a workable framework for analysis, user classification is rarely so simple. For instance, it is important to distinguish between 'domain experts', who are knowledgeable about the application domain, and expert users, who have knowledge of the designed computer system, and usually of the domain as well. Users therefore tend to fall within three dimensions: frequency of use, experience of computer systems, and knowledge of the domain, although frequency of use may itself vary with time. Some users may be casual and use the system only when they want to; for other people the system may be part of their job. Within a user population there may be a mix of people who have used the system for a long time, i.e. skilled users and new recruits, who will be novices. Variation occurs even within individuals over time. Expert users may rotate jobs and not use a system for several months, during which time they will forget their knowledge and may regress to a novice state. In spite of these difficulties, measuring user characteristics is worth while because it enables the designer to tailor and customise the interface to the users' needs (see the adaptability principle, Section 2.8) and select the level of support which is appropriate to most of the users.

3.3.2 Measuring User Characteristics

To start classifying users, some basic metrics are required. These are a mixture of anticipated usage patterns and observed abilities of the user population. The critical factors are how often people use a system, how much they already know about the system and how much they may be prepared to learn.

The choice of these measures is linked to expected user performance when operating the system. For instance, frequency of use will affect how skilled users become, while discretionary users are usually less tolerant of poor interfaces than users who have no choice about using a system. The impact of domain and application knowledge is more difficult to assess directly. Domain experts are likely to be more demanding about the system functionality and care will be necessary to ensure the design is compatible with their task model.

The important measures are:

- *Frequency of use*: how often will the system be used? Frequent users build up skills and become experienced quickly; if use is infrequent, then skill build-up will be slower and a more supportive interface may be necessary. The variation in usage frequency over time is also important. If frequent users have gaps between using the system, then they may forget key information and require help facilities.
- *Discretionary usage*: use of a system may either be compulsory, i.e. part of someone's job, or may be an optional extra; for instance, a data entry clerk may have to use the sales order processing system as part of the job duties, but it is up to a manager whether to use a spreadsheet for forecasting or not. All designs should be good, but interfaces for discretionary users have

to excel in ease of use and attractiveness to users; otherwise the system may never be used.

- *Computer familiarity*: most users have some experience of computers but the degree of experience varies. This measure will have important implications for how much training may be necessary to attain operational skills, e.g. use of keyboard and mouse as well as the system itself.
- *User knowledge*: some users may have considerable knowledge of computer programming and operation. These expert users have the ability to extend the functions of a system and its interface; consequently, they will need a flexible interface with extensibility (e.g. by macro programming facilities) to satisfy their aims. User knowledge needs to be subdivided into domain expertise, i.e. how much the users know about the application domain and knowledge of the designed system.
- *General abilities*: this is a measure of the general knowledge and intelligence of users. It is necessary to judge the level of interface sophistication which users can deal with and how much they may be expected to learn about an interface. General abilities can be acquired from educational qualifications.
- *Physical abilities and skills*: the physical characteristics of user populations and workplace design properly belong to the realm of ergonomics. Information should be gathered at this stage, especially if new equipment and the workplace environment are being designed. The objective of ergonomic analysis is to choose equipment which is designed to meet human needs; however, such considerations are beyond the scope of this book and the reader should consult Galer (1987) for further details. The relevant skills within the context of design of interface software are experience of any interface-related skills such as typing, use of mouse, etc.

Using these measures, user populations may be scored on a simple scale (e.g. 1–10 where 1 = low frequency, 10 = high frequency). It is important to establish a picture not only of the average characteristics of the population but also of the variation, as the interface will have to try to satisfy different types of user. This information forms part of the interface human requirements specification which feeds through into the strategic choice of interface type.

3.4 User Models

User models come in several varieties, depending on the interest of the authors. The terminology is further confused by ambiguity about who constructs the model, and what is being modelled. User models can be inside the user's head (often called mental models); the designer's idea of what is inside the user's head (conceptual models); and, finally, a piece of software enshrining the designer's model (embedded user models). Some categories are as follows:

- The *user's model* of the system: these models exist inside people's heads and are the result of learning how to use a system. They are usually incomplete and often inaccurate.
- The *designer's model*: this is the model held by the designer of the user's task and other relevant information. Designer's models result from task analysis and become part of the implementation.
- The *system image*: this is the external manifestation of the implemented system which the user sees and interacts with. Modelling therefore completes the circle, for it is from the system image that users will acquire their user model of a new application.

In interface design we are concerned with acquiring the user's mental model of a system in the form of a designer's model which is used to help construct the interface. However, user models exist for a variety of other purposes. Some model an individual user for the purposes of making the machine adapt to that person, while others are more theoretical models of how people may work at a cognitive level. To put user models in perspective, the following types are current in the human–computer interface literature:

- *Theoretical cognitive models*. Such models are constructed by psychologists in order to understand human mental processes. Theoretical models explain and predict how we memorise, reason, problem-solve, etc.; however, they do not have any domain-specific detail; hence, their predictions are limited to very small examples of interaction or high-level predictions when context is less important. Information processing models, as used in Chapter 2, fall into this category.
- *Cognitive task models*. These describe human activity and mental processing and have at least some origins in more theoretical models. They describe the mental activities carried out by a person in a domain. Problem-solving models such as GOMS (see Chapter 2) fall into this class, and may be used as a basis for HCI design.
- *Performance prediction models*. These are related to cognitive task models but add an extra dimension of metrics to predict human performance. Two main schools are *operational performance,* exemplified by the keystroke level model, which aims to predict how long it will take an 'ideal' user to complete a short sequence of interaction, and *learning performance models*, which attempt to predict learning time and probably errors using some measure of complexity, e.g. Cognitive Complexity Theory or Task Action Grammars.
- *System models of users*. These models are inspired by CBT (Computer Based Training) interests and adaptive interfaces. They are embedded in many applications for intelligent help, explanation and tailoring the system's response to the user. The model attempts to capture the knowledge held by a user about a system and other properties which may be in-

ferred from interaction such as a skill level deduced from error counts and task completion time. It is common to start with a stereotype of the user (e.g. knowledge appropriate for a novice, intermediate or expert user) and then update the model by monitoring interaction. Other system models in intelligent tutoring systems are expert or tutor models which hold rules and knowledge for tutoring. In adaptive interfaces the model describes the user's knowledge in terms of plans and procedures and the system uses the model to predict the most appropriate action to take. (See Chapter 10 for more detail.)

- *Models of user characteristics.* These models are used to classify users in broad terms of skill and ability, as described in Section 3.3, and may also be called user profiles. User profiles may be implemented as a configuration file containing preferences for an individual user which are then used by the system to tailor its interaction to that person.
- *Task models.* These identify the user's concept of how a task is constructed in terms of its functions and operational sequence. TKS is an example of a task model, which usually describes goals, procedures, actions and objects. Some task models, including TKS, may also hold information about the domain. User task models are an attempt to discover how much users know about the system in terms of its operation and what their expectations are about how it will work. A further distinction is often made between task and device models:

    - *user's task model*: describes what the user knows about the system, and expectations about how to operate it.
    - *device model*: this is a result of the designer's models and is a physical manifestation of how the system can be operated, e.g. commands, permitted mouse manipulations, etc.

The importance of user models lies in the compatibility principle; the more an interface conforms to users' preconceived notions of how it should appear and operate, the easier it will be to learn. When the user's and device models are not in harmony, problems will arise. User models may have varying degrees of accuracy; for instance, there is the designer's model of what he thinks the user expects, and the user's model of what he expects of the system. It is the analyst's job to make sure that these models coincide.

- *Domain models.* These models hold other information which may not be present in the task model, such as the system structure expressed either in terms of visual metaphors (e.g. an office and its components) or in a verbal classification of system components. Domain models describe objects, their classes, relationships, and links to activities in task models.

For the purposes of design, models of the users' task, domain and characteristics provide directly usable input. Theoretical and cognitive task models have less relevance to HCI design at present, although in the future such models may be embedded in CASE tools as intelligent assistants for designing interfaces. System models of users are becoming more common as applications become more sophisticated. Any system which adapts to the user requires an embedded model, and as more software has intelligent help, and tutorial facilities become standard features, these models are becoming a necessary part of design.

3.5 Domain Models and Metaphors

Task models have already been described, but they omit much vital information for design of graphical user interfaces. This is where domain models are important. Most users construct mental models of systems based on their past experience of similar computer systems. Experienced users are more likely to have well-formed models than are novices. When the system is first encountered, the user's model may be vague but it will grow as experience increases. It is the interface designer's responsibility to make the interface conform as far as possible to the user's previous model and, if no previous model existed, to present a clear structure of the new system and make assimilation of the new system model as easy as possible.

One means of presenting a model of the system to the user is via an interface metaphor. *Metaphors* are information which helps us understand something and exploit analogical memory. The information is similar to the domain which we are trying to understand, but it transfers some understanding by reference to general properties. Metaphors come in different scales, e.g.:

- *Metaphor in the small*: most linguistic metaphors such as 'this job's a dead end', 'the user manual is as clear as mud' fall into this class. Examples of small-scale visual metaphors are circle, square and line shapes in graphical palettes in drawing packages. Small-scale metaphors help explain the properties of objects or how they may be used.
- *Metaphor in the large*: these give more information and help organise other facts that may be contained within smaller metaphors; hence, they supply a context for interpretation. The classic example of a general metaphor is the desktop now used in many graphical user interfaces (GUIs). The metaphor provides knowledge which places other objects in their context of use; hence, the desktop suggests how filing cabinets, folders, in-trays, etc., may be used.

Metaphor is closely related to analogical memory and problem solving by analogy. Indeed the boundary between the two is hard to define, although analogy usually conveys more knowledge about a problem and involves more abstract knowledge which links two apparently unrelated domains. *Domain models* are important for capturing the knowledge, which can then be used for metaphor design. The principal components of domain models for the purposes of GUI design are:

- Objects, properties of objects, logical relationships, and their classes.
- Physical structure of the domain, spatial organisation of objects and other structures which otherwise may not be modelled, e.g. in a library domain the layout of physical structures such as shelves, issue desk, short loans sections, etc.
- Description of activities, as found in the task model, which are associated with objects and physical structures.

Domain models record the user's views of the system in two ways. First, there is a static view of the system structure in terms of objects and their relationships which may be expressed in visual or linguistic terms. The models describe objects, relationships and activities with the users' terminology for objects and operations within the system. The descriptive labels form the semantic, language-based view of the system. Second, there is an expectation of system operations, or the dynamic behaviour of objects, which is relevant to the design of direct manipulation, e.g. how user actions can be expressed in mouse movements: select, drag and drop, etc. Furthermore, in many domains users' movements may express actions in the physical system layout which can be directly transformed into manipulations in GUI designs.

In a library, for instance, users may view the system as books which reside on shelves which are organised in stacks which, in turn, occur in subject areas, all of which may be visualised in terms of a hierarchy. There may be other parts of the library which serve specific purposes, e.g. a reference section, temporary stacks, books to be reshelved, and the issue desk, which are seen in spatial terms as a network. Such domain model views can contain a rich description by which users organise their knowledge about the current system in terms of a physical layout or map (see Figure 3.6).

Domain analysis

This term is often used for a type of exhaustive systems analysis for all the functions in an organisation. In HCI we use domain analysis in a broader sense. It serves two purposes:

- Gathering information on the physical aspects of the domain which are involved in system activity, e.g. structures, objects and their spatial layout which can be used for interface metaphors in GUI design.
- Analysis and modelling of the system environment to gain a wider picture of how the system will fit into its environment. This is particularly necessary for distributed systems and group-work support.

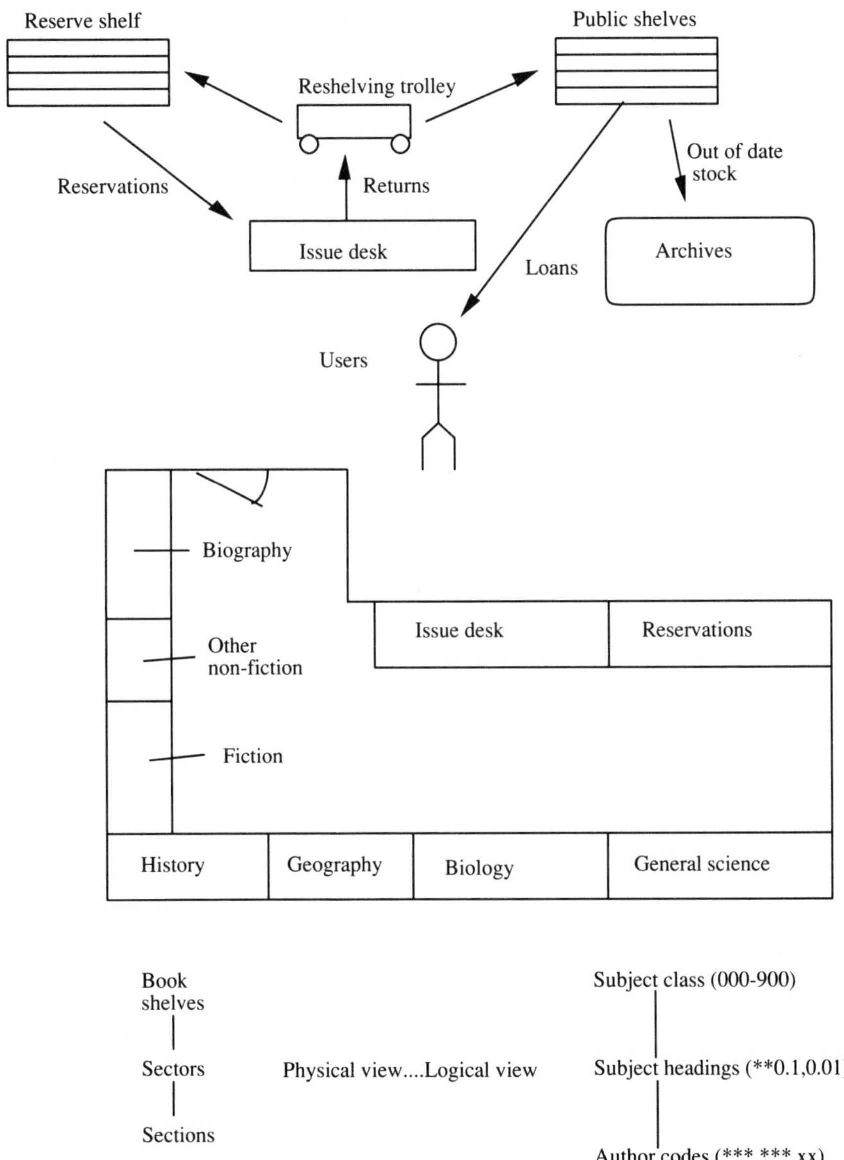

Figure 3.6 User view in terms of a conceptual model describing a library: in physical terms of layout and book movements; and in logical terms of book classification.

The first level of domain analysis and models is important for presentation of the interface because the user's visual image of the system may be directly transferred into an iconic form. It encourages questions of the type:

- What activity happens where, and what objects are involved?

- What physical movements of objects happen in the domain?
- How are physical movements related to logical (task) actions?

In domains which involve physical actions, e.g. chemical plant control, the concrete metaphor can be transferred directly into the graphical user interface. A sketch of the domain can be used to design the GUI image: for instance, in the chemical plant the layout of pipes, valves, and reaction vessels in reality would be faithfully represented by the graphical picture in the user interface. Design of GUIs for more abstract domains represents more of a challenge, and this issue will be revisited in Chapter 5. Domain modelling can also help dialogue design because the view can also reflect the functional organisation of systems components from the user's angle.

The second level of analysis takes a wider view of the system beyond single users and their tasks. Many systems involve co-operative work between a group of users. People communicate by a variety of means, so it is important to understand not only what people do but also how they communicate, negotiate and co-operate to get a job done. Domain analysis in the large has some similarities to the 'rich picture' constructed by software systems methods, an informal diagram of activities, people, information flows, etc. (Checkland, 1981). In HCI we are concerned with physical structures and objects as before, but also people's roles, their location and communication. This prompts questions such as:

- How many people co-operate in the system, and what are their roles and responsibilities?
- Where are they located and does each person do all their work in one place?
- How do people communicate, by informal means as well as by technology?
- What sort of information do they communicate?
- Are there any observable means of co-operation, negotiation or authority in the group?

Information may be gathered by interviews, although observation is often necessary to study group communication patterns. The results are recorded partly as sketches to show the layout of the system objects, structures and environment. User locations, roles and communication channels can be annotated on the diagram to give a picture of how the system works *in situ*. User roles can be integrated with task analysis, as each role will be composed of several tasks; likewise, objects can be cross-referenced to the task model.

The purpose of this type of domain analysis is twofold. First, it gives the designers further information to help them choose the appropriate technology for the system. This is important for data input/output and inter-user communication. For instance, should speech technology be used, or is the environment too noisy; should touch screens be used for data entry rather than keyboards on the factory floor; should a messaging system be introduced to support communication, and so on? All these questions at the level of user interface technology and interface devices require a thorough understanding of the domain. The second motivation is design of groupware systems. In many applications communication between co-operating users needs technical support. Study of communication patterns and user roles helps here. In some computer support co-operative work (CSCW) systems, the task itself and the object acted upon are shared. In this case the location of activity in space and time is an important input to design. CSCW design is returned to in Chapter 11.

3.6 Information Analysis

This step specifies task-related information needs. In practice task and information analysis will proceed concurrently.

The main objective is to specify what type of information is required during a task. First, a classification of information types is proposed, then the taxonomy is used to describe information requirements. The information requirements are transformed into a specification of the presentation interface in the context of a task design. The information types are 'tools for thought' to help refine descriptions of the necessary information content. These descriptions are derived from either a data analysis or a task analysis using source documents where appropriate.

3.6.1 Taxonomy of Information Types

A pragmatic approach is taken to classifying information, starting with values and attributes, entity relationship type data, facts in text-based documents, and progressing to more complex information such as task-related knowledge, i.e. how to do something and abstract facts referred to as concepts. Information can be broadly divided into static data about objects and dynamic data describing actions, events and changes in the environments. Dynamic information types are based on the schema of Task Knowledge Structures (Johnson *et al.*, 1988). The static information types are based on entity relationship terminology and are defined as follows in approximate ascending order of complexity:

Static information types

- *Entities or objects*: information belonging to some 'thing' of interest in the universe of discourse, be that a concrete object (a customer, ship, aircraft) or a more conceptual thing (e.g. mortgage, bank account, reservation).
- *Attributes*: data items or isolated facts which describe an entity, its status and history. Attributive information can be subtyped into status, historical, descriptive, spatial, and quantitative information, e.g. a person has a title, a record of employment, address, religious belief, a job location, height, weight, etc.

- *Relationships*: links between entities which indicate some functional dependency between the two, e.g. cargo is loaded in a ship.
- *Value domains*: values which belong to attributes, for instance salary in the value domain of £0–20 000.
- *Domain properties*: facts or states pertaining to the universe of discourse which may not be attributable to any particular object, e.g. information about physical layout in scenes, and temporal information, e.g. air corridors on a map of the airspace for air-traffic control.
- *Propositions*: assertions about some object or state in the universe of discourse; for instance, a cup may have attributes of volume, colour and material, but assertions about its use, e.g. 'holds liquid', 'is used for drinking' are propositions.
- *Concepts*: higher-order aggregates of objects, relationships and dynamic information which explain some part of the world. For instance, concepts could be knowledge about how something works (e.g. steam engines) or a rationale for causality (e.g. explanation of the rainbow spectrum).

Dynamic information types

- *Plans*: knowledge composed of goals which are organised in an order, e.g. plans for organising workload allocation in an office.
- *Procedures*: knowledge composed of actions and objects organised with the control constructs Sequence, Selection and Iteration, e.g. procedures for allocating loans to bank customers, calculating interest payments.
- *Actions*: elementary mental or physical activities, e.g. check order, select supplier, evaluate risk, allocate materials.
- *Rules*: these have a condition consequence-action structure and express activity declaratively rather than in procedures, e.g. If Book loan date is more than 30 days ago Then recall Book from loan.
- *Heuristics*: rules of thumb which have a less deterministic consequence, i.e. the action is advisory and may, or may not, have the desired effect, e.g. if tasks cannot be described in 10–12 lines of procedure, then try further decomposition.
- *Events*: messages recording some change of state in the world. These may be regarded as triggers for action or as a transient datum which does not belong to an object, and are therefore more closely related to static information.

The categories are not completely orthogonal, so classification may not always be unique; on the other hand, the informal definitions preserve ease of use, which more formal definitions may impair. The assessment feeds into design to specify the source of information. For instance, rules and heuristics may have to be designed, and propositions and concepts are more likely to be text-based explanations derived from bibliographic sources, whereas entity relationship information is more readily accessed from standard databases.

3.6.2 Information Analysis Procedure

The information types are used in 'walkthroughs' in which the analyst progresses through the task model asking questions about the information needs at specific steps. At each step the level of information/knowledge is assessed and the quantity and quality of information required may need to be modified with respect to the user's knowledge. For instance, trained users will require little task knowledge, whereas novices will require considerable task knowledge as prompts, help screens and instructions. The walkthrough uses lower-level goals in the task hierarchy (i.e. sub-goals which are not decomposed further), with analysis steps and questions as follows:

1. Progress through the task description for each goal and determine the answers to the following questions:

   - What are the information inputs to this task-goal?
   - What are the information outputs from the goal?
   - What other information is required to achieve this goal?

   Information may be a necessary input for task action, or created by task action, i.e. output. Other information may be required throughout the task: for instance, continuous monitoring of data, or knowledge about how to carry out the task. Datastores on DFD (data flow) diagrams are good indicators of information required by a task-goal.

2. For each goal check each action within the procedures to ascertain:

   - What input information is required for this action?
   - What output information is produced by this action?
   - Is any other information required to help the user complete this action?

At each Selection or Iteration step:

- Is any information required to help the user take a decision?

and for the whole procedure:

- Is any information required throughout the procedure?

Actions will usually require input of simple data, although for more complex actions several information types may be required. The quantity of information will depend on the granularity of the task analysis as well as the complexity of the domain-task. Similarly, decisions may require a single fact or attributes from several entities to be tested for a complex decision. Continuous information necessary for the whole procedure is likely to be status messages and historical data.

Although requirements should, ideally, be described without prejudice to an implementation, defining information needs often necessitates a view about the likely implementation. For automated processes simple input data items will be most common. This may also be true for simple, physical human actions, although human cognitive actions in problem solving may require support with more complex information. Furthermore, in user-operated tasks, novices will require considerable task knowledge to help them operate a system. Allocation of information types to task models is therefore iterative and requirements develop as the user interface design progresses.

An important distinction to bear in mind is whether information is required to be processed within the task or whether information is needed to help the user perform the task. To illustrate the point:

- *Operational information* is required as input; hence, in a library loans system, task operational information for the task action 'loan book' is the reader details, book identity, date, etc.
- *Task support information* is required to help a user carry out the task, although it is not a necessary input for all users. For the action 'fine reader' when book returns are overdues, a set of heuristics could be provided to give the librarian policy for mitigating circumstances when fines may be waived. Novice librarians may need the information; experienced librarians will already have such information readily available in their task knowledge. The task model annotated with information requirements is illustrated in Figure 3.7.

The following questions can help elucidate needs for manual and semi-automated actions in the perspective of operational and support information:

- What information does the user need to carry out the action manually?
- What information should the user supply to the computer as input?
- What supporting information should the computer supply to help the user complete the task action?

The answers to these questions are linked to specification of the presentation interface, so the needs will unfold gradually as the nature of the task support is clarified. Another important need is to discover which data items are important or vital for task operation. This will feed through into presentation design for highlighting key information for the user's attention. Important items for the user's attention (e.g. warning or safety critical information) can be specified by further annotations on the task model.

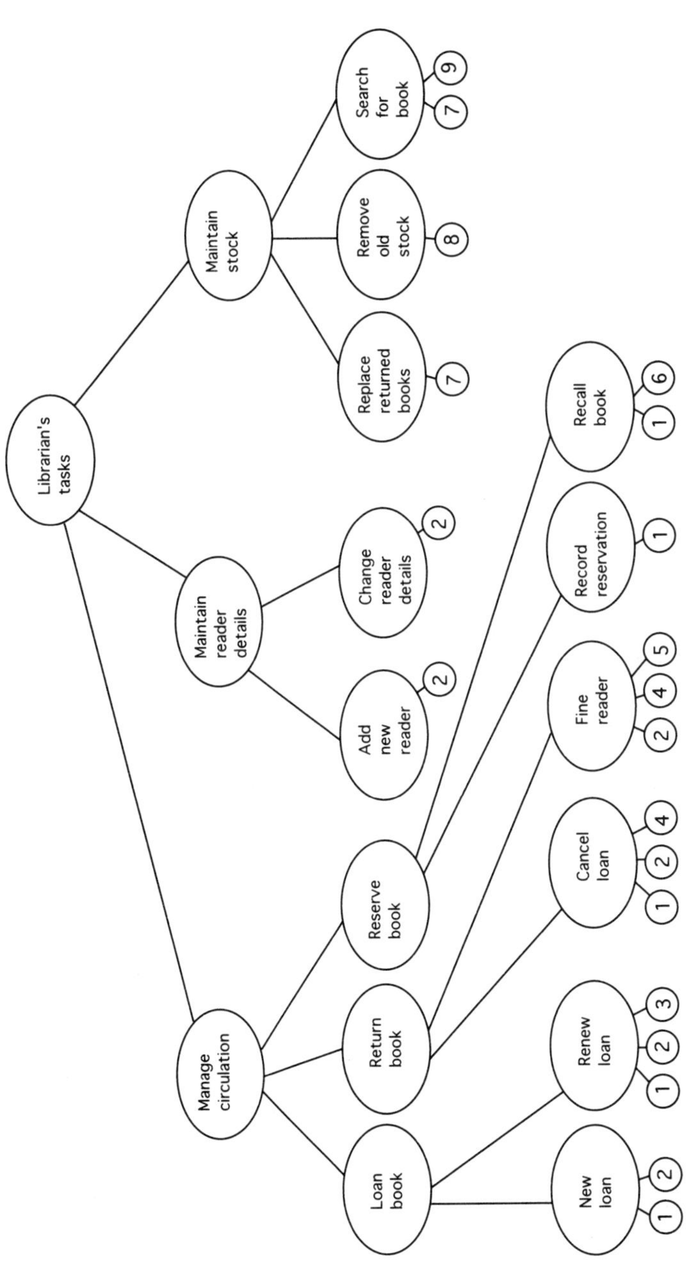

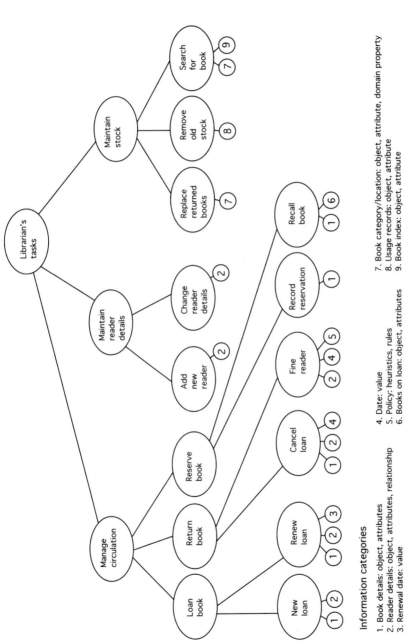

Information categories

1. Book details: object, attributes
2. Reader details: object, attributes, relationship
3. Renewal date: value
4. Date: value
5. Policy: heuristics, rules
6. Books on loan: object, attributes
7. Book category/location: object, attribute, domain property
8. Usage records: object, attribute
9. Book index: object, attribute

***Figure 3.7** TKS goal tree of librarian's task after information analysis.*

3.7 Task Design

Task design aims to reorganise the initial task model to design support for users so that the computer co-operates with them to achieve a job of work. Task support design is a creative activity which comes from experience; however, some guidance can be given. The essence of task design is to answer the question 'How can the computer help the user to achieve the task goal efficiently and effectively?' This can go beyond automated support for the way users currently work. Computers empower users by enabling them to do jobs more creatively, and even to carry out many activities which were previously nearly impossible. Task design may therefore involve task synthesis, i.e. design of completely new ways of working.

Other parts of task design involve organising the workflow and the grouping of tasks into coherent units of activity which become part of a job description. This involves synthesising tasks with differing characteristics into a job suitable for people, and planning the work so that the workload is matched to the personnel resources available. The first part of the process is deciding what activities in the application are more suitable for people or for computers.

3.7.1 Task Allocation

Tasks vary in complexity in physical and mental dimensions. Design aims to create human tasks which are neither too demanding (i.e. composed completely of very complex steps), nor too simple, which may lead to the operator becoming bored. Variety is desirable in any task. Task complexity also has to be matched to personnel ability; hence, the capabilities of the user have to be considered when designing tasks. It is no use giving someone a stimulating yet overdemanding task in relation to their abilities. A compromise has to be reached which ideally should give people tasks which stretch their abilities, thereby encouraging them to develop new skills and widen their experience, while not going beyond their abilities, as this could cause despair and frustration.

Within each task, actions are allocated to either the computer or the users, or to both users and the computer. Compared with computers, people excel at heuristic, associative tasks but are poor with high volumes of data and repetitive tasks. Generally, users should receive tasks which require initiative, judgement and heuristic reasoning. On the other hand, computers should get repetitive checking, calculations and data handling tasks. Data entry, data retrieval and decision support are examples of mixed tasks in which human and computer interact to achieve an objective. Mixed tasks require further refinement to specify the human and computer components.

Allocation produces two task networks: one human task network and one for the computer system. Both networks can be designed using data flow diagrams to illustrate the logical sequences of activities. The human network will form the basis of operating procedures and the user manual, and the computer network will add to the system specification. Task allocation can be done on the data flow diagram at the level of a process/task but this level obscures much of the operational detail. Hence, it is preferable to allocate parts of the system to either human or computer at the action level. The steps are:

1. Inspect the data flow diagram and mark tasks as either for the computer system or the human system, or joint tasks.
2. Take the joint tasks and allocate actions within each task to either human or computer.
3. Specify new computer actions to support human activity.
4. Construct new computer system and human system task networks.

In the task sequence illustrated in Figure 3.8, most of the repetitive checking is given to the computer, with the human operator supplying the input. However, in the Raise-Bulk-Order function there is a complex step which involves a trade-off between delivery date and sourcing the stock from one or more suppliers. This decision involves local knowledge of delivery dates and heuristic judgement to find the best delivery date versus number of suppliers trade-off, and consequently this task is allocated to a human. It may be possible to computerise this function with a small expert system but the designer should preserve human interest and activity in a system, so this step is left uncomputerised.

The design elaborates separate human and computer actions in terms of human actions and computer support for those actions, e.g. displaying information, suggesting options, giving warnings, etc. Further actions may be added to provide the information necessary for the user's task. For instance, the computer may be required to provide decision support for the human operator. In the above example, finding the best suppliers involves browsing down a list with different combinations of product categories and suppliers. How the interaction for decision support will operate has to be designed and agreed in consultation with the user. Task interaction diagrams (see Figure 3.9) can be used to cross-check the networks and start planning the user system dialogue. These diagrams allow the following validation checks to be seen by inspecting the sequence of the computer support and human task actions:

- Are all joint human-computer actions supported by the computer?
- Do all human actions have the necessary information provided by either a computer display or documentation?
- Is information provided for user decision making?
- Are outputs from fully automated actions communicated to the user where necessary?

Task interaction diagrams work if tasks are simple and have a linear nature; however, cross-referencing complex interaction rapidly defeats the diagrammatic notation. Other notations such as matrices to cross-reference user and system actions are an alternative means of checking out task designs.

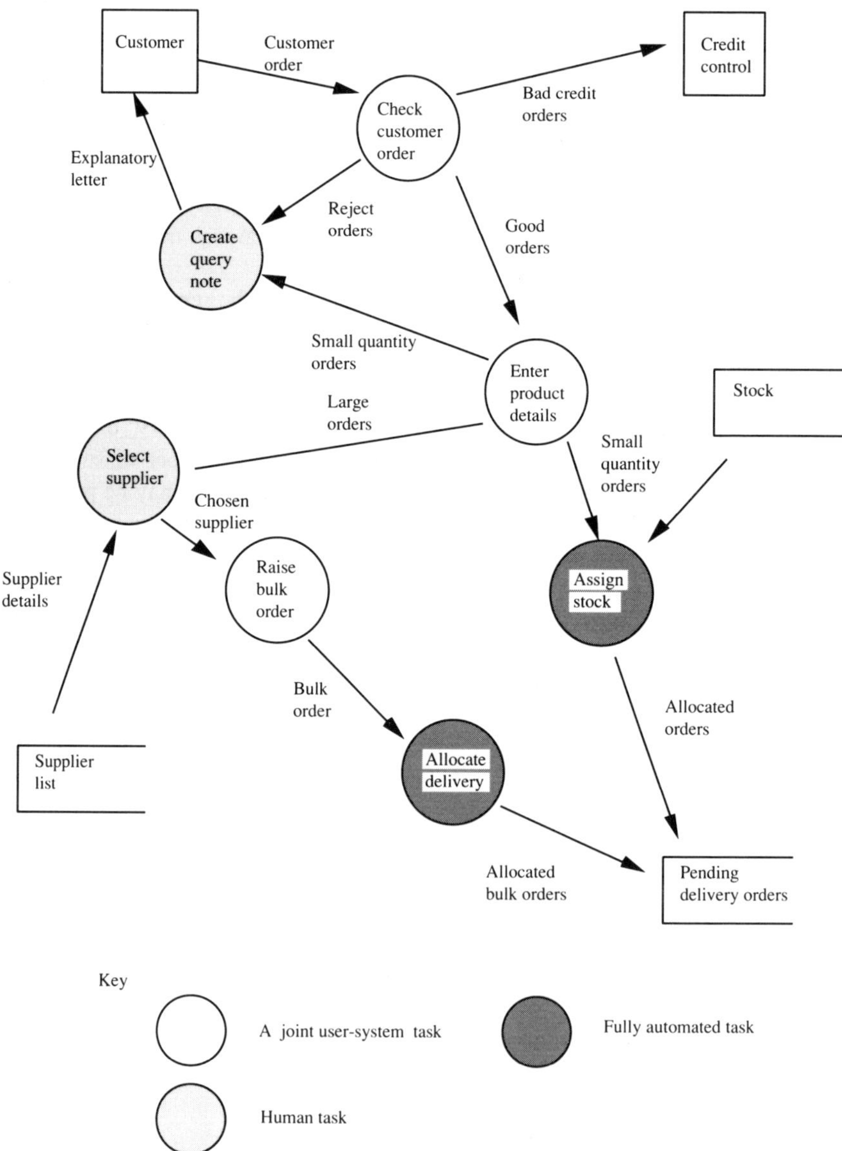

Figure 3.8 Task model at the design stage: data flow diagram of order entry task, showing fully automated, semi-automated and human-operated tasks.

Some tasks naturally occur in sequences, while other tasks may be fragmented and each sub-task can be performed independently. Processing a sales order or a library book loan are examples of structured tasks composed of a series of sub-tasks carried out to achieve the goal. On the other hand, many office tasks are unstructured: a manager may write a memo, arrange a meeting, answer the phone or analyse sales figures in an unpredictable sequence. In this case there will be no human task network, just a set of unrelated tasks which the user needs to access individually. Consequently, the specification may be composed of a set of 'mini-tasks' which cannot be composed into a coherent superordinate sequence.

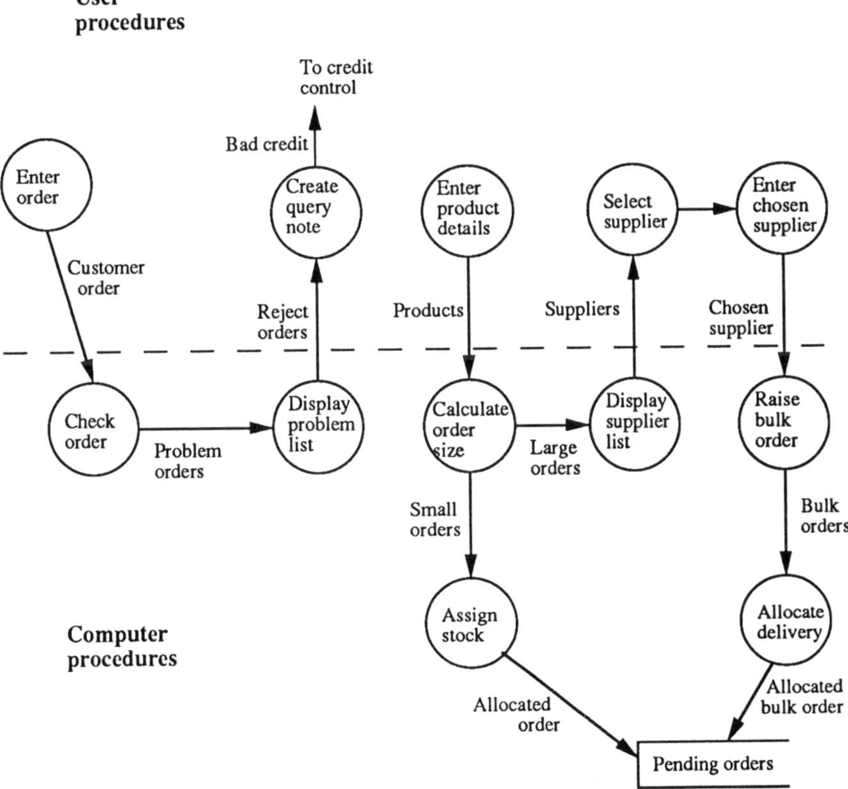

Figure 3.9 Task interaction diagram for order entry task.

A further consideration is to provide break or rest points within the task. A continuous sequence of activity causes physical and mental strain which can lead to loss of concentration and errors. Careful design of tasks with break points at regular intervals allows concentration to be refreshed by a 'closure event'; this is a short period during which the cognitive processor can be reset. Closure events should be planned at logical end-points in a sequence, e.g. at the end of a record, after each query, etc. If there are no natural break points in a sequence, closure events will have to be imposed on long task sequences at intervals of 2–5 min, depending on complexity of the activity involved.

Finally, the mental load on the user should be estimated. The objective here is to reduce overloading on short-term memory, so at each task step the quantity of information required by the user should be calculated. The design is then checked to establish whether the information is readily available to the user in a display or whether it has to be held in short-term memory. Memory loading is particularly important at decision points and error recovery within tasks, and care should be taken that users do not have to hold too many facts in working memory. Also, users should have all the information available for the action they are engaged in and not have to remember data from previous displays.

3.7.2 Work Modules and Job Design

Task design in its fullest sense involves job design, which aims to match task demands to the operator's abilities and to provide jobs which give people the correct amount of interest, responsibility and satisfaction. To treat such matters in detail is beyond the scope of this book; the aim of task design within this limited context is to provide a better understanding of the designer's problem when designing the human part of an interface. The human side of the interface forms the basis of system operation manuals, training documentation and user guides.

Tasks should be measured on a simple scale to establish their human factors properties:

- *Complexity*: in terms of reasoning, judgements and decision making.
- *Concentration*: attention to detail, and the monitoring activity necessary to complete the task successfully.
- *Responsibility*: importance of task in overall system, consequences of task failure.
- *Variety*: variability of task in one of the above measures.

A small number of tasks are combined into one work module. A work module is an identifiable piece of work which will be performed by one person to fulfil one system objective. For example, the tasks involved in order entry could be grouped together: data input, customer credit clearance, resolution of errors and credit queries. Another work module could be order progress chasing: determining where orders are in the system, identifying key late orders, investigating reasons for delays and proposing solutions.

Work modules should be balanced in terms of complexity and concentration. Too many repetitive undemanding tasks will cause attention to wander; on the other hand, too many demanding tasks will cause fatigue. The correct balance should provide stimulation and interest without fatigue, ideally by a mixture of undemanding routines mixed with more challenging decision making. Task flow within modules should be examined to make sure overloading does not happen. Overload is caused by too many things happening at the same time. Several tasks may require the user's attention simultaneously: consequently, swamping the user's working memory and information processing capacity which deal with conflicting and urgent demands. As a result nothing gets done, leading to task failure.

Task design and non-functional requirements

Non-functional requirements are performance-related criteria that a system has to achieve. Examples are volume of throughput, accuracy of output, speed of processing, response times, etc. Tasks have to be designed to achieve non-functional requirements within the constraints of available manpower and the software design. Poor design can lead to overloading of users and consequently stress. Task overload may not be apparent within normal operating procedures; instead it occurs when errors occur or the unexpected happens. If the demands of error processing are poorly or incompletely specified, there may not be time allowed in the working day to correct them. Expected frequencies of errors should be calculated and work time allocated to the resolution of such errors.

Another common cause of task overloading is peaks in workload. For example, in many transaction processing systems inputs come in bursts, e.g. telephone orders at the end of a day, a peak of mail orders in the morning. Calculations should be made for the time it will take to process input at peak loading as well as at average input rates. Manpower has to be allocated to deal with the load within the constraints of cost, because peak rates at one part of the day usually imply low rates at other times. It is uneconomic to have staff employed for processing the peak load completely unoccupied at other times. Part of the task designer's job is to plan the workload so it is as even as possible. This is done by simple estimates of task completion times, allowing for the number of transactions expected as the system throughput. This gives required activity time in hours, minutes, etc., which is matched against the available hours calculated from the number of operators, and length of the working day. Allowances have to be made for rest periods, staff training, illness, etc., so planned availability is never 100%. Manpower is then allocated to carry out the planned work, matching the skill levels of individuals to the demands of the work.

3.8 System Environment and Support

Interfaces do not exist in isolation. The interface functions in an environment which influences its performance and may impose constraints upon it. Design of the interface/task environment has three considerations:

- Physical design of the workplace. This subject is within the realm of ergonomics and readers are referred to Galer (1987) for more details.
- Design of interface support documentation. This consists of the user manuals, technical documentation, training courses and training manuals.
- Design of electronic user support. This involves on-line help, tutorial systems and explanation.

3.8.1 Design of User Documentation

User manuals can be based upon the human part of the task specification. Two types of documentation are produced for most systems:

- *User Operations Manual*: this gives instructions on how to use the system.
- *System Technical Documentation*: this is intended to explain the structure and internal workings of the system and may be produced at different levels of complexity for system support programmers and skilled 'local expert' users.

User manuals should be clear, concise, and well structured. It is a well known complaint that users never read the manuals, a symptom usually of poor manual design. Users have two broad requirements of documentation:

- *Education*: to find out about the system and how to operate it in its early stages of implementation.
- *Aide-memoire*: to access a specific piece of information quickly, often in an emergency.

These demands conflict. The first requires a well-structured guide which leads the user systematically through the system, while the second is for direct access to a specific point. Add to this people's propensity not to read massive amounts of documentation and the problem becomes apparent. It may be solved by writing three separate documents:

- *the training guide* which introduces the user to the system, aimed basically at education.
- *the quick guide* for users who are too lazy to read the whole training guide and need only the bare minimum of information to start using the system.
- *the reference guide* for trouble shooting and aide-memoire later on.

The training guide should be well-structured, to lead the user through various facets of the system one at a time, allowing one area of knowledge to be acquired before moving on to the next. Quick guides should contain commonly used command sequences with minimal instructions for operation and exhortations to read the training manual if the user gets into trouble. Minimal manuals which introduce only sufficient functionality to get users started and leave out much error trouble-shooting have proved to be particularly effective (Carroll, 1989). Users can then gradually progress on to more complex functionality and documentation as their learning progresses. Reference guides should be laid out in an itemised manner with indexes and clear access paths to data. More general guidelines to help user assimilation of information, which can be applied to all guides are:

- Structure information in a hierarchical manner: chapters, sections, paragraphs, etc.
- Label sub-divisions with clear headings and codes to show the relationship: 1, 1.2, 1.2.1, etc. Indentation can be used to further clarify hierarchical classification
- Paragraphs and sentences should be short and to the point.
- Instructions and text should be jargon-free, unless the user's own terminology is being used.
- Procedures should be laid out sequentially and numbered to show the steps.
- Important steps should be highlighted using bold characters, different fonts, colour, or icons.
- Use pictures, diagrams and visual methods to illustrate points if possible.
- Keywords should be placed in the margin to provide direct access to specific topics.
- Point-by-point summaries should be given at the end of chapters.

Many of the above points are illustrated in Figure 3.10, which shows part of a well-designed user manual.

3.8.2 Help and Tutorial Systems

A well-known problem with paper documentation is that users don't read it. The solution, which is becoming more common, is to put the documentation on-line; however, this does not solve the problem immediately. Careful design is necessary. On-line documentation can be provided in a variety of ways: on-line help is most familiar, although tutorial guides and explanation systems are becoming more widespread as standard features in applications.

On-line help

As with documentation, users have three main needs:

- What does this command/function do?
- How do I operate it?
- How do I correct it when it has gone wrong?

Changing Keyboard Modes

You can turn keyboard modes on or off by taking the action listed in the following table. Indicators in the status bar show what modes are active.

If you want to	Do this	Status bar message
Add more cells to the current selection—cells need not be adjacent.	Press SHIFT+F8.	ADD
Extend the current cell selection to other cells.	Press F8.	EXT
Keep the keypad in Num Lock mode.	Press NUM LOCK in Microsoft Excel for Windows; SHIFT+CLEAR in Microsoft Excel for the Macintosh.	NUM
Place the decimal point in the position you specify.	Choose Workspace from the Options menu and select the Fixed Decimal check box.	FIX
Replace existing text rather than adding to it.	Press INS with the insertion point in the Formula bar (Microsoft Excel for Windows only).	OVR
Scroll through a document while keeping the active cell stationary.	Press SCROLL LOCK.	SCRL
Type all keys in uppercase.	Press CAPS LOCK.	CAPS

Recognizing Mouse Pointer Shapes

The mouse pointer takes on different shapes, depending on its location on the screen and on your actions in Microsoft Excel. The following table shows the mouse pointer shapes and describes the mouse action you use with each pointer shape.

Pointer shape	Screen location	What to do
⇖ or ⬉	On the menu bar, scroll bars, charts, and graphic objects, and on a worksheet when dragging cell contents between rows or columns	Point and select, or drag to a new location.

Figure 3.10 Example of layout in a user manual (courtesy of Microsoft Inc.).

The first two imply description of the system functionality and operation procedures. This information should be directly available from the design. Diagnosis of errors and problems is more difficult, as the designer has to anticipate what may go wrong in the future.

The user's first problem with help is how to access it. Old-fashioned help systems were constructed as a separate hierarchy which the user browsed until the topic of interest was found. The advice then had to be remembered while returning to the main system. This creates working memory problems, so better-designed help systems are context-sensitive; the advice is appropriate to the part of the system being used. Context-sensitive help involves embedding help within each function or designing a mechanism for tracing where the user is in a dialogue and then retrieving the correct text, so that if the error was discovered after a 'Cut and Paste' command, advice on this topic is given rather than on the whole word processor.

Help systems should be provided in context-sensitive and in browsing hierarchy versions. The former is used for trouble-shooting and the latter for system exploration. Another sophistication is to adjust the level of advice by the user's model. A simple way of achieving this is to allow the users to set their preference on a control panel. The system then gives verbose, detailed help or shorter explanations, according to the setting on a scale of expert to novice user. Error diagnosis in help systems is difficult. It may be possible to trigger context-sensitive advice from error messages but this depends on an analysis of likely errors. This can be difficult at design time when the product does not exist. If a prototype or similar product does exist, observation of user problems (see Chapter 9 on evaluation) can allow 'usability bugs' to be recorded. Advice can be constructed to solve these problems and then included in the help system.

Tutorial systems and explanation

These support sub-systems are aimed at training the user on first encountering the application rather than trouble-shooting later on. Tutorial guides and learning programmes fall into this category.

Tutorial systems should take the user through a guided tour of the main components of the system, explaining, for instance:

- Background explanation of concepts and functions in the application.
- User interface metaphor if appropriate.
- Operational guidance, system commands and actions.
- Explanation of system objects, screen icons, feedback messages.
- Possible errors and misconceptions.

Guided tours need to explain by example, so the tutorial system has to be scripted. This necessitates programming a dialogue which leads the user through the application, trying out sample problems on the way. Ultimately, tutorial systems can become very complex; however, effective systems can be designed using simple procedures and rules to control the dialogue according to the user's progress. Typical components of a tutorial dialogue are:

- A guided tour with demonstration. The system explains a function and then simulates the operation of the computer system. The user just presses Return to progress to the next stage. This strategy does not allow any interaction, so it is not so effective in promoting learning.
- Guided learning with hands-on interaction. The system explains a function and then invites the user to try the computer command. In this case the real system is used and the user can make errors. Although this strategy is more effective, it does involve more work for the developer. The tutorial programme has to track the user's input, diagnose errors and provide advice on problems.

Often a hybrid strategy is a good solution where the user can have hands-on experience, but the possible actions are limited, thus simplifying the system problem in diagnosing what may have gone wrong.

Rules cause the tutorial script to branch according to user errors or preferences. Users should be given the opportunity to go back to re-do a stage or to jump forward if they are experts. Other rules can be used to invoke alternative strategies; for instance, if the user makes a mistake once and receives an explanation and then makes the same mistake again, a different explanation should be tried, such as offering an analogy.

Explanation is closely related to tutoring, and both contribute to a distinct area of research in Intelligent Tutoring and Advisory systems. Moreover, explanation facilities are a sub-system in knowledge-based systems. These systems are dealt with in more depth in Chapter 10. Hypertext is often a convenient means of implementing tutorial and explanation sub-systems, as different information can be linked together in a scripted sequence.

3.9 Summary

The HCI development process starts with requirements analysis. This uses stakeholder analysis to focus on understanding the task fit of a proposed system and its impact on users. A distinction is made between primary operator users and the people who may have some secondary interest (i.e. stake) in the system. This attitude is then assessed in design collaboration workshops. This technique can be used to assess the desirability and ranking of proposed functions. Additional uses are to analyse the introduction of information technology for competitive advantage.

Task analysis is similar to functional analysis as practised in systems analysis and design. Top-down functional decomposition is used to break tasks down into smaller components which can then be specified in detail. The HCI techniques of Task Knowledge Structures and Analysis Technique may be used for this purpose or standard software engineering notations, e.g. data flow diagrams can be adapted for task analysis.

Besides task analysis, analysis of user characteristics is important. Qualities of frequency of use, general ability and computer experience contribute towards measures of user sophistication and support. These measures can then be used to plan the type of interfaces suitable for a user population. Users can be approximately categorised as Naive, Novice, Skilled and Expert, depending on their previous experience.

User models have several different objectives. User characteristics, user task models and domain models are the more important models for interface design. User task models attempt to capture the user's knowledge about how a system is expected to operate, while domain models capture the user's perception of system structures and more physical information for the user interface metaphor. Domain analysis and modelling cover physical aspects of the system and its environment. This information is used in metaphor design, selecting interactive technology and CSCW applications. The closer an interface conforms to these preconceptions the easier it should be to use.

General interface design starts with task design. Allocation of actions and tasks to either human or computer or both is the first step. Allocation is best carried out at the detailed level of actions. Joint human–computer tasks and actions may need further analysis. Task networks are drawn up for the human and computer system.

Task design then reorganises the human task network to create designs which allow for human limitations. Task support design is a creative process which attempts to design interactive systems which help people to do a job of work creatively and effectively. Task and procedural sequences should include closure events to prevent fatigue from continuous attention. Tasks are combined into work modules and jobs. Task combination aims to produce jobs which have the correct degree of stimulation while not overloading the operator. Care must be taken to avoid task overload, especially with processing transaction peaks and error cycles.

System support design involves documentation and training manuals. Structuring the information and simple clear layouts are vital. Manuals have to support trouble shooting as well as education, and good access paths should be provided to information. User support can also be provided interactively by help and tutorial systems. Help systems should be context-sensitive to give information appropriate to the user task. Tutorial systems need to lead users through the system with examples and provide explanation.

Further Reading

Further details of task analysis and job design can be found in Bailey (1982) and Damodaran *et al.* (1980). Details of TKS can be found in Johnson (1992). More on documentation and minimal manuals can be found in Carroll (1990).

Questions and Exercises

1. Try a task analysis in a familiar domain such as a library. What are the goals of the assistant librarian who handles loans and returns? What other functions are involved, e.g. searching for books, recalling overdue books, reserving books? How are these goals, with their associated procedures and actions, organised?
2. Construct a TKS goal tree and a Data Flow Diagram from the above analysis. How do these notations compare?

3. Look at the following narrative description. Carry out a task analysis, making assumptions where necessary.

   Underground train driving London Underground trains are operated by a single device which controls the speed and braking of the train. This device, the 'dead man's handle', is a safety device to ensure that the driver must take action for the train to move. The device is a lever which can be pressed down and rotated. The train will only move if the lever is pressed down. Rotation controls the velocity of the train; the greater the rotation the more power is applied to the electric motors. Braking is controlled by depression of the lever. If the lever is not depressed, the brakes come on; when fully depressed, the brakes are off. This is the safety device so that, if the driver is incapacitated, the brakes will automatically come on.

   The driver has to attend to signals between stations and at the end of each station. Red signals stop, green go and amber proceed with caution. Other input comes from the guard or station staff, who give instructions when it is safe to start the train after the passengers have finished boarding the train. Every journey consists of many stops and starts at each station. The driver has to decide when it is safe to start, accelerate the train, brake on entering the next station and stop at the appropriate point. At the end of each journey the driver has to take the train into the switching track, wait until the points have changed and then start the return journey. The work continues in this manner until a rest break after a set number of journeys. Interruptions can occur when there are passenger problems or other emergencies. These may be notified either by a light showing that the emergency handle has been pulled or verbally from the guard over the intercom. In this case the driver has to stop the train at the next station, then evacuate the train, explaining as far as possible to the passengers what has happened.

   When you have constructed a task model, imagine you have been asked to automate this job as far you feel it is appropriate. Perform a task allocation and comment on the rationale for your decisions. Suggest your ideas for task support design.

4. Returning to the library example, construct a profile for users of your system assuming the application is

   (a) A circulation control system for use by librarians to control loans, returns, etc.
   (b) A general reader facility for searching and reserving books.

5. Construct a domain model for the library application. Describe the objects and structures which are important as lists and informal sketches. How could the domain model be used in task design of:

   (a) A circulation control system for use by the librarians?
   (b) A browsing facility which allows users to explore the sections of the library and search for books?

4 Interface Components and Interaction Styles

User interfaces are now commonly built from a set of components with support tools into UI development environments. Most operating systems now provide basic UI building blocks and a means of integrating and calling them from a programming language. Interfaces composed of these components often have a similar appearance and behaviour. This so-called 'look and feel' is enforced by vendors of the operating system and its UI construction environment. The more common look and feel UI styles are:

- IBM's CUA (Common User Access), which is implemented on all IBM operating systems, e.g. PS/2, VMS, RS-Unix.
- Apple Macintosh and its successor Bedrock. The Apple Mac environment is only available on Apple machines through the MacApp developers toolkit; Bedrock, however, will be a portable environment.
- OSF/Motif. This is the common style for Unix operating systems using the X-Windows management system.

These 'look and feel' UI styles are becoming *de facto* standards for interfaces. They have the advantage of helping consistency across applications in that the interface always looks similar and should behave in approximately the same way; however, styles have their limitations and toolkits only solve the surface-level problems of interaction. UI styles may help to give a consistent means of controlling menus but they give little help in designing the interactive metaphor. Even within one style guide, it is amazing how different designs can be created for the same type of application (e.g. word processing). This is because the style guides are only passively enforced. The development environment provides a toolkit of building blocks. These building blocks have some built-in elements of the style, although most of the style relies on paper guidelines to help the designer use the components in a consistent manner.

The building blocks provided by the UI toolkits are:

- buttons;
- boxes;
- windows;
- icons;
- function keys.

These are often called 'widgets'; they can be used to compose larger parts of the interface. Several different types of design have been created for human–computer interfaces. Most interfaces use more than one design type, while the overall design aims to provide the correct level of sophistication and support for the user population. The simple design types are:

- menus;
- forms.

These are often combined into graphical user interfaces; other means of interaction are provided by:

- command languages;
- natural language and voice.

Each type has different qualities and capabilities; consequently, when choosing the correct interface for a particular set of user requirements, designers have to be aware of the merits and limitations of each particular type. This chapter surveys the building blocks for user interfaces and then examines different means of interaction.

4.1 Basic Components

4.1.1 Radio Buttons

These are also called push buttons. A selectable area in a menu box is labelled with an option. Instead of typing a reply code the user just points and selects the desired button. Buttons are often used for question and answer interaction with limited choice menus, e.g. Cancel, Save, Quit-no save, when you wish to finish word processing a document. Buttons highlight when selected and can be 'greyed' out to show that they are non-selectable during certain stages in a dialogue. Buttons can be used in menus, form-fill interfaces and other styles.

Toggles are a variant of buttons based on a two-way choice. Pushing the button flips from one choice to another; another push changes it back again. Toggles are used for rapid parameter choice (e.g. trace on/trace off in a programming debugging system). Toggles are used with a variety of menu and forms interfaces.

4.1.2 Boxes

Boxes come in different kinds for input, output and dialogue:

- *List boxes.* These contain a set of choices in a window. When the list is long, scroll bars are used so the user can view the whole list. List boxes are used for entering data in form-filling dialogues, and most menus are composed of list boxes. Some list boxes allow users to enter their own free form option into the list, and may provide some search capability.
- *Data entry boxes.* These are for alphanumeric input and may be formatted (e.g. date fields in DD.MM.YY order or not). A prompt for data entry is usually placed before the entry field. Validation routines can be attached to the box for simple type checking, e.g. numeric/alphanumeric, range checks. For text entry simple word processing facilities such as word wrap and backspace editing should be available. Data entry boxes are the principal component of form-filling dialogues but they also appear in style sheets and other parts of the interface.
- *Message boxes.* The purpose of message boxes is to supply message output to the user for advice, feedback and guidance as well as conveying the results of system processing. A limited reply set is added so the user can either cancel the message or take appropriate action. Message boxes are components of dialogue boxes and a ubiquitous part of the interface for help and error messages. An example is illustrated in Figure 4.1.
- *Dialogue boxes.* These implement a small sequence of interaction, combining message boxes with buttons, data entry boxes, lists, etc. Dialogue boxes often implement a group of related user actions in a task, and handle the prompts, user replies, system feedback, error processing and display of results. If the interaction is based on transactions, a dialogue box will handle one transaction and is a useful way of structuring the dialogue to provide coherent units with breakpoints (see Chapter 3 on task design). An example of a dialogue box would be to handle a book loan in a library system. This involves the related actions of acquiring the reader's name and the book title and then authorising the loan.

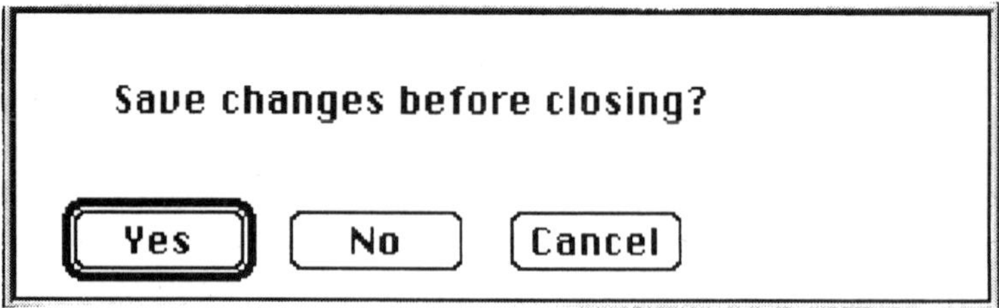

Figure 4.1 Message box: Apple-Macintosh user interface.

4.1.3 Windows

Another facet of GUI interfaces is the ability to have several different working areas at once and more than one view on a single object. Such features are supported by windows. Windows subdivide the screen space so that different operations can take place on the screen at the same time. Windows come in two basic types:

- *Tiled*: the screen is divided up in a regular manner into sub-screens with no overlap.
- *Overlapping*: windows can be nested on top of each other to give a depth illusion. Complete or partial overlapping is possible and windows can be dynamically created and deleted.

Windows have many uses. Screen areas can be separated for error messages, control menus, working area and help. If there are phases in a dialogue when computer control or a sub-dialogue is needed, a control window can be opened and two or more processes can be run at once in different windows. In this manner windows allow multitasking in a suspend-and-resume manner. There is evidence that people work concurrently on several tasks in offices, so windows can be suitable for support of office activities. Windows are also useful for monitoring information. The status of background or suspended tasks can be held in a window so the user may periodically monitor what is going on.

Windows usually come with built-in controls for resizing, moving, opening and deleting. The nature of the controls differs slightly between user interface styles, but most use sliders to control the view port so the window can be moved across a large document. Other controls allow for the window size to be altered or its location on screen to be changed; see Figure 4.2.

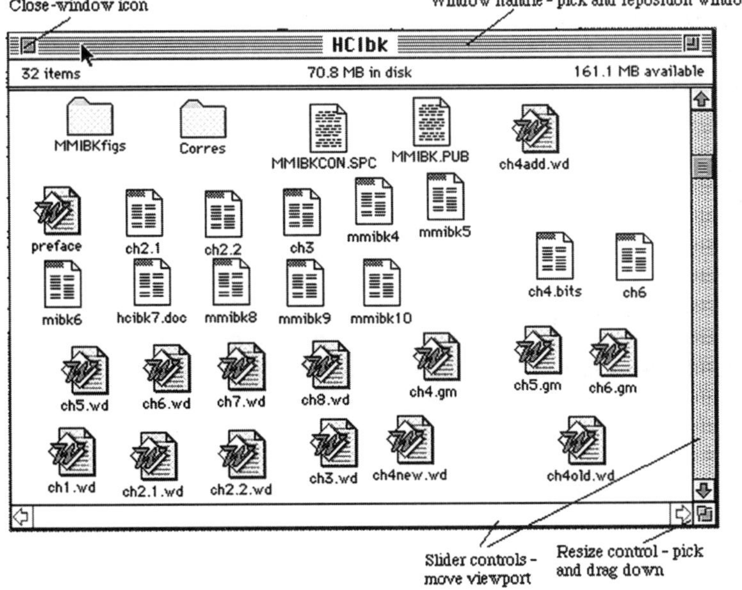

Figure 4.2 Window controls: Apple-Macintosh.

Although windows are very useful, they have some disadvantages. If too many windows are created, the screen becomes cluttered and mistakes will be made as attention is distracted by changes in a window not being worked on. Increased window clutter also incurs the penalty of an unstructured display, and search times increase with complexity.

Use of windows is still a matter of active research, so few definite guidelines can be given for their use. The following tentative advice may prove useful:

- For novice users simple tiled windows usually suffice; overlapping windows create unnecessary complexity.
- Use windows for task swapping (e.g. from editing to file management and back again) but keep multitasking to a minimum.
- Avoid frequent change in the image of windows not being worked on. The changed image will distract the eye and attention from the task in hand.
- Close old windows which are not directly related to the current task. Old windows create clutter.

Windows and direct manipulation interfaces require advanced interface software and a high-resolution VDU. Such software acts as interpreter between the application software and the user, managing all the interaction and communication.

4.1.4 Icons

Icons were pioneered by Xerox in the Star system and later by Apple in the Macintosh interface. The key idea is that pictures of objects in the system create a visual impression modelling the user's everyday experience. In this way the Xerox Star system has icons for objects in the office, e.g. in-trays, filing cabinets, folders, calculators and wastepaper baskets. Operation of the system is by picking objects and moving them with the cursor. For example, to delete a file, you move a folder into the wastepaper bin, following the metaphor of everyday life of throwing waste paper into a bin. Figure 4.3 illustrates the use of icons for a personal computer interface. Icons are a very effective technique if the icon pictures are realistic, because the learning time is reduced and operation becomes easy for inexperienced and experienced users.

To be useful an icon has to be realistic so users can recognise the object or command which is being represented. Symbols may also be used; however, symbols initially are meaningless shapes, and to be useful they have to be associated with an object. That association has to be learned. An absolute boundary between symbols and icons is illusory because as soon as a symbol's meaning has been learned it will become a meaningful image. On the other hand, an icon may be ambiguous or have no immediate meaning, even though it is a complex and apparently realistic image. Pictorial communication is essentially bound to the interpretation of images made by individual users.

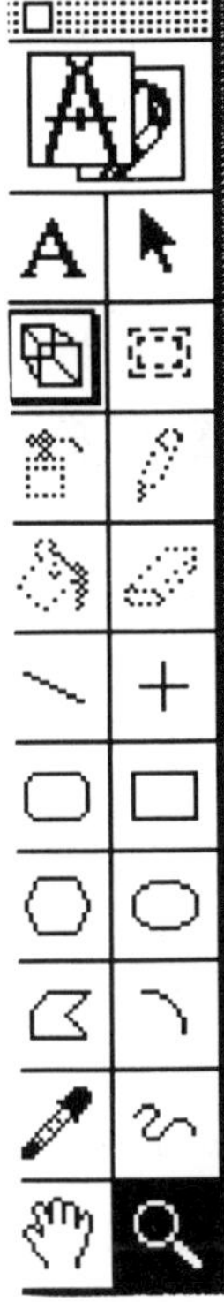

Figure 4.3 Illustration of icon design from Aldus SuperPaint for the Apple-Macintosh.

Icons, however, suffer from individual differences in interpretation and therefore usually have to have some clarifying text associated with the image. Also, they take up a considerable amount of space on VDU screens, so the technique is not economical for displaying a large number of choices. Icons work well for concrete objects such as files (a filing cabinet) and messages incoming (an in-tray full of paper), but their descriptive power is poor for more abstract concepts, e.g. commands for validating, linking and sorting.

Icons also present some problems when operational sequences need to be displayed; for instance, cut and paste operations in a word processor, or global find and replace, or checking spelling. Some iconic representations can be found, such as scissors and a paste brush for the cut and paste metaphor in word processing; but as concepts become more abstract the expressive power of icons wanes. Icons also suffer from problems of ambiguity. One picture may be interpreted in different ways by different people; for instance, the dustbin (or trash-can) can be misinterpreted as a message basket or as a secure place by novice users. As a precaution against ambiguity most iconic systems have some text explanation associated with the icons. The problem of ambiguity in icons can be seen in Figure 4.4. Poorly designed icons can lead to incorrect interpretation and sometimes to undesirable emotional reactions, even though the message is interpreted correctly.

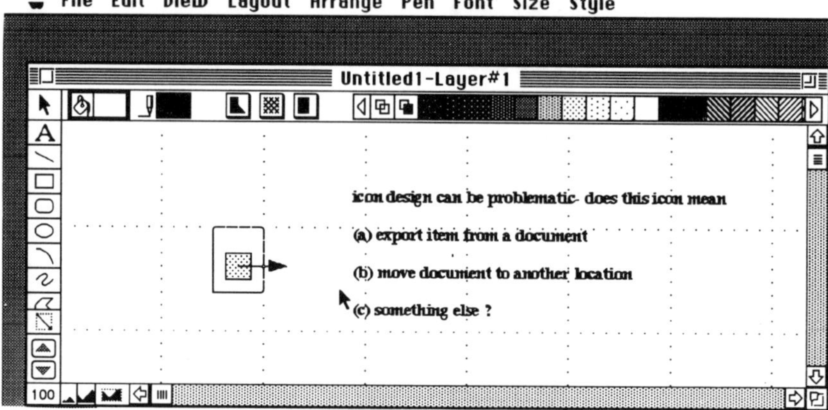

Figure 4.4 Icon design, illustrating some of the problems of ambiguity. A further test is to try to guess the purposes of the remaining icons in this MacDraw Pro application.

Some advice to follow on the design of icons is:

- Test the representation with users.
- Make icons as realistic as possible.
- Give the icon a clear outline to help visual discrimination.
- When showing commands give a concrete representation of the object being operated upon.
- Avoid symbols unless their meaning is already known.

The size of icons is a matter of compromise. If the image is too small, then visual discrimination suffers; too large an image, however, consumes valuable screen space. Consequently, there is a premium in keeping icons reasonably small. Size is integrally related to complexity of the icon image. Simple symbols can be effective in dimensions of 0.5 cm square (e.g. the Apple-Macintosh window expand/contract symbol); more complex images need to have dimensions of the order of 1 cm.

4.2 Interactive Devices

As well as displays, interfaces require some means of communicating feedback from the user. The QWERTY keyboard is the ubiquitous means of communicating user input; however, other devices have become commonplace.

4.2.1 Keyboards and Function Keys

Function keys are a hardware equivalent of menus, with options allocated to special keys on the keyboard to save screen space and alleviate the reply coding problem. Function keys can either be hard-coded or soft-coded. Hard-coded functions are permanently allocated to a particular, clearly labelled, key. This approach is good for a single application on dedicated hardware, such as a word processor, when functions are not going to change. However, for most systems function keys are soft-coded.

With soft-coded keys the command is allocated to the function key by the application program. One or more commands can be allocated to each key; but as more commands are linked to a single key, user confusion will mount because of the problem of keeping track of which mode the system is in. For instance, in one context the F2 key may mean delete a word, and in another context it may mean save a file. To help users a partial menu has to be displayed on the screen showing the allocation of options to keys, thus mapping the keyboard layout on to the screen. Alternatively, cut-out templates can be overlaid on the keyboard to show the allocation of commands.

Even so, function keys become limited by mode changes. Most computer hardware suppliers provide 10–12 function keys. Important keys should have a constant function in any context (e.g. F1 is always help, F2 is always escape). The remaining keys can be dynamically allocated to 2–3 functions each before user confusion mounts. Hence, the overall options in a system which can be usefully implemented with function keys are limited.

4.2.2 Pointing Devices

These are the most common means of cursor control and, hence, interaction in direction manipulation interfaces. The *mouse* is a simple device for translating motion of a wheel or ball on a desktop to displacement of the cursor on the VDU screen. The cursor movement follows hand movement reasonably faithfully. Some GUIs allow the sensitivity of mouse movement to be tuned under user control. A variant on the mouse theme is the *tracker ball*, essentially an upside-down mouse where the user moves the ball directly, rather than the mouse, thus indirectly rotating a ball or wheel. *Joysticks* are slightly different in that they allow explicit direction control by displacing the stick left–right or up–down. The distance or speed of movement is interpreted from the degree of movement from the vertical, resting position. Joysticks have proved popular when motor control has to be rapid and accurate, as in games interfaces.

4.2.3 Gesture Devices

Data gloves are an important means of communicating gesture and their use goes beyond pointing by allowing the whole hand to be used as an interactive device. Data gloves are indeed gloves worn by the user. The glove has a series of transducers which measure and monitor the position of the fingers, change in the shape of the hand, e.g. bending fingers and clenched fist, and the relative position of the hand in space. The signals from these sensors can then be translated via software into an image of the user's hand on the screen. Data gloves are an essential part of virtual reality in which a three-dimensional world is portrayed on screen with an image of the user's hand. This allows gesture-based communication so you can grasp and pick up objects, point to them, manipulate them with finger movements, and so on.

4.2.4 Other Input Devices

Other means of interacting are being experimented with, such as *gaze detection* enabling users to point with the eyes, and haptic interaction by use of *foot pedals*. So far none of these has proved more effective than the ubiquitous mouse and keyboard.

4.3 Simple Control Dialogues

The most simple type of control uses question and answer dialogues in which the computer asks whether a particular option is required or not and the user just gives a Y/N reply. Slightly more complex examples can move towards a menu-based system. These dialogues, although easy to use, are tedious after experience and slow to operate. Because each step has to be answered each time, experienced users can quickly become frustrated with repetitions which they know are just wasted effort. Consequently, these dialogues should only be used with naive users or novices who are likely to remain that way. Question and answer dialogues are easy to use and learn because the prompts should give complete instructions to inform the user what to do by listing the valid responses. This interface type is also easy to program, as replies can be validated by simple conditional statements or against a small look-up table.

When using these dialogues, some guidelines to follow are:

- Only one question at a time. Asking multiple questions may seem quicker but the question-answer link will burden the user's short-term memory
- If the previous answer is needed later in a sequence, re-display it; otherwise, errors are caused by short term memory problems
- Keep sequences compatible with the source document or user model. If there is a precedent for the sequence of questioning, keep to it.

4.4 Form Filling

Forms are commonly used for data entry but can also be an effective means of implementing data display and retrieval. The essence of the method is to use a VDU display which is similar to the layout of a paper form with which the user is familiar (see Figure 4.5). The display has a form title, prompts for the various fields, markers to show where the data should be entered and messaging areas to guide the user. The cursor is software-controlled to move from one field to the next, either automatically or by using the Tab or Return key. Data can be retrieved, displayed and edited using the same display.

Ready **ORDER ENTRY** Date 12/12/94

Customer code <_ _ _ _ _ _ _>

Name <_ _ _ _ _ _ _ _ _ _ _ _ _ _ _ _ _ _ _ _>

Address <_ _ _ _ _ _ _ _ _ _ _ _ _ _ _ _ _ _ _ _>

<_ _ _ _ _ _ _ _ _ _ _ _ _ _ _ _ _ _ _ _>

<_ _ _ _ _ _ _ _ _ _ _ _ _ _ _ _ _ _ _ _>

Postcode <_ _ _ _ _ _ _ _>

Previous order <_ _/_ _/_ _>

	Catalog No.	Quantity	Unit price	Sub-total
Item 1	_ _ _ _	_ _ _	____	____
Item 1	_ _ _ _	_ _ _	____	____
Item 1	_ _ _ _	_ _ _	____	____
Item 1	_ _ _ _	_ _ _	____	____

Press TAB to move to next field

ENTER to save
E to exit
C to change record

Figure 4.5 Form filling interface for a mail order system.

Forms have the advantage of a familiar layout. All the information is shown on the VDU and as long as the form is well designed, the sequence of operation should be self-explanatory. In data entry dialogues, form filling is accompanied by on-line validation and data editing. Data entry screens may be composed of buttons, toggles, menus, picking lists and fill-in fields. The dialogue guides the user during data entry and supplies error messages, and editors to correct errors. This is dealt with in more depth in Chapter 6 on dialogue design.

The basic components of form filling dialogues are:

- *Fill-in fields.* These allow users to type input or use a pen device to enter characters. Fields may be either validated or not, and defaults may be set in fields when the values can be expected with confidence (e.g. current date in order date). Some fields may be mandatory, in which a reply must be made, or optional and hence can be skipped by the user.
- *Lists.* Picking lists allow data entry from a known set of alternatives. The user points to one or more items on the list, which are then entered for processing. Small lists may use buttons or a palette of options.
- *Validation editor.* This allows mistakes in data entry to be detected and then notified to the user in a meaningful message for correction by the user.

Some guidelines for form-filling interfaces are as follows, but the influence of the design context should be considered when putting these into practice:

- *Appropriate validation*: validation occurs incrementally when the user presses the Return key after each field, rather than waiting to the end of a record. This saves the user making further errors dependent on a mistake at the beginning of a data entry sequence.
- *Explicit movement*: autoskip/autotab between fields is not usually advisable, as unskilled users find the unexpected movement distracting. Use Tab or Return or arrow keys for explicit user-controlled movement between fields.

Local navigation within the form: it helps if users can move between fields to fill them in in their own order. A mouse gives most flexibility, although arrow keys can also be used to move up and down a form.

- *Explicit cancel*: if the user interrupts an entry sequence, the data already entered, including the current field, should not be deleted. This allows reconsideration of a cancel action which may have been a mistake. Make cancellation an obvious action which is not easy to take without an extra confirming step, e.g. Delete Order: are you sure? (Y/N).
- *Provide feedback*: users should be able to see what they have entered. If several entries can be placed on one screen, the previous transactions

should still be displayed. Feedback messages should be given to users to inform them of the next action which is expected.

- *Allow editing*: ideally, this should be allowed both within a transaction and after it has been completed; hence, users should be able to edit a field that they are currently entering and to go back and change fields entered previously. A consistent method of editing should be adopted.
- *Auto format*: users should not have to enter redundant digits and characters such as leading zeros, e.g. enter 79 not 0079 to fit a PIC 9(4) field. Entry should not be space-sensitive, e.g. both A. Name and A. Name should be acceptable.
- *Show valid entry responses or values in prompt*: if the reply set is known as a range or set of valid replies, then the user should be prompted with them, e.g. enter discount value in the range of 1 to 10.
- *Entry at user's pace*: users should be able to control the speed of data entry; forced work schedules will be resented.
- *Explicit completion*: the users should be able to communicate that they have completed the data entry.

4.5 Menu Interfaces

Menus are used most frequently as an access mechanism; however, they can also be used for data entry when there is a choice between a limited number of items. Menus are simple to program and easy to make 'bullet proof' for the users, that is all possible invalid responses are trapped by the program and an appropriate error message is displayed. The user can select valid choices, escape and possibly a help option, but all other keys invoke error responses.

Menus are a common component of computer interfaces, yet sufficient attention is rarely given to their design. Menus work by users associating a reply code with an option displayed on a screen. Reply codes may be either numeric or characters. Character codes can be mnemonic and suggest the meaning of an option; however, this method has the problem of running out of letters to represent options, e.g. the E for edit and E for exit problem. The solution to duplicates is to use a longer code but this hinders the advantage of giving a response in a single keystroke. Numeric codes, although they contain no meaning, are not a hindrance to efficient menu operation.

An alternative to using a reply code from the keyboard is to use a mouse, or to have a revolving band type of menu in which the space bar controls selection by successively highlighting menu options. The user picks the currently highlighted option with the Return key.

Menus are limited in the number of choices which can be displayed on a screen at one time. Ideally, this should be no more than nine choices; more than this overloads short-term memory and increases the search time. As a result systems with many options have menus organised in hierarchies to provide a logical access path. This is simple for inexperienced users but slow and tedious for expert users, who have to page through many menu levels to access the option they want.

It is important that the hierarchical organisation conform to the user's model of how options and functions within a system should be grouped; otherwise, the task of learning the menu hierarchy is made more difficult. Navigation in menu hierarchies presents two problems for users:

- Keeping track within the hierarchy, the 'where am I?' question.
- Tracing a path through the hierarchy, the 'where have I been?' question.

To help users navigate, status information about the hierarchical level and part of the sub-system being accessed should be displayed on the top of the screen. To improve pathway tracing, a backtrack facility is helpful so users can return to the last menu with a single keystroke. A further extension of user control is to give users 'escape to the top' commands. Features in a poor menu design and a better alternative are illustrated in Figures 4.6 and 4.7.

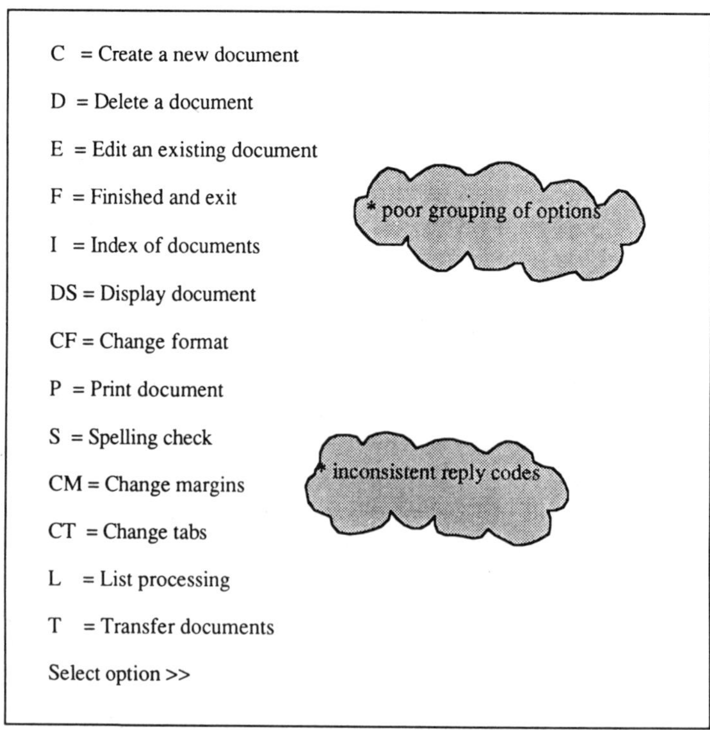

Figure 4.6 Illustration of poor menu screen design.

WORD PROCESSING MENU ? for help

No document selected General options Office>WP

Editing Commands

C = Create a new document
E = Edit an existing document
X = Exit

Formatting Commands

M = Margins change or set
T = Tabs change or set
F = Font size and type

File Commands

I = Index of documents
V = View document
P = Print document
D = Delete document
R = Rename document
S = Spelling check

Sub Menus

L = List processing
T = Document transfer

Select option >>

Figure 4.7 Illustration of better menu design.

How many options to display on a menu has been the topic of considerable research. There is a trade-off between depth and breadth in a menu hierarchy. Making the hierarchy broad by placing many options on one menu means that users have to spend longer searching through the list of options; however, there are fewer levels of hierarchy to descend. If the hierarchy is deeper with many levels and fewer options per menu, then the search time per menu is shorter, although the menu level descent time is increased. Intuition suggests there must be an optimal compromise and some studies indicate that this is so, with 3–4 levels and menus containing 7–9 options being best.

However, the efficiency of broad menus can be increased by structuring the options into groups. In smaller systems the breadth-first design may be advantageous because it cuts out traversal time of a menu hierarchy; but for large systems a clear hierarchical structure may be required to help the user comprehend the system, in which case the depth style may be better.

A problem with all hierarchical menu structures is that users soon learn part of the tree and wish to traverse from one option to another without going up and down the hierarchy. To accommodate this desire a menu by-pass facility can give direct access to options. Options are addressed using a page number principle, with the numbers being derived from the menu responses at successive levels, e.g. option X has an address of 134 as an alternative to typing 1 at the top menu, 3 at the second level menu, etc.

In summary the guidelines for menu design are:

- Group logically related options together either as menu blocks or in separate menu screens.
- Order menu options by the usual criteria, e.g. operational sequence, frequency of use, importance, etc.
- Indicate the reply expected and associate it with the option.
- Title the menu according to its function.
- Give the user feedback about menu levels, errors, etc.
- Provide escape routes and by-passes.
- Bullet-proof the replies, e.g. if 1 to 7 are options and 0 is escape, make sure any other keystroke is followed by an error message and not a program failure.

A disadvantage of menus is that the whole screen is usually consumed by the menu, leaving no space for a work area. If menu choices are required at several points in a dialogue, the necessity to replace a work area with a menu screen can become disruptive. This problem can be solved by using pop-up/pull-down menus on systems supporting such facilities.

4.5.1 Types of Menu

Menus can be implemented in a variety of ways. The choice within the constraints of specific user interface development environments is from the following:

- *Pull-down menus.* These menus are pulled down from a top-level menu bar positioned at the top of the screen. Selection is by pointing with the mouse to the menu bar; this causes the pull-down menu to be displayed; then the option is chosen by pointing (see Figure 4.8). Some designs include cascade menus, where the sub-menu appears at the side of the first menu. The existence of the sub-menu is cued by an arrow pointing sideways; when the menu option is highlighted, the sub-menu appears to the side. Cascade menus have to be kept active by keeping the mouse button down; hence, the depth should be limited to 2–3 sub-menus, as otherwise users have problems in walking along the cascade and keeping the cursor on the route. Once the option has been chosen, the menus are rolled back into the top-level menu bar, so the working screen is only temporarily obscured during the choice.

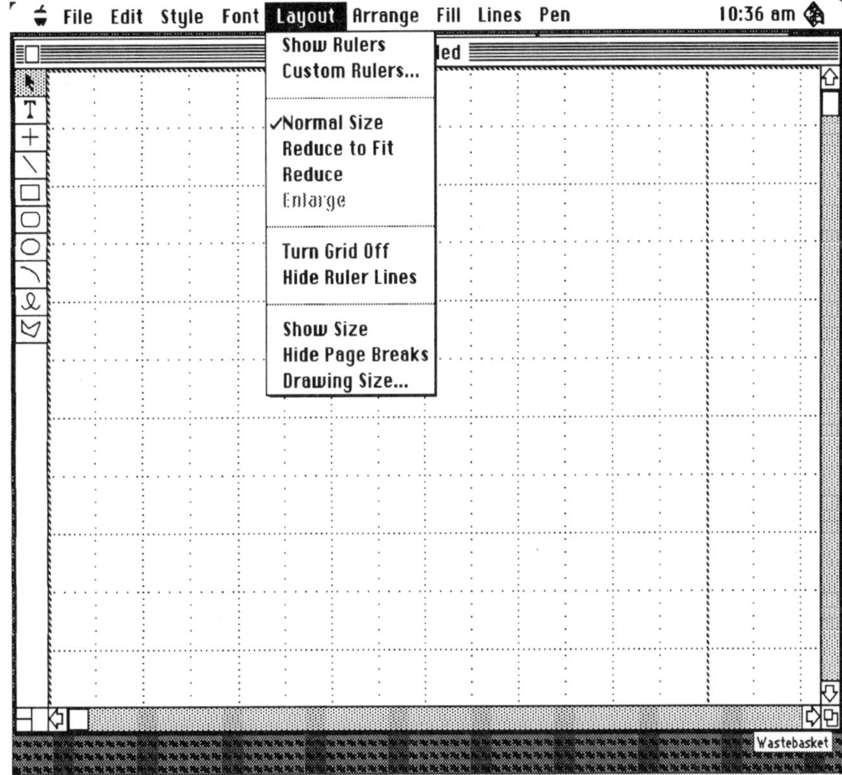

Figure 4.8 Pull-down menu

- *Pop-up menus.* These can appear in any part of the screen. This type is used with a multibutton mouse in which one button is a display-menu command. The pop-up menu appears wherever the cursor happens to be on screen and selection proceeds as before by pointing to options which are highlighted. No upper-level menus are visible as a menu bar. This type of menu is useful for the non-hierarchical options, such as setting parameters, (e.g. fonts, character size in word processing), and has the advantage of being operated without having to go through the menu bar. Once the parameter is set the pop-up menu disappears, leaving the working area visible.
- *Palette menus.* These present options as a set of icons and are common in graphical packages for choosing shapes (see Figure 4.9). Each icon is essentially a button which selects an object or an action. Icons can be used

to represent objects (e.g. shapes in a drawing package), parameters (e.g. colour, texture or line thickness in drawing) or actions (e.g. commands for save, copy, delete, etc.).

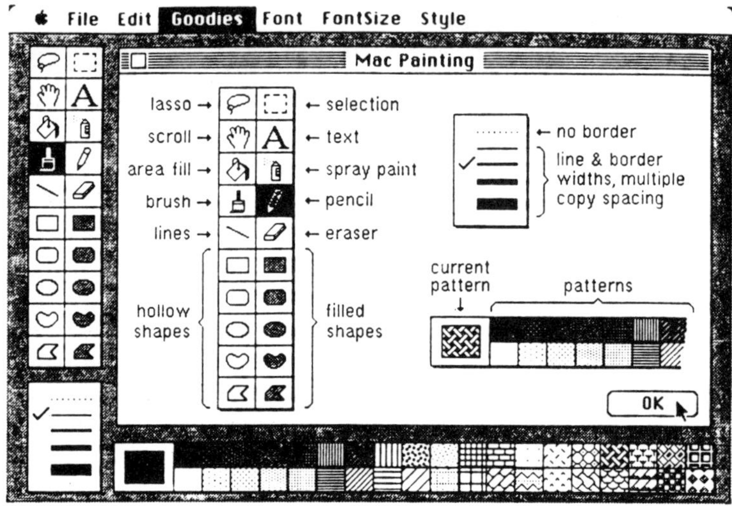

Figure 4.9 Palette menu from Microsoft's MacPaint for the Apple-Macintosh.

- *Style sheets.* These are a mixture of menus and form filling and are used to set properties of an object being worked upon or customise interaction according to a set of preferences. Menus, buttons, toggles and value entry fields are used to set parameters (see Figure 4.10); for instance, a favourite use is to set document parameters in word processing, line spacing, heading format, column format and spacing, etc.

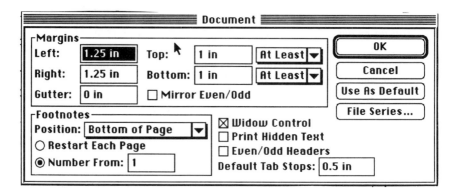

Document
Margins
Left: 1.25 in Top: 1 in At Least
Right: 1.25 in Bottom: 1 in At Least
Gutter: 0 in Mirror Even/Odd
OK
Cancel
Use As Default
File Series...
Footnotes
Position: Bottom of Page
Restart Each Page
Number From: 1
Widow Control
Print Hidden Text
Even/Odd Headers
Default Tab Stops: 0.5 in

Figure 4.10 Style sheet user interface component for changing document parameters, etc. in Microsoft's Word for the Apple-Macintosh.

4.6 Direct Manipulation (DM)

This term was coined by Shneiderman (1987) to refer to interfaces which include icons, pointing and the features which have now become associated with WIMP (Windows, Icons, Mouse, Pop-up menu) interfaces such as the Apple Macintosh. The central idea of such interfaces is that the user sees and directly manipulates representations of objects in the system, rather than addressing the objects through an intervening code, as in command languages or menus. These interfaces are now commonly referred to as Graphical User Interfaces (GUIs).

Objects are shown as icons which can be pointed to with a mouse or a similar cursor control device, thereby allowing objects to be selected. Selection then invokes a system operation, e.g. calls an option in a menu or selects a file. Direct manipulation goes further by allowing objects to be moved around the screen using a dragging operation. In this way new associations between objects can be formed, e.g. a file can be placed in a folder (a sub-directory in non-DM interfaces); and operations can be performed on objects, e.g. a message placed in the out-tray creates the 'send-message' action in an e-mail system. The advantage of direct manipulation is that the computer system models everyday operations more naturally than do older styles of interface; and the more directly an interface models reality, the easier it is to learn.

The essential features of DM interfaces can be summarised in a set of principles:

- *Explicit action*: the user points at and manipulates objects on the screen.
- *Immediate feedback*: the results of the user's actions are immediately visible, e.g. when an icon is selected it is highlighted.
- *Incremental effect*: user actions have an analogue/sequential dimension, e.g. as an icon is dragged across a screen display it moves continuously, following the movement of the mouse rather than suddenly jumping to a new position.
- *Intuitive interaction*: interaction matches the user's conceptual model of how the system should operate and the display shows pictures of familiar objects.
- *Learning by onion peeling*: the complexity of the system is gradually revealed in layers as the user explores system facilities.
- *Reversible actions*: all actions can be undone by reversing the sequence of manipulations.
- *Prevalidation*: only valid interactions have an effect, so that if the user points at an object and this makes no sense in terms of the current task, nothing happens on the display.

The interface supports the user's task by portraying a realistic 'virtual world' on the screen. Operation is supposed to be immediately obvious and no error messages are required, because invalid interaction has no effect on the interface image. The interface presents a metaphor of the application to provide the context for interaction. As this should be based on the users' domain model, it should be compatible with their expectations. Learning, in theory, should be automatic, as the interface suggests the possible actions. Try this claim out on yourself with Figure 4.11. Is the metaphor employed by the graphics package obvious?

Figure 4.11 Control metaphor based on a video-recorder analogy.

Although such interfaces have undoubtedly been successful and have had a major impact in some products, they do pose problems for designers and users. In many systems the 'virtual world' has no readily available physical metaphor to help the designer; also, the intuitive model of interaction may be absent if the user is new to the task. The lack of error messages can be frustrating for some users and lead to uncertainty; in addition, learning can be hindered by the lack of explicit representation of all the system facilities. In spite of this, direct manipulation does create usable and appealing user interfaces.

The DM idea has given rise to another acronym, WYSIWYG (What You See Is What You Get), which was initially applied to word processors. This refers to the system output in which the results of the user's actions are immediately apparent in the display. Old-fashioned text editors had embedded format commands which controlled the layout of the text, such as '.PP' for a new paragraph. WYSIWYG editors use direct manipulation to format text, delivering the exact image of what the user sees, and, hence, eliminating the necessity of remembering format control commands.

4.7 User Interface Design Environments

The next step beyond providing user interface components as a library of building blocks is to construct support tools that systematically guide designers in developing user interfaces. Such tools as the HCI equivalent of CASE (Computer Aided Software Engineering), although regrettably few, have been integrated with mainstream software engineering tools, so most UIDEs (User Interface Design Environments) remain as research prototypes.

One quest has been to separate the user interface from application software. If this were possible,then user interface could become portable between applications. User Interface Management Systems (UIMs) were an attempt in this direction. UIMS started with the influential Seeheim model (see Figure 4.12),

(a) Seeheim model

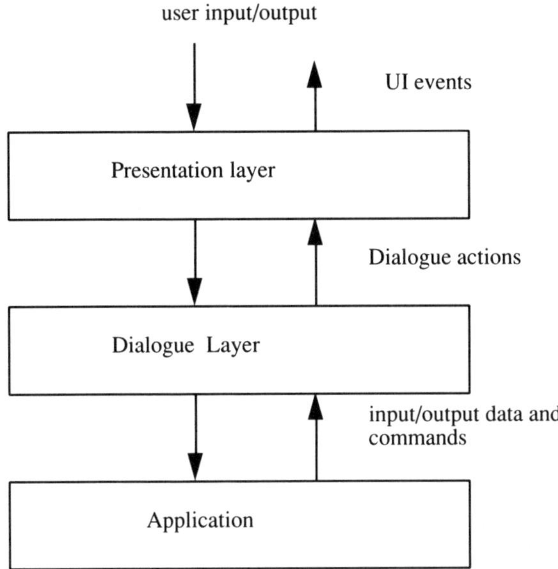

(b) Agent model PAC (Coutaz 1990)

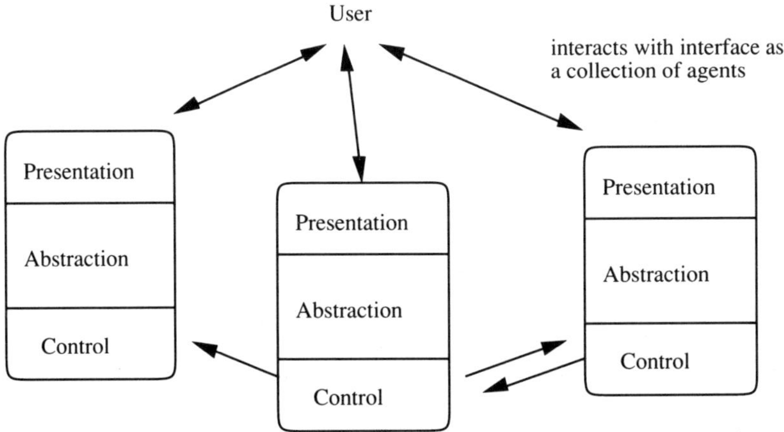

Figure 4.12 User interface development environments. (a) Seeheim model; (b) Bass and Coutaz agent model (PAC).

which proposed three layers: a presentation layer which dealt with surface level display and input/output; a dialogue layer which controlled the user system conversation; and finally the application which carried out the functional processing of the system. If mappings could be developed between each layer then separability could be achieved. In practice designing presentation and design layers has been possible but achieving separability between the application and dialogue has proved less tractable. The problem is that the task resides in the application to an extent, but the task also influences the dialogue structure. If the task model is made implicit, in the dialogue layer, then it is no longer portable; alternatively, if the dialogue is controlled by the application, then separability is compromised.

The UIMs debate has been overtaken by object oriented models which see the interface as a set of collaborating agents, each with a specific role. One of the more influential agent-based models is PAC (Coutaz, 1989), which proposes three major components:

- *Presentation agents* responsible for displays and low-level input/output handling.
- *Activity agents* which carry out the task-related processing in the interface and include task-related dialogues.
- *Control agents* which oversee the cooperation of other objects and ensure the whole interface interacts in an orderly manner.

PACs objects can be specialised for different UI components and task roles. They also communicate with other objects representing fully automated transaction processing.

Other research has concentrated on development environments. Here the challenge has been to construct a set of modelling tools to support the user in specifying the task models and then give some means of transforming the task into an interface design. This is usually achieved by libraries of UI components as described earlier in the chapter. An early, and successful, example of library-based UIDE is the GARNET environment (Myers, 1991). UI templates may be built into UIDEs for tailoring according to user taste or to conform to style guidelines. Further templates may be supplied for typical user interface operations, such as editing a list, handling multiway selections, setting parameters in style sheets, etc. These reusable objects help construction of user interfaces at the operation level (see HUMANOID system; Luo *et al.*, 1992); however, few templates have any notion of typical tasks beyond the syntactic level of editing, simple presentation templates, and processing user choices.

Besides providing diagrammers for task modelling and UI component libraries, more advanced UIDEs have added active guidance to help the designer transform task models. The guidance comes as matching rules which try to detect properties of a task procedure and then suggest suitable UI components to match it. Unfortunately, such rules are limited by the sophistication of the UI library and the domain task knowledge possessed by the UIDE. In practice this has meant that active guidance is restricted to the syntactic level of UI design, leaving definition of dialogue structure and task support still within the creative domain of the designer. In spite of this UIDEs hold considerable promise of improving the design process, especially when they incorporate design rules for usability. The ADEPT environment (Johnson *et al.*, 1993) follows this path by building not only a task model user TKS, but a user model as well. These are transformed into a user interaction model and thence mapped to user interface components. Rules suggest usability refinements such as setting the verbosity of prompts and help to match skills level in the user model, etc.

UIDEs, however, still have a long way to go. To attain commercial success, integration with CASE tools is necessary, and more active guidance incorporating design guidelines is required for added value. Also, most of the tools are still restricted to simple interaction style and components and so do not support development of complex GUIs, or of other styles such as command and natural language interfaces.

4.8 Command Languages

Command languages are potentially the most powerful command interface, but more power brings with it the penalty of being more difficult to learn. The common feature of command languages is that little or no supportive information is displayed for users, who enter commands in locations indicated by prompts which are often a cryptic $ or * symbol. The command then invokes the system operation which the user requires; when the operation is complete, the command prompt returns. Because little information is displayed, command languages are very economical in use of screen space.

The great advantage of command languages is the sophistication and flexibility of the interface. If a system has a large number of functions and those functions may be required in different combinations, then a command language is a good solution. This is because various functions can be combined into sentences using a grammar. All command languages have a word set, called a lexicon, and rules which state how words may be combined together, which is a grammar. The lexicon contains command words with encoded meanings to help recognition and remembering of the command functions. The grammar uses the principle of nesting complex commands in phrases and substituting complex commands as a sub-routine identified by a simple name. In this manner the interface becomes a sophisticated and extensible method for system control.

The penalty of command languages is that users have to learn a code and some form of grammar; this takes time and makes command languages difficult for beginners. The user also has to have some knowledge about what the system does, because little information is displayed on the screen. A further disadvantage is the development effort required for command language interfaces. Simple command interfaces can be implemented using keywords or a code set, in which case only lexical checking is required to validate commands against a look-up table. As soon as the language has a syntax, a parser has to be built to check and interpret input. This becomes an increasingly demanding task which, taken to its logical extension, becomes compiler writing for programming languages.

4.8.1 Command Language Lexicons

Command languages need words to identify objects and operations. Objects will be devices, files, etc., which the commands of the language operate on. Objects will usually be described by nouns, and command actions by verbs. Both word sets should be as meaningful as possible. However, one objective of command languages is brevity of input; hence, coding of identifiers is usually necessary. The basic choice when shortening a word is to truncate or abbreviate.

Truncation removes the latter part of a word, leaving (N) characters at the front, e.g.

DIRectory CATalogue DELete DISplay DEVice

This is an effective technique if the front of a word communicates its meaning. Another advantage is that truncation can be used in two modes. A full version of the word is provided for novices, while experts can use the short form. The problem with truncation comes from duplicates between words sharing common leading characters, e.g.

DELete DELay
DISplay DISconnect

When this happens, a further character may have to be added to remove the ambiguity. Unfortunately, this violates the consistency rule, as users may have to type in either three or four characters, depending on the word. There is a trade-off between risking ambiguity in a command word set and the effort a user has to expend entering commands. Ideally, users should be able to invoke commands with a single keystroke; however, single-letter commands are most likely to create ambiguities as the command word set grows. Most operating systems use three-letter commands to prevent ambiguity. Longer commands also improve ease of memorisation.

The alternative to truncation is compression. Characters are removed at various points in the word, leaving sufficient letters to convey the meaning. The resulting compressed words should, as with all codes, be the same length. Simple elimination of vowels or consonants rarely produces good code words;

instead, mnemonic techniques of front–middle–back compression using syllabic emphasis give the best results. The main disadvantage of compression techniques is that they cannot be used in a long and short form; also, the memorability may not be any better than a truncated code. Consequently, command languages have tended to favour truncation coding. Compression codes become more advantageous in large systems with extensive word sets in which truncation is no longer a viable option.

4.8.2 Command Language Syntax

The rules which govern how command words may be combined together vary from simple association rules to very complex grammars. Generally, three gradations in command language complexity can be described, although there is no rigid boundary to each category:

- *Keyword.* A simple command as a single keyword invokes an operation. Single nouns and verbs are used to identify objects and invoke commands, e.g. DIR to show the directory. Command keywords may be used in very simple combinations, such as the Command/Object associations of a verb/noun pair, e.g. Type Myfile. Few grammatical rules are present; consequently, the word combinations are limited. The expressive power of the language is dependent on the size of its word set.
- *Keyword and Argument.* In these languages the basic word may be qualified by added arguments to enhance the behaviour of the basic command, e.g. DIR/SIZE, DIR/OWNER, DIR/PROT, to list the directory according to file size, ownership and read/write protection of the files. This gives more flexibility to the language, as one command can now be used to do several different things, depending on the argument. Rules are introduced to govern the set of permissible arguments per command and how they are combined. Unfortunately, many command languages add punctuation which is totally redundant and confusing, just to govern the argument position, e.g.

    - lpr -Pdiablo myfile (a printer command in Unix, in which the printer type (diablo) is the argument).
    - Keyword and argument command languages still have relatively simple rules for combination of words which can be validated using look-up tables.

- *Grammar-based languages.* These are the most complex, in which a full syntactic structure allows very complex commands to be written. A set of rules defines the phrases which may be derived by combinations of command words. The rules dictate which word types may occur where within a command word string, just as English grammar constrains the way sentences are formed. Many command language grammars mimic natural language grammars to help learning, although the types of sentence are simple when compared with natural language.

Command languages become much more complex if simple phrases can be built up into more complex expressions. In the case of English the grammar dictates the way in which phrases are composed into sentences. The rewriting rules of a grammar can allow many layers of nesting using a recursive principle, so very complex expressions can be constructed. As a result command strings have to be parsed using recursive techniques familiar to compiler writers.

Command languages with a hierarchical grammatical syntax have the complexity of programming languages and are indistinguishable from them. The other property required for full programmability is the ability to store several command strings together in a file. This facility allows users to extend the system's functions by producing new combinations of commands in programs. Examples are .COM and .BAT files in DOS and shell programs within Unix.

4.8.3 Design of Command Languages

Commands can be derived from the task model actions and their associated objects; also, task goals and procedure names can be used when the command calls an automated function. A single command should be provided for each function, as duplicate commands will only confuse users. The level of sophistication of the language should be matched to the user's characteristics. Generally, full syntactic command languages should be reserved for sophisticated users; however, many users can use complex command languages, provided good training and support are given. If users have a considerable amount to learn, then a layered approach should be adopted. Release a restricted simple set at first, then let users progress on to the full command set when they feel confident with the simple version.

Command language specification concerns drawing up the command lexicon and syntax, adding error messages and the help sub-system. Error messages should be planned with care. Errors should be anticipated at several levels: lexical misspellings, syntactic errors, semantic misunderstanding about usage of a command, and run time errors from the underlying software. The error interpreter should aim to give informative messages which relate the type of error to an explanation of its most probable cause.

Command language design involves design of an input parser, error message interpreter and run time system. These are systems and compiler design issues which will not be treated further here. In summary, interface design guidelines which should be addressed are:

- Limit unnecessary complexity. The larger the lexicon and the greater the number of grammatic rules, the harder the language will be to learn.

Eliminate duplicate rules and synonyms.

- Command word codes should be consistent. If EXIT has been used for the escape command, do not use QUIT in another part of the system.
- Punctuation and use of delimiters should be minimised.
- Entry should be flexible and forgiving. Double spaces between words should be ignored and misspelling corrected if possible.
- Command words and syntactic sequences should be natural and familiar; e.g. use COPY from file to file, and not PIP destinationfile=sourcefile.
- Allow editing of the command string rather than requiring the user to retype it.

4.8.4 Data Retrieval Languages

Data retrieval is usually effected by a command language, which provides the user with a means of choosing what is to be displayed and to some extent how. These languages are English-like but the user has to learn a syntax and identifiers for data entities and their attributes. The usual form is as follows:

> Search for Data (and display with set format) from Entity with Attributes = X and Display Attributes, X, Y, and Z.

```
SELECT TITLE
FROM BOOKREFS
WHERE $$ INPUT
     (SELECT $$
     FROM PUBLIST
     WHERE T$ INPUT
          (SELECT T$
          FROM AUTH
          WHERE NAME = "Jones"))

Result

Software development: A rigorous approach
Jones C.B.

Practical systems analysis
Jones A.N.O.
```

The basis syntax is Select (variable/attribute name) from (entities/relations/sets) where (boolean expression). SQL can use nested syntax to express successive selections from entity sets, in this case titles, publishers and authors. Matching conditions for attributes are specified in WHERE clauses.

Figure 4.13 Example of a data retrieval query in SQL (Structured Query Language). In English the query is 'Find the titles for books in the publication list where the author's name is Jones'.

A typical query in the SQL query language is illustrated in Figure 4.13 on the previous page. The basic syntax is to Select (variables/attribute values with display format) from an Entity set where (conditions define the values or constraints). The conditions are matched to find the individual records or entity instances. Formatting instructions have increased in complexity with successive versions of SQL and now allow quite sophisticated presentation capabilities. The attributes to be displayed from retrieved records can be selected, records can be sorted on one or more keys, grouping can be defined according to record numbers of sort-key breaks, e.g. all records relating to one sales branch are displayed in one block, and so on.

People often have difficulty using data retrieval languages. Most problems stem from poorly designed syntax and confusion about logical operators, e.g. AND, OR, >, <=, etc. Many users confuse logical quantifiers such as Greater Than with Greater Than or Equal To; also, compound conditions cause further problems with AND and OR conditions being mixed up because English does not distinguish the exclusive XOR from OR but may be Both conditions. Most databases have a built-in query language which is beyond the interface designer's influence; however, if a data retrieval dialogue is being designed, the following points should be considered:

- The names of entities should be natural and descriptive and not terse and obscure. It may therefore be necessary to translate the database schema terms into more user-friendly language.
- Query syntax should follow natural language as far as possible. Questions have an imperative syntax, e.g. Find information on subject (*x*). Natural expression of queries involving related information should also be followed, e.g. Find information on sales in Countries of southern Europe. Query construction can use a restricted natural language.
- Users should not have to remember the names of attributes and entities. Attribute and entity lists should be displayed in pop-up menus or help screens.
- Many searches proceed in steps as the user selects a set of likely records and then chooses from among the first set. An output file should be provided for search results, and this file should then be the input file for the next search. This method is better than one complex nested search because it reduces errors caused by incorrect syntax or by mistyping long command strings.
- Logical operators should be clearly specified on help screens with examples of their impact. Clarifying sentences in English may be given after a query has been formulated as user feedback. For example,

SELECT CUSTOMERS Where Account-Val >= 20,000

- This search will find customers with accounts over £20 000 and customers with accounts equal to £20 000.

Data retrieval is a task suitable for decomposition into a logical sequence. Most data retrieval involves three or four steps:

- Finding which parts (or entities) of the database to query.
- Formulating the query logic and syntax.
- Refining the search if it is iterative.
- Formatting the results for printing or display.

Data retrieval interfaces should make the task steps explicit and provide support for each step in turn. Too many data retrieval languages try to do everything at once, which may benefit the expert but is of little use to the vast majority of inexpert users.

4.9 Natural Language

Natural language should be the ideal human–computer interface because it is the user's natural method of communication. Unfortunately, it has limitations from the user's viewpoint and poses considerable computational problems. Natural language may be input either directly as speech or via a keyboard. Spoken input is quick but the problems of deciphering speech are enormous and limit current speech recognition systems to vocabularies of a few thousand words. Typed input is verbose and time consuming for average users, who are not expert typists and are prone to making typing errors.

The major problem for natural language understanding is that meaning is generated at several different levels. First, there is syntax, which dictates how correct sentences should be formed; but to derive true meaning we need a framework of knowledge about words, their meanings and relationships. This information brings in the 'semantic' level of interpretation. Unfortunately, this is often not enough, because the meaning of a word can depend on the context in which it was uttered. To build a true natural language interface necessitates making computers mirror this process. This implies building a machine with a vast knowledge base of word meanings comparable to human intelligence.

Not surprisingly natural language interfaces are currently practical only in limited problem domains. By limiting the domain the quantity and complexity of knowledge required can be restricted to manageable proportions. Some limited natural language interfaces are practical for databases in which the interface has knowledge about the data items and a restricted set of words which the user may employ.

Natural language, like command languages, consists of a lexicon and a grammar. Unlike command and programming languages, natural language has many more rules for syntactic composition, which allows more flexible expression and ambiguous interpretation. This section does not cover the complexity of natural language understanding in depth; instead, the aim is to give an impression of the complexity of the problem and then guidelines for use of natural language interfaces in the light of those problems.

4.9.1 Syntax

Language is composed of words (called lexemes in linguistic jargon), which can be classified into nouns, verbs, adjectives, etc. Grammatical rules state how word classes can be combined to make well-formed sentences, e.g. 'He must go to the station to catch the train' is correct English; the equivalent in German is, 'He must to the station the train to catch go' – 'Er muss nach dem Bahnhof den Zug erreichen gehen'. The rules state the composition of sentences in terms of sub-components, noun and verb phrases, which in turn are composed of word classes. The composition rules vary between languages and can be very complex. English has approximately 20 000 rules and grammarians estimate that the known rule set is not complete, and is evolving with time.

Sentences can be decomposed using parsing strategies which test a sequence of words against the permissible combinations. Syntax, however, can only tell the listener whether a sentence conforms to the grammatical rules of a language. To generate meaning, the semantics dimension is needed. To illustrate the point, syntactically correct phrases can be constructed which are obvious nonsense; for instance, 'the square beliefs taste nice' is clearly meaningless, yet the sentence parses correctly as follows:

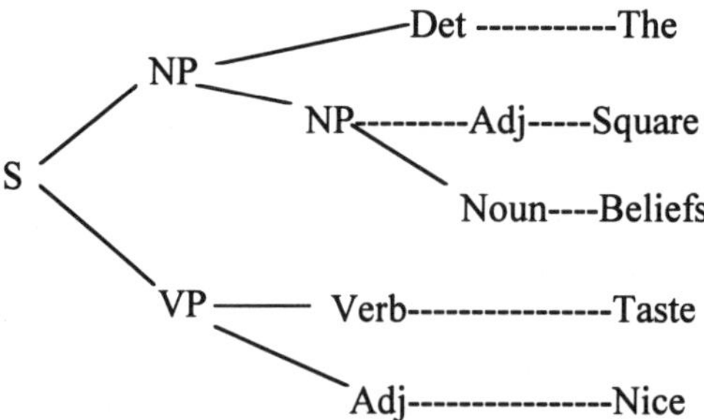

4.9.2 Semantics

Semantics is concerned with generating meaning from knowledge about words and their associations. It forms the link between language, memory and experience. Semantic rules can be built into grammars in an attempt to eliminate nonsense sentences; however, not all semantic rules and classifications are exact, and building a complete semantic grammar is very difficult. Many words are lexically identical, yet have different meanings, e.g. bank (as in put money into) and bank (as in sit upon by the river). Semantic ambiguity forms the basis of puns in which two meanings can be applied to the same sentence, as in the following example from an encyclopaedia entry for Nell Gwynne, one of King Charles II's mistresses:

Gwynne, Nell – see under Charles II.

Semantic ambiguity can be compounded further by inadequacies of syntactic rules. An example of syntactic incompleteness is the lack of any scope rules in natural language grammars. Programming languages are full of such rules which define the structure of programs in terms of control constructs, e.g. While...End-While, If...End-If. Natural language has few scope rules. Consider the sentence:

> Jane's mother put the birthday cake on the special jubilee plate because she knew Jane would like it.

Did Jane like the cake or the plate? The sentence is ambiguous because the pronoun reference (it) has no scope rules about how far back it can refer.

However, to understand language, people do not rely on semantics and syntax alone. To generate more complex understanding, the context of the speaker and listener is required. This is called the pragmatics of language understanding.

4.9.3 Pragmatics

Consider the statement 'He is supporting the reds'. This could have a very different meaning, depending on whether the reader was aware that the speaker was referring to a Communist Party meeting or a supporter of Liverpool football club. Another problem is when idiom and vernacular language are used, for instance, 'she is going to the dogs' could mean that she is going greyhound racing, a plausible explanation in East London, or, more likely, that she is suffering some decline due to personal problems, an interpretation in idiomatic English. Pragmatics is the application of knowledge about the speaker, the surroundings in which communication took place, with other factors such as gestures made by the speaker, and past experiences of interactions between speaker and listener.

From the above, it should be apparent that language understanding is a very complex matter which is inextricably linked to knowledge about the world. While computer systems can be built to successfully parse sentences, constructing a true understanding machine is more difficult. One approach is to equip the computer system with a lexicon of words and associated facts, so the parser can resolve ambiguity and avoid errors of misinterpretation. The power of such systems is dependent on the size and complexity of their lexicon, which rapidly becomes a vast knowledge base, unless the scope of the domain can be restricted. Therefore, most practical natural language systems restrict understanding to a small specialised area of knowledge so the lexical/semantic knowledge base can be constructed with a fair expectation that it will be reasonably complete.

4.9.4 Problems with Natural Language Interfaces

People are overambitious in their assumptions about machine intelligence. They tend to expect computer systems to understand complex sentences, incomplete and ambiguous utterances such as they would use with their fellows. This projection of human qualities of understanding on to computers means that users quickly reach the limits of the system's abilities and misunderstandings occur.

Apart from the inadequacies of language-understanding systems, there are further problems caused by the inaccurate way in which we use language. Consider the statement attributed to a nameless judge: 'It takes no training to distinguish between the false and that which is untrue.' Many people would automatically correct the error and restore the sense of the statement by altering untrue to true, probably unconsciously. Computer programs have great trouble in making such inferences. Other inaccuracies and ambiguities are frequently found in the following constructs:

- *Statements of time*: the ordering of events is often unclear, e.g. read the following instructions:

    - Please sign the list for a taxi.
    - Registration forms should be handed in at the desk.
    - Please fill up the seats in the centre of each row first.
    - Before entering the dining room please wash your hands.

  It is not clear how long the time interval should be between the actions and which instructions should be executed first if the sentences are treated as a list. Knowledge that one has to register before entering the conference may help. Likewise, statements such as please telephone immediately, as soon as possible, or soon, all have different meanings for individual people.

- *Quantifiers*: words such as many, some, often, sometimes, are all vague. Their meaning is derived from the reader's knowledge about the subject being discussed. Two readers may ascribe very different values to the same quantifier in the same context, e.g. some students are lazy; is it 0.1%, 1%, 15% or more in your opinion?

- *Logical operators*: English and most other languages do not distinguish between the computer inclusive/exclusive OR, so people use 'or' when they mean 'or, and, both sometimes' and vice versa. Consider the statement:

  > A large vehicle is one considered to be over 32 feet long or 9 feet 6 inches wide or 38 tons laden weight and not licensed to carry passengers.

  Does the large vehicle possess all three initial properties, or only one, and, does the 'not' condition have to be true? People tend to confuse 'either/or' with 'maybe both' and 'sometimes and'.

- *Numeric comparisons*: logical operators of the type 'greater than' are confused with 'greater than or equal to', e.g.

  > Find all staff with salaries more than £20 000. Most people would include staff with salaries of exactly £20 000 as well.

4.9.5 Design of Natural Language Interfaces

In view of the substantial problems of natural language processing, the main guideline is to restrict interaction to a small domain of knowledge. With current technology successful natural language interfaces can be constructed using single-word recognition, as this does not have the problems of syntax and largely ignores semantics. Understanding sentences is more difficult but possible in restricted circumstances. Natural language query systems for databases have been successful because knowledge of the database entities, attributes and synonyms is restricted to a domain; hence, natural questions and conversations can be held. Other examples are co-operative advisory systems (see also Chapter 10), in which the range of language can be determined beforehand, e.g. tourist information about a specific town or city.

With the current state of the art of language understanding systems it is advisable to:

- 'Back-translate' the user's input so that meaning can be clarified by a further dialogue. This is helpful in reducing ambiguous statements.
- Design dialogues to obtain values for linguistic quantifiers such as 'some, many, more'.
- Interrogate users about new terms so that they can be incorporated into the knowledge base.
- Avoid giving the impression of understanding too much, or outputting statements which imply reasoning.

4.9.6 Speech

If natural language is input by a keyboard, it loses much of its advantage because it is too verbose. Speech interfaces can harness the full power of natural language. Unfortunately, speech introduces the further problem of deciphering words from a nearly continuous physical sound (see the section on hearing in Chapter 2). People are often ungrammatical in written communication, and in speech they are even more lax with the use of language. Spoken communication is full of unfinished phrases, ungrammatical sentences and mispronounced words. Furthermore, words are spoken in a variety of dialects and speakers use intonation in the voice to convey meaning; for instance:

> Find the glass – this can be a question with a meaning 'have you found the glass ?'; or it can be an order with a different intonation.

Speech recognition systems have to deal with all of these problems. Speech recognition varies according to the range of voices to be recognised. Two categories can be used:

- *Speaker dependent.* These systems have to be trained to recognise a limited set of speakers. Intelligent algorithms detect the differences in intonation between each speaker and the machine learns the individual's pattern of speech. Speaker-dependent systems are given good voice recognition accuracy of up to 95–99%, although as they have to be trained they cannot be used for public access. These systems can deal with a wide range of words, with vocabularies of 2000–5000 words being possible. As we normally use about 8000 words in everyday speech, speaker-dependent systems can deal with diverse sentences.
- *Speaker independent.* In these systems any speaker can be recognised. Furthermore, no training period is necessary, as the system has been configured to recognise general voice qualities with variations. The penalty is that recognition rates are not as good (circa 90%, or worse with non-standard speakers); the vocabulary has to be more restricted, usually in the range of 1–200 words.

Single-word recognition systems can handle a wider vocabulary but this does not give syntactic or semantic language recognition. For example, IBM's speaking typewriter relies on isolated word recognition and can handle up to 20 000 words, but it does so by simple phonetic processing. Continuous speech is more problematic. The translation of some words from phoneme (sound) to lexeme (written word) is unfortunately dependent on understanding meaning, either because one word sounds the same as another, as in boar and bore, or because of mispronunciation, or because one word is used with different meanings, e.g. bank. Speech is transient, and if the meaning cannot be deciphered quickly, the system rapidly becomes overwhelmed with more input. With current technology real-time language understanding with speech is just possible; continuous speech understanding is possible with simple sentences, and more complex ones in limited domains. The main problem arises with the poor quality of human speech. This means that speech recognition/understanding systems have to rely heavily on feedback and error correction dialogue to clarify the meaning of users' utterances.

4.10 Summary

User interfaces can be constructed from basic building blocks supplied in development environments. Building blocks, such as messages boxes, buttons, toggles, lists, windows, etc., can be used to construct different types of interfaces. Communication of user responses to the computer is generally by keyboards, although mouse pointing is also common. Other pointing devices such as tracker balls and joysticks have some advantages. New forms of interaction by data gloves may be necessary in virtual reality interfaces.

Simple command interfaces use question and answer dialogues or menus. Menus need a hierarchy in large systems, which makes access slow. By-pass techniques can help for experts. Breadth–depth trade-offs can be made and menu formats designed to optimise recognition. Function keys are a hardware-assisted menu design which economise on screen space but are limited by the number of keys provided.

Icons, windows and pop-up menus are all part of direct manipulation interfaces which work by users picking and interacting directly with objects via a screen image metaphor instead of an identifying code. The screen presents a virtual world based on the user's view which contains an intuitive metaphor to guide interaction. Icons have limitations of realism and ambiguity in large systems. Windows provide multiple views on tasks but may be distracting if overused. User interface design environments are a collection of support tools which enable designers to model tasks and then map dialogue models to user interface components. Some environments include active guidance rules to help mapping; however, little integration with CASE tools has occurred, limiting their effectiveness.

Complex command interfaces use command languages or natural language. Both consist of words and composition rules for sentences, called a grammar. Command languages have relatively few grammar rules but can provide a powerful and flexible interface. Care has to be exercised in choosing abbreviations for command words. Natural language has a vast number of composition rules, but in spite of this, it is still inherently ambiguous. People decipher meaning using semantic and pragmatic knowledge. The inability of machine systems to store sufficient knowledge for sophisticated understanding means that users expect too much of language interfaces and tend to exceed the system's capabilities. Limited natural-language interfaces can be used for dialogues about restricted areas of knowledge.

Further Reading

Shneiderman (1987) gives a good survey of command and control interfaces and deals with direct manipulation in more detail. For UIDEs and more details on PAC see Coutaz (1989) and Luo *et al.* (1993). Bass and Coutaz (1991) is the book to consult for good survey on UI architectures and their components. For more details on design environments, style guides and UI components, try Hix and Hartson (1993) or Myers (1993).

Questions and Exercises

1. How do graphical user interfaces differ from the more classical styles of interaction such as full screen menus or form filling interfaces? What principles of HCI are realised in GUIs?

2. What problems do icons cause in interpretation? Examine icons in the interface of a GUI version of a word processing package, e.g. Microsoft Word, WordPerfect. How could you improve the design of icons for format marks (e.g. tab, margin, indent)?

3. Discuss the merits of command language and natural language interfaces for a specific application such as data retrieval. Compare the usability advantage and problems with each interface style.

4. Compare the different types of menu provided by graphical user interfaces. What improvements have pull-down/pop-up menus made over full screen menus?

5. How should icons be designed to represent objects which have a concrete and abstract identity? What guidelines would you follow in their design?

5 Media and Modalities

The theme of this chapter is the means by which we interact. *Multimedia* will be considered as various forms in which information can be presented. This is linked to *multimodality*, which will be treated as communications channels between user and computer. *Hypertext* is reviewed as a different means of presenting information in a non-linear manner. Add different media to hypertext and we have *hypermedia*. Add three-dimensional images, sensory wrap-around and gesture modalities and this produces *virtual reality*. All these technologies personify the technical push part of HCI which creates new means of interacting and, hence, the potential to achieve new ways of working with computers. However, technology is only part of the story. With new opportunities for interacting come new challenges in design. Technically innovative interfaces can still be bad designs unless principles and methods for user-centred design are applied. In this chapter the objective is to explain the basis for interactive technologies. This forms input to presentation design in Chapter 7.

5.1 Multimedia

A medium is a means of conveying a message. In communication it is common to separate these:

- *Message*: the content of communication between a sender and receiver.
- *Medium*: the means by which that content is delivered. Note that this is how the message is represented rather than the technology for delivering a message such as a telecommunications network.

Computers used to be limited to alphanumeric character displays and low-resolution graphics. With the advance in technology this is changing and computers are increasingly supporting multimedia. So what are these media? Definitions can be considered at a logical level of how the message is presented to people and a physical level of how the message is stored inside a computer. Logical media types are:

- *Alphanumeric text*. This covers the ASCII character set of numbers and letters familiar in text displays, and numeric tables.

- *Static images.* These may either be realistic pictures taken from film or video recordings or drawn by people as cartoons, sketches, etc. In this class subdivisions can be proposed for:

    - *pictures*: images derived from photographs;
    - *diagrams*: symbolic images which have to be learned in some way;
    - *sketches and informal images*: drawings, designs and other visual material which does not fit into the other categories.

- *Moving image.* Films, cartoons and all animated images. As with still images, these may be either realistic pictures, as in films, or created by people, as in cartoons.
- *Sound.* Audial messages which are not spoken language. The message may be natural sounds, such as bird song, the composed sounds of music, or just plain noise.
- *Speech.* Language communicated audially. The categories of media are often related to the modality of communication and this difference is apparent in language. The message in text and speech may be the same; however, it may be delivered in either a printed form by a visual modality or in a spoken form by audial modality. Modality is dealt with further in Section 5.2.

5.1.1 Formats and Storage

At the physical level media may be stored by different techniques. Indeed one medium is often represented in several ways. Text, for instance, may be encoded as 7-bit ASCII or 8-bit EBCDIC. Images are either stored as a pixel array or as vectors. Pixel storage represents images as a series of dots (or pixels, an abbreviation of 'picture cells') which have different qualities of greyness on a black–white scale. An image is composed of many pixels (1024 times 1024 for most high-resolution computer screens). For colour the red, green and blue properties of each pixel are encoded. This becomes very expensive in storage, as 24 bits are necessary for high-quality colour. To reduce storage demands, various encoding algorithms have been invented which only code necessary information, such as differences within an image rather than areas which are the same. The JPEG (Joint Pictures Expert Group) algorithms are now widely adopted by most computer systems for compressing and decompressing images to economise on storage. Vectorised images are more economical to store, as the whole image is not represented; instead shapes which compose the image are encoded in algorithms for drawing them (e.g. curved lines, polygons, cylinders, etc.). Vector graphics are effective for drawings but less useful for realistic images where pixels are necessary for detail of texture, shading and colour.

If storage is a problem for still images, then for moving image it becomes severe. Moving image on film or video tape is encoded in an analogue medium. This may be bulky to store as video tapes or film spools, and cannot be manipulated by computers except via an analogue playing device such as a projector or VCR. Computer-based moving image has to be digitised into pixel format and this is when the storage demand becomes huge.

A short clip of film will contain more than 30 separate images per second, so 10 seconds' worth would consume 200–300 Mb of disk space uncompressed, assuming 307 200 pixels per frame with 640 × 480 VGA resolution using 24 bits per pixel for good colour coding gives 921 600 bytes per frame at 30 frames per second (NTSC American video standard – 25 per second for European PAL) gives 23 040 000 bytes. Compression is essential and algorithms adopted by the MPEG (Moving Pictures Expert Group) are now used by most systems. These algorithms work in a similar manner to still-image compression by looking for the changes in an image and, with film, between two images as well. Algorithms may be either 'lossy', in that when the movie is decompressed, some of the detail is lost, or 'lossless', as all the detail is preserved. Not surprisingly, lossless algorithms achieve lower compression on storage (about 10 times reduction), whereas lossy algorithms can achieve 20–30 times reduction. Even so, storing moving image consumes megabytes. Multimedia with moving images therefore requires storage capacities afforded by optical disks.

Sound in comparison is less of a problem. Storage demands depend on the fidelity desired for replay. Full stereo with a complete range of harmonic frequencies can take 100 kb for 5 min.

5.1.2 Multimedia Devices

In view of the large demands made by multimedia on storage, special devices are necessary. Most multimedia is stored in CD-ROM: Compact Disk – Read Only Memory. These are optical disks which are written by lasers burning digital code into the disk. This is then read by another laser. Once written, it can not be changed; hence read only memory. Some read–write optical disks do exist and will become more common in the future. Currently CD-ROMs store around 500 Mb per disk, but disks can be stacked in platters and multidisk-reading devices called 'jukeboxes'. This raises the storage capacity to many gigabytes. There is a storage standard for uncompressed data, ISO 9660, but this only really applies to text. Most image is compressed and there are three rival standards:

- *CD-I* (Compact Disk – Interactive), marketed by Philips and Sony. This is designed as a stand-alone system for home entertainment and uses standard

TVs as display devices. There is a version which allows more integration with standard computer systems, CDI-XA (eXtended Architecture).

- *DVI* (Digital Video Interactive), supported by Intel and IBM, which is intended to be integrated with standard computer software and comes as a plug-in board with software drivers. This provides analogue to digital conversion, image data compression and interactive control of video-based multimedia.
- *Quicktime* from Apple is also interactive, and supports control of video-based media, including scripting type controls.

As yet no winner in the standards race has emerged. CD-I is likely to remain in the home entertainment niche, but the computer sector may have an industry-wide set of standards in the near future. The Interactive Multimedia Association (IMA) is an industry body which brings together nearly all the major players in multimedia technologies (e.g. Apple, Sun, IBM, Hewlett Packard, Adobe, Intel, to name just a few). Their vision is to create a raft of industry standards for the whole area of distributed networked multimedia client–server environments. This is summarised in Figure 5.1.

At the *lowest level* are multimedia system services which provide the basic transport from a media serving device to a system requiring media services. The conceptual architecture has media storage devices which store media in a format, probably compressed. A transport network delivers the compressed data to the client system. A rendering device then decompresses the media, and possibly changes the format. The media are then passed on to the client in the required format. The services are built on top of the COBRA architecture (Common Object Broker Request Architecture) or the OMG (Object Management Group).

The *second layer* of media control services allows different media to be played and synchronised on a variety of different machines and operating systems. This provides the basic stop/start/playback type controls with synchronisation between event tracks. By using event tracks different media can be played according to predetermined sequences. This layer also has container data structures to define complex multimedia objects with their own access paths and, hence, presentation. A container could have text documents with an embedded still image and then a movie within that.

The *final layer* is a scripting language for overall control of multimedia applications. This will be a programmable authoring language to control the presentation of different media, in presentation sequences.

While the details of the IMA standards are still being worked out, in the near future the transport, compression, storage format and control of multimedia will come as a standardised set of transportable facilities for all the major operating systems (e.g. Unix, DOS/Windows, Apple Bedrock).

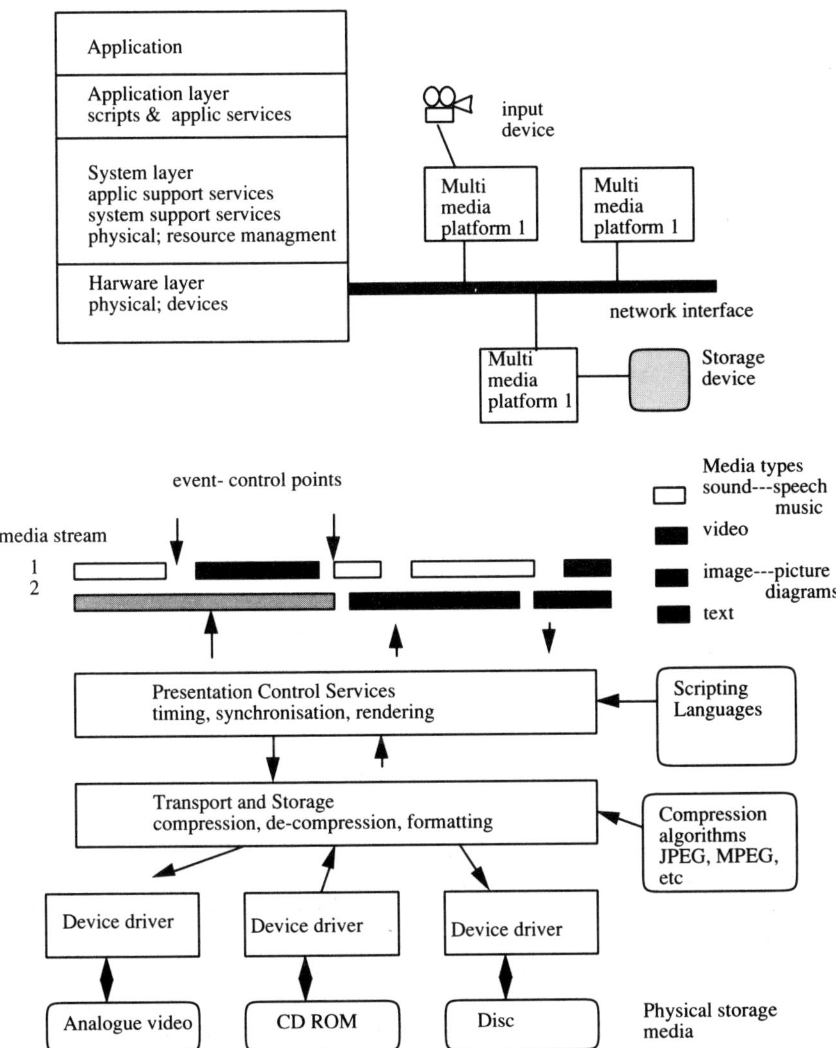

Figure 5.1 Multimedia architecture (adapted from IMA reference model).

5.1.3 Media Types

Media have logical properties which are important for design. First the differences between dynamic and static media have to be considered.

Dynamic media

Sound, speech and moving image are dynamic or time-varying media. The temporal dimension marks these apart from other forms, as design has to consider:

- How can the media be controlled over time? Can the speed of presentation be changed, and what controls exist over presentation? In visual media the controls are those familiar from VCR technology: fast forward, rewind, freeze frame, stop and start. Figure 5.2 shows an animated image displayed at different resolutions. This is linked to the presentation speed, as there is a trade-off between the number of frames per second which can be displayed and the image resolution. Coarse-grained images take less storage so faster replay is possible.
- How can the media format be changed? Can the image be expanded (zoom in)? Can the sound be filtered, changed in amplitude, frequency, etc?
- Are sub-components of the dynamic medium addressable directly or indirectly? Direct addressing is achieved by format codes within the medium, e.g. frame numbers on a film allow access to frame 101, etc. Indirect addressing has to be effected by use of a clock as no format markers are present in the medium itself; hence, going to the start of a Mozart symphony is achieved by starting to play the sound 30 seconds from the start, having timed the start position.

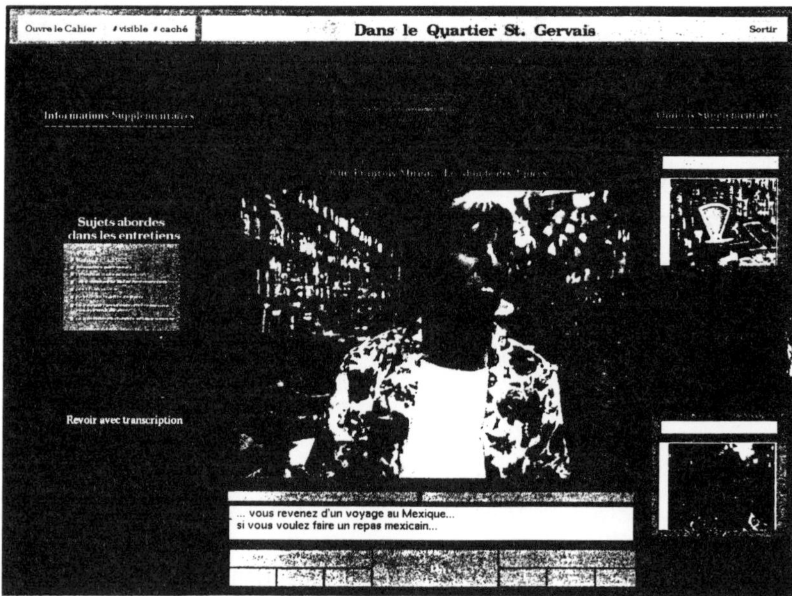

Figure 5.2 Multimedia interface showing use of animation and graphics (courtesy of MIT project ATHENA).

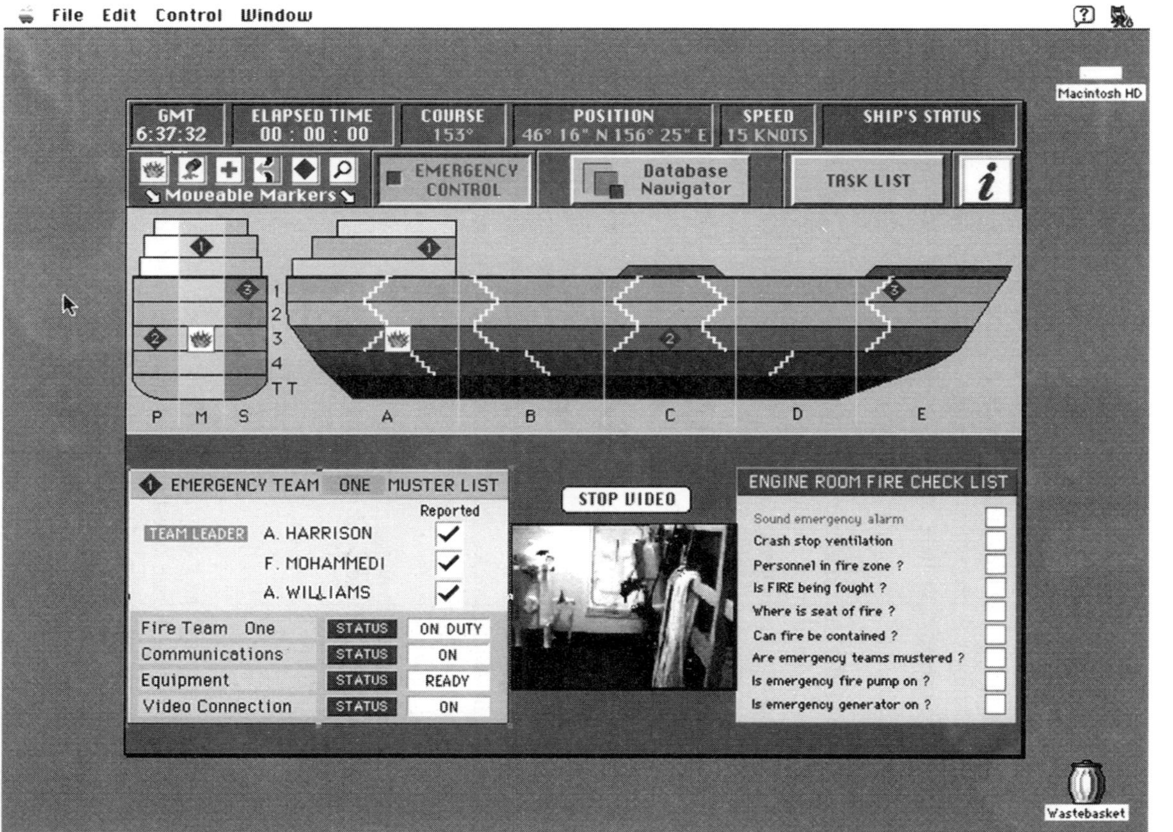

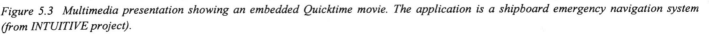

Figure 5.3 Multimedia presentation showing an embedded Quicktime movie. The application is a shipboard emergency navigation system (from INTUITIVE project).

Answers to these questions are necessary for planning multimedia presentations, so media can be co-ordinated in a script which controls delivery of a consistent message between different media. Time-varying media present a particular problem in synchronisation. Two media may have to be played at the same rate, for instance a sound channel for a movie or sub-title texts co-ordinated with a range of frames in a movie. Scripting languages and standards are emerging which enable this sort of co-ordination. The Quicktime language from Apple has been influential as a means of controlling time-varying media. This is used in the Quicktime animation viewer, illustrated in Figure 5.3.

Some psychological properties of media were touched upon in Chapter 2. The important qualities to bear in mind when designing with dynamic media are:

- Dynamic media tend to dominate by attracting attention from static media.
- Retention of detail from dynamic media is poor; this is because the quality of information is potentially vast and we deal with this by filtering the gist.
- Dynamic media can easily overload human information processing. If we have to extract a complex message from dynamic media, then the pace of presentation may over-run our ability to comprehend and memorise the message.
- Co-ordination of the message between separate dynamic media requires care. Because dynamic media tax our processing abilities, presentation of two different messages concurrently is a bad idea. The message on one medium (e.g. sound track) should be congruent with the other (e.g. film). Even slight discrepancies are noticeable, such as when a film has been dubbed and the speech no longer matches the movement of the speaker's lips.
- User control over dynamic media is highly desirable, so that people can replay sequences if they did not manage to hear or see all of the message first time.

Static media

Text, numeric displays and graphics are static in the sense that they have no time dimension. The design questions, however, relate to similar properties to those for time-varying media:

- How can the display be controlled? Controls are often part of the standard GUI environment, e.g. sliders to pan or move along a static medium.
- How can the media format be changed? The answer to this and the following question depends on the storage format and the capabilities of the presentation device. Text formats can usually be changed in size (point) and shape (font, bold). Images can be scaled by zoom in and out.

- Are sub-components of the medium addressable? For text, individual characters are addressable, but in images the answer depends on semantic encoding. The ability to address and, hence, interact with part of an image depends on the ability of the computer's object management system to discern shapes; then, interpretation of the shape as an object depends on whether it has been indexed. Semantic encoding involves giving image sub-components an identifier and descriptive attributes.

With static media there is generally more potential for interaction, as the storage format often allows more addressability. This gives the designer more freedom in planning interactive effects between the media to show links between different messages. The important cognitive properties to bear in mind for static media are:

- Visual media tend to dominate over text, primarily because images can be scanned quickly, whereas reading is a more attention-demanding process.
- Many different messages can be extracted from one image. Interpretation of a message in an image depends on the user's attention and knowledge about the image contents. For instance, one person may extract a wealth of detail from a map, whereas another may see little except strange icons. Memory for image detail is generally poor unless people's attention has been drawn to specific facts. Extraction of information from diagrams requires learning the syntax and semantics of a symbolic language.
- Reading is a sequential process whereby we assimilate a message by progressively chunking the meaning as we read phrases, sentences and paragraphs. Good sentence structure and layout help this process. Memory for detail in text messages is generally better than for image, although only the higher-order chunks will be recalled accurately; hence, the story plot may be remembered although the words will not be.

Visual media are useful for conveying certain types of message, e.g. spatial and event-context information, whereas text is more useful for instructions, procedures and giving abstract information. The different properties of static and dynamic media types are exploited in media selection rules. The control and addressability properties are important for planning interactive effects which help direct the user's attention to important information within one or more media.

Media may be embedded within each other as complex composite objects, e.g. it is possible to place a movie clip within a text to illustrate part of a story. Embedded media formats are called *containers*. These storage structures have an index which gives the address and control characteristics of each media type within the container. The Bento container format from Apple is one potential *de facto* standard in this area, which defines a portable format for composite multimedia objects.

Multimedia is invariably described with multimodality. Sometimes these terms are wrongly taken to be synonymous.

5.2 Multimodality

Modality is a means of communication relating to our senses. For that reason multimodal systems are often called multisensory. People use principally vision and hearing, and to a lesser extent touch, taste and smell. Modality has another meaning in HCI, as a mode of interaction in a context which determines how something should be interpreted. This, however, is another debate (see Chapter 6); here we shall concentrate on modality as a communication channel. Two principal modalities are used by people:

- *Vision*: all information received through our eyes, including text and image-based media.
- *Hearing*: all information received through our ears, as sound, music and speech.

In addition, we use two other modalities:

- *Haptic*: information received via the sense of touch. This is closely related to motor-based action with many computer devices, e.g. keyboard, mouse, joystick.
- *Gustatory–olfactory*: so far, the use of our sense of taste and smell has been of limited use with computers.

The main problem with multimodality comes with combinations of voice, vision and haptic modality via pointing. Outbound multimodality happens when two channels are used with different media, e.g. a voice explanation of a diagram. Inbound multimodality occurs when we communicate with a computer using two channels, such as speech and pointing, as shown in Figure 5.4. The former is a problem for multimedia presentation scripting and will be returned to in Chapter 7. The latter raises problems of dialogue design which are examined here and have implications for Chapter 6, which investigates dialogue design in more depth.

Input multimodality raises a timing problem. Should pointing come after, before or during speech? Two forms of multimodality are possible:

- *Asynchronous*, in which communication in one modality must be before or after the other.
- *Synchronous*, in which input from both modalities may occur at the same time.

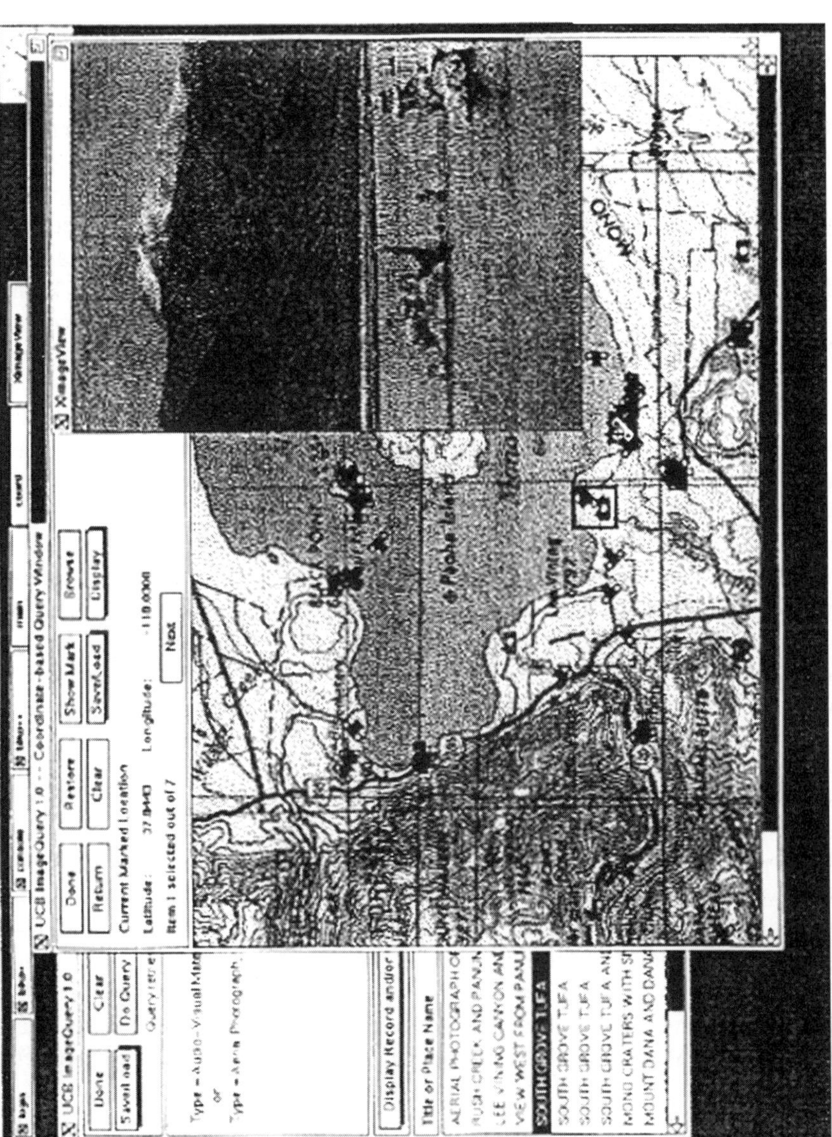

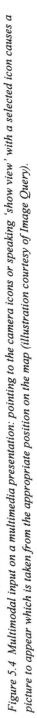

Figure 5.4 Multimodal input on a multimedia presentation: pointing to the camera icons or speaking 'show view' with a selected icon causes a picture to appear which is taken from the map (illustration courtesy of Image Query).

Synchronous multimodality is more difficult to process but more natural in human terms. Research into natural multimodal dialogue is still in its infancy. We have very little evidence to say when pointing should be interleaved with speech. For instance, pointing may be used for commands as well as for referring to objects. Commands are arguably as easy to speak as to point to, although the user may forget a command name. Objects, however, especially collections of objects, are more easily referred to by pointing. This may lead to the assumption that pointing should generally come after speech in an <action, object> syntax, e.g. the user speaks 'show me these', points to several icons representing objects. The reference to 'these' is called deixis and the computer system has to find the identity of the object being pointed to and substitute the objects instead of 'these'. Unfortunately, there are references between turns in a dialogue as well as within them. For instance, it is quite natural to say 'I am interested in these tools' while pointing at a collection of tools icons; this could be followed by the command 'attach them to the system'. In this case the dialogue interpreter has to search back to find out to what 'them' refers.

This necessitates keeping a dialogue history of the objects which have been referred to. The current object is the topic focus in linguistic terms, and the problem is to decide how many objects are in focus and for how long. These are questions for advanced natural language interfaces which incorporate multimodality, and as such are beyond the scope of this book. The upshot of multimodal interaction is that the order may be either way, i.e. speech before pointing, which is more natural; or vice versa because <object action> syntax is more common in direction manipulation, so, if speech is substituted, pointing may come first. The system has to maintain a tie marker to decide whether a point belongs to a dialogue act or (see page 252) is the beginning of a new one. Research systems are only just starting to address these problems.

Gesture

Use of pointing raises the problem of gesture. *Mouse-mediated interaction* is a primitive form of gesture, but it is limited to point at, drag and drop. We use a wide range of gestures in human–human communication, so considerable research has been devoted to seeing whether gesture can be effective as another communication modality. *Hand-based gesture* has made most progress. Pointing, grasping and hand motions can be communicated via sensors on a data glove (see also Section 4.2). This allows the computer to recognise and interpret the hand's shape as a particular gesture for grab-object, select, move forward, etc. (see Figure 5.5). We make a wide range of gestures with our hands and arms, so the potential for this communication is considerable. Unfortunately, much gesture is culture-specific and idiosyncratic, so, whereas thumbs up is fairly reliably interpreted as a positive affirmation, tapping the side of one's head can mean a wide variety of things in different European countries.

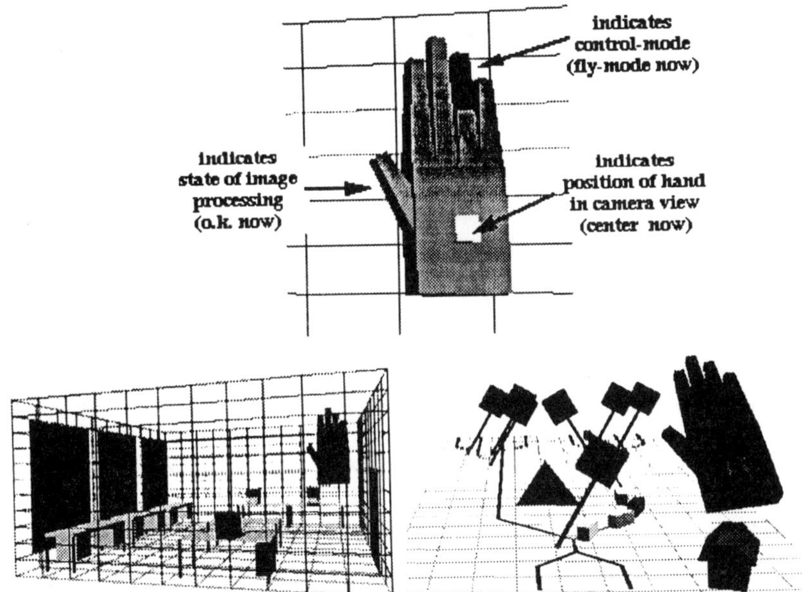

Figure 5.5 Gesture in a virtual reality system. The hand is used to fly forward, point and select object in the virtual world (illustration courtesy of Siemens Ltd.).

Head gestures are also unreliable. Head movement from side to side may signal a disagreement in Europe, but in India the reverse is true.

Gesture, therefore, is open to ambiguous interpretation. It also requires considerable image processing capabilities to recognise the position of a person's head or arm. Furthermore, gesture is often used in human–human communication to back up what is being said verbally, so the justification for such complex and potentially error-prone means of human–computer communication seems dubious.

Gaze, however, may have some potential as a type of gesture. We fixate on objects with our eyes. Gaze detection devices can track the direction of our gaze, giving the potential for us to point by looking. The disadvantage is that gaze is permanently active; it is not something we can shut off, so it is hard to restrict the effect. If the computer highlighted everything we looked at, it would rapidly become annoying. Gaze may be used when combined with another device which acts as a context switch for gaze on/off. This could be used for eye-direct pointing when other pointing devices cannot be used. Current gaze detection devices are expensive and intrusive for the user, so the impact of this technology may be limited for some time.

5.3 Hypertext and Hypermedia

Hypertext owes its heritage to the foresight of Vannevar Bush (Bush, 1945) who looked forward to the day when reading material could be accessed in a non-linear manner. His proposal for a Memex system was the ancestor of hypertext. The first computer-based system was implemented by Doug Englebart in the mid-1960s, although the term 'hypertext' was coined more recently by Ted Nelson in the Xanadu project (Nelson, 1987). The idea is simple. Text fragments are connected by access paths so the text can be read in a variety of different ways. Information can be combined by many different pathways, thus maximising the interrelationships. Essentially the idea takes cross-referencing and indexing as found in encyclopaedias to its logical end. In Nelson's vision Xanadu becomes a giant network of information access paths ultimately linking everything that anyone has ever written. To date more prosaic implementations have been limited to smaller domains, but hypertext has become an important means of supplying documentation and authoring tutorial software and a novel means of information browsing.

Hypertext consists of components of data and an access structure. This provides a graphic pathway through the data. Two different types of hypertext are possible, depending on how the data is stored:

- Card-based hypertexts: the base unit of information has a preset size as a 'card'.
- Document-based: this type has a less rigid notion of data storage, which can be any size or shape; links can form paths within the documents as well as between different documents.

Both types of hypertext consist of *nodes* and *links* which together make a *pathway*. The fundamental elements are:

- *Data* contained in the nodes in the hypertext graph. Nodes may be documents or pieces of text as small as single words.
- *Buttons* or *hotspots*: these are associated with nodes as active areas in a document which signify links to other data. They form the starting points for hypertext links and may also be called *anchors.*
- *Links* are the arcs between hypertext nodes and are activated by the user's selecting a button. The effect is to take the user to another piece of information. Hence, in text describing the battle of Waterloo, selecting the name 'Wellington' takes the reader to another text on the biography of the Duke of Wellington. In some systems links may be typed (e.g. supports, contributes towards, contradicts, etc.).
- A set of standard operations for *navigation*, such as 'next card', 'previous card', goto home (start card).

Most systems provide facilities for designing the database, such as graphics tools and texture palettes for the background of the document/card. The ability to import text and images is also important. Some systems allow data entry fields so the user can input values and selections to determine their path through the network. Two types of document access may be supported:

- *Intra*-document hypertext: the document has hotspots (words, paragraphs or images) which cause a jump to another location within the same document.
- *Inter*-document hypertext: the nodes of the hypertext are small documents in their own right, usually referred to as cards. Access paths link cards and each card may have several anchors, or starting points for links as buttons and hotspots.

Most systems support both forms of access but some are specialised towards the interdocument variety, e.g. Notecards.

The topology of hypertext nets and access paths is summarised in Figure 5.6. Most links form chains via which the user can explore different connections; some, however, are simple annotations and just lead to a pop-up footnote, returning the user to the same place within the original text. Menus and button panels can be used to provide a choice of links to follow. Most hypertext systems support a simple programming-by-example way of building the database and its links. Some also give keyword search facilities so that information can be accessed when the link structure fails. There is no standard architecture for hypertext systems and separation from the database remains a considerable problem. An idealised view is the three-layer model of the Hypertext Abstract Machine (HAM) with a presentation layer for input/output, an intermediate layer and then the database (see Figure 5.7). The main problem is how to support anchors in the intermediate layer, which may also be part of nodes which should, as data, be in the database layer. Current hypertexts contain the database within the system, thus merging the two layers.

The ability to handle different media upgrades hypertext to *hypermedia*. The access structure remains the same; all that changes is the database, which may now contain film, sound, still images, etc. Hotspots may be objects in an image; graphics have to be encoded so that parts of the image can be selected, leading to a link. This can be done either by placing icons overlaying the image or encoding buttons/hotspots directly as selectable objects. Most hypertext systems handled graphics from the outset, so the main addition for hypermedia is the use of dynamic media. These do impose a limitation on anchors and links to other parts of the database, as a dynamic medium must be played until it has finished before the next link can be made. Some systems provide icon anchors on a pictorial summary of animated media to allow links to within a film clip (e.g. goto frame number N).

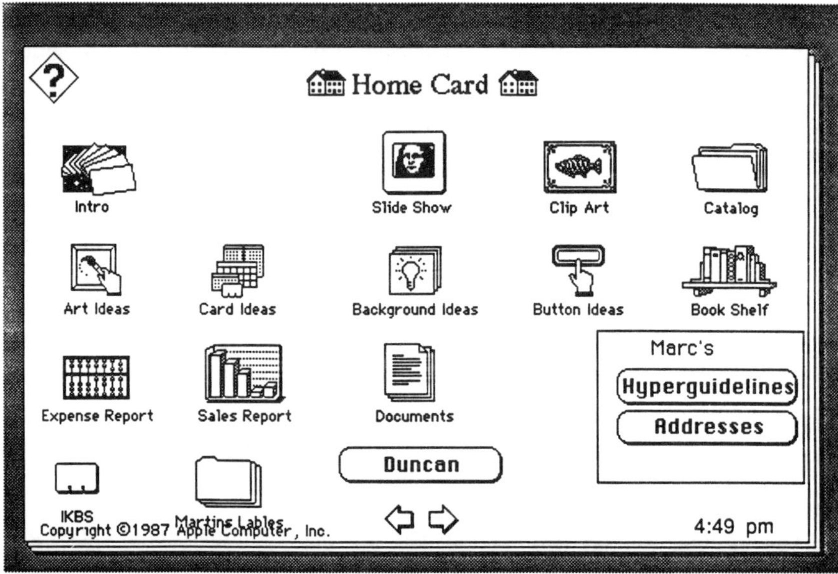

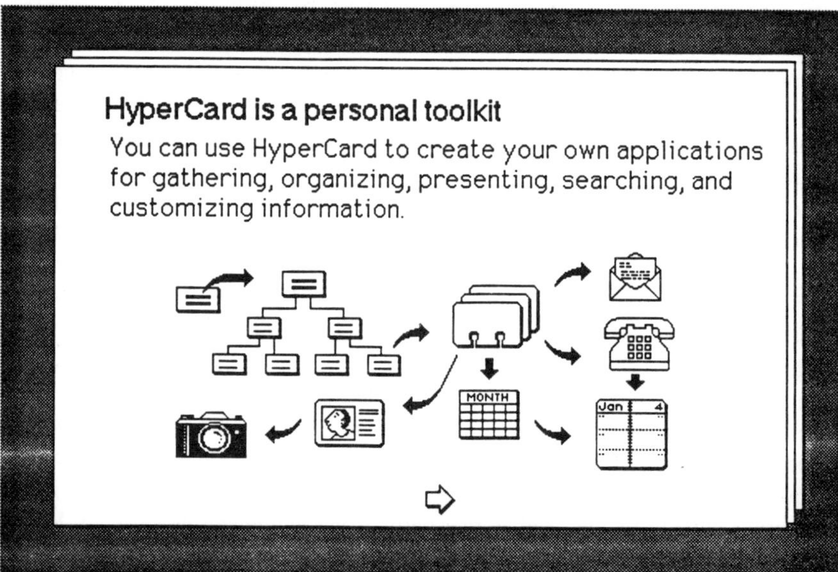

Figure 5.6 Hypertext, illustrating cards as nodes and connections (links) between cards (HyperCard application courtesy of Apple Inc.).

Hypertext systems come in a variety of formats. Some adhere closely to the card format, e.g. Xerox Notecards and Apple HyperCard. The metaphor consists of stacks of cards which are connected and relate to one topic or theme. The idea is that the stack is like a pile of memo cards on a topic. The whole system is composed of a series of stacks which may be arranged in a hierarchy.

Others, e.g. Guide and full document hypertexts, allow more flexible format and connections can be made within a document as well as between a document or card and another one.

Besides providing a database and access structure, hypertext systems also have a scripting language for more flexible design of information pathways. In non-programmed mode hypertext systems are developed by example. The user creates a card and specifies the links by pointing to the next card to be accessed from a button. The hypertext system then automatically creates a program script with the necessary 'goto card-address' instructions. These interpret data entered by the user and determine the link address by an algorithm or calculation. The user's progress through the database can be controlled in a sophisticated manner by a program with the usual structured constructs of Sequence, Selection and Iteration.

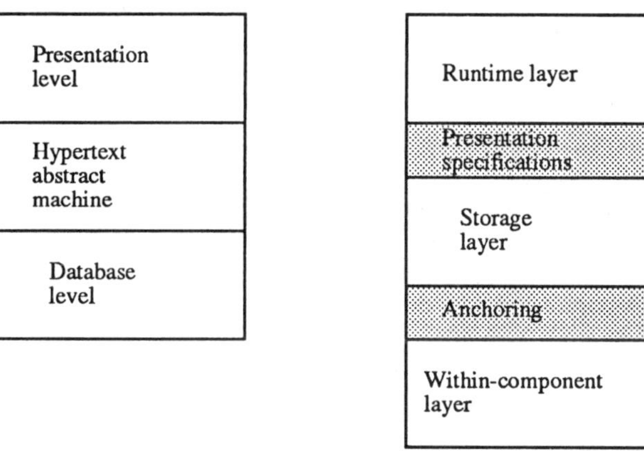

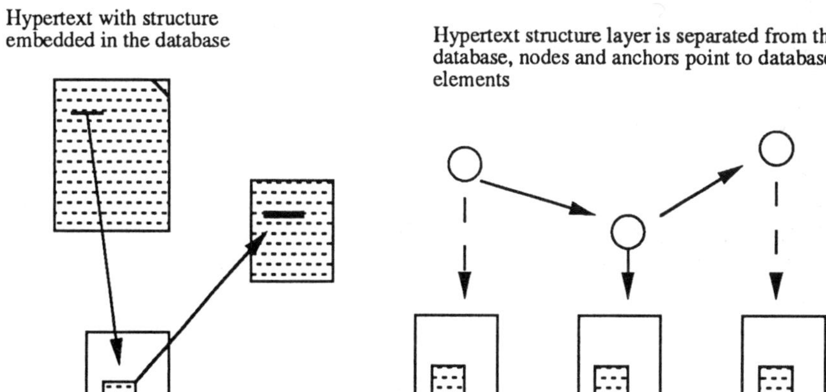

Figure 5.7 Hypertext Abstract Machine and Dexter models of hypertext systems. The Dexter model adds Within-component and Anchoring layers to give more structuring between the database and user interface.

Navigating in hypertexts

Studies of user interaction (Belkin *et al.*, 1985) with hypertext systems have shown different search strategies:

- *Random*: no particular order is observable.
- *Scanning*: users sample different parts of the hypertext without systematically exploring any part in depth.
- *Spike exploration*: the user follows link pathways, although the search may not be directed to any specific goal, and side tracks are evident in the trace of the user's search.
- *Searching*: exploration follows pathways in a directed manner towards an information-seeking goal. Fewer diversions down side tracks occur in searching.

Hypertext systems need to support the user's information-seeking task. Unfortunately, hypertext systems assume a fixed database and link structure. This can be made more flexible by scripts, but the user is still ultimately limited to the pathways provided by the design. More open-ended hypertext environments, e.g. Microcosm (Hall *et al.*, 1992) provide scripts and query facilities which allow the user to access data in host databases. Preformed queries can be attached to hotspots, or terms in hypertext nodes can be submitted as query parameters. This is more flexible, as the hypertext can then provide an access path to a wide variety of data without having to become a database as well. In this case the division between hypertext links and database query languages becomes blurred.

Skill in good hypertext design is a matter of sound information analysis for the pathways between related items (see Chapter 7), and use of cues to show the structure of the information space to the user. One problem with large hypertexts is that users get lost in them. Navigation cues, waymarks and mini-map overviews can help to counter the effects of disorientation. *Mini-maps* give an overview of the hypertext area while another display shows the local part of the network (see Figure 5.8). This gives the user a reference context for where they are in large networks. *Filters* or user views for part of the network can also help to reduce complexity to a sub-set of nodes and links that the user is interested in. Having typed links helps filtering views. Other facilities for user navigation are *visit-lists* containing a history of nodes traversed in a session. The user can then backtrack using the visit-list as a trace pathway. Visit-lists and all nodes can be tagged with the date when they were accessed so users can find out they have been in a particular part of the hypertext and when, as illustrated in Figure 5.9. Finally, *bookmarks* are a good means for users to tailor a hypertext with their own navigation mementoes. Bookmarks, also called waymarks, are iconic/text tags which may be placed on hypertext nodes to remind the user about important nodes.

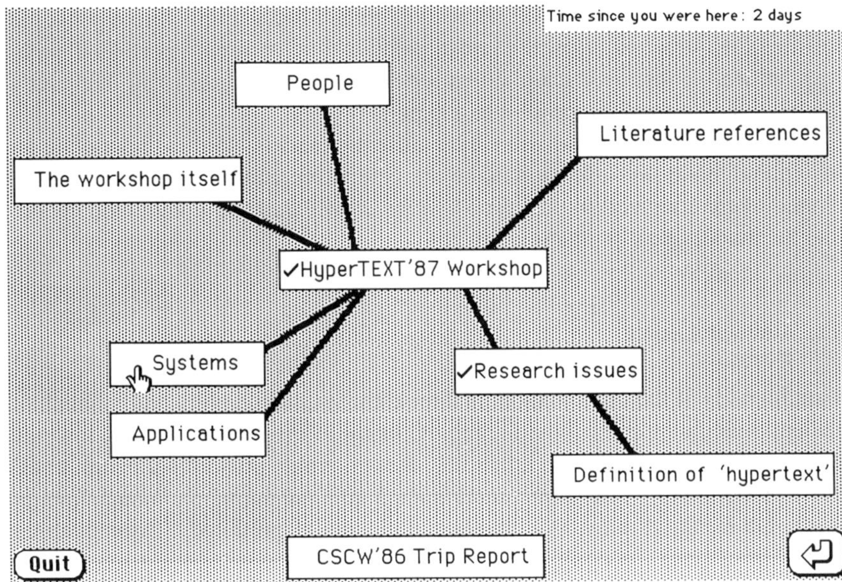

Figure 5.8 Hypertext mini-map for conceptual orientation (courtesy Jakob Nielsen).

History list

Click on the name of an article to jump back to it

(time since you read the article)	
6 min.	Book covers: Front cover of Main HyperTEXT'87 Report
6 min.	Chapter Overview Maps: HyperTEXT'87 report overview
6 min.	Chapter Overview Maps: Hypertext research issues
6 min.	Hypertext systems: Classifying hypertext systems (Frank Halasz)
6 min.	HyperTEXT'87 Trip Report: Definition of Hypertext
5 min.	Hypertext systems: HyperCard (Apple)
5 min.	Literature references: As We May Think
5 min.	Vannevar Bush: Quotes from As We May Think
5 min.	Literature references: As We May Think
5 min.	Hypertext systems: HyperCard (Apple)
5 min.	HyperTEXT'87 Trip Report: Definition of Hypertext
3 min.	Hypertext systems: Classifying hypertext systems (Frank Halasz)
3 min.	Hypertext systems: Writers using Xerox NoteCards
3 min.	CSCW'86 Trip Rep : Hypertext, NoteCards
3 min.	Hypertext systems: Writers using Xerox NoteCards
2 min.	Hypertext systems: Symbolics Document Examiner
2 min.	Chapter Overview Maps: Hypertext people
34 sec.	Hypertext people: Is Text Data ? (Andy van Dam)

Quit

Time since you were here: NEVER

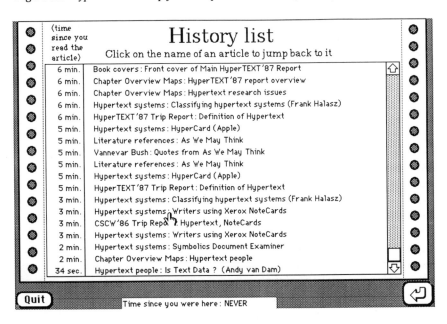

Figure 5.9 Visit-list of nodes for tracing back in hypertext (courtesy Jakob Nielsen).

Another problem is not knowing where to get started. Guided tours or tutorial programmes can help to solve this problem by taking the user on a preset exploration of the hypertext. However, guided tours do militate against the spirit of free exploration in hypertext because they enforce a particular pathway. Overall, constructing a good hypertext is based on translating the user's model of the information space into a hypertext graph.

Unfortunately, individual users have different models, so this may not be an easy task. Too many links will make the system too complex and increase the chance of the user getting lost. Too few links will frustrate a user who cannot find the associations he or she wants.

5.4 Virtual Reality

Virtual reality is the combination of three-dimensional graphics and interactive devices which simulates some feeling of 'being in the picture'. In VR systems the user is encapsulated in an artificially created reality projected through small VDU screens worn as glasses (see Figure 5.10). As the whole visual field is subtended by the display, this creates the illusion of presence. This capitalises on a view of visual recognition and comprehension proposed by Gibson (1966), who describes the interaction between visual process and the senses of balance and spatial judgement. Gibson was concerned with the link between peripheral and central vision on judgement of motion. VR systems exploit peripheral vision to give the feeling of motion in the virtual world, so when the user moves forward parts of the image go past the viewer, giving the feeling of motion.

The other part of VR is telepresence. This combined with the graphics gives the feeling of being there. Telepresence is delivered by a device which allows part or all of the user to be monitored by the computer and represented within the display. The most common device is a data glove holding sensors to detect finger movement and motion of the user's hand. This movement is mimicked by a hand displayed in the virtual world. Movement forward causes the display, and the user perception thereof, to go deeper into the virtual world. Telepresence can be enhanced by wearing other sensors to detect head and body movement, so the computer can monitor and present the user's body within the virtual reality. In addition to its use in VR, telepresence has many other applications in robotic control. The robot operator has a VDU display of the robot's view and a set of controls for manipulation. Well-designed systems give good hand–eye coordination so the operator can control a device which may be many miles away. Applications include robots in hazardous environments such as repairing nuclear reactors and tele-operation of space probes.

VR systems started in military applications as head-up cockpit displays. Images containing flight data were projected on to a special visor so the information appeared to be superimposed on the pilot's normal view of the world. It is a small step from superimposition to full immersion or the feeling of being 'there' in the computer-generated environment. Virtual reality comes in two major variants:

- *Desktop, or non-immersive reality*. This uses a normal VDU display which shows a 3D graphical world. The user interacts with this via a data glove and the telepresence is shown by an image of the user's hand on the screen. By using gestures and motions of the hand the user can move within the display and grab objects.
- *Full immersion virtual reality*. These systems require the user to wear VDU headgear so the whole visual field is filled with a 3D graphical image. Telepresence is simulated either by an image of the user within the reality or by a hand. Interaction is much richer as the user's position can be monitored by a data glove and sensors to detect motion of the head and whole body.

Figure 5.10 Virtual reality: illustration of head-mounted VDU display, and images of a VR environment as seen by the user.

In full VR systems (see Figure 5.11) users can look around the virtual world by turning their head, move through it by walking or more usually by moving their hand to signal motion. Too much movement is discouraged, as this leads to collision with real walls while in the virtual world. Objects can be grabbed, picked-up and manipulated. Telepresence provides kinetic feedback through data gloves so touch can be felt. Body suits of sensors are being developed so users can feel when they bump into virtual objects. Ultimately the sky is the limit with this technology. In the current state of the art, computing power is still labouring with the vast computational load to update large 3D images in real time, so the reality can appear jerky as the user looks around. The 3D imagery will soon be totally realistic and smooth. Interaction with agents in the VR world via complete telepresence may become a standard feature, so we can enter a VR world and interact not only with objects but also with simulations of people. These possibilities have been termed cyberspace and a new generation of computer junkies has arrived to worship this technology, the cyberpunks who will play VR computer games.

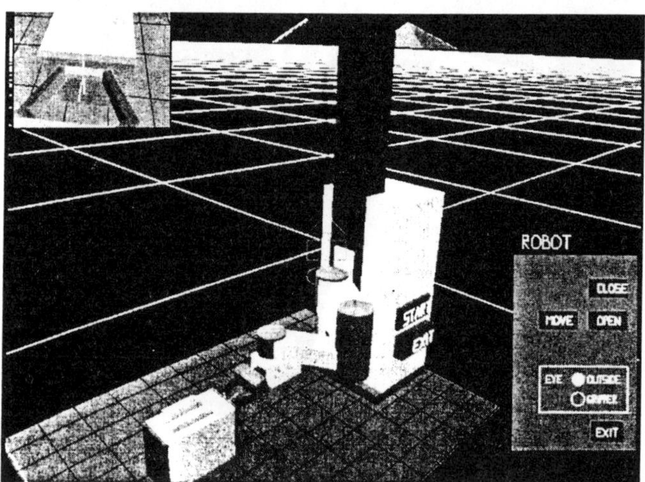

Figure 5.11 Virtual reality environment for computer supported co-operative work.

More serious uses of VR systems are beginning to emerge. Envisioning design by VR allows users and designers to check out an artefact before it exists. This is a form of virtual prototyping to validate requirements and design quality, and the applications have ranged from aircraft designers checking out structural designs, architects walking through new buildings, to truck designers investigating driving positions. Education is another area with vast potential. The ability to move or fly through landscapes for geography lessons, or virtually travel down blood vessels in an anatomy class, are just some of the possibilities.

In spite of all the technology, the design problem of interaction will still be there. 3D graphics give users orientation problems, and further research is required on navigation and waymarking. The sense of presence is still not well understood. Users will be able to get lost and disoriented in virtual realities and the means of control are still primitive. Different forms of interaction become possible with virtual tools which can be manipulated to mimic real tasks, e.g. using a drill in a virtual dentist's training environment: experience without the patient's pain. Other virtual tools may become inactive devices for computer control. Intelligent agents can be presented in VR environments to carry out co-operative tasks. These are just some of the possibilities.

5.5 Summary

Multimedia is a combination of different ways of presenting information: image, moving image, sound, speech, and text. The medium delivers the message. Media are divided into time-varying (moving image and sound) and static varieties. Moving image, in particular, consumes vast amounts of computer storage, so compression techniques are necessary; even so, only small durations of video can be played on computers at present.

Multimodality refers to the means of interaction with computers: direct manipulation, use of gesture or speech. When different modalities are used, they have to be integrated to one message. Messages can be categorised as having a communicative function and these are called dialogue acts. Speech and pointing is the most common form of multimodality.

Hypertext is a novel form of presenting information in a non-linear manner. Information may be in any form; hence, hypertext can support hypermedia. Information is contained in nodes connected by links. Links provide access paths so that users can browse through a network. Scripts allow different pathways to be programmed into a hypertext network.

Virtual reality is the ultimate extension of interaction with a 'wrap-around' display which is worn by the user as VDU glasses. This gives the feeling of complete immersion within the computer display. Alternatively, an ordinary computer screen with pseudo-3D display can be used. VR systems use gesture extensively for interaction. The technology is still immature, as updating complex 3D graphics requires large amounts of processing power. Applications are developing as the technology matures.

Further Reading

See Conklin (1987) and Nielsen (1993a) for further information on hypertext and hypermedia. For an example of 3D graphical interfaces for information retrieval, see Card *et al.* (1991). More examples of multimedia systems and technology can be found in Waterworth (1991, 1992).

Questions and Exercises

1. Multimedia is often used for teaching and training. How could multimedia be used to teach part of the course you are taking? Where would the material come from, and what problems may be encountered in converting it into a computer-based form?

2. Design a multimedia application for teaching part of a course which you are familiar with. Script the presentation of each medium and if possible design story boards to illustrate your design in outline.

3. What problems would you expect to encounter when delivering task-based information by moving image? For instance, imagine you are designing a multimedia presentation for emergency evacuation of your building in case of fire. You have to instruct people where to go, what precautions to take and how to deal with hazards (e.g. fire, smoke, fumes, locked doors, etc.).

4. What problems does hypertext solve which are inherent in ordinary text-based displays or standard media such as books? How far can hypertext solve these problems?

5. Design a hypertext system to guide your colleagues around the course you are taking. Specify the subject matter (nodes) and the different associations (links) which people may want to explore. To extend the idea as a project, implement the system using a suitable hypertext tool and evaluate it with your colleagues. What pathways do people follow and did your specification meet the users' needs?

6 Dialogue Design

Interfaces should serve people; therefore, when selecting the interface type human requirements come first, followed by system requirements. This chapter takes task, user and domain models from Chapter 3 and transforms them into a dialogue design. Modularity of user interface software is reviewed, followed by design of dialogue sequences. Representation of dialogues in network diagrams is described together with detailed design of interaction sequences. This chapter covers the dialogue part of the design process which proceeds concurrently with presentation design, described in Chapter 7.

6.1 Transformation from Task to Interface Design

The user profile specifies the level of support needed and the desirable level of sophistication (see Chapter 3). Highly skilled expert users who use a system frequently will require a sophisticated interface to fulfil the complicated functions which they wish to undertake and to give them the ability to extend the system's properties to suit their own needs. Users who are skilled but lack background knowledge about the system structure are less likely to need the flexibility to extend the system's powers, even though they will still require a quick-to-use and sophisticated interface. High-frequency users who lack knowledge about the system structure and have low to moderate ability are unlikely to be able to deal with sophistication and need a supportive but quick-to-use interface. Users with good knowledge of the system but who will have an intermittent pattern of use will require a sophisticated interface with a high level of support because the low frequency of use will lead to the interface characteristics being forgotten.

Inevitably users in a population will rarely fit neatly into one category, so the eventual choice depends on trade-off decisions which try to satisfy as many different types of user in the overall population as possible. Finally, consideration of the user's domain model may have implications for the choice if there is a strong structural metaphor in the view. If the user views the system in terms of a map or a spatially linked collection of objects, then a graphics user interface is advisable.

So far the interface specification is composed of a set of task descriptions, and system requirements. The next step is to subdivide the whole interface into modules which can be mapped on to physical structures such as dialogue boxes, help and error windows, menus and command lines.

To do this, interface design uses the same principles as Structured System Design. For those who are unacquainted with structured design, the basic idea is to divide up the system (or interface) into parts, called modules. The contents of a module are determined by the axiom of cohesion, 'one module one purpose', so, for example, a data-entry module accepts data but does not have editing operations mixed up with it; editing is done by another screen or overlay. This notion is related to functional decomposition carried out in task analysis; therefore most tasks should show good cohesion. The justification for introducing this criterion into interface design is identical with that employed in system design, namely cohesive modules are easier to identify, understand and maintain. This principle can also be applied to object-oriented approaches. HCI adds user interface objects to model interactive tasks within the problem domain. These objects handle events for user dialogue and the data structures involved in task processing. As user interface design widgets (e.g. dialogue boxes, windows; see Chapter 4) are reusable objects, the user interface can be seen as an aggregation of dialogue control/task support objects with surface-level UI widgets.

6.2 User Interface Design Process

Defining interface modules presents the same problems as defining modules or objects in system design: where are the boundaries and how big/small should a module be? Interface design, fortunately, has a starting point to guide these decisions in task analysis. The task sequence should be examined and the break points noted. Break points occur at the end of any series of sequentially related operational steps; in reality this means when there is a pause, for instance, at the end of a record during data entry, or when one life has been lost in a space invader game. The sequence between break points should form one cohesive sub-task which becomes one logical interface module. Close mapping of tasks to interface objects may not always be possible, especially when error and exception sequences may interrupt tasks.

The interface is designed first as a set of logical modules using input from task design, and then the modules are organised into a structure by addition of an access mechanism. Access mechanisms are the way in which users address data or functions provided by the system, and can be hierarchic, network or direct. In SSADM this step is a logical grouping of dialogue elements, which is taken from the input/output structure. To this we may add the further advice:

- Dialogue sequencing (the result of grouping) should reflect the task structure, i.e. one dialogue sequence should achieve one goal.
- Additional dialogue sequences should be added for user support, e.g. help system, tutorial sub-system, and error recovery.

- The dialogue sequences are arranged in an overall order according to the task structure. The sequences should therefore be ordered according to the task goal structure.

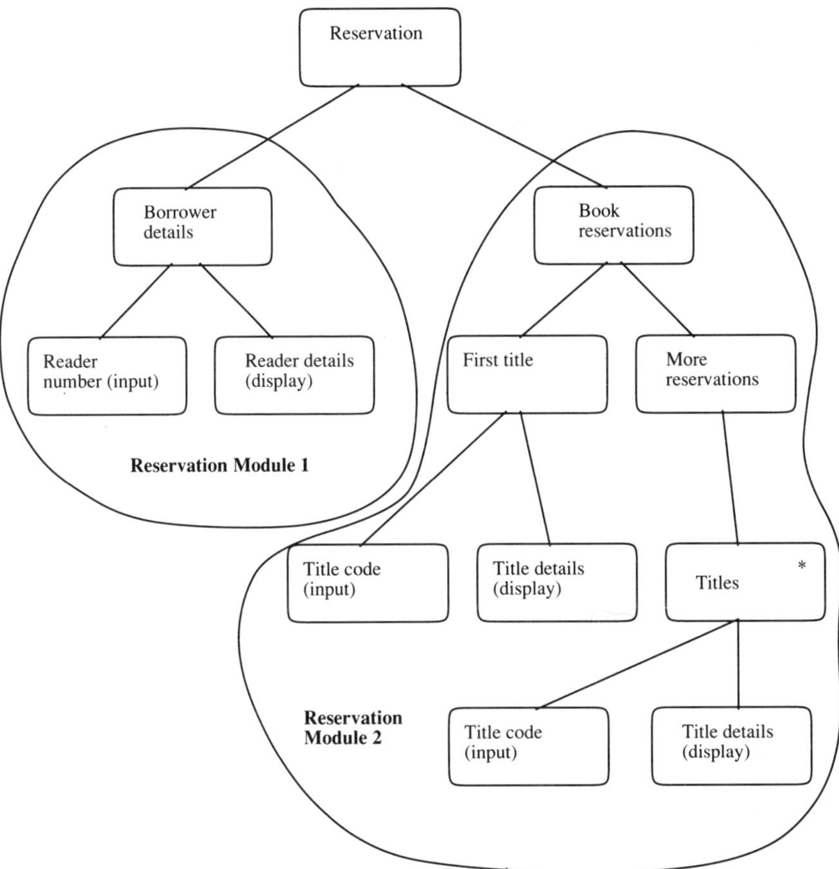

Figure 6.1 Logical groupings of dialogue elements (following SSADM). The dialogue elements (message boxes, data entry actions, etc.) are organised in a sequence reading left to right.

The logical dialogue modules, each one of which implements a dialogue sequence, are mapped to UI components such as dialogue boxes and windows, depending on the target UI style and software environment. The interconnection between UI components and valid pathways between them can be illustrated on dialogue navigation diagrams, used by structured methods such as Information Engineering (see Figure 6.1). In some cases this may be the end point of design if components such as dialogue boxes can be used to implement each group. However, even when sophisticated UI components are available in design environments, it is still necessary to design the dialogue flow. UI components and style guides do not always ensure usable dialogues.

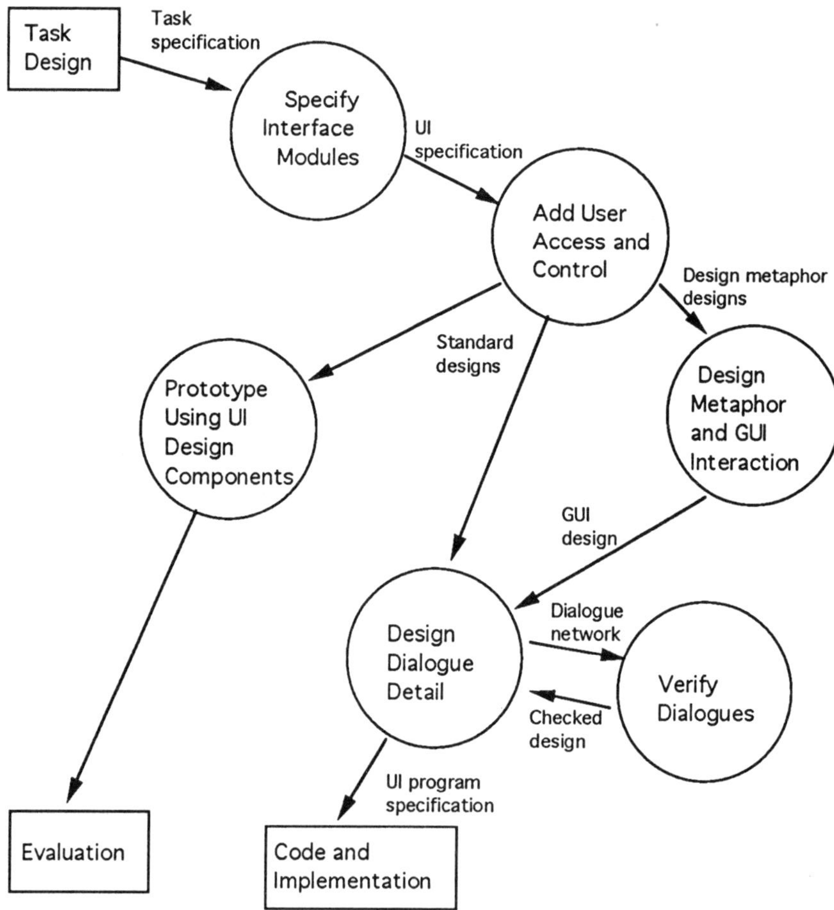

Figure 6.2 Data flow diagram of stages in dialogue design.

Each module is decomposed into discrete steps, each step being a single question and answer between person and machine. This follows Norman's model of user–system interaction (see Chapter 2). The steps are then re-assembled into a detailed dialogue design which describes how the interface communicates with the user. The detailed design aims to incorporate good HCI practices and provides some means of verifying that the design adheres to those practices. The steps involved are first designing the dialogue structure, then the access paths, followed by either prototyping the design with interface design tools (fourth-generation languages, screen generators) or detailed design of each step before implementation. The steps are summarised in Figure 6.2.

Which route is followed will depend on the complexity of the interface. More complex interaction in which the dialogue is critical should be designed in detail.

6.2.1 Adding User Access and Control

As user access is not part of the task description, it has to be added as part of the new system. The aim is to synthesise the user's domain model and the goal structure from the task model. With luck these will agree but sometimes the analyst may perceive a network of linked tasks which the user sees as a set of independent tasks. When in doubt the user knows best.

The user's view or the user requirements for system operation may state that certain modules must be available on demand while others should be organised in sequences to achieve a particular task. Depending on the type of interface chosen, the modules will be linked together either as a hierarchy or as a network.

If hierarchical access is being used, the module grouping will be influenced by the user's view as well as by the logical relationships of functions. Users may have several views which relate to different parts of the system. There may be a physical layout view and a logical classification view, the former expressed as a type of map and the latter as an abstract hierarchy. Access paths should reflect the way users currently view their system, a view which should have been discussed and agreed with them.

For instance, librarians may view a library system as a hierarchy of rooms, stacks, shelves, and then books for a physical layout part of the system. In contrast, for retrieval and literature searches, the view may be one based on a current book classification system, such as Dewey or Library of Congress. But the issue desk may be conceived as a network of tasks such as checking the borrower's library ticket, recording the loan, and date stamping the book.

6.2.2 Metaphor Design

In GUI implementations the first problem to solve is choosing the interface metaphor. Information collected in the domain model should help metaphor selection. Often applications will naturally suggest a physical metaphor. In this case the sketch of the application environment can be transferred directly from the physical real world into a graphical picture of that world. Structure from the domain model becomes the background of the metaphor, while interactive objects will become icons capable of responding to manipulation. Four main design concerns have to be addressed in GUI metaphors:

- Selection and representation of the conceptual metaphor. This is the screen image of the application virtual world. This gives the user the context of interaction and suggests how things should behave. It is composed of graphics and icons depicting structures in the application environment.

- Representation of interactive objects in the metaphor. These objects will respond to interaction. The entity relationship model should suggest which objects are necessary; further indications come from the task and domain models. The objects should be represented as realistic icons. The starting state of the objects is cued by positioning them by or within an appropriate structure within the metaphor, e.g. in graphical drawing packages shape primitives such as circles and lines are shown in a palette.
- Design of manipulations to implement user actions. User actions from the task model have to be mimicked in the interface. This can be done by commands via menus and buttons; however, good DM design should try to implement actions related to the application transaction by manipulation. This enhances the look and feel of the basic metaphor. The range of manipulations with mouse devices is limited to point, select, move, and drag and drop. However, these can supply a rich set of micro-metaphors for action when combined with structures in the conceptual metaphor.
- Design of micro-metaphors for control actions and representation of commands. Actions may be directly expressed by manipulations using the conceptual metaphor, or may require a separate mini-metaphor to be deigned. For instance, in graphics packages (see Figure 6.3) putting arrows on lines requires a mini-metaphor to set the property of where the arrow points. This metaphor was not too clear in the first version of this package.

The interface screen design for the library loans sub-system is illustrated in Figure 6.4. The main metaphor of interaction, derived from analysis of the users' domain model, shows structures in the application world. The library is divided into three areas: the stock area itself containing the issue desk, short-loan collection, ordinary book stock, reserved books, and the reshelving stack; the reader area within the library; and the out-of-library area. The principal objects in the ER and task models were Book and Reader and accordingly these appear as icons on the interface.

The task model specifies user actions of loan, return, renew and reserve book. Other actions performed by the librarian are reshelve book and authorise loan. Actions relating to the main transaction, i.e. the loan and return of books, are implemented by drag and drop manipulations. Actions are performed on book icons by dragging them between different screen areas representing system structures. Hence, dragging the book icon from the issue desk to the reserve stack models the action of book reservation. Book icons can be picked from any part of the stock area, so the object management software has to decide in what context a book has been picked (e.g. from stock, from short loans, on the reshelving stack, issue desk, etc.) and what the appropriate actions are for that role. Thus book icons picked on the issue desk may be loaned,

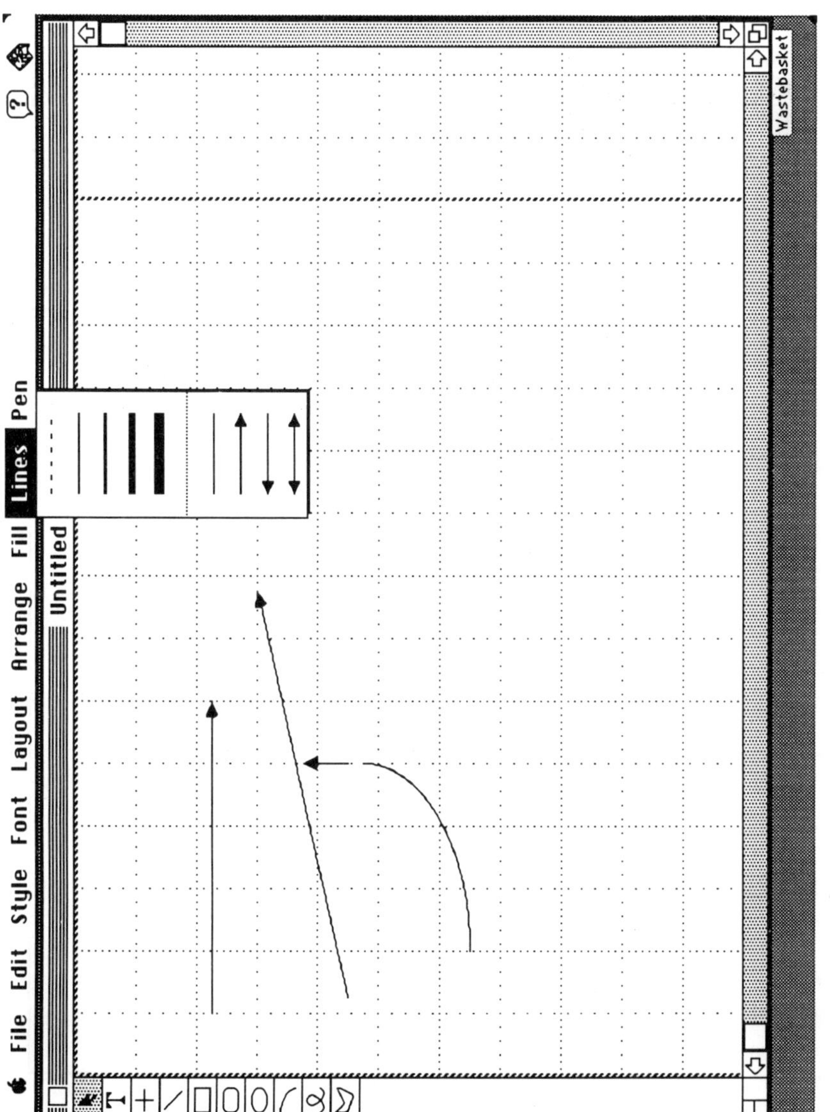

Figure 6.3 MacDraw I screen, showing the arrows menu and arrows on curved arc problem.

reserved or returned by moving them to the out-of-library, reservations or re-shelving stack, respectively.

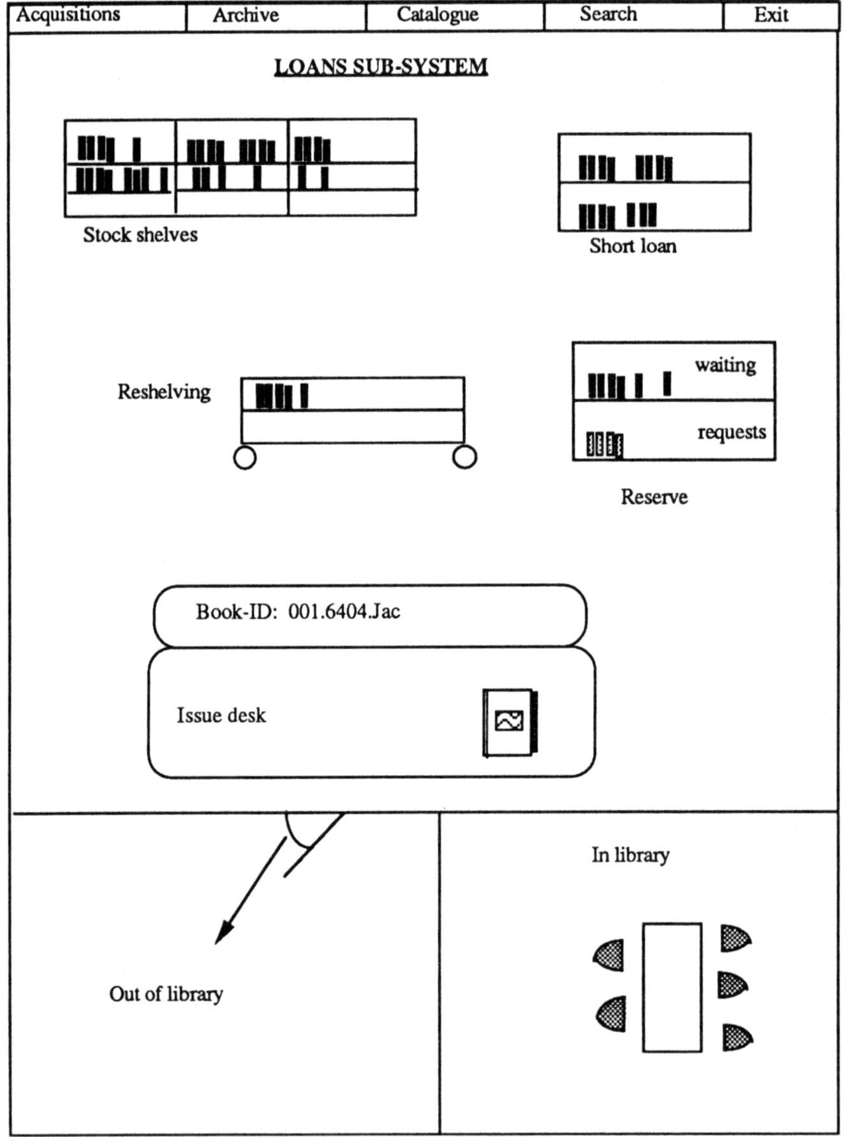

Figure 6.4 Screen design for library loans system interface.

Control of the display context requires a status indicator to be created which tracks where the icon is on the screen and thereby controls the permissible manipulations. To illustrate the point, the book icon has to know where it is on the screen as well as where it is in its life history. The book object in the 'issues desk' area can be moved into the reservation area, the user area for loans or the reshelving area if it is a return. This choice will be further constrained by the status record of the particular book in question (e.g. if on loan and already renewed three times it can not be loaned again). Interaction is controlled by the object role specification within the object management process, in consultation with the status record containing the life history of a particular book.

6.3 Principles of Dialogue Design

Design continues by elaborating the dialogue to add actions for user control of the system and to provide support as help screens, etc. Before proceeding to detailed design, the principles upon which dialogue design is based are reviewed.

Many guidelines for good design have been proposed, and while no definitive set exists, there is a certain consensus which is becoming enshrined in ISO standard 9421 (ISO, 1994). The following is a distillation and a sub-set of recommendations by several authors. For further details see Brown (1988), Apple (1987) and Smith and Mosier (1986). The principles relate only to control of the dialogue; separate guidelines are necessary for presentation of information and these are dealt with in the next chapter.

- *Feedback*: always provide users with messages to inform them what is going on, especially if there is going to be any significant delay in response time. Failure to do so leaves users wondering whether they or the machine is at fault and often causes them to press Return or Control-C to find out what has happened.
- *Status*: provide a message informing users which part of the system they are in. In large systems users may forget which facility they are using, resulting in their issuing the right command in the wrong context. This can have unfortunate consequences.
- *Escape*: allow users a method of terminating an operation and escaping from options. Many operations are selected accidentally and one of the most frustrating features of a bad interface design is being locked into an option you never wanted.
- *Minimal work*: try to save users' effort when operating the interface. This can be effected by using the minimal number of dialogue steps necessary (e.g. don't use two question and answer steps where one will do) and by reducing the amount of typing with abbreviations and codes. Long-winded dialogues may be supportive at first but users quickly learn and slow multi-step dialogues soon become frustrating.
- *Default*: set default replies whenever there is a predictable answer; again this saves the user work.

- *Help*: provide on-line help whenever possible. Help messages should give information which guides the user towards diagnosing what went wrong. Help should be layered or nested so that the information pertains directly to the option or facility which the user wants to know about.
- *Undo*: mistakes will be made and users will want to backtrack in a dialogue sequence and start again. The interface should provide the ability to go back and recover a previous state, e.g. in word processing the previous version of the paragraph being edited.
- *Consistency*: the format and execution of commands should be consistent throughout the interface. For instance, the escape command should use the same code (e.g. E to exit) at all levels and should have the same effect (e.g. terminate the operation and return up one level in the interface hierarchy). Consistency reduces the amount users have to learn about an interface.

Guidelines, of course, are only useful if they are applied, but their application will often require compromises between two or more conflicting factors (e.g. should feedback and acknowledgement be given at every step of the dialogue or will overattentive messaging merely annoy the user?). Design decisions will remain human value judgements involving trade-offs between contradictory demands; however, guidance can be given as to where guidelines should be employed to ensure the design process is methodical, if not perfect.

6.4 Putting Principles into Practice

The basic sequence of the dialogue steps is taken from the Structured English task description; the steps within each module need organising into a coherent order and supplementing with additional steps so that the dialogue provides the correct choices for users at the correct time, gives appropriate messages and allows the user control over the interaction. The first step is to refine user and system actions, from the task allocation (see Chapter 3).

- *User actions*. These are commands and input data, usually communicated by the keyboard and mouse, although other modalities may be used.
- *System actions* are responses by the system to user action. System actions should appear as feedback which conveys the change in the system's state to the user.

Interaction follows a cycle of user and system action, following Norman's model (1986). The designer's job is to ensure this process is smooth and the user is never left guessing what to do next or puzzled about what has happened to the system. User and system actions are linked to computer processing by the following relation:

User action —causes→ System action —changes→ System state

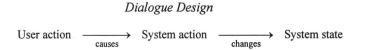

The system state should serve as a prompt to suggest the next action to the user. Interaction can be defined as a series of triplets in this manner (see Hix and Hartson, 1993). However, interaction, especially with graphical user interfaces, is also about searching for cues for commands and objects. A more elaborate view is presented in Figure 6.5 (page 169). This summarises pathways of interaction within a task–action cycle. The model still has Norman's action cycle with the gulfs of execution and evaluation embedded in it, but it adds an entry point from the task goal and user actions of searching for interface features to cue future actions, and, in GUI metaphors, gives a context for interpretation. Even with good design, interaction can and will go wrong. A further part of the model gives error and recovery pathways. The model can be used as a 'tool for thought' when designing. Each stage requires support in the design, e.g.:

- Search for candidate features: requires cues for action, either in a metaphor to give the context for action or in menus to guide the user towards the appropriate action.
- Try (or guess) feature/action: should be helped by good cues to identify the action; however, it may not always be possible to give a direct prompt in GUI interaction; hence, the UI metaphor plays a crucial role in suggesting the available system actions to users.
- Recognise and evaluate change: this is the gulf of evaluation which should be bridged by making the change in system state explicit (see observability principle, Section 2.9), and helping the user evaluate what has changed.
- If an error has occurred (attempt to interpret change), then simple slips should be apparent from the interface, e.g. attempting to select an unselectable object should be communicated by some feedback, maybe a warning sound. If errors are not slips, then the system should guide the user in interpreting the problem.
- Help systems support creating candidate explanations and trying out the repair action.
- The system should support learning. The user will discover features accidentally, but the system should support the user in deciding how useful the newly discovered system action may be. Metaphor and help systems are important for this purpose.

Walking through the dialogue can help the design in a formative sense, and evaluation in a summative sense; this theme is returned to in Chapter 9.

Good designs can be realised intuitively using the guidelines and HCI principles combined with usability evaluation, but further improvements can be made, if not guaranteed, by planning the dialogue detail using network diagrams to show the interconnection between each question and answer step. This may be necessary when interaction is critical, as in command and control, or in safety-critical applications. The ability to trace pathways through a dialogue has two great advantages. First, it enables designs to be verified to ensure that bad practices are eliminated, such as answers which cause the system to crash and leave the user in limbo without a message; and second, guidelines can systematically incorporate good practices into a dialogue design.

Several techniques are available for detailed design. Most diagrammatic methods owe their heritage to state–event transition diagrams. These map the progress of sequences of events within a system and have two basic components, a state which is an object or entity at rest and an event which is something causing one state to finish and an object to change from one state into another.

Translated into dialogue terms, a state will be the computer awaiting a user's reply; there will usually be a message associated with this state as either a prompt or feedback message relating to the last reply. The user's reply is an event which the interface has to deal with. It changes the interface from one state into another as the computer reacts to the user, issuing messages and performing actions until it requires more human interaction. In this way the whole question and answer sequence in a dialogue can be described and planned.

Grammars specify interaction as rules for system action and a response according to user action. Combinations of rules can be nested to give structure to the dialogue, as sub-dialogues. Grammars, however, hide the connectivity between user and system actions, although rules are useful for defining exceptions, conditions and features which may interrupt normal interactions, e.g. help, errors, undo, and escape.

State charts (Harel, 1988), as their name suggests, focus on the stative part of interaction rather than action. These diagrams show the structure of a dialogue by nested states. Each box represents a state and going across a box boundary specifies an action (or state transition). Arrows between the boxes denote the valid transitions which user actions can cause. Jackson diagrams can be used as an alternative means of representing dialogue states and events. This notation has the advantage of showing the event sequence so the flow of a dialogue can be traced (Sutcliffe and Wang, 1991) Furthermore, Jackson diagrams are a familiar notation in structured programming, so the same notation can be used to represent the user–system interaction and the structure of the user interface software. Jackson diagrams (see Figure 6.6 on page 170) read from left to right starting at the base of the sub-tree. Only the lowest-level boxes are atomic events (e.g. messages from the computer, or user actions); upper-level components just add structure to improve the clarity of the diagram. These diagrams can be used to illustrate the design at several levels from a task design through to dialogue detail.

Each technique has its merits and disadvantages. To illustrate detailed design and incorporation of guidelines into the specification, I shall use dialogue network diagrams, which owe their heritage to Cognitive Complexity Theory (Kieras and Polson, 1985).

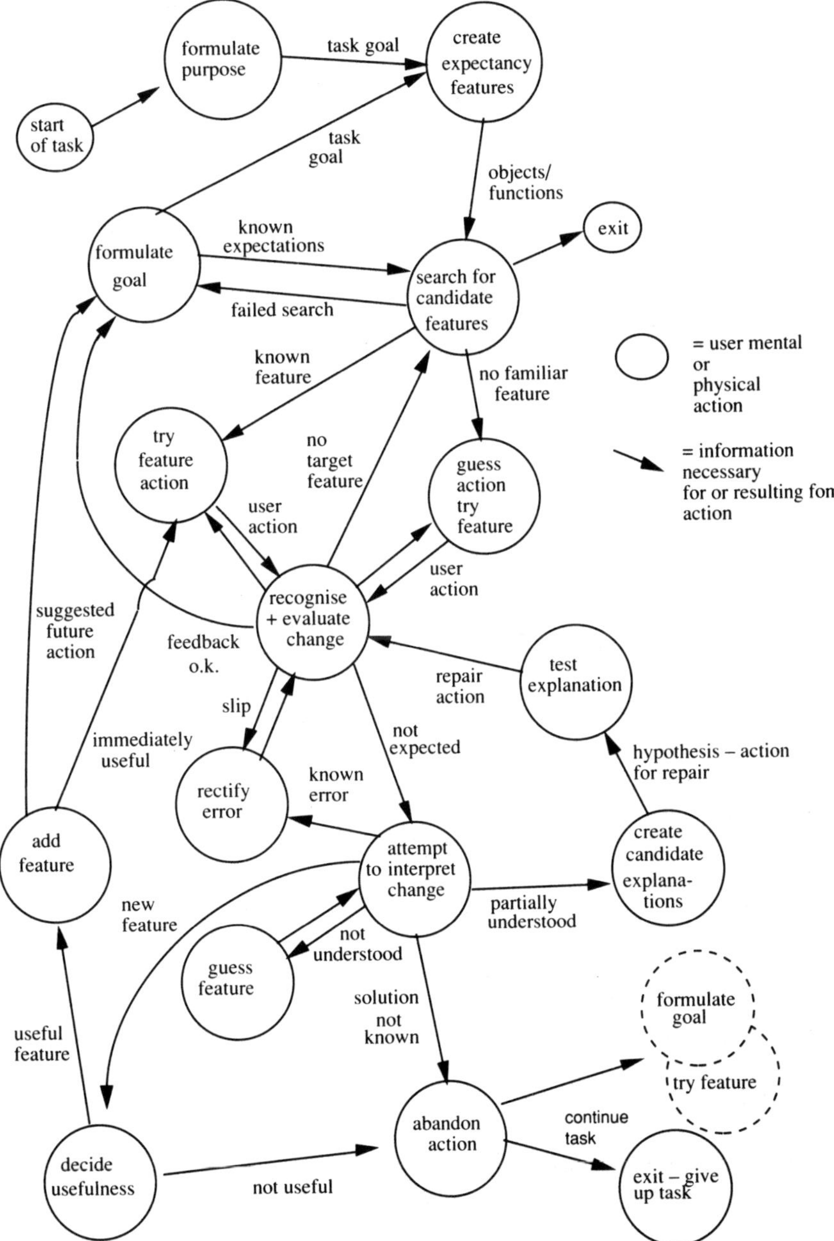

Figure 6.5 Model of action with direct manipulation interfaces.

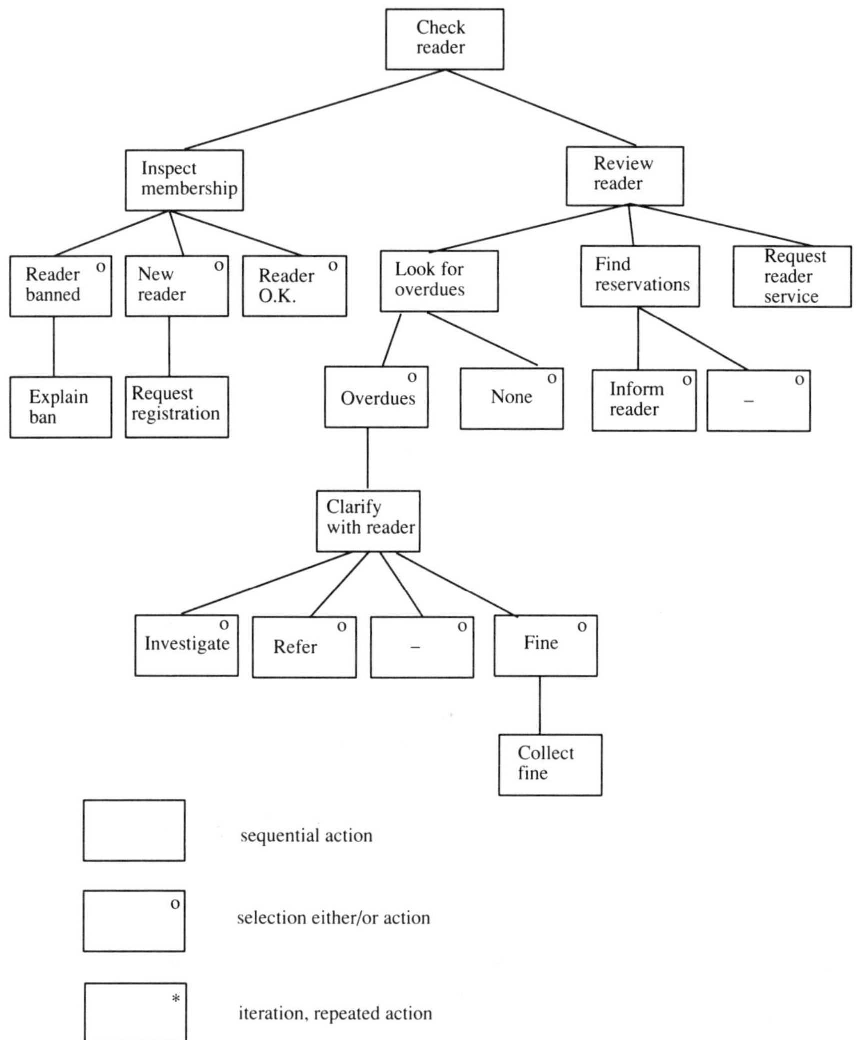

Figure 6.6 Jackson process structure diagram: Check-ReaderID high level dialogue specification.

6.5 Dialogue Network Diagrams

In dialogue network diagrams a state (or question) is represented as a circle, which is a resting state in the human–computer dialogue when the computer requires human intervention before proceeding to an event (or answer). This is represented by an arc, which shows the change between two states, each arc being dependent on the characteristics of the user's reply (e.g. valid data, invalid data, escape command). Each arc is annotated with the conditions which cause it to be invoked. These conditions can then be cross-referenced to systems and program design documentation.

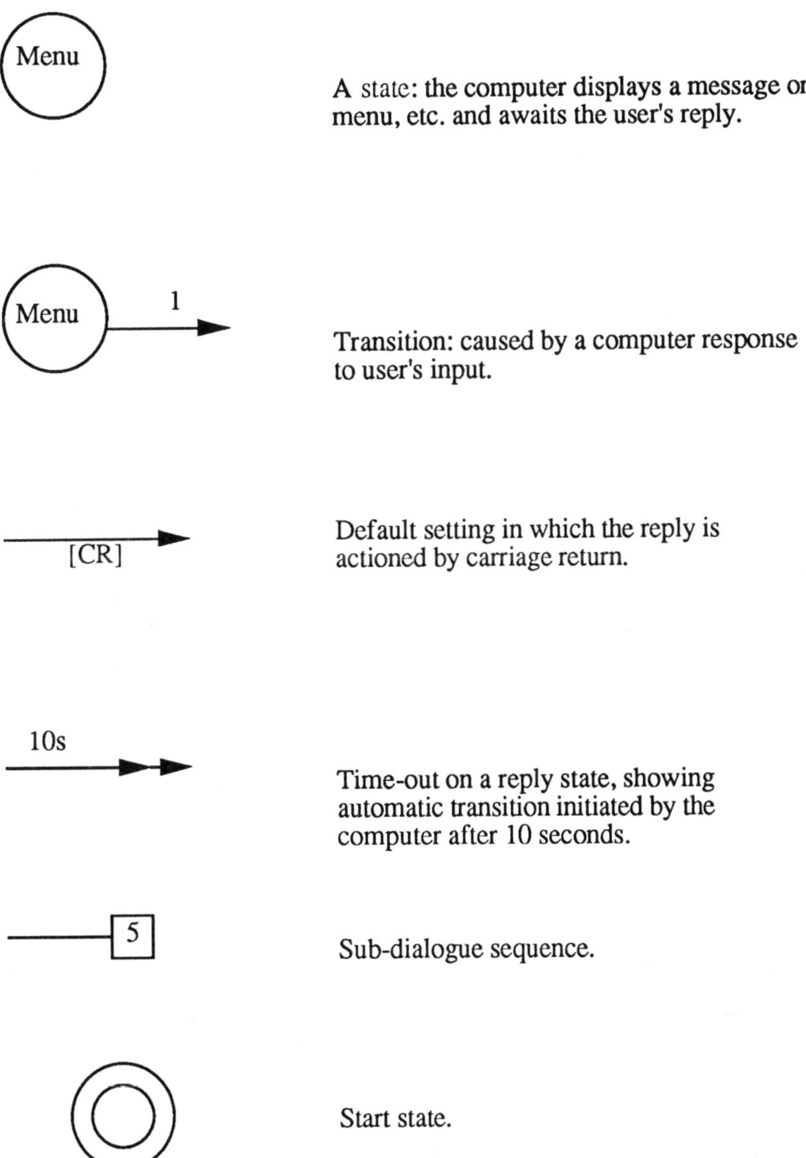

Menu
A state: the computer displays a message or menu, etc. and awaits the user's reply.
Menu
1
Transition: caused by a computer response to user's input.
[CR]
Default setting in which the reply is actioned by carriage return.
10s
Time-out on a reply state, showing automatic transition initiated by the computer after 10 seconds.
5
Sub-dialogue sequence.
Start state.

Figure 6.7 Dialogue network diagram components.

Diagrams read from top to bottom and concurrency can be expressed by two parallel sequences of circles and lines in one diagram, each showing, for instance, activity in separate screen windows. In some cases concurrency will need to be expressed within one sequence, e.g. when a long-lasting status message is displayed, it is useful to illustrate its presence throughout the dialogue. In this case a circle is used for a message state and a dotted line indicates its presence during the dialogue, although there is no state–event change.

The transition between states may involve several events from the computer viewpoint, but these can safely be ignored if there are no implications for the user–system dialogue. However, if there is going to be a significant delay in response time before the computer can accept the next command, then this is a significant dialogue event which is shown as a bar on the event arc representing a delay due to computer processing time.

Other features illustrated are default settings of replies, the defaulted arc being marked with a double arrowhead; and timeouts, when the computer controls transition between states after a certain time period if it has not received a human reply. Diagram components are illustrated in Figure 6.7 on p. 171.

Network diagrams can be nested hierarchically to deal with complex sequences. A square is used to represent a call to a sub-dialogue sequence which is labelled on the top-level diagram. For instance, in a command language the interpreter will be called when a command string has been entered; the parse sequence may be shown as a sub-dialogue (possibly using a different notation such as a parse tree). The system action may involve considerable processing in the form of a complex algorithm or procedure. Parts of the functional system may be cross-referenced to circles (system states) to denote that an automated procedure is carried out at this point. If this implies a delayed response time, then a feedback message should be given to the user. A sample sequence is illustrated in Figure 6.8 opposite.

Dialogue diagrams are not suitable for the design of complex command languages, where other techniques such as syntax graphs and grammars have to be used; but for dialogues with moderate complexity, network diagrams work well.

6.6 Checking the Design

One of the advantages of network diagrams is that they provide a quick visual cross-check to ensure that principles of good design have been employed. This can be carried out by checking the destinations of arcs. Most circles should have at least three arcs leading from them: a normal reply; the invalid reply leading to an error message state followed by return to the previous dialogue step for re-input; and an escape route to exit from the step to a previous break point in the dialogue.

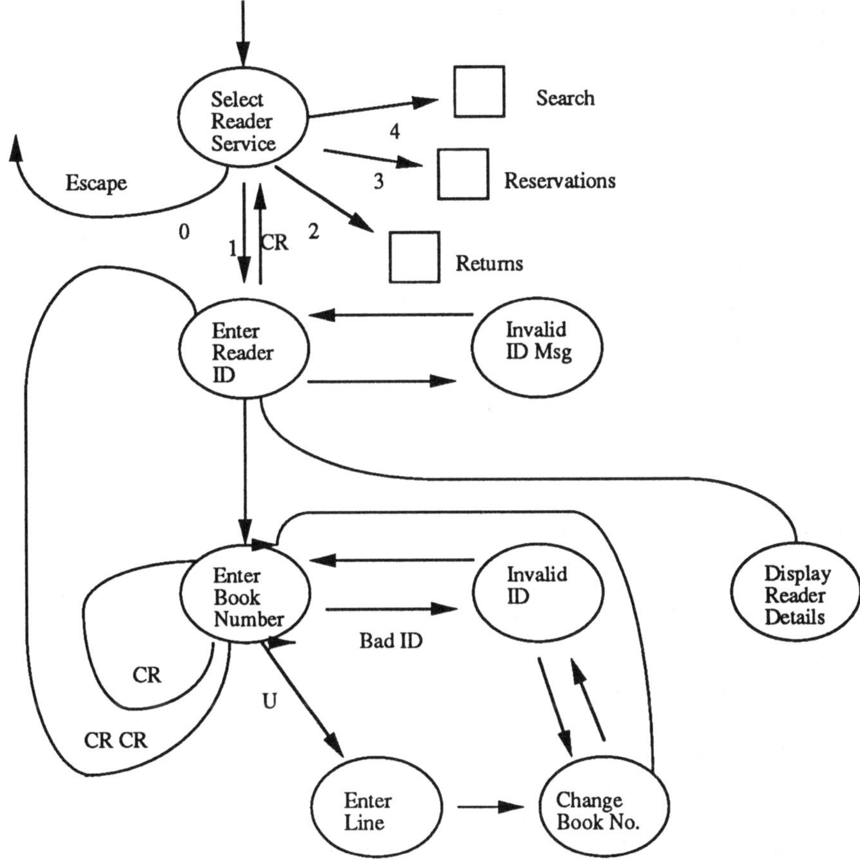

Figure 6.8 Dialogue network diagram of library loans menu.

More sophisticated implementations may have five arcs from each data entry state:

- Normal user action leads to the next system state.
- Error leads to an error message state and eventual return from error sub-dialogue.
- Escape terminates the sub-dialogue and returns to the next level back or to the beginning of the current sequence.
- Help arc leads to a message state and waits before returning to the previous dialogue step.
- Undo arc forms a separate dialogue sub-sequence of its own.

Dialogue networks can be verified in two ways, first to ensure that the connections make sense, e.g. error pathways terminate with a request for further input, escape routes take the user out of an operation at a sensible place; and second by checking that the appropriate number of arcs is present at each step to ensure that design guidelines have been adhered to. For instance, in menu selection dialogue steps can be checked to ensure an error pathway is present, an escape route is provided, all options are present and optionally help and backtracking facilities are present.

Network diagrams can also check the efficiency of a design. A large number of steps with only two branching arcs following simple questions (of the Yes/No type) should be viewed with suspicion. Such a dialogue is likely to be too long-winded for all but the naive user.

Sequences can be examined for defaults; if there are none, each step should be examined to determine whether preset replies could be included. Backup information, such as status messages, should be included if not already present. By following through the dialogue sequence on a diagram, good design principles can be incorporated, although it should be remembered that good designs cannot be guaranteed, but are finally dependent on experience.

6.7 Formal Specification of Dialogues

Formal specification has two motivations. First, by expressing specifications in a formal language inaccuracies and inconsistencies can be discovered; and second formality can help improve the reliability of computer systems by proving facts about software behaviour. Human–computer dialogues lend themselves to formalisation, as they can be described in precise terms as sequences of state transitions. If dialogues are deterministic (i.e. the sequences can be reliability predicted), then they can be expressed as finite state automata or in set theoretic formalisms. If interaction can be formally described, two benefits can arise. First, the behaviour of the software which implements the interface can be proven to be correct; hence, the system should be more reliable. Second, if basic principles of human–computer interaction can be formalised, then design can be verified for usability. Formally verified UI software could ensure good design of reusable software modules which can then be incorporated into any number of interface designs.

The essence of formal description is to break dialogues down into primitive steps, composed of:

- *Events*: changes to a state which occur as a consequence of user or system action.
- *States*: periods between events when the system does not change. States can be divided further into state of the interface (i.e. displays) and states of

objects in the underlying system. This allows correspondence between objects and their representation, such as icons, to be specified.

- *Operators*: actions which cause state transitions, that is the change from one state to another.

Set theoretic formalisms describe states of objects, so the interface can be described according to the states which objects possess (e.g. selected, not selected).

The behaviour of software and dialogue can then be rigorously described according to the preconditions and post-conditions for actions as follows:

- *Preconditions*: are the necessary states which must pertain for an action to occur, e.g. the object must be selected (icon highlighted) and be a file icon before it can be moved.
- *Post-conditions*: these describe the state which is the result of action having taken place.

By testing chains of pre- and post-conditions, so that the post-conditions from the last action become the preconditions for the next, the behaviour of a dialogue can be proven. Further tests can be performed to ensure no unsafe condition ever occurs within a dialogue. This is done by asserting invariants (i.e. states which must never change) expressed as conditions which must never be true (e.g. an object cannot be deleted while it is still in use or selected) or which must always hold. The specification can then be tested to see whether any of the invariants are infringed.

Several formal methods have been adapted for use in HCI. Languages familiar to computer scientists, such as set theoretic formalisms (e.g. Z; Sufrin, 1982), event algebras and CSP (Communicating Sequential Processes) may be used to formalise interface behaviour (Alexander, 1987). Other authors have used algebras (Harrison and Barnard, 1993) to describe dialogue sequences and algebraic formalisms to describe a set of interactions for a system (Dix and Runciman, 1985). The techniques of formalism differ in their expressive power and flexibility, but all aim to demonstrate a finite description of dialogue behaviour. While formalism can deal effectively with the computer side of interactions, it is less suitable for describing what people may or may not do. Formal description of displays and cues for human action has made less progress, as these are often complex states, e.g. metaphors, graphical user interfaces composed of many different components which may affect action. Approaches using deontic logics which express obligation (i.e. must and may type conditions) such as Modal Action Logic may be able to tackle these problems.

The critical point is what to formalise. Besides describing sequences of interaction, the power of formality really needs to be deployed to ensure that good usability properties are built into design. Unfortunately, many of the guidelines derived from psychology are heuristic and dependent on context for interpretation. This makes formalisation in their current state of precision practically impossible.

One answer to this has been to look for generalised principles of interaction which may be sufficiently reliable and context-free to allow formalisation. Generative rules could then be designed for each context of a design rather than a large rule set which tries to account for all the different contexts of interface designs. Generative User Engineering Principles (GUEPs; Harrison and Thimbleby, 1985) have attempted to progress in this direction. GUEPs are derived from general human factors principles, such as 'interfaces should exhibit what you see is what you get'. This concept can be refined into statements of cause and effect and from there to a set of assertions which describe how the interface can and cannot behave, e.g.

- Any operation provided by the system will have an equivalent effect on the screen as in the data.
- No hidden side-effects may occur (data may not be modified without a corresponding screen display to inform the user).
- It is always possible to generate a visible description of the data which is available to the current toolset.

While GUEPs have the potential to improve interface design, their application would need to be evaluated in practice. Also, because GUEPs are dependent on improvements in psychological knowledge for the production of general principles which may be formalisable, it impossible to say how complete, or even sufficient, a set of GUEPs would have to be to ensure a good interface design.

While most formalisation of dialogue has used existing software engineering languages, one more specific HCI model has been produced, the PIE model. This links user commands which are considered as a history (P= Programme of commands), to effects which result in a state change to the system (R) and display change (D); see Figure 6.9. A state transition function 'do-it' takes the current system, a user command, and produces a new effect which in turn has a manifestation in the display and system state. To this basic model a function (O) is added to specify the user's process of exploring the current display (e.g. by scrolling). PIE models allow formal reasoning about the associations between changes in the computer system and communication of those state changes to the user, e.g.:

P a command C to delete an object by pressing the delete key;
I the interactive function which interprets the command;
E the effect caused, composed of;
  D the object vanishes from the screen;
  R the object is removed from the system database.

While such formal models can help design the properties of dialogue and suggest how the presentation interface should change, they can say little about how the visual interface is designed. Perception of state changes, design of metaphors, etc., are not as yet amenable to formalisation.

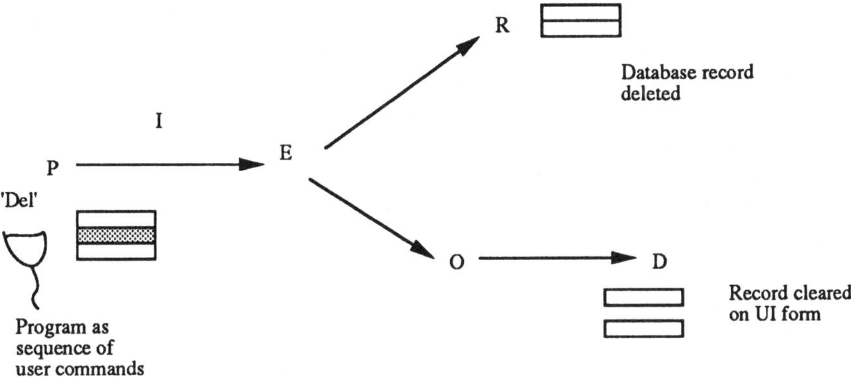

Figure 6.9 Formal model of human–computer interaction.

Formal methods in interface design face the same problems as they do in software engineering. Many formalisms become cumbersome, not to say unworkable, with large systems; in addition, formalisation creates a learning problem for the average designer. Hence, formal methods have an interface design problem all of their own: how to hide the mathematical formalism from those who wish to use it but do not want the learning burden of a formal language. Formalism of human–computer interaction will probably make slow progress in the short term because of the variability of possible interactions between people and computers and because of the context dependency of current knowledge. But formalism will continue to be a necessary aim to link interface design with advances in the formal design of software and eventually to specify types of interaction in more rigorous terms. This presupposes that we shall eventually succeed in understanding the cognition of interaction.

6.7.1 Transition to Programming

State transition sequences map naturally to program language construction of Sequence and Selection, although some notations are more effective in showing the structure of dialogues and its mapping to program structure. Jackson diagrams described early are useful as a notation which spans interaction and program specification.

Whatever the specification language, there is still a question of modularity in design. Increasingly programming languages, such as Visual BASIC, are providing constructs for user interface event handling. User interface events are captured by the message loop associated with a window. The UI software then dispatches the event to the appropriate piece of code to process it. The software runs and then returns to the interface as a 'call-back'. While the design still has to link the UI events to the appropriate piece of code, messages and dispatch of events are handled by the operating system. Programs therefore do not have to have a hierarchical calling structure of main, sub-routines, etc.; instead they are constructed from a series of events handlers which are triggered by user action.

This raises the question of how large an event handler should be. This may not be a problem if object-oriented specifications have been adapted. Messages are sent to objects where they trigger methods. These are the event handlers and return a call back to the user interface. Object-oriented implementation often uses co-operation between a UI object provided by the style guide environment (e.g. window, dialogue boxes, etc.) and system object written by the applications developer. Interaction is processed by a series of shallow and deep event handling loops, so if an event only requires a UI response (highlighting an icon), then this is handled in the UI object, whereas an event requiring an application response (e.g. updating the database) is passed down to the system object.

If object orientation is not being used, event handlers correspond to state transition sequences specified in dialogue network diagrams. Implementation finally depends on the programming environment being used. Increasing user interfaces will be constructed from reusable components (see Chapter 4), so the programming involves co-ordinating the responses of UI objects and linking UI events to the application.

6.8 Summary

Detailed design starts by mapping the task design to interface modules employing the principle of cohesion as a guideline. The access mechanism, modelled on the user's task, is added to the design to provide user control and the overall design expressed in an interface structure diagram. Access also depends on the task structure, which may suggest a hierarchy, network or, in an unstructured domain, direct access to task fragments. Dialogues are based on task sequences, but additions are made to incorporate good design practices for user guidance and support, e.g. undo, help, escape, default and feedback.

Dialogue sequences are designed using network diagrams which show all the possible pathways through a dialogue as a series of state–event transitions. Nodes represent states which are computer messages and displays; arcs are transitions and annotated with the human reply which triggers the transition. Network diagrams can be verified by visual inspection to ensure good design practices are adhered to. Escape, help and undo arcs are expected at most dialogue steps and pathways should contain messages giving relevant feedback.

Further Reading

Hix and Hartson (1993) describe the User Action Notation for describing dialogues. A good summary of formal approaches to dialogue design is given in Dix (1991) and Harrison and Thimbleby (1990), while Thimbleby (1990) argues for formal approaches with a stimulating and different perspective on dialogue and HCI generally.

Questions and Exercises

1. Design a dialogue for a cut and paste facility in a word processor. Specify this as a dialogue network diagram, or using a technique of your choice (e.g. statecharts, grammars). Check your specification for errors using UI design guidelines.

2. Using the specification created in question 1, list the design features you would add to support interaction.

3. Imagine you are designing a GUI system for library loans. Sketch the interface as a storyboard to show the sequence of actions, and manipulations, for checking out a loan. This should include acquiring the reader's ID, validating it, handling invalid reader IDs, entry of the book details and then recording the loan. Use the dialogue cycle to check out your storyboard design. What extra features would you add to support normal interaction and error recovery?

4. Discuss undo facilities. When can undo be applied in dialogue, and how can it be implemented in a system design? Use a word processor or graphics package with which you are familiar, as a test case. How far back in a dialogue can you undo? What are the problems in recovering a previous system state? Would you design undo differently from the package you have studied?

7 Presentation Design

This chapter gives general principles and guidelines for the display of data. Presentation design for most interfaces involves screen design, although other media, such as voice, are increasing in importance. This section concentrates on the general approach for VDU screen design.

Presentation design aims to display information as efficiently as possible for human perception, structuring the display to draw attention to important items of information. Presentation design is concerned with general structuring of the display and detailed design of field formats. The following guidelines apply primarily to VDU screen displays, although most principles may be applied to hardcopy reports as well. The designer should be aware that reading VDU screens and reading printouts do differ. Procedures for screen design are described first, followed by investigation of attention and highlighting, use of colour, messaging, abbreviations and codes, and screen layout.

7.1 Information Delivery

The presentation interface is elaborated in tandem with task design, and description of the user–system dialogue. The main needs of presentation specification are:

- Specification of what has to be displayed.
- Description of the logical structure of the information and any task-related requirements for its organisation or drawing attention to specific items.
- Specification of when information should be displayed during a task.

The task model has already been annotated with the users' information requirements (as depicted in Figure 7.1; see also Chapter 3). For manual tasks the information requirements feed into design of procedure manuals, operating instructions and forms. Checklists, notepads, *aide-mémoire* lists and forms design will be the result of information specifications for user-operated tasks. The end point is to describe a number of documents which will help the user complete the task. For partially automated systems a more detailed level of specification is necessary.

So far we have captured the user's information requirements; the next stage is to describe the available resources to satisfy those needs. Usually the data will be available in paper form (e.g. reports or instruction manuals), so the designer's task is to convert it into an electronic display. However, the data may

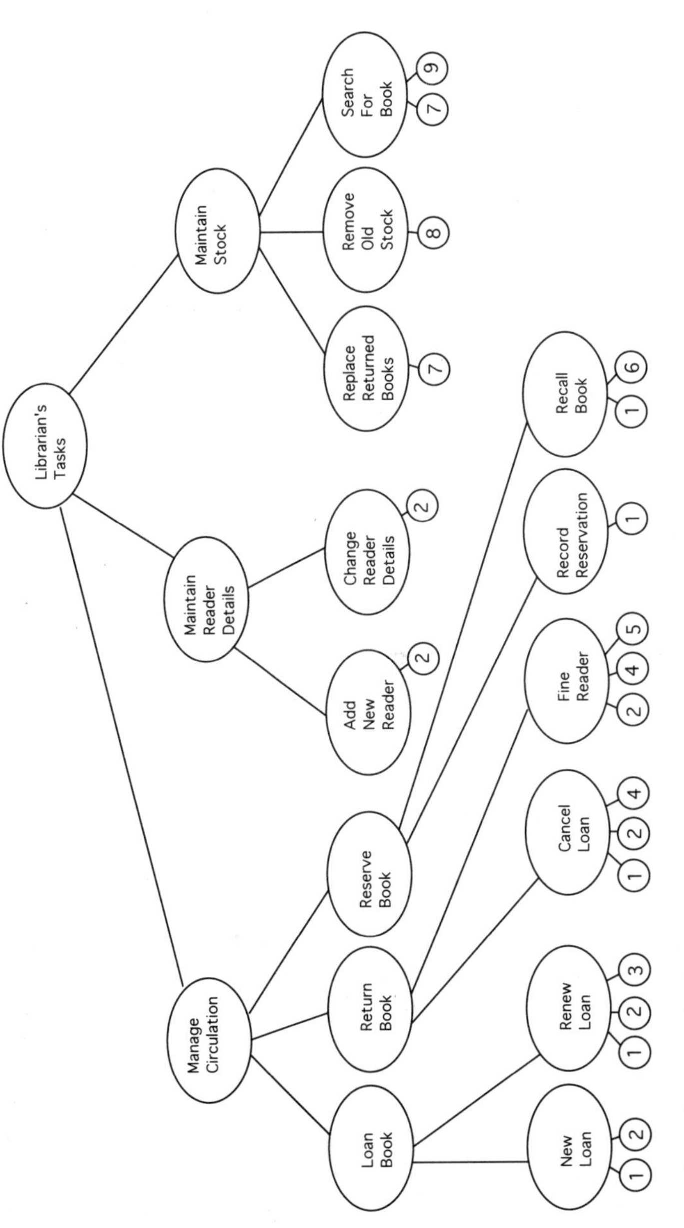

***Figure 7.1** TKS goal tree of librarian's task after information analysis.*

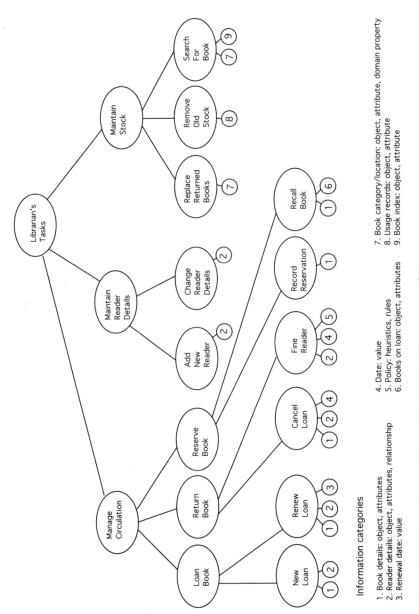

already be in a database or in other media such as digitised images, so it is necessary to decide whether they can be accessed by a query language. The next step involves identifying the target data resources and then designing the presentation interface in the light of the requirements and resources by selecting displays, hypertext, data retrieval languages or a mix of all these methods. Figure 7.2 opposite gives an overview of the method stages.

The data sources will often be identified during task/domain analysis and therefore be readily available as documents or scanned text/images. However, for some requirements the resources may not exist and these will have to be created anew by the designer. Some resources may be updated and, hence, may be classified as:

- *Static*: the data are not expected to change during the lifetime of the application.
- *Dynamic-instance*: the data may change at the instance level although the type will remain constant.
- *Dynamic-schema*: data types, i.e. entities in the schema, may change, as well as instances.

Table 7.1 Decision matrix: information resources analysis and presentation planning

	Information Resources		
Requirements	*Static*	*Dynamic Instance*	*Dynamic Type*
Single Item**	Displays	Preformed Queries	Query Templates Query Language
Information Group**	Displays	Preformed Queries	Query Language
Linked Items*	Hotspots Linked Displays	Linked Queries	
Pathway*	Hypertext	Linked Queries	
Unpredictable	Query Language	Query Language	Query Language

** = sequential; * = non-sequential

The changeability of resources has an impact on presentation design, as dynamic data can only be presented via a query interface. Resource analysis for presentation design involves comparing the resources with the properties of the information requirements. Table 7.1 above gives a comparison matrix to guide selection of the appropriate mix of presentations as follows:

- *Information displays*: these are hard coded into a dialogue so that the information displayed will be the same each time. Some decoupling can be achieved by updating the display contents on a disk file; however, changing the display content requires some intervention. If the information needs are known at the instance level, a display is created to support the task set.

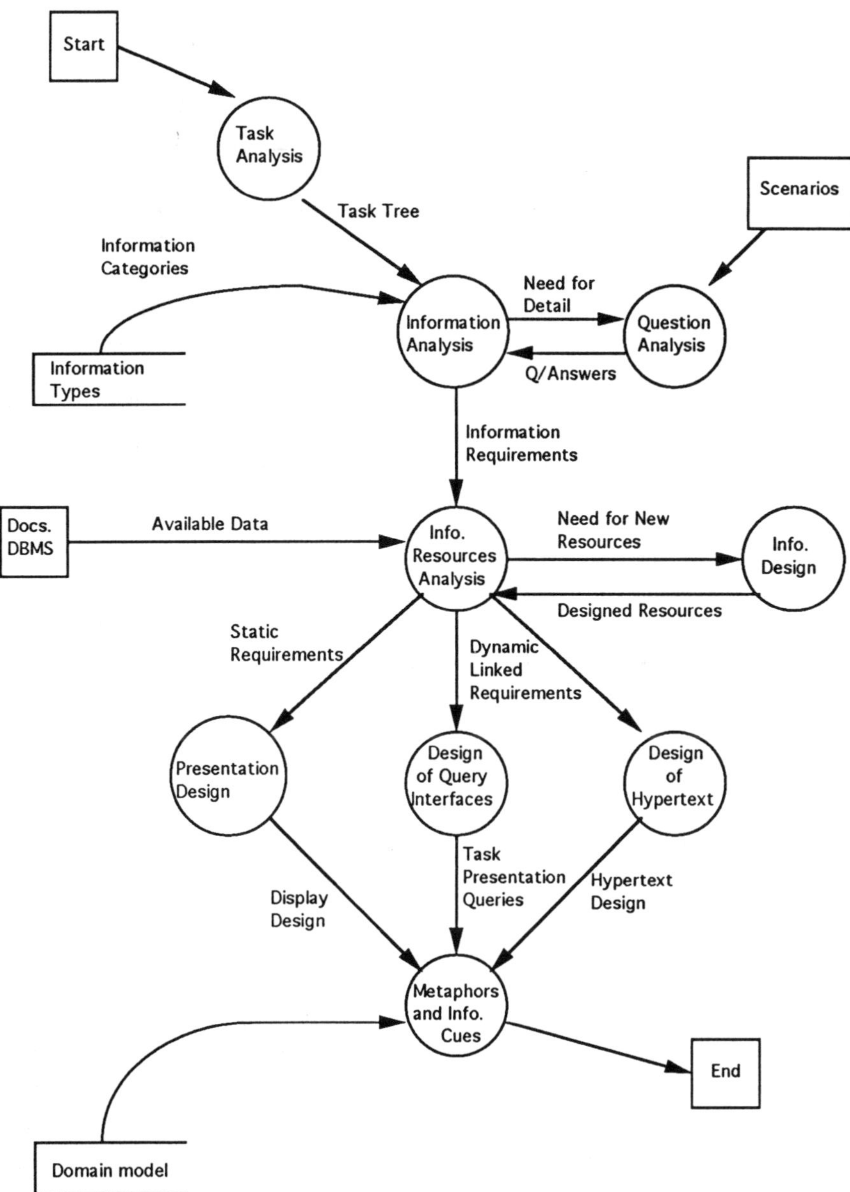

Figure 7.2 Method overview, shown in data flow diagram format.

- *Preformed queries*: the contents of displays in this case are determined by a query which is known at the design stage but executed at run time. The content of these displays is therefore determined dynamically according to the state of a database. Preformed queries can then be triggered automatically or by user action.

- *Query templates*: these are a variation of preformed queries which allow some user configuration, so the entity and attributes may be specified in the templates but the user has to complete the constraint clause.
- *Hypertext*, following the standard definition as a non-linear, linked set of data items. Links between data items are constructed at design time. Some flexibility is possible by scripted control of links.
- *Linked queries*: the display contents are determined by preformed queries but associated links between information requirements are added, so the interface functions as a hybrid between hypertext and a query language. If links have been identified, then either a linked query or a hypertext interface will be necessary, depending on how changeable the data resources are.
- *Query languages*: any open-ended query language which allows full syntactic and semantic expression of data retrieval needs. For most databases this will be SQL. When requirements are difficult to determine or the data resources are very volatile, then the only option is a query language.

If query patterns cannot be determined beforehand, then an information retrieval tool (e.g. SQL) will have to be used; however, assuming that questions can be predetermined, it should be possible to link them to specific steps within the task. Two possibilities can be followed:

- To embed queries within the user–system dialogue. When a user action is completed, the system automatically triggers a data retrieval request to the target database. The system presents the results as the next dialogue step.
- To make query submission under user control. Queries are presented in menus which may either be separate from the main task-related dialogue (i.e. in a hierarchy of menus as a query sub-system) or linked to the main dialogue. In the latter case completion of a user action causes the system to display a menu of queries appropriate to the task stage.

In decision support systems queries are more likely to be under user control and may be used to supply information from databases into models, spreadsheets and formulae for 'what if' type analysis. When needs are only partially known, query templates are used, leaving the user to fill in the extra details; alternatively, for more well-determined needs, queries may be completely constructed at design time. However, queries may not occur in isolation. Information seeking may start with one question and then progress to linked information, depending on the user's need for query extension. Linked queries introduce the concept of information pathways, which are familiar in hypertext systems. Design of the presentation interface may require a mixture of information retrieval, information displays or hypertext. Two main design strategies are possible:

- When the pathway has several information nodes, a hypertext implementation is more appropriate. The design problem is then to define the access links indicated in the analysis and other anticipated exploration pathways. Patterns of hypertext browsing (e.g. Belkin *et al.*, 1985) can be used to refine pathways; overviews and mini-maps can deal with conceptual disorientation.
- When simple links or shorter paths are specified, preformed queries or linked queries are the appropriate implementation. The cues for preformed queries are either hotspots on a graphical user interface or hypertext buttons. Either a master interface can be designed with menus of preformed queries, although this only addresses a 'star'-type path from one source, or, more often, the information types will be chained. In the latter case, cues for the next step in the query path have to be designed using hypertext or hypermedia concepts of buttons, hotspots and active nodes.

7.2 Selecting the Presentation Medium

The designer may have a choice of media (see Chapter 5) for displaying information. The choice between text-based or visual media will depend on the resources available and the demands of the task. However, if the information can be displayed in two or more media, then selection guidelines are necessary. Text- or linguistic-based media are generally more suited for display of detail whether this be instructional information for procedures or data such as numeric values. Graphics, on the other hand, are good for summarising information and showing abstractions from raw data. Visual images, diagrams and sketches can all be used effectively to show spatial data and relationships in a variety of forms, e.g. hierarchy diagrams, networks, etc. Time-varying media such as speech and moving images are effective in drawing users' attention and conveying restricted messages; however, people rarely remember much detail from moving images, so these are unsuitable for giving detail.

Heuristics offer high-level advice about media combinations to use and situations to avoid, while guidelines give more targeted advice about selecting media for information types. Some heuristics to follow are:

General heuristics

- Present the same material on two modalities if available; this reinforces the message and provides alternative views on the same subject matter. Although this adds redundancy to the presentation, repetition can be

advantageous for explanation and training applications. In less educational, more direct task-based applications, redundant presentation of the message is less desirable.
- Use text and still images for key messages. Temporal media do not allow time for people to retain detail in memory, as they must attend to the next part of the message, so static media are necessary for display persistence. Key messages can be assimilated and checked if necessary.
- Use text for instructions. Detail of how to do things is best presented in text-based language, preferably bullet pointed for clarity. In some cases use of moving or still images can reinforce instructions, but text is necessary for display persistence.
- Use sound for warning. Dynamic media are best for attracting attention, as movement and change automatically seize attention (see Section 2.6). Sound is more advantageous for warning, as it can be used to interrupt an ongoing presentation on another (i.e. visual) channel; moreover, sound can be used as speech to add content to the warning message.

Selection guidelines

These advise in more detail on choice of presentation media for specific information types. The information types will be have been added to the task model during information analysis (Chapter 3).

- For objects with physical properties and spatial object relationships, prefer visual media.
- To depict physical object composition, such as components for assembling a motor car engine, prefer visual media.
- To describe physical situations or events when context information is important, use visual media to show the scene/context where the event took place.
- For abstract objects with complex relationships, use visual media in diagrammatic or schematic form to show the relationships. These may be networks, hierarchies, sets, and so on. Complex interrelationships are often well summarised as a diagram and visual formats allow connectivity to be traced.
- For procedures and operating instructions, language should be used, preferring text for persistence. This allows users time to check instructions and scan for details, as well as reading the procedure in a sequential manner.
- To describe abstract object properties and values, use language and numbers, preferring character display for persistence. This is simply because abstract description in images is more difficult.
- To depict event sequences, or a history of action, animation should be used or a sequence of still images if more detailed information has to be

extracted from each image. People tend to extract only the 'gist' of an animated sequence and remember salient events or a summary of what was shown.

- For warning messages, speech or sound should be used to draw attention, backed up by visual warning signals. This redundancy in signalling is a useful safeguard for more safety-critical applications.
- To summarise procedural information or complex object relationships, visual media can be used with text. Diagrams portray the framework within which to interpret individual objects, while text may be necessary to describe the objects themselves.

As with many guidelines, some are just stating commonsense; however, many are founded on cognitive studies of perception and experiments with multimedia, and the references can be found at the end of the book. As with all guidelines, application has to be considered in context, and one guideline offers no guarantee of good design.

In addition to design guidelines, the following validating heuristics can be used to check the combination of media to ensure that attention and human information processing are not overloaded. The main problem with multimedia is making sure that different messages do not arrive at the same time and that one channel does not swamp the user's attention to the detriment of another. Validation checks are as follows:

- Do not present different subject matter on separate channels; if the message content is different, it will create an interference effect, for instance a news story being spoken while an unrelated image is shown. In this case one or the other channel will be attended to, and the user will be confused. Congruence of message is difficult to judge, for instance if a map was displayed to locate the region where the news story came from, then this could be assimilated, but if an image of a person involved in the story was shown in the wrong part of the story, then an incongruity results. Validation of continuity of message is best effected by user testing.
- Do not present a large amount of information on non-persistent media, as most people have limited ability to retain information in working memory. This is a simple consequence of working memory and our ability to process only a small quantity of input information detail at once.
- Present only one time-varying medium (animation or sound) at a time. People have some ability to time slice between concurrent presentations, as multiple images in pop videos demonstrate, but information retention is poor. Two sound channels just interfere. Attention can only be directed effectively to one source at a time.

- Visual and verbal channels may be used concurrently so long as message continuity is maintained (as in heuristic i). This combination is common in film sound tracks, although it is less effective in text sub-titles, as attention has to be time sliced in between text and image in one visual channel.
- Beware that temporal media (animation, sound) will dominate over static media (text, images) and visual media tend to dominate over verbal, although with static media visual dominance is less pronounced. Change is always an attention switch and temporal media are inherently changing, so it is hard to concentrate on another message while moving image or sound is being played. Consequently, important messages should be placed in the visual channel in concurrent visual/verbal presentations.

When there is a choice over the medium, for instance with numeric data, then, generally, information in a graphical form is assimilated more easily than in text and tables. However, graphical presentation requires interpretation if the data is transformed for display, e.g. by changing tables of values in line graphs, histograms, pie charts, etc. The abstraction of data into visual form can help to convey more abstract messages such as trends over time using a line graph, or a cluster of individual points in scatter diagrams can suggest a set. However, the presentation may lead to users perceiving different facts than would be apparent from reading the raw data, for instance the trend which is easy to see in a line graph may disguise the variation within the sample. Graphs are useful for showing trends in data, creating impressions of differences, but are not so useful for accurate and detailed analysis of values.

The choice of media, or whether to transform data into graphs, should ultimately be made by the user. A general guideline is: for detailed analysis in which values are important, character display should be used. In contrast, if overall qualities of the data need to be communicated, and values are not critical in the analysis, then graphs are a more effective medium.

7.3 Specification of the Presentation Interface

First the information requirements have to be related to the dialogue design. As the dialogue design is based on the task, the sequence and content of data displays follows the information requirements annotated on the task model. Alternatively, specification for information presentation may come from tracing the associations between information categories. This can be taken from parts of standard software engineering techniques such as Entity Access Paths in SSADM (Longworth and Nicholls, 1987), which traces users' access needs across entity relationships. This may be necessary in applications without a strong task model, such as decision support. In this case the data and entity relationships' potential usage suggests the sequence and grouping of presentation.

Once it has been decided what information should be displayed, the next problem is to group data into presentation units which can be mapped to output devices, e.g. message boxes, windows, reports, speech generators, etc.

Grouping will depend on the timing of presentation and on the logical structure of information. To help timing, bar-chart-like diagrams (see Figure 7.3) can be used to specify when information groups should be displayed during a human–computer dialogue. Different diagramming techniques may be chosen according to the preferred notation for the dialogue. For instance, dialogue network diagrams can show information needs attached to states. A variety of techniques can be used to cross-reference presentation to dialogue designs, depending on the preferred software engineering notation. Bar charts cross-reference to state transition diagrams or Jackson structure diagrams (see Figure 7.4). Continuous information displays are more problematic but a duration/sequence convention could be adopted for the network diagram. If state charts (Harel, 1988) are preferred, then information displays can be annotated on to the appropriate state box, although some care is necessary to differentiate input and output information. Concurrent information, however, needs to be represented as being continually present in the high-order state.

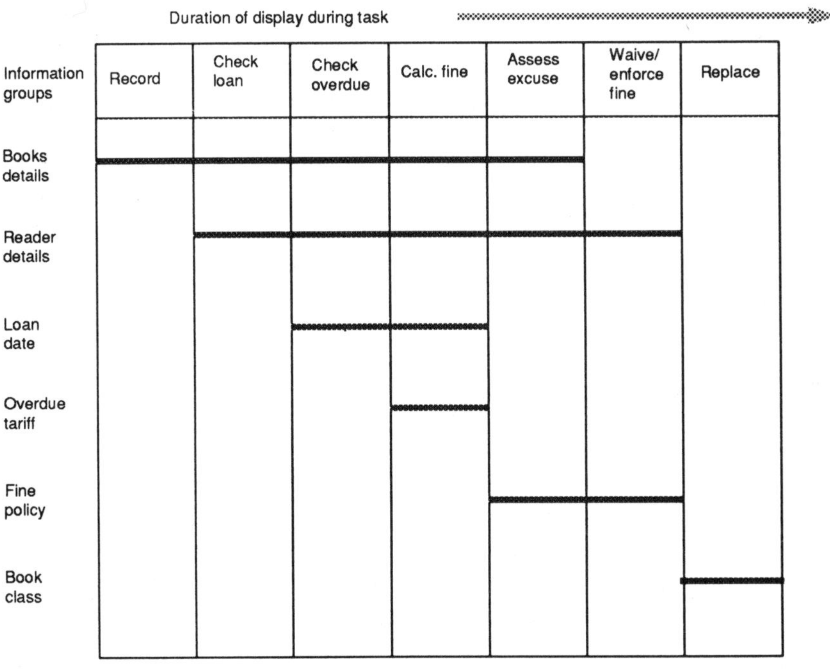

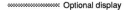

Figure 7.3 Display bar chart.

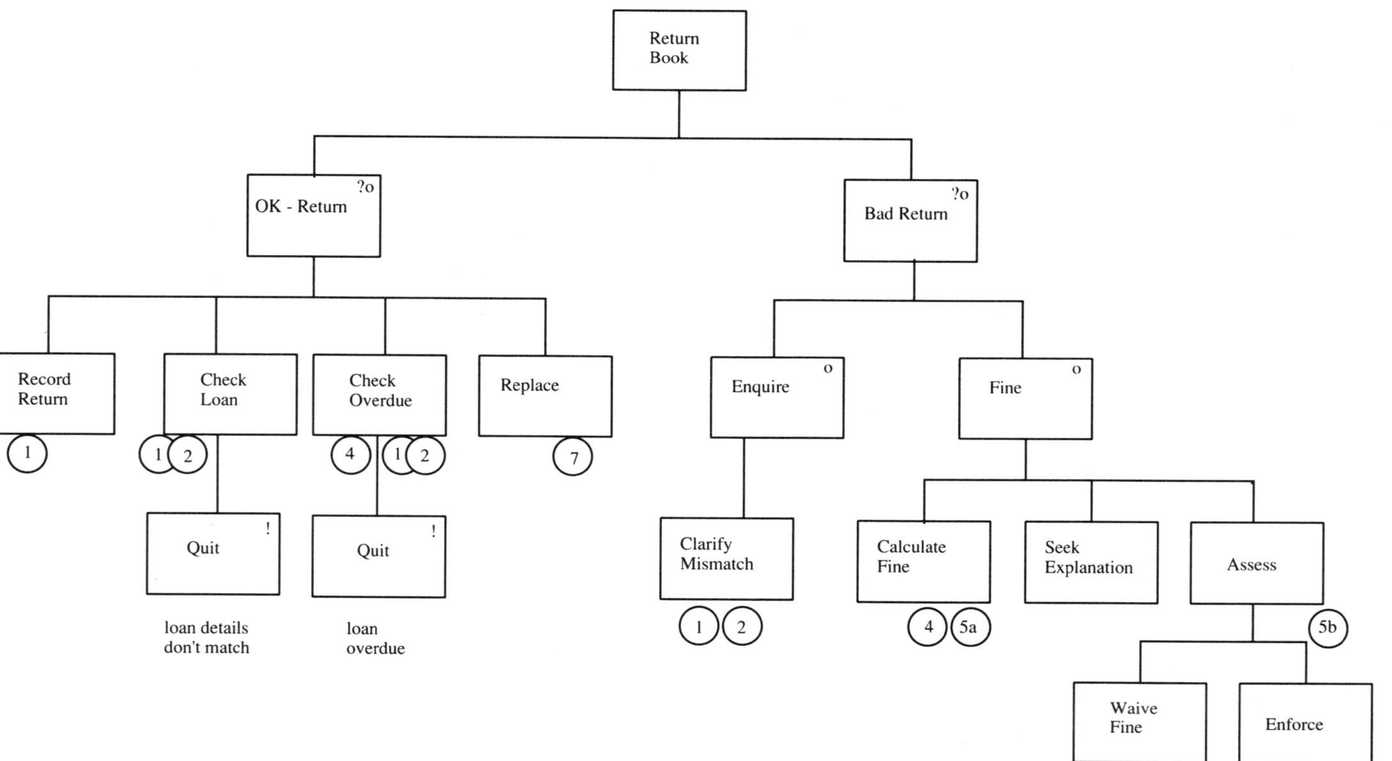

Figure 7.4 Jackson process structure diagram for librarian's task.

Planning the presentation sequence applies to all displays. More detailed design differs according to whether sequential, linked information for hypertext or non-sequential, grouped displays are required. Another consideration is the level of planning which can be achieved. In some cases the data may be resident in a database and volatile (i.e. updated frequently). In such circumstances presentation design becomes information retrieval interface design.

7.3.1 Presenting Retrieved Information

If the information source contains data which are updated frequently, then detailed design of a static display will not be possible. The type of data may be known but the instance (or number of instances) cannot be determined at design time. In this situation, the problem changes to specification of an information access interface, and general design for presentation of the retrieved results. While the presentation can be planned in outline, e.g. the approximate order and location of presentation windows, detailed design of formats is only possible if preformed layout templates can be used. If this is the case, then presentation templates can be attached to preformed queries to determine the layout of the retrieved data. When a data retrieval language is used, the ability for output depends on the formatting instructions provided by the language.

Design for information access also involves defining preformed queries and possibly linked query links. Information groups can be taken from the task information model, or display planning bar chart, although grouping and ordering should also take other user requirements into account, e.g. grouping according to the user's view of priority, importance, security, etc. Queries can then be placed in the appropriate part of the dialogue to generate the necessary information. Alternatively, preformed queries may become an information access sub-system with menus of queries, editable templates, etc. Query templates may be tailored so the user can specify the instance of an entity, e.g. for a Salesman's details query, the area and ID of the sales person are entered by the user.

7.3.2 Presentation Planning

Presentation planning requires two questions to be answered:

- How much information should be displayed at once?
- In what sequence should groups of information be displayed?

Presentation sequences will probably be already known (see Section 7.2), although in decision support systems without a strong task model, information display may be the main purpose of the interface. In these cases presentation sequences have to be planned to account for user needs.

The trade-off between concurrent *versus* sequential presentation revolves around increasing search time in more cluttered displays *versus* reducing working memory load if information has to be compared, evaluated, etc., from different displays groupings. Several different information types could be presented at once, if screen real estate is available. The first decision is whether the user has to work with separate information groups. If so, then the burden on working memory should be reduced by concurrent presentation. Concurrent presentation is also advisable to save the user work, because having all the necessary information visible in a tiled display permits rapid scanning. Otherwise the user has to swap between overlapping windows.

Sequential presentation may be necessary if screen real estate is limited; otherwise it should be reserved for less important information needs. These may be identified as secondary information types which help task operation, even though they are not vital. Alternatively, the user model may suggest that novices need additional information. Ordering and grouping of data will have been partially determined during task-information analysis (see Section 3.5). Screens, windows, lists, messages boxes, etc. (as in Chapter 4) can be specified directly for each information group or dialogue network diagrams can be used to determining display subgroups according to closure events implied by the task design. Dialogue diagrams also suggest when help, prompts and error messages should be displayed.

The end point of presentation specification consists of:

- List of information groups cross-referenced to the task model.
- Specification of information groups.

These lists may be taken from the data or task information analysis.

- Specification of structure and organisation data within information groups.
- Diagrams cross referencing information presentation to the dialogue design using graphical notation or simple lists.

7.4 Presentation Design

To be effective, displays need to be structured. Overcrowded displays cause mistakes in reading, and eyestrain. Effective presentation has to solve a dilemma of displaying the maximum amount of information on the small space of a VDU screen while at the same time not overcrowding the screen with too much data. If too little data is displayed, the user will have to page through endless screens to find the data needed; display too much and users have the problem of not seeing the wood for the trees.

In applications with a weaker task model, the objective of grouping data is to place data items which will be used together in the same place and make it easier for the user to find related data items. Examples of grouping by usage are placing figures for comparison together, such as planned budgets and actual spend. Grouping by category uses the identity of some object the data belongs to, e.g. branch, district, regional sales figures, or some quality associating the data items, for instance, all counties with above-average rainfall. If the usage cannot be anticipated, then a compromise is to group data belonging to entities using the results of data/task analysis. When data usage requirements are ill-defined, or user needs produce conflicting groupings, data retrieval dialogues and user customised displays have to be designed.

Description of data items amplifies the amount of information already present on data dictionary entries by adding information needed for presentation design, such as prompts, field size and display format. A typical data item description may be:

Data name	*Size*	*Type*	*Req*	*Validation*	*Prompt*
Customer name	30	X	R	LUT	Cust name
Address	30	X	O	New cust	–
Address city	20	X	O	–	City/town
Post code	7	X	O	–	Post code
Vehicle type	15	X	R	LUT	Vehicle
CC	4	9	R	Range	Engine CC
Cover	1	X	R	LUT	Ins cover
Period	2	9	R	Range	Cover durn
Start date	6	D	R	dd/mm/yy	Start date
Driver age	2	9	R	Range	Driver age
Years exp	2	9	O	Range	Driver yrs
Other drivers	20	X	O	–	Ex drivers

Data grouping in order by:

Driver details
Policy sought
Driver experience

Validation may be by look-up table (LUT), reference list, range check, check digit, etc. An extra column may be added to specify the effects of validation failure (fatal, warning) and the error message issued to the user.

Supporting data has to be added to the basic requirements for:

Screen title
Status information: screen page, file display, current system function
Section headings

Messages and prompts
Instructions and help

Display areas are allocated for data display/data entry, control, error messages, titles and headings. User characteristics have a bearing on the amount of support information which should be provided. Screens for naive users will require complete prompts and detailed explanatory instructions, although the amount of instructional and prompting material necessary will decrease as user expertise increases. Abbreviations and short prompts should only be used with skilled users or with novice users who may be expected to acquire skills quickly through frequent use. A screen sketch is prepared showing the approximate layout as depicted in Figure 7.5. The sketch is then refined using detailed guidelines to create a screen layout specification on a VDU layout chart.

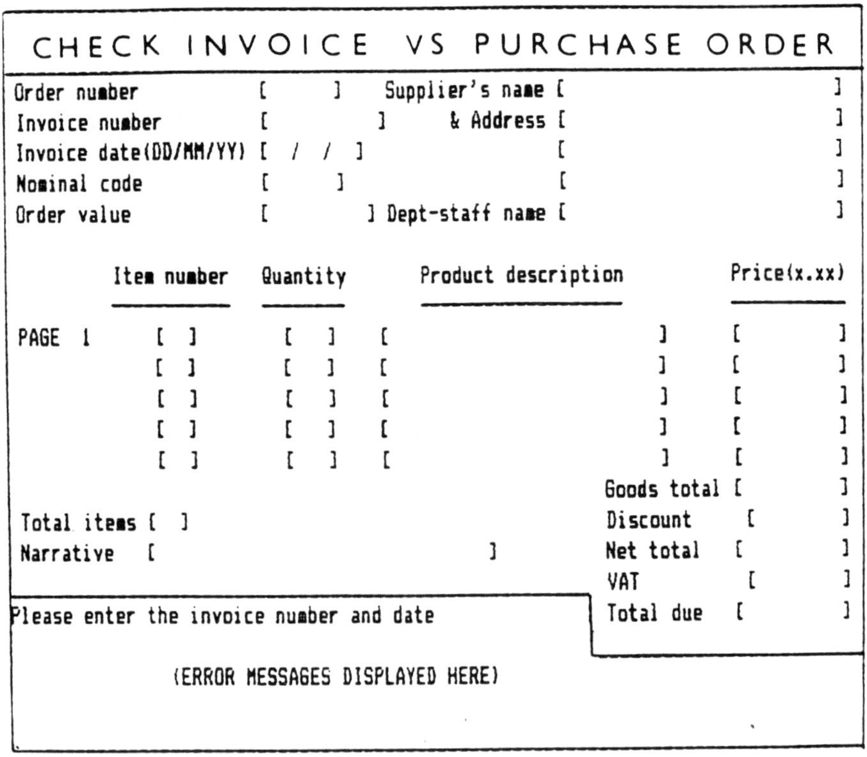

```
CHECK INVOICE VS PURCHASE ORDER

Order number             [      ]   Supplier's name [                    ]
Invoice number           [         ]     & Address [                    ]
Invoice date(DD/MM/YY)   [ /  / ]                  [                    ]
Nominal code             [      ]                  [                    ]
Order value              [        ] Dept-staff name [                    ]

         Item number   Quantity      Product description          Price(x.xx)

PAGE 1      [ ]         [  ]   [                          ]    [          ]
            [ ]         [  ]   [                          ]    [          ]
            [ ]         [  ]   [                          ]    [          ]
            [ ]         [  ]   [                          ]    [          ]
            [ ]         [  ]   [                          ]    [          ]
                                               Goods total [          ]
Total items [ ]                                Discount     [         ]
Narrative  [                        ]          Net total   [          ]
                                               VAT          [         ]
Please enter the invoice number and date       Total due   [          ]

           (ERROR MESSAGES DISPLAYED HERE)
```

Figure 7.5 Screen design showing division into data entry, command and error messaging areas.

Once the contents and overall structure of the display have been decided, more detailed design is carried out to create a mock-up of the display.

Presentation design is an iterative process which benefits greatly from user testing. Specification is little substitute for showing users what they are about to see, and storyboarding, prototyping or Wizard of Oz techniques are invaluable ways of eliciting feedback (Gould, 1987). Storyboarding is one of the cheapest techniques for creating mock-ups of screen designs. These can then be explained to the user with a script describing the task scenario and user–system dialogue. Prototypes and Wizard of Oz techniques give a more realistic feel to the use of information in an application.

The display storyboards or prototypes are tested with users for acceptability. Early user testing of interfaces is a good way of obtaining feedback not only on screen designs but also on the functionality of the system itself. When users see part of the system, they invariably venture opinions, whereas written specifications may be accepted without any feedback. In summary, the steps in presentation design are:

- For task-related dialogues, plan the presentation sequence according to the task structure.
- Using the dialogue specification, plan into screens, display boxes and windows, using closure events to determine boundaries of sub-dialogues.
- In applications without a strong task model, identify user requirements for information, and criteria for groups and sequencing.
- Design presentation detail, adding headings, titles, prompts, help and error messages to the application information.
- Describe in detail the format of data items and messages to appear on the screen using display guidelines.
- Mock up or prototype screens and test with users; redesign as necessary.

Design guidelines for messaging, use of colour and general formatting are given in the following section.

7.5 Detailed Display Design

Structure within information groups is a matter of detailed design for which numerous guidelines have been proposed (e.g. Brown, 1988; Tullis, 1986; Galitz, 1987). This section describes a sub-set of the more important issues which the designer should attend to. These are: highlighting important information; and, to attract user attention, use of colour, messaging and abbreviations. Key data for important and safety critical actions will need to be highlighted following any annotations for information emphasis on the task model.

7.5.1 Attention and Highlighting

One of the most important effects when presenting information is drawing users' attention to important items. This is achieved by highlighting information, but the technique has to be approached with care. Overdoing highlighting can make screens tiring to read and may cause physical discomfort if too many attention-seeking stimuli are used. Also, if too much information is highlighted, then the user cannot possibly attend to it all, a situation which can lead to task overload and poor performance. The objective is to highlight only when strictly necessary and then to use the techniques judiciously so as not to overdo the overall effect.

Data can be highlighted by the following visual attributes which are placed in approximate order of effectiveness for attracting attention:

- Movement (blinking or change of position).
- Shape/Size (character font, shape of symbols, text size, increased size of symbols).
- Colour.
- Brightness.
- Shading/Texture (different texture or pattern).
- Surroundings (borders, background colour).

Movement is by far the most effective stimulus for gaining attention. People are very sensitive to movement, as the eye has specific detectors for that purpose. After movement, size and shape are effective but their utility depends on scale and context. Odd, unusual shapes attract attention by being dissimilar to their surroundings; likewise larger text sizes or different fonts attract attention. However, smaller differences between the background and highlighted item are less effective, e.g. 9 pt and 10 pt Times text are not easily distinguishable. Colour is also effective but again the scale of the effect depends on how the attributes are used. Colour is a complex subject in its own right, and is reviewed in the following subsection. Complete black and white contrast to the normal image in inverse video makes a very effective stimulus. Brightness is not so good. People can only distinguish a few levels of brightness, so it can only be used sparingly. Overbright images are unpleasant to read and should be avoided.

Shading can be used to draw attention to part of the screen and does not run a high risk of presenting too strong a stimulus. Surrounding screen areas by drawing explicit boundaries can also be used. Text may be underlined or surrounded by a box; the background can be shaded or coloured. As well as using attributes of the displayed item and its immediate surroundings, highlighting and attention markers can be designed as indicators or warning icons. Care has to be taken that the user population interpret the warning icon as the designer expects.

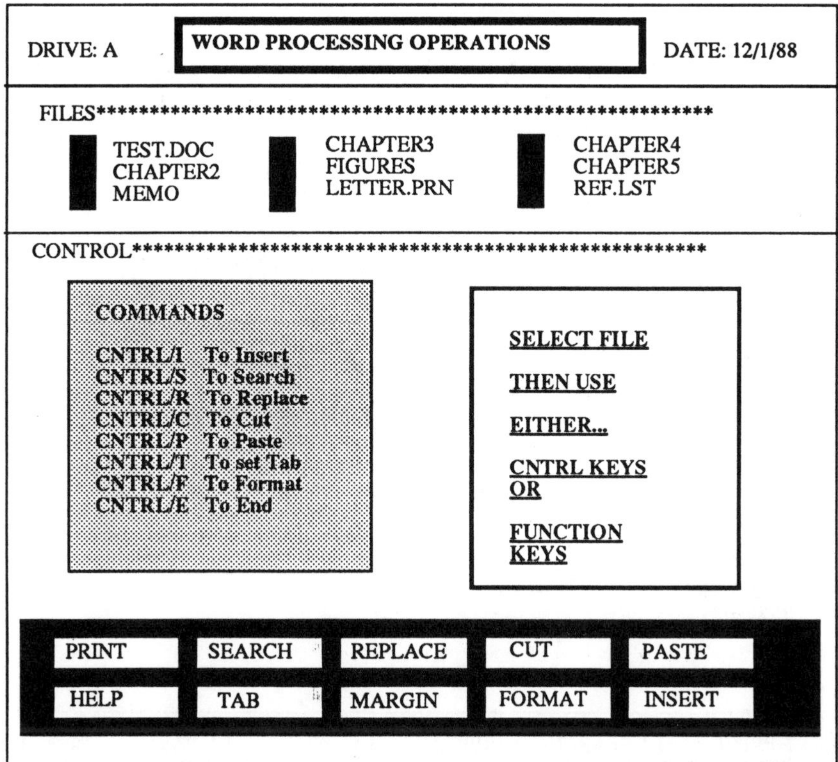

Figure 7.6 Example of too many stimuli on an overcrowded screen. The use of highlighting in several different parts of the screen results in too many strong stimuli competing for attention.

The design should achieve a pleasant display which guides the user to important data items but does not present too many conflicting stimuli. In Figure 7.6 the screen has been overloaded with attention-seeking stimuli. This screen would fail to achieve its objective and be unpleasant to the user. A better design is illustrated in Figure 7.7, in which attention-seeking display has been limited to the minimum necessary items.

7.5.2 Use of Colour

Colour is a very effective technique for highlighting and may also be used for grouping information, differentiating between information, and coding simple messages (red = danger). Colour also has aesthetic qualities and properly used makes displays appear more pleasing and restful than black and white. Visual resolution of detail is better in monochrome, so there is a trade-off between the impression made by colour and the amount of detail that can be displayed. Colour is a strong stimulus which it is easy to overuse.

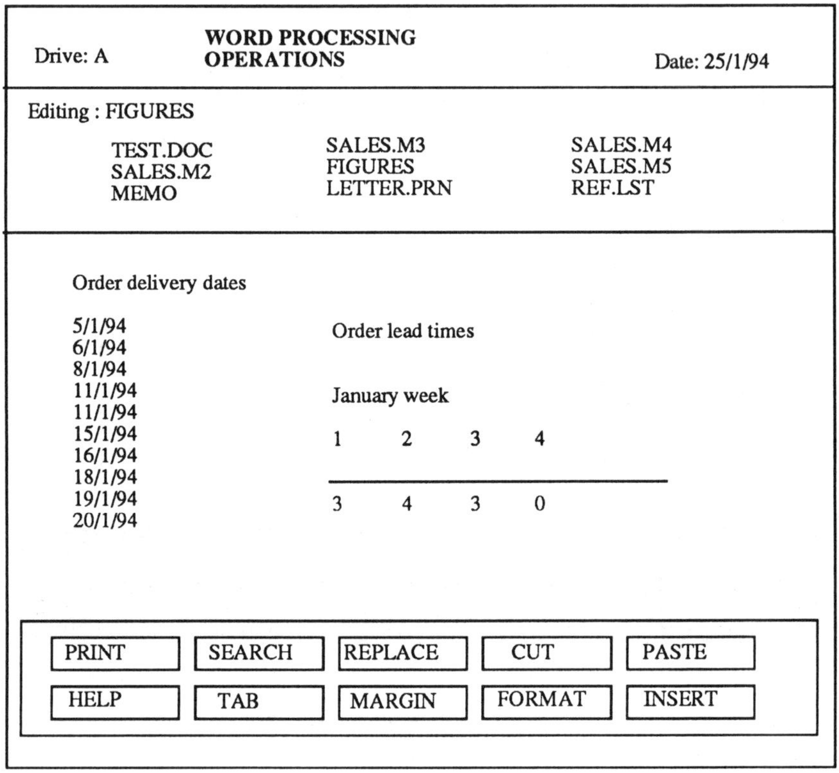

Drive: A **WORD PROCESSING OPERATIONS** Date: 25/1/94

Editing : FIGURES

TEST.DOC	SALES.M3	SALES.M4
SALES.M2	FIGURES	SALES.M5
MEMO	LETTER.PRN	REF.LST

Order delivery dates

5/1/94
6/1/94
8/1/94
11/1/94
11/1/94
15/1/94
16/1/94
18/1/94
19/1/94
20/1/94

Order lead times

January week

1	2	3	4
3	4	3	0

PRINT	SEARCH	REPLACE	CUT	PASTE
HELP	TAB	MARGIN	FORMAT	INSERT

Figure 7.7 Example of better screen design. The use of highlighting has been restricted to the minimum necessary and the screen is less crowded.

Colour has three qualities:

- *Wavelength*: this determines the basic colour in the spectrum from red to blue. Wavelength determines the energy in colour bands, so red has less energy and tends to be less visible than blue, while the mid-spectrum (yellow) is most visible.
- *Saturation*: the amount of white mixed with a colour or the mixture between any two colours; hence a low-saturated red with a lot of white in it is a pink or rose colour. Low-saturation colours are more restful on the eye and should be used for display background. Saturation can be applied to mixes of all primary colours, so an orange is a mixed saturated red with yellow.
- *Brightness*: this is the measure of the colour luminance; however, it also

intersects with wavelength. Some colours therefore appear brighter than others. This is because our eyes are more tuned to the middle of the spectrum; hence bright yellow is a good warning colour, visible from distance.

All three qualities interact to give subjective impressions which are poorly understood and further discussion of this topic is beyond the scope of this book (see Further Reading for references). Despite imperfect information on the effects of colour, some guidelines may be given:

- Limit the number of bright colours in one display to a maximum of 5 or 6. Most pastel shades can be used for background.
- Display unhighlighted information in low-saturation pastel colours, e.g. unobtrusive pale colours.
- If colour is being used to code information, make sure the user understands the code.

The guidelines for colour coding and use are:

- To show status: red = danger/stop, green = normal/proceed, yellow = caution.
- To draw attention, white, yellow and red are the most effective.
- To order data, follow the spectrum (red, orange, yellow, green, blue, violet).
- To separate data, choose colours from different parts of the spectrum (red/green, blue/yellow, any colour/white).
- To group or show similarity, use colours which are close neighbours in the spectrum (orange/yellow, blue/violet).

Note that colours have different qualities of subjective brightness and that colour also affects shape resolution. Characters and detail which require good visual acuity should be displayed in high contrast such as black on white or yellow on brown; background material is best displayed in blue, which appears most restful. The common colours have visibility characteristics:

- *Red*: low symbol luminance, poor visual acuity.
- *Yellow*: good visibility over a wide range of luminance, best visual acuity.
- *Green*: good visibility over intermediate range of luminance.
- *Blue*: good visibility at low luminance, poor acuity.

A final note of caution when using colour is to remember that 9% of the male population is colour blind, with red/green blindness being most common. Although colour blind people can discriminate colours using black and white shades, the designer should check that use of colour is not going to impair performance of colour blind users.

7.5.3 Messages and Abbreviations

Presentation of text occurs in design of titles, heading, prompts, error messages and control instructions. A few simple guidelines should be adhered to whenever text is being used:

- Keep the wording simple: avoid computer jargon, although use of user jargon words may be necessary.
- Be concise: do not include any words and phrases which are not strictly necessary.
- State the positive rather than negative.
- Use a polite but not overfamiliar tone. Use of 'please' always helps but too many 'have a nice day' or 'hello I'm your friendly XX computer' messages irritate after a few days.
- Use the active voice of verbs rather than passive voice, e.g. 'to Cancel order press C', not 'Orders are cancelled by pressing C'.

Messages should always be given in full unless space constraints make this unavoidable, in which case abbreviations will be necessary. Codes may be necessary as a further form of abbreviation, if space or keystrokes are at a premium, as in data entry dialogues with keywords or command languages.

Abbreviations should be consistent: try to avoid exceptions to the rule. Abbreviations should be of the same length, the number of characters being a trade-off between typing time and clarity. One approach is to abbreviate either by truncation or by compression, thereby producing a mnemonic code, that is a meaningful code in which the abbreviated word contains some clue to the identity of the whole word. Truncation removes trailing characters from a word, leaving the front few characters to convey the meaning, e.g. DIRectory. Generally, truncation is the easiest and most effective technique but it does run into problems of duplicates. With larger code sets truncation becomes a less viable technique and compression has to be used. (See Subsection 4.8.1.)

7.6 Summary

Presentation design takes the task/information requirements and dialogue specification as a starting point. Presentation sequences will generally follow the task-goal structure; however, in applications with weaker task models, information grouping and sequences have to be designed according to user-defined criteria. Information resources need to be considered to decide on the type of presentation. Static information displays are sufficient when data does not change; however, customisable displays and preformed query interfaces will be necessary for more volatile data. In extreme cases, only the data retrieval language can be provided. Interrelationships between information items suggest the need for hypertext-type interfaces.

When data is present in different media, a further choice is necessary about which medium is most suitable for displaying information of a specific type. Selection rules advise on which dynamic and static media to use according to the type of media and the sequence of presentation. Presentation sequences require more planning. Information display dialogues may map directly to presentation units such as boxes, windows and screens; however, segmentation of the dialogue according to the task break points may be necessary. Dialogue segments are then mapped to screen areas, boxes and windows, adding supporting information for prompts, help and error messages.

Detailed design needs to consider use of highlighting; but too many strong stimuli can create unpleasant designs. The range of attention-seeking stimuli in approximate order of potency is movement, shape, size, colour, brightness and texture. Colour should be used sparingly and care is required when attempting to colour-code information; although, as a method of improving the overall appeal of design, colour can be very effective. Messages should be concise and relevant with no jargon. Abbreviations may be necessary whenever there are constraints of display space.

Further Reading

Galitz (1987) covers presentation design guidelines for screen and report layout. Marcus (1992) is a good survey of issues in graphics presentation design and also provides guideline advice. For more detail on colour Travis (1991) provides comprehensive treatment.

Questions and Exercises

1. Critique the display in Figure 5.4. What poor design features does this display exhibit?

2. How would you design a hypertext interface to help readers access this chapter? Analyse the contents of the chapter from your view and specify the segments of text and images, and the links between them.

3. How should information presentations be designed for decision support systems which use both external statistics liable to updating, and a model which contains more stable data? Economic forecasting is such an example. Try specifying the information necessary for a decision support

system to forecast price inflation.

4. Design a multimedia presentation for teaching HCI. Assume you have the contents of this book, a video recording of users interacting with applications, and images of computer screens and other necessary illustrations. Voice recordings of key points are also available. Focus on one instructional task, perhaps use of colour in interface design, and plan a multimedia presentation for teaching students about colour usage.

8 Information Systems User Interfaces

Methods only get used if they are practical and economical for the task in hand. One of the first requests from practitioners is for a cut-down version of a method, so that the desired effect can be achieved in the minimum time. This chapter aims to give a lean version of HCI design which can be applied to smaller systems or by organisations who do not wish to take complex methodology on board. As quick methods are only practical with iterative development and prototyping, the recommendations are set in this context.

Prototyping poses the question of why the use of structured methods and a systematic approach to design are necessary. Prototyping and 4GL development are fine so long as they are not used on complex systems, but the boundaries of their effectiveness are limited by the following conditions:

- Applications have to be small enough to be developed by one person acting as an analyst-programmer. Large systems require communication between people, integration, and, hence, a systematic approach coupled to standardised notation of models as provided by structured methods.
- Applications are restricted to information systems where the prime purpose is to provide reports on business transactions. More complex applications with many algorithms and computation exceed the power of 4GLs.

Given these limitations, a large number of applications can be, and have been, developed by end users. The authors of structured methods have recognised this fast track of systems development and created cut-down versions to suit prototyping, e.g. IE-RAD, Systemcraft. Even with prototyping, methods are necessary to guide analysis, and in interface design guidelines are still necessary to ensure interfaces are well designed.

Information systems require rapid development to produce reports and query screens, and carry out simple transaction processing in response to business needs. This chapter gives guidelines for designing the two basic interfaces of such systems, data entry and data display.

8.1 Prototyping and Iterative Development

Prototyping is a key HCI technique for system development. A *prototype* is a partially constructed application to enable the user to assess some of the system's functionality and dialogue look and feel. Prototypes may be either *vertical*, in that a small part of the system is implemented in depth with complete functionality; or *horizontal*, when most of the system is implemented at the user interface level, although much of the functionality is missing. A prototype may be throw-away and just used for testing ideas, or it may be the first version of the eventual implemented system. These evolutionary prototypes grow in functionality with successive versions and gradually become the working system. Evolutionary prototypes save effort, as no code is discarded; however, they may not produce maintainable systems, as the code structure may be poor.

Prototyping tools allow rapid generation of user interfaces and functional programmes. There are two categories of tool, simulation-type packages and true prototyping tools. Of the former, hypertext is useful for HCI prototypes, as dialogue can be mocked up and made partially functional by links. More sophisticated tools, such as Macromind Director, provide facilities for making simulations of systems which look realistic and show some dialogue behaviour. The simulation tool provides a scripting language for designing the prototype behaviour. Other scripting-type packages can be used for prototyping (e.g. Icon Author), even though they were primarily aimed at the computer-aided learning market. Prototypes produced by simulation software must of necessity be thrown away, as no actual functional code is written.

True prototyping tools such as 4th Generation Languages (4GLs; e.g. Focus) incorporate screen and report design tools with a high-level procedural language. The rise of end user computing in the 1980s was empowered by 4GLs which gave people the ability to rapidly design and program their own systems. Prototyping and iterative design are very much part of 4GL development and these advances have improved usability by simply allowing more freedom to test and change design quickly. However, a weakness of many prototyping tools is the stereotyped nature of interaction they offer. Most only provide interfaces built from menus, form filling, message displays and dialogue boxes.

Variations of standard programming languages, such as Visual BASIC, have been developed as prototyping tools. Visual BASIC allows interfaces to be designed rapidly by composition of UI components (i.e. dialogue boxes, menus, windows, etc.). The language is designed around the user interface, with event handler routines to process user input into dialogue boxes and windows. Functional parts of the application (e.g. calculations, algorithms) can then be attached to input event handlers to complete the loop: input – validate – process – display.

Prototypes can be constructed very quickly with sophisticated graphical user interfaces. After early evaluation functional parts of the system can be added in later iterations to evolve the prototype towards a working system. The Smalltalk language has provided user interface development libraries for a number of years, while more recently Microsoft have developed user interface foundations classes as reusable UI objects for rapid prototyping and development. These extensions to programming languages facilitate evaluation prototyping, as the user interface can be constructed very quickly with limited functionality. This is evaluated and further functionality added, with UI design refinements as the prototype progresses.

Scenarios

Another important component of iterative design is scenarios. These are descriptions of a prospective application sketching out the domain of use and how an application will address a particular problem. Scenarios are used in requirements analysis. A variant of this approach is to script a typical sequence of interaction, called a 'use case'. This illustrates the functionality of a product as well as giving some idea of how the interaction may occur. Scenarios require simulation and prototyping tools to be effective. Different levels of presentation and simulation can be used with scenarios for requirements analysis and validation.

Storyboards are a paper-based simulation technique. Screen designs for the new application are created using a graphics drawing package, or sketched manually. A series of screens illustrates key steps in the dialogue to give some impression of how the new system will operate. This creates the storyboard or outline script of interaction. Even though storyboards are a minimal means of representing a new design, they can elicit invaluable feedback. They can also be used to plan more comprehensive simulations.

Evaluation

The final link in iterative development is testing. This is carried out by usability evaluation techniques, which are described in more depth in Chapter 9. However, as many usability evaluation techniques can also be time consuming, a quick economical technique for assessment is required. Such a simple yet effective method is heuristic evaluation (Nielsen, 1990; Nielsen and Molich, 1990), which uses a set of design principles similar to those described in Chapter 2. These are:

- Simple and natural dialogue which matches the user's expectations.
- Good use of graphical design and colour, following the structuring principle in Chapter 2.
- Simplicity and relevance of messages and information displays.
- Use of the users' languages; avoidance of jargon and obtuse messages.
- Mappings and metaphors, following the compatibility principle.
- Minimising the user memory load by consistency in displays and commands.
- Provision of feedback to keep the user informed.

- Clearly marked exits, all options having an escape route.
- Provision of shortcuts, following the economy principle, setting defaults, fast-path menus, etc.
- Good errors messages, which inform the user what has gone wrong and how to fix it.
- Prevention of errors by prevalidation, e.g. if an option is not relevant to the user's task, 'grey it out' as unavailable. The interface should prevent the user getting into dangerous situations.
- Help and documentation in a relevant form, context sensitive and not overwhelming to the user.

The heuristics require more background reading for interpretation, but an evaluator who has studied the HCI principles in Chapter 2 or the fuller description of the usability heuristics given in Nielsen (1993b), should be well able to assess a prototype design. The design or specification is vetted against these principles to detect usability errors. The evaluator should preferably be a potential user of the system, although anyone who is not the designer will suffice. The evaluator goes through the interface trying out as many features as they can, of mentally walking through the features in a storyboard. Design problems are noted against one or more of the usability heuristics and this critique is discussed with the designer. This method may be used by non-HCI experts and it is claimed to trap up to 70–80% of the potential errors. More evaluators, up to an optimum of five, trap more errors; and HCI experts do not find significantly more errors than non-expert evaluators. Improvement is left to the designer's judgement. This method is cheap yet effective.

Fast-path HCI development is based on a concept of repeated cycles of refinement rather than a waterfall-like development process. Delivery of quality designs is achieved by iterations of specify – prototype – build – evaluate – redesign. The agenda of steps for prototype development is:

1. *Requirements analysis*: this is an essential first stage in any system development. Investigating the user-required goals in terms of functionality and information provision develops a 'wish list' of system features.
2. *Task analysis:* at least in outline, some analysis of what the user wants to do is essential. The task model produced may be at the goal level but this should be sufficient for task allocation and task support design.
3. *User analysis*: some profile of the anticipated user populations is necessary, at least to establish possible customisation of the system by configuration files. *Domain analysis* is advisable but this may be less important in small-scale systems which are likely to have standard user interfaces (e.g. form filling and menus, rather than GUI metaphors).

4. *Map task goals* to user interface design components supplied by the prototyping environment, e.g. dialogue boxes, messages, windows, menus, etc.
5. *Storyboard- and scenario-test* the design. Incorporate user feedback in design improvements.
6. *Validate* the design using heuristic evaluation. This gives a check list of usability features which should be preset in a design. Any omissions should be cured.
7. *Design and implement* the prototype using available tools.
8. *Usability-test* the prototype using diagnostic evaluation techniques to discover design errors and their reasons. Improve the prototype and iterate steps 7–8 as long as users are not satisfied with the design, and while resources for development allow improvement.

This basic cycle may be changed if simulation tools are used, in which case there is a transition from prototype-simulation to full-scale development or evolutionary prototyping after one or two cycles.

Most prototypes have two standard interfaces which are found in most information system applications. The next section reviews design guidelines for those interfaces.

8.2 Information Systems

Information systems carry transaction processing and provide information for business purposes. Typically they are composed of three main components:

- *Data entry and validation*: these components gather input data necessary for a business transaction, e.g. the details of a sales order.
- *Transaction processing and database update*: the input data is processed, some calculations carried out and the database or master file updated, e.g. the order is cross-checked against stock and goods are allocated to the order. The stock and order files are updated.
- *Report generation*: to provide management information on the process, e.g. orders processed per week, stock turnover by item, order value for each salesman, etc.

The user interfaces for such systems are:

- Data entry and validation to accept input data. These are often *form filling dialogues.*
- Data display interfaces as *printed reports and query screens.*

- Simple command dialogues to allow the users to run different parts of the system according to their choice. These are usually *menu-style dialogues.*

Fourth generation languages usually provide generation facilities for the user interface as screen painters, report writers, menu design facilities and business graphics routines. The designer/user employs high-level tools to interactively plan the layout of screens, placing input fields and titles by pointing. Additional user interface components such as dialogue boxes, buttons, etc. (see Chapter 4) are also provided. While these make development of the user interface very rapid, they can nevertheless allow poor designs.

In the remainder of this Chapter the design problem of data entry and display interfaces will be examined. Menus have already been covered as a dialogue style in Chapter 4.

8.3 Data Entry

Data entry interfaces are the part of computer systems with which end users spend most of their time. These interfaces are also one of the most error-prone parts of computer systems and have given rise to the acronym GIGO (Garbage In Garbage Out). The design should aim to prevent GIGO and make data entry as efficient and pleasant as possible for the user.

Most of the dialogue will be specified in the task design, but data entry dialogues invariably require elaboration to deal with editing and correcting errors. The dialogue should be planned with break points for closure events which become more important the longer a sequence is. In a short transaction with 5–7 entries, a break after each record may be permissible, although longer transactions will need break points within a record sequence. The general objectives for data entry are to save the user work, and to make entry error rates as low as possible. This is achieved by keeping the user's memory load as low as possible, making the interface predictable and consistent, protecting the user from making mistakes, and automating as much of the data entry as possible.

Reduction of the user's workload can be achieved by:

- Setting defaults for commonly entered items.
- Using codes and abbreviations.
- Automatically filling in previously entered items, e.g. taking the customer's name and address from file.
- Using pointing responses and selection from a list, if entry is from a limited set of choices.

Most data entry tasks involve a transaction. Transactions in most information systems are described by a paper document, a form which is created and then processed by the system (e.g. customer order, hospital admittance record, export shipping document). The input–user interface should be based on the design of the paper forms as far as possible to preserve compatibility with the user's knowledge of the existing system. As part of the overall system, design may involve the design of data capture forms; it is worth considering this topic in more detail.

8.3.1 Forms Design

Forms play an important part in most people's lives and are the source of most data entered into computers. Data capture can be an error-prone process because people may mistake instructions, skip fields, give information in the wrong format, make transposition errors, or write illegibly. Good form design can reduce these problems.

When designing data capture procedures, the following factors should be considered:

- Data should be collected at source as far as possible.
- Data should be entered on to the data capture document (a form) by the originator of the data.
- Avoid transcription of data from one form to another, since it is an error-prone process.
- Automate the process if possible by automatic data capture devices, e.g. OCR (optical character recognition); see Subsection 8.3.4.

Forms should be designed for ease of data collection rather than extraneous factors such as fitting into envelopes, and saving printing costs. They should have a consistent design as far as possible within a system and organisation. The more consistent that designs are, the more uniform users' expectations become, and consequently their learning burden is reduced.

It may be necessary to capture optional as well as essential information. The designer needs to identify who will fill in the form, and strike a balance between having one form which tries to suit all people and many different forms, each one tailored to a particular type of user. The all-purpose form suffers from errors of people filling in irrelevant information and completing the wrong sections. Tailored forms, on the other hand, suffer from people having difficulty getting the right form for their needs and accidentally filling in the wrong one. How many individual data sources to target on one form is a trade-off decision.

Generally, one form should have one purpose and the number of alternative form types should be kept to a minimum.

Forms consist of three main components:

- Data entry areas.

- Supporting information, and instructions.
- Titles and headings.

Data fields should be ordered and grouped according to frequency of use, importance, functional relatedness or sequence of use: whichever is most significant for the user. Within each group, fields are ordered in sequence of entry. For transactions, fields will generally be grouped in functionally related blocks, e.g. in an order form: customer details, order date and delivery details, and products ordered. Data groups should be separated by clear boundaries and the complete form should not have a surface area more than 40% full of data fields and printed messages.

Three types of prompt may be used: caption before, caption above, and caption and box designs. The caption and box design is favoured because it gives the best visual link between the caption and the data entry area, encourages readable input, and gives a better visual structure to the form.

Guidelines for general form design are:

- Make selections explicit. If there are alternatives within a form, of the type 'If A fill in section 1, else fill in section 2' make sure that separate sections are clearly marked. The else condition should give clear navigational guidance with arrows and Goto section (x) instructions.
- Many forms are filled in by two or more people. Typical of these are the 'For office use only' sections on forms. Sections for different people should be clearly separated, and if any transcription from one entry to another is necessary, related fields aligned as closely as possible.
- The effort of form filling should be kept to a minimum. When replies come in limited sets, use tick boxes, circle the answer or cross out the alternative. This makes replies neater and less effort is demanded from the user. On the whole, tick boxes are the most economical movement.

8.3.2 Data Entry Dialogues

Form-filling dialogues are the most common data entry interface for information systems. The principal aim is to model the user interface on the data entry document so that the user is familiar with the layout, and transcription from paper to computer follows a sequence the user knows. Dialogue aspects such as editing incorrect data, error messaging and validation have to be added. Handling errors is one of the more complicated parts of data entry, which necessitates creating new dialogue sequences for errors messages and correction. Dialogue networks can be used to design these pathways in detail (see Chapter 6). Data entry dialogues aim to prevent errors happening and, when they do, to make correction a simple matter for the user.

Data entry dialogues should give the user positive control over the sequence of communication rather than attempting to help the user with design tricks such as automatic skip to next field. Such features can cause frustration when they are not required, but, more importantly, they conflict with what people normally expect. Most people expect data entry to be like filling in a paper form by hand, in which case you have to explicitly move to the next field. However, automatic skipping to the next field may be justified for skilled users with high transaction volumes, in which case speed and efficiency considerations are more important. This trade-off illustrates how context affects the interpretation of guidelines.

The user's input should be accepted in a variety of formats and automatically reformatted for computer processing. For instance, users should not have to enter redundant digits and characters such as leading zeros, e.g. 79 not 0079 to fit a PIC 9(4). Input should not be space-sensitive, e.g. both 'A. Name' and 'A.Name' should be acceptable.

Prompts should indicate to the user what value is to be input and show the valid replies either as a range or as a limited data set, e.g. 'enter discount value in the range of 1 to 10'.

8.3.3 Validation and Error Correction

Data entry is notoriously error prone. Errors may be caused by omission of a field, incorrect data being entered in a field, and number/letter transpositions. Data validation attempts to check that all mandatory fields are filled in, and that the data entered is correct, or at least reasonable. Some commonly used validation methods are look-up tables, and reference files; e.g. checking data entry values against customer numbers, account codes, part types, etc. Other techniques include range and type checks or testing for reasonable data by comparing them with other known values.

Validation errors may be classified into three categories and different error correction actions specified for each.

- *Fatal errors*: errors which make a nonsense of further processing, such as invalid account codes, customer names. In this case the user must either re-enter a correct value or abort the entry; no other action must be allowed.
- *Warning*: errors which are caused by highly unlikely values. Processing should be halted, and the user invited to re-input. However, an over-ride should be given so the user can input the original value, which may be the exception to the reasonability rule.
- *Advisory*: errors which are caused by unlikely values. Processing may not necessarily be halted but a warning message should be given so the user can halt either immediately or at the end of the transaction to check and possibly edit the data.

Validation messages are placed in a consistent part of the screen reserved for error control.

Error messages

Messaging is important for conveying the type of error and giving users instructions for their correction. As with all computer messages, the wording should be clear, simple, concise and relevant.

Error messages have often been one of the most user-vicious parts of interfaces. There is no excuse for 'Syntax error' or 'Invalid field'. Error messages must be informative and jargon-free, and attempt to tell the user not only what is wrong but also why, with an explanation of the correct course of action to put it right, e.g.

Start date: 1/10/94
Maturity date: 12/9/94

Error: the Maturity date should be after the Start date. Please re-enter either date in dd/mm/yy format.

Data entry invariably requires data editing. The dialogue should allow the user to check input fields to ensure that errors not trapped by validation are found and corrected, as well as guiding the user to correct those errors detected by validation. There are several different methods of implementing editors, for instance:

- Prompt errored field and re-enter in a pop-up box, e.g.

  Delivery Date error: month out of range: 12/13/93
  Please enter in dd/mm/yy format: --/--/--

  This method can be effective when a long sequence of data is being entered. The incorrect entry should always be shown to prompt the user. The main disadvantage is that the prompt for re-entry may obscure data already on the screen.

- Address errored field to re-enter, e.g.

  1. Customer number
  2. Customer name
  3. Customer address
  4. Vehicle type
  5. Policy period
  6. Policy type

  Errors: 5. Policy period too long – 12 months max.
  6. Unknown policy type – valid reply codes CMP 3RD 3FT TMP

Type field number to edit
(1–6 or 0 to escape)

This method may be useful in input sequences when errors cannot be detected immediately.

- Edit/skip correct fields, e.g.

Customer Name:	J. Smith
Address:	The Willows
Address:	Sunnydale Avenue
Address:	Milton Keynes
Vehicle Type:	Ford
Make:	Escort
CC:	1300
Policy:	C
Durn:	12 mths

Press Tab to skip to next field
or Enter to save

Edit/skip field editors are quick to use and display the whole of the entry for checking with error messages. The user moves between fields using the Tab or Return key and types over the incorrect data. The disadvantages with this technique are tabbing past the errored field by mistake and the tabbing time taken in long entry sequences.

While form filling is probably the most popular of current data entry interface techniques, it is time consuming to operate and inappropriate if the set of replies is limited and predictable. In these cases other entry techniques such as picking lists and input menus can be applied. However, all data entry takes time and any automation pays dividends.

8.3.4 Automating Data Entry

The objective is to get the computer to read the input transaction data. This may be in numeric or alphanumeric form. If it is printed, then optical character recognition techniques can be used via scanners. Otherwise a code system has to be devised so a more specialised reading device can be used.

Bar codes

These are special optical codes in which goods are labelled with a unique combination of vertical stripes which code a number by the presence or absence of bars in certain positions (Figure 8.1). Bar codes are a ubiquitous feature of supermarket packaging. The code is read by a special light-sensitive wand or bar code reader which picks up the dark bands as it is traversed across the coded area and translates the sequence of bars into a code according to the presence or absence of a dark band at position x, $x + 1$, etc. The computer compares the bar code sequence against a look-up table and computes the number of the stock item.

Bar codes are a good example of considerable investment by computer manufacturers on behalf of the users (the supermarkets) to help them automate data entry.

Figure 8.1 Bar code for automatic data entry. The vertical bars correspond to digits, according to the position and thickness of the bar.

Scanners and optical character recognition (OCR)

Computers used to have trouble reading printed text because it is very variable. To cut down the variability standardised computer-readable character sets were proposed by the European Computer Manufacturers Association (ECMA). Their stylised format enabled computers to read characters by pattern matching; however, this approach was of limited use because of the expensive printing requirement.

Modern scanners and OCR systems can deal with printed text in a number of different fonts and sizes by learning the characteristics of a type face. After a few trials the computer system learns the rules for a typeface and incorporates the rules in its pattern-matching algorithms. Scanners combined with OCR software convert text and image into digital formats. Images are stored as pixel arrays, while text is converted into ASCII characters. Scanners/OCR can be used to automate form-filling data entry, as the paper form can be scanned in as an image and data extracted as the alphanumeric characters.

Recognising handwriting still presents problems; although some systems can recognise handwritten capitals and numbers, continuous script still defeats most machines, probably because human handwriting is variable and only too often illegible.

Voice data entry

Use of speech is the other main opportunity for reducing the burden of data input. Text can be entered by speech recognition devices which now have the capacity to recognise a wide vocabulary in slow yet continuous speech; hence, spoken data can be entered into the main transaction processing system. However, speech systems still have a noticeable error rate, and this becomes higher for speaker-independent systems. If the whole data entry dialogue is speech driven, then the system requires at least limited natural language understanding to deal with error repair commands. This has limited speech input applications in the past but speech will become a more effective medium for input in the near future.

8.4 Data Display Interfaces

Display design has to resolve what data to display and then how much information to place on a screen. Display too little and users have to page through many screens to find the data they need; display too much and search times increase. The general aim is to display information which is appropriate for the user's task without overcrowding the screen.

To decide what to display, the following guidelines may be employed:

- Display only necessary data. Anything which is not directly related to the user's requirements should be omitted.
- The data on display should be related to the task the user performs with the data.
- The quantity of data per screen, including titles, headings, etc., should not cover more than 30% of the total area.
- Group data in a logical manner. Data groups may come from task information analysis; otherwise, group data relating to the same transaction (e.g. a customer order), or by frequency of use, sequence of operations or function, according to the user's views.
- Order data according to criteria which are meaningful to the user. Key fields and identifiers should be placed at the top left-hand side of displays; other data may be ordered by importance, frequency of use, sequence of normal usage, mandatory then discretionary items, etc. Sort items by one or more keys.
- Show abstract qualities of the data if required and use graphics to illustrate those qualities (trends, associations, differences).

While screen layout is being planned, there are other general display guidelines which should be considered:

- Codes and abbreviations should be kept to a minimum. Data displays should be immediately comprehensible to the reader without having to translate codes.
- If several displays are being planned, try to establish a consistent format. If users know where to expect information and how it will be presented, they have less to learn.
- Provide clear headings, titles and other wayfinding information to help user navigation within and between display frames.
- Avoid overfussy displays; inclusion of too many subsections impairs visual searching and locating data. Use of delimiters such as &&&& ****** $$$$$$$ should be avoided, as these only increase screen crowding and add no extra information.
- Use the users' conventions and keep to their terminology. The typical example is UK or American date conventions, which are dd/mm/yy and mm/dd/yy format, respectively.
- Highlight important data with colour, text size, underlining or by use of a different font.

After the display structure has been designed, detailed design depends on whether graphics or character displays are being used.

8.4.1 Text and Tabular Displays

The presentation problem is how to lay out screens and format the data so they are easy to find and pleasant to read. Displays may be either pure text, or tables and lists, and more frequently a mixture of both.

Continuous capitals for text should be avoided because reading rates for capitals are slower than for mixed text. Capitalisation should be used as in printed text and occasionally for emphasis.

Text in English should be left justified and the right margin may be ragged, as this does not impair readability. If both right and left margins are justified, equal spacing between words is preferred over unequal odd-shaped gaps, which distract the eye precisely because they are unequal.

Captions in tables should be placed above columns and captions and prompts should be placed before the data and separated by a space or delimiter:

City: Manchester   Population: 1,546,000

Data fields should be left justified for text, and either justified on the decimal point for real numbers, or right justified for integers:

Compiler	System time (minutes)	Number of users
COBOL	161.68	123
FORTRAN	23.1	12
APL	54.56	21
RPG III	0.75	1

Users should be given a flexible means of accessing displays by page and scroll controls. In page control, part of the previous display should still be visible at the top/bottom of the new page for continuity. When using scrolling, the speed should be under user control so that unwanted data can be skipped with a fast scroll and more interesting data can be inspected with a slow scroll.

8.4.2 *Graphical Displays*

Graphics are effective because they abstract qualities from data and present information in a more 'chunked' form. But that can introduce bias into interpretation of data, and designers should exercise care when choosing graph types and layouts.

Users may want to show a particular quality of the data for demonstration purposes, for instance, trends, grouping, differences. Some of the graphical treatments of data commonly encountered in information systems are:

- *Association*: the graph is to show how two measures or classes of objects are related in absolute terms (same value) or co-vary in some manner.
- *Difference*: the antithesis of association; here the aim is to show how items differ by an absolute magnitude or show opposite patterns in variation.
- *Exception*: this is a special case of difference related to a set of items. The objective is to show the 'odd man out' in a set.
- *Trend*: aims to show a pattern in a set of values over a range, usually an increasing or decreasing trend.
- *Grouping*: this is a special case of association which aims to show relationships between many objects in a population. The inverse effect to clustering is a measure of *scatter*. An example is the clustering of weight and height measurements for individual people around the average values of 70 kg and 1.7 m.
- *Distribution about a norm*: the graph is to show how a group of data items are spread around the average value for the population. Normal distributions are balanced with an approximately equal number of items above and below average, with most values clustering around the average. Other distributions may show skew, more points either above or below the average; or kurtosis, more points spread away from the average than expected by statistical definition of a normal distribution; see Figure 8.2.

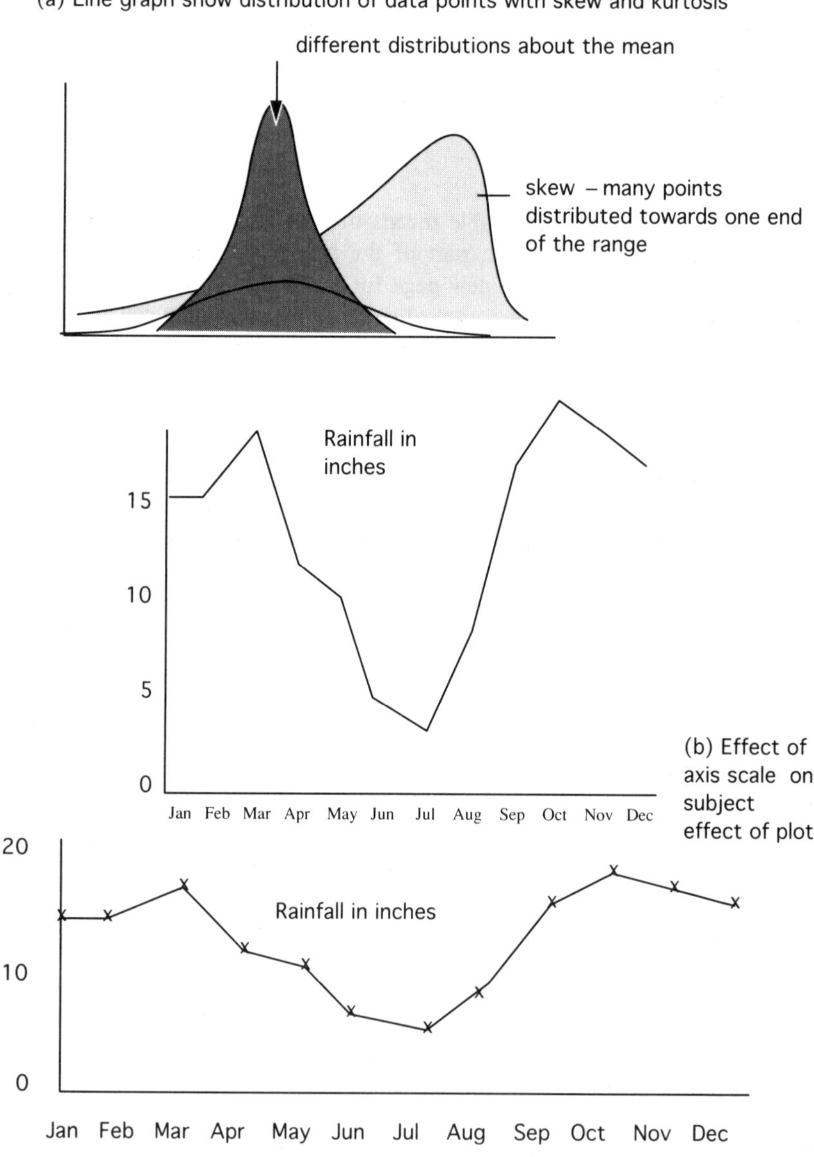

Figure 8.2 Line graphs, illustrating different plots.

The designer's choice of graph types is set by the application package or 4GL environment. Most support standard chart types such as line graphs, pie charts, histograms and scatter plots, as illustrated in Figure 8.3 on page 220.

Choice of which to use depends on the characteristics of the data, although some guidelines to consider are:

- If data values are related to a time dimension, then line graphs are generally appropriate.
- For distributions around an average, use line graphs; for clustering of individual measures, choose a scatter plot.
- For set memberships and percentage data, pie charts can be effective.
- To compare differences and associations when there is no organising dimension, histograms are a reasonable choice.

Design of graphics is a complex subject in its own right and interested readers can explore the topic in books by Tufte (1990) and Marcus (1992).

8.5 Reports

This section examines design of hardcopy printed reports. Too many reports contain too much data. Overcrowded reports cause longer search times as the reader has to track down a data item in a morass of print. High print densities also increase transcription error rates, as figures close together are mistaken. A report with more than 50% of its area covered by print, including headings and any format characters (e.g. $$$$), is overcrowded. Aim for an upper limit of 40% of the total area in print.

Report crowding does pose a dilemma when several pieces of information are required together. If the information is separated on to different pages, then the user has to turn pages to find all the data, burdening short-term memory while doing so. Place too much information on one page and overcrowding may result. There is no ideal answer to this trade-off judgement, but on balance excessive crowding should be avoided.

First the type, function and expected usage of a report should be established. A report's function may be either to convey information from one system to another, e.g. an invoice, or to summarise information about a system, as in a management summary, or a historical record, simple listing, etc. Some categories are:

- *Transaction reports:* these contain the results of input data which has been processed and is to be passed out of the system. Transaction reports often carry information between systems. Examples are order forms, delivery notes, invoices, purchase orders, pay slips.
- *Information reports:* these contain data describing system processes and the state of system objects. The information is consumed by managers and system operators to monitor, control and modify the system's behaviour. Exception, monitoring and analysis reports and management summaries all

fall into this category.

- *History and archive reports:* these are a special case when information is needed over a long time period to describe a system's history. Data which may be required in the future is also held in archive reports.
- *Browsing reports:* these are the simplest report type and are the hardcopy equivalent of the query screen or file listing. Information is generally presented in an unsophisticated format so that users can sift through it in a variety of ways.

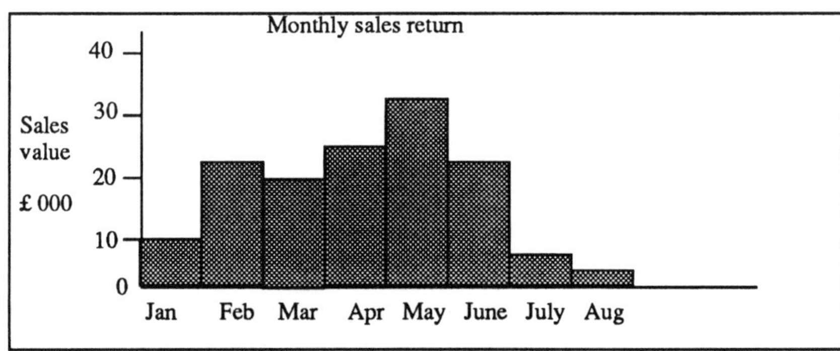

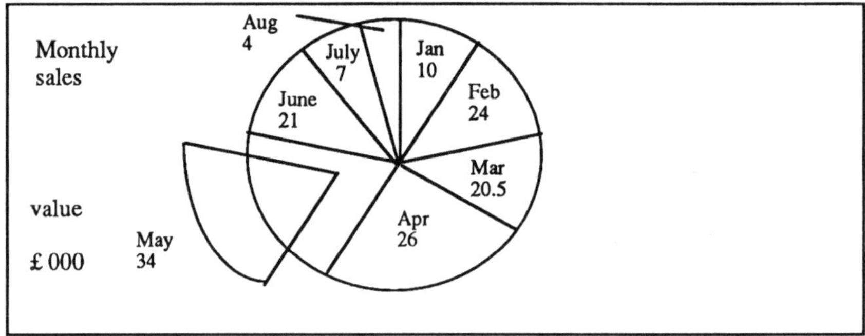

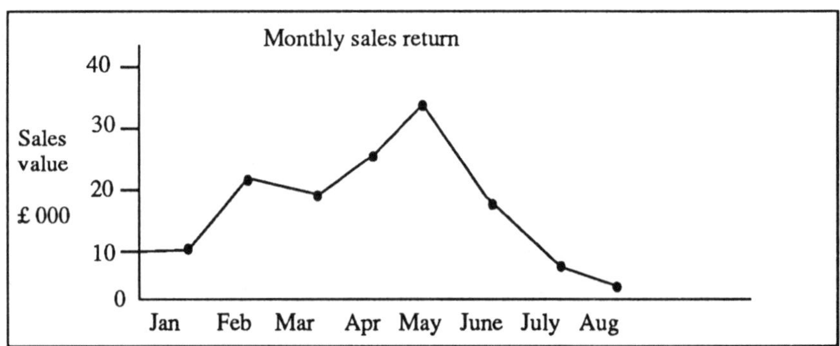

Figure 8.3 Types of business graphics charts.

The function of a report may influence its layout; however, general formatting guidelines can be given for all types.

8.5.1 Report Design

Transaction and information reports require most design, although some structure should be given even to history and browsing reports. Transaction reports often have similar contents to input forms, and forms design guidelines can be applied. Transactions are generally indexed by a unique code which should be clearly marked and placed in the top right-hand corner, since this helps leafing through a pile of reports to find the reference number. These reports often use preprinted stationery, so it is advisable to print a dummy page first to check on printer alignment of the print fields on the preprinted template.

For all reports, general layout guidelines apply as they do to screens and other presentation media. First, the purpose of the report should suggest a clear and concise title. Decide on the report contents in consultation with the user. Structure the information into groups and blocks of related items. Grouping may be by entity-related data in transaction reports, or by purpose according to the user's criteria. Order the groups and blocks according to the user's needs and reading sequence, e.g. importance, cost, frequency of use, sequence of use.

In addition, the following factors should be considered which may affect the report structure:

- *Frequency of production*: is the report required on demand or at a specific time, e.g. daily, weekly, monthly? Is all the information required at the same time? Timing requirements may lead to some information being placed in an on-demand report while other items may only be required at weekly intervals.
- *Volume of production*: how many copies of a report are required, and will the same number be produced each run? Reports with different volumes may have to be run separately, as a long print run will require operations staff to set up printers, whereas a single copy could be printed without any operator intervention.
- *Timing and accuracy of information*: the timing of a report can be influenced by how up to date the data has to be and the value of information which is not completely up to date. If slightly inaccurate information is permissible (e.g. close of business yesterday), then overnight printing of reports is tolerable; on the other hand, if information must be totally up to date, then an on-demand report is necessary. Accuracy also pertains to the numeric values. Calculation to five decimals may be needed on an engineering report; in contrast, a cost forecast may be acceptable with an accuracy to the nearest £100.
- *Security*: this concerns how sensitive the information is and what precautions have to be taken to ensure it is not seen by unauthorised

personnel. This influences the devices on which it is printed and arrangements for distribution.

After formatting and layout design, pagination should not be forgotten:

- Number pages and title each one. An unnumbered page which has become detached from a report can be very irritating.
- Date and time stamp the report each run. Sooner or later the fact that it was the weekly report before Christmas will be important.

Finally, when the detailed report layout has been designed, the users' opinions should not be forgotten. As with most aspects of the human–computer interface, users should be consulted about designs, and changes made to accommodate their views. In display and report design early consultation is advisable before the detailed layout is planned, as well as final acceptance testing.

8.6 Summary

Data entry interface design should aim to make tasks easy for the user and to minimise the input workload. The user should be in control of data entry sequences and actions should be made explicit. Forms design is important for data capture documents. Logical layout and formatting are the most important factors of forms design, although clear prompts and instructions are also important.

Data entry can be achieved using a number of dialogue design techniques. The most common interface style is form filling, which is useful for complex and open-ended data in which the reply set cannot be predicted. When the reply set is better known, picking menus or keyword command input may be used. Where possible, data entry should be automated. This can be achieved using optical character recognition, bar codes, or voice. The use of voice in particular may increase for remote data entry and in environments where keyboards may be inappropriate.

Display design involves structuring information to help people read and understand it. Data items should be grouped and groups ordered according to usage. Important data should be highlighted to ensure that attention is drawn to them.

Data displays may be either textual or graphic. Text displays should not be overcrowded and space should be used to separate items of information. Display control dialogues are designed to help users progress through a body of data according to their needs. In simple cases this will be by scrolling; more advanced access is by data retrieval query languages. The syntax and structure of such languages has to be designed with care. Graphical displays make use of human chunking abilities by abstracting qualities of data. Designers have to choose a chart type according to the data set being analysed and the type of analysis treatment.

Reports should be analysed to determine their function. This may dictate the structure of a report and should suggest its title. Reports have transaction, information, listing or archive functions. Information is ordered and grouped to optimise efficient access. Detailed formatting of columns, text and decimals has to be designed to make the appearance of a report consistent and pleasing to the eye.

Questions and Exercises

1. Discuss the problems of designing a form-filling interface when the transaction is long, i.e. the quantity of data which has to be entered for each record is composed of many fields (an Inland Revenue Tax return is a good example!).

2. What are the problems inherent in validation and error correct for data entry? How can data entry mistakes be detected and corrected to save the users work and frustration?

3. Discuss the limitations of automatic data entry. Take a Point of Sale system as an example and then extend it to home shopping via TV. Assuming that two-way communications are possible from a home TV set to a central computer, how would you design a data entry system for home shopping?

4. Should reports be prototyped or designed or both? Discuss the merits of designing reports for users, and whether evaluation paper-based designs can help improve readability.

5. What are the problems in using query languages for data retrieval? How would you improve on SQL or any other data retrieval language you are familiar with?

9 Quality Assurance

This chapter deals with the quality assurance part of HCI, evaluation and usability. Different types of evaluation are reviewed and quality definitions of HCI as usability and utility are described. These are related to design principles encountered in Chapter 2. First, the HCI definition of quality, i.e. learnability, memorability, effectiveness and flexibility, is reviewed. This review is followed by description of usability evaluation, that is the testing process for user interfaces. Evaluation may either aim to check that an interface has achieved some standard of benchmark, or be targeted as design improvement via diagnosis of usability errors.

This process of evaluation is similar for benchmark or diagnostic evaluation. Tasks have to be constructed to test the interface, a cross-selection of users chosen and the evaluation session prepared. Various data collection techniques are used, ranging from observation and interviews, through questionnaires for opinions and attitudes, to think-aloud protocols to capture the user's reasoning about why a problem occurred. Data analysis techniques, such as counts of errors and time to complete tasks, are described with different types of evaluation approach applicable to specifications, designs, prototypes and products.

9.1 Evaluation and Usability

Ensuring a human–computer interface is usable is one of the most important parts of HCI. Evaluation of human–computer interfaces should be carried out in conjunction with prototyping development and on complete products produced within the more traditional analysis-design implementation life cycle. Quality assurance is seen, only too often, to be the last stage of product development; however, testing and checking that designs are appropriate should be a continuous process. Two types of evaluation are distinguished:

- *Formative*: evaluation and testing carried out during the development of a product. Tests may be carried out on specifications and designs as well as on prototypes. Testing should provide feedback to inform and, hence, improve the design.
- *Summative*: evaluation when the product exists. In this case the results of tests add more to the sum of knowledge about a product. If the results can also be used to improve the design, so much the better.

Eventually the boundary between summative and formative evaluation becomes blurred, especially when iterative development is used.

Evaluation consists of a set of concepts which define what qualities should be tested, procedures for carrying out the tests and then a means of interpreting the results. Usability supplies the concepts, which can then be refined into a set of goals for evaluations. Techniques, measures and metrics are used to assess the achievement or otherwise of usability goals. First, it is important to establish the reason why evaluation is necessary. There are two main motivations for usability testing:

- *Benchmark testing*: evaluation to establish whether a product attains a certain standard. This may be done to obtain a quality certification and, as HCI becomes increasingly subject to standards recommendations by ISO (see ISO 9421 part 12), it may be possible to obtain a quality certificate such as the British Kitemark. Alternatively, benchmark evaluation is used to test whether a product attains usability goals set by market analysis.
- *Diagnostic testing*: this aims to pinpoint the poor design features by observing users' problems or examining recordings of dialogue sessions. These are usually videoed and then inspected for signs of user frustration, users' errors and misconceptions. The reason for the problem is analysed and recommendations made to improve the design.

In addition to these types of evaluation, experiments in the psychological tradition may be used either to compare two similar designs or to test the effect of a specific design feature. Experiments control the context of interface operation carefully to give precise results about the design under test. However, experiments are only possible if the environmental conditions for the test are strictly controlled. This introduces an artificial context which cannot take the working environment into account. Context effects can be important. A product may appear to be usable in the laboratory but when in an operational environment the story can be different. A simple example would be testing a voice interface in the laboratory and in a noisy factory.

Concern over the artificiality of laboratory evaluation has led to the practice of contextual evaluation which takes place in the working environment (Whiteside *et al.*, 1988). While this approach is much stronger on ecological validity, i.e. the test relates closely to the context of use, it sacrifices objectivity and analytic power. This is because the test environment is not controlled; if the user is interrupted in the middle of a session, then the vital error may be missed. In spite of these limitations, contextual evaluation is a powerful means of diagnosing usability flaws. On the other hand, for benchmark testing a more controlled evaluation is desirable.

Before progressing to consider evaluation techniques, the concepts of interface quality have to be examined.

9.2 Definitions of Quality

There is no single measure of a good interface, but a set of important qualities of an interface from the user's point of view can be defined. The first distinction is between how well an interface (and therefore the application) helps a user perform a task, and how easy the interface is to operate. These concepts are referred to as *utility* and *usability*:

9.2.1 Utility

This is a measure of how well an interface (and the system) helps the user to perform one or more tasks. It is linked to the functionality of the system (what you can do with it) and the task fit, e.g. how well the interface matches what the users want to do and their perception of how to do it (the task). Good utility is a result of effective requirements analysis, accurate specification and creative design. It is therefore not easy to measure, but it can be assessed by testing prototypes and design mock-ups with users. Early testing of design utility can save considerable costs in changing designs later on. Evaluation techniques for utility, such as user testing, scenario and use cases, simulation and design validation, are shared with requirement engineering (see Chapter 11). The result of utility testing should be feedback for design improvement.

Utility is difficult to measure. Attitude data from questionnaires can give some feel for task fit, but more comprehensive analysis requires elucidation of a user task model. A subjective assessment measure could be *percentage of users satisfied with the application.*

Ultimately, utility is demonstrated by how many people used the application or bought the product. However, even though parts of an application may have high utility, other parts may never be used. The concept of coverage can be used to assess overengineered applications.

Coverage is the quantity of system facilities which are used. While not all users can be expected to use all parts of the system all of the time, if some facilities are never used by any users there may be design problems. Coverage is measured as: *frequency of facilities used by x% users within a set time period.*

A well-engineered product should have high utility and good coverage, although this is not easy to achieve, especially in general-purpose applications. Providing more facilities to please different types of user can increase the product's utility for a user population. This has to be traded off against making an overengineered product too complex for an individual user. This has an impact on usability.

9.2.2 Usability

This refers to interface operation. An interface has good usability if it can be learned quickly, is easy to operate and can be remembered. Usability is related to utility because some applications may be complex, and in spite of the very best endeavours of the designer, complex applications take some learning. The relationship between complexity and usability is difficult and still the subject of some debate; however, complex applications can be designed which are easy to use. Dealing with complexity should be part of the designer's, not the user's, task. Most evaluations have concentrated on assessing usability with a small number of measures, typically task completion time and error rates. Usability can be decomposed into the following components (after Shackel, 1986). Each component is given with metrics which can be used to assess it and an example of a target goal for a benchmark-type evaluation.

- *Effectiveness*. This is a measure of how well the interface, and, hence, the system, performs in achieving what the user wants to do. This can be measured in terms of:

    - Error rates lower than a target level.
    - Task completion time within a set target time.
    - Usage of system facilities above a minimum target frequency.

    A typical usability goal for effectiveness may be:

    > 95% of the users complete the test tasks within 10 minutes with an error rate of less than 2% of the transactions processed.

- *Learnability*. This measures how easy to learn a system is and can be quantified with measures of:

    - Decreased error rates over time from the start of system usage.
    - Decrease in task completion time from the start of system usage.
    - Increase in user knowledge about system facilities over time.

    A sample usability goal may be:

    > 95% of the users can learn to use the system commands to complete the set tasks of the effectiveness goal with 20 minutes of tutored training before the test.

    Another possibility is to set learning goals over successive sessions:

    - Errors should decrease to less than 2% and task completion times of x minutes should be attained by 95% of users after 5 sessions.

- *Memorability*. It is important that an interface remind the user so that, when returning to use the system after some time, the user does not have to relearn it. Memorability is closely linked to learnability, and is measured either by comprehension/memory recall tests or by usage tests after an elapsed time period. Example measures are:

- Correct recall of system facilities, operational procedures or command names.
- % system facilities or commands recalled after time period T.
- % system commands explained adequately after time period T.

A usability goal for this component could be:

> 95% of the users should be able to recall and accurately describe 90% of the system commands 7 days after training.

- *Attitude/satisfaction.* Attitude is the subjective part of usability which quantifies user satisfaction with the system. It is measured by rating on a scale typically 1–7, where 1 = bad and 7 = excellent. Typical measures are:

  - User satisfaction exceeds a target rating.
  - User-perceived problems are kept below a set level.
  - User motivation to use the system exceeds a set baseline level.

  A usability goal for user satisfaction could be:

  > 95% of the users rate the overall system quality as being 5 or better on a 7-point scale.

  Attitude is a hybrid measure which captures both usability and utility. If an overall metric is required for an application, this can be expressed as 'acceptability':

  $$acceptability = satisfaction + usability$$

  where satisfaction is measured by questionnaire and usability is assessed using the metrics of effectiveness, learnability, etc.

All usability measures require goals to be set based on reasonable expectations for the system before the evaluation is carried out. These will depend on the complexity of the application, the target user population, and the environment of training and use.

9.3 Techniques for Evaluating Human–Computer Interfaces

These depend on the purpose, i.e. whether benchmarking or diagnosis is the aim. Measures of evaluation may be either objective, i.e. derived from controlled collection of data, or subjective, i.e. based on intuitive judgements and opinions gathered from users. Diagnostic analyses may use objective measures such as error counts to pinpoint critical features of an interface design, and combine this with a subjective approach using questionnaires to record attitude to design features. Data collection techniques vary in their intrusiveness. Observing users is intrusive, as users are only too well aware of an evaluator watching what they are doing. This can lead to abnormal reactions and reticence in critiquing applications, so it is important to reassure users that it is the product which is on trial, not they. Data collection by logging, on the other hand, is unobtrusive. The user's normal work should be uninterrupted, although permission to record the user's activity should be sought beforehand. Evaluation often uses a mixture of intrusive and unobtrusive techniques. Whatever the aim, evaluation requires a means of data collection and analysis.

9.3.1 Data Collection

Broadly, five approaches to data recording may be followed:

- *Observation.* The evaluator sits beside the users and records what they do by a tape-recorded commentary or writing interaction details on check sheets. This type of recording intrudes on the users because it is difficult to ignore the observer's presence and this can lead to bias if the user is distracted. Evaluation sessions may be video recorded and subsequently analysed by playback for diagnosis and collecting more objective behavioural data from the recorded film. Video recording can be less obtrusive if the camera is hidden behind a one-way screen.
- *Think-aloud protocols.* This technique goes further than observation by asking users to think aloud about what they are doing in terms of mental activity, decisions and reasons for decisions. While this method is intrusive, it is one of the few ways of getting a record of the user's mental activity during interface operation. The data is open to the user's subjective interpretation about what was happening but it can be an invaluable source of data for interpreting the reasons for a mistake. Users vary in their ability to verbally report what they are doing and many facts may be left unsaid, just because the user assumes they are obvious to the evaluator. Protocols also demand considerable concentration so the naturalness of interaction will be affected. With these provisos, protocols can be an effective means of capturing diagnostic data, although full verbal reports are time consuming to decode and analyse.

- *Interviews*. Interviews should be structured so the evaluator has an agenda of questions which are to be answered. The interview may be the main form of evaluation, i.e. the evaluator gathers the users' reactions after they have used a product. Alternatively, interviews may be combined with observation and form a debriefing session after a test session. In this case it is useful to note problems during the session and then follow up the reason for user problems during the debriefing. Post-test interviews can be used with video recording to ask users to 'walk through' problems and explain why a design feature caused a problem. This can be expanded into a retrospective protocol in which the user is asked to think aloud and talk through the recorded interaction.
- *Monitoring*. Interfaces may be monitored by recording the user and systems actions as keyboard, screen and mouse events. Monitoring may be carried out by logging system commands and terminal I/O signals with operating system facilities or by specialised line monitors. Recording the input–output traffic is non-intrusive, as the user should not be disturbed by the measuring. Events then have to be interpreted as user commands and system actions and collated to give reports of interface feature usage, error rates, frequency of command use and duration of usage.

  Monitoring allows objective data to be gathered, although lack of knowledge about the context in which the measures were collected may lead to difficulties in objective interpretation. For instance, even though errors may be detected, the reasons why they occurred are not captured. Users may make a simple slip or a mistake because they do not understand the system. Both appear as single errors on a system log.
- *Questionnaires*. Questionnaires are useful for collecting subjective data and some semi-objective data about users' reactions to a product. This technique is necessary to discover users' attitudes and opinions. Questionnaires can be augmented by interviews to gain further understanding about particular points such as misunderstandings about a dialogue, and difficulties in using an interface. This technique is useful when users are remote and cannot be visited by the evaluator; furthermore, questionnaires are an economical means of getting a large evaluation sample. The main problem is getting a good response without a bias. Offering a reward for filling the questionnaire can help to increase the response rate and to motivate a cross-section of users to reply rather than just a few dissatisfied ones.

  Questionnaires should use either a semantic differential technique in which the questions are posed with prompts on either end of the scale, e.g.

  effectiveness of the help system

	1	2	3	4	5	6	7
useless							very good

Or a scale with the same numeric response scale but an agree/disagree prompt:

command names were consistent throughout the system

	1	2	3	4	5	6	7
disagree							agree

Responses are totalled and represented either as histograms showing the frequency of response in each category, or as a collated score given as a net positive value. This is calculated on a scale of –3 to +3, e.g.:

Clarity of feedback messages

–3	–2	–1	0	1	2	3
0	4	6	10	5	4	1

total responses =30

0	–8	–6	0	5	8	3

net value = +2

(response *x* weighting)

Questionnaires can be used to comprehensively evaluate an interface design (Ravden and Johnson, 1989) by providing a checklist of usability principles against which a design can be measured. However, many usability problems double classify against more than one criterion, so it is not always clear how such checklist questions help in finding the responsible design flaw.

9.3.2 Procedures for Benchmark Evaluations

Benchmark evaluations use quantitative measures to assess the performance of a product against preset usability goals. The steps in a benchmark evaluation are as follows:

1. *Set usability goals*. These will depend on the target market for the product or the profile of use for in-house applications. The characteristics of the target user group and the complexity of the task should be considered when setting goals. The goals become part of the non-functional requirements for the system and in marketing terms may also be critical success factors.
2. *Develop product or prototype for testing*. Benchmarking may be carried out more than once and, if a prototype fails to achieve usability goals,

design improvements indicated by diagnostic evaluation should improve subsequent versions.

3. *Design evaluation tasks*. This can be difficult to get right. On the one hand, a range of tasks is required to test all the systems facilities; on the other hand, too many tasks may test the tolerance of users. A compromise has to be reached in testing the more important aspects of a product if it has a large number of functions.
4. *Select users*. It is important that the users represent the type of people who will use the system during its operational life. Users should be selected for a cross-section of abilities and experience, balanced for age and sex. The more users in an evaluation the better, as more confidence can be expressed in the result.
5. *Carry out evaluation*. Benchmark testing may be done in controlled environments such as usability laboratories equipped with video cameras and one-way viewing screens. Alternatively, contextual testing may be used in the user's workplace. The advantages and disadvantages of each approach were reviewed earlier. Data on task completion times and errors are collected. At the end of the test a questionnaire may be used to collect attitude data.
6. *Analyse results using usability metrics*. These are error counts and task completion times, although more sophisticated metrics can be used, such as errors per unit time and ratio of errors to commands. Several metrics can be found in the documents available from the Esprit MUSIC project (Bevan *et al.*, 1994). Results are compared with the 'gold standard' set for the application. If the product fails to make the grade, the reasons why should be analysed using diagnostic techniques.

A more rigorous form of benchmark evaluation is to use controlled experiments to assess the usability of a design feature or to compare two products for the same task. Experiments control the context and use empirical measures which are objective and quantitative but pay a penalty in that only a small number of features can be tested in any one experiment. Evaluation experiments generally use a between-groups design, e.g.

- Experimental group one – carry out the task with product one.
- Experimental group two – carry out the same task with the second product.
- If possible, it is good practice to include a control group as a baseline for measuring the experimental groups:

  - Control group – carry out the task without either product.

The data collected is the same as for usability benchmarks, e.g. errors and times, although other data may be used, such as frequency of command usage, recall tests of commands, etc. Designing effective experiments is difficult, especially with complex artefacts such as computer systems. The reasons why one product may be better than another can be complex. Commands and other design features are rarely independent of the whole design, so it is difficult to interpret the reason behind quantitative differences between products. Experiments are more powerful when one specific feature of a design has been varied, e.g. to test the effect of ordering options in a menu, one group has ordered options, while the other group has randomly ordered menus. In this case the effectiveness of one design feature can be objectively assessed. Unfortunately, experiments are very expensive in resources so they are rarely used in commercial evaluation. If quantitative measures have been collected, a variety of statistical techniques exist to assess the results. Further details of experimental techniques can be found in Johnson (1992).

Quantitative techniques have their uses but to understand the reasons behind usability problems a combination of techniques is necessary. For instance, it may be found that help screens in a system are rarely used. There are five possible interpretations for this observation:

- Users found the system so easy to use that they rarely needed to refer to the help screens.
- Users found the help screens so good that they only needed to use them once or twice.
- Users found the help screens so bad that they gave up using them after an initial attempt.
- Most users didn't know the help screens were in the system.
- Users found the command to access help screens difficult to use.

To find out the answer to this question, data collected from logs would have to be combined with questionnaire data, and an experiment may be necessary to quantify how useful the help information was.

9.3.3 Procedures for Diagnostic Evaluation

In this case more emphasis is placed on discovering the reasons why a design caused problems for the user. Analysis of data can either be intuitive or quantitative. Objectivity, however, does not just depend on the approach but also on the method of data recording. Three approaches can be employed:

- *Expert judgement.* A human factors expert is employed to assess usability defects. This may be done by simply inspecting the product or by observing users operating the product. The experts make recommendations for design improvements. Design improvement depends on the number of problems discovered by the experts; this in turn is dependent on how thorough (and good) they are.

- *Guidelines and checklists*. Evaluators who are not human factors experts can also use a set of HCI guidelines as checklists (e.g. ISO 9421). A specification may be assessed by inspection or products tested with tasks, using the guidelines either as a means of diagnosing why errors have occurred or as a means of static analysis to ensure the product passes all the guideline recommendations. In the latter case the evaluator (or user) assesses conformance by rating the product on a scale (Ravden and Johnson, 1989). Heuristic evaluation (Nielsen, 1992) may also be used as a diagnostic technique on products. As a means of interpreting errors, guidelines/checklists often produce multiple causal categories for one error, so their power to indicate design improvement may be limited.
- *Walkthroughs*. This approach extends the guideline approach by systematically encouraging the user/evaluator to step through a sequence of actions while testing each step against a list of desirable qualities. Walkthroughs are based on a model of interaction, and this suggests the type of questions which should be asked about the design at specific stages of the walkthrough (see Sutcliffe and Springett, 1992; Lewis *et al.*, 1990).

A typical evaluation session is composed of similar steps to those in benchmark evaluations:

- Design evaluation tasks, prepare evaluation environment.
- Select users, brief them and reassure them that it is the product that is on trial.

During the evaluation session:

- Give users a pretest questionnaire in order to gather data on their background experience and characteristics.
- Provide a training period if users are unfamiliar with the product.
- Run the evaluation session, recording users' problems. Problems often come to light through users' verbalisation, which may not be complimentary about the designer's ability. Problems may be more difficult to detect with quiet or reticent users. Problems should be classified as either:
    - *Critical incidents*: when a user encounters some problem with the design which causes disruption to the normal flow of interaction. Care has to be exercised to ensure that simple pauses for thought are not interpreted as incidents.
    - *Interaction breakdowns*: the completion of the task has to be abandoned because the user cannot find a way to recover from an error or a means to complete the necessary action.

In both cases the design feature associated with the problem should be noted.

- De-brief the user with follow-up questions on the problems noted during the evaluation session. As an optional extra a post-test questionnaire may be used to gather attitude data.

A good set of procedures is given in the York Manual (Wright and Monk, 1989); the manual advises a semi-interventionist policy of asking the user to verbalise the reasons why the design has created a problem when a critical incident or a breakdown has been detected. However, the reasons for errors may be difficult to ascertain, and analytic techniques may be required.

Analysis techniques

The first treatment is to total the error frequencies for each user by design feature. The resulting table can be inspected to discover which design features cause the highest error frequencies. These are the obvious candidates for attention, but the distribution of errors across users should also be inspected. A design feature with a high error frequency may be caused by one or two users making repeated errors. This points towards a feature being a problem for some users, whereas a feature which caused all users to make errors is clearly more problematic. However, if the errors were not repeated, then users may have learned the design rationale or found a way of working around the problem. The real problem is when a feature has high error frequencies for all users. Figure 9.1 shows that the arrows facility for line drawing was the feature most prone to error in use.

Error taxonomies may help understanding of the problem. A simple classification which distinguishes between action and cues for interaction is:

- *Feedback errors*: the system gives no feedback after a user action, so assessing what has happened is difficult.
- *No prompt or cue*: the system contains the action needed by the user but the cue to identify it is absent.
- *Misleading cue*: the system gives an inadequate cue so the user either uses an inappropriate action or uses a system function incorrectly.
- *Missing action*: the system does not possess the required action.
- *Incompatible action*: although the system does have the required function, it does not match the user's model for the action.

	Misleading cue	Expectancy of an action that is not possible	Hidden functionality	Inappropriate functionality	Missing/ ambiguous feedback	Total
Palette selection		5			7	12
Arc				2		2
Freehand				4		4
Polygon					1	1
Palette default	1					1
Copy	1					1
Duplicate	1					1
Flip				2		2
Rotate				1		1
Arrows	18	16	13			47
Grid			1		1	2
Cursor			1		2	3
Drawn objects		2	5		3	10
Text		3			3	16
Layered window	1			1		2
	22	26	21	9	17	95

Figure 9.1 Analysis of MacDraw I errors by design feature and error type.

Classification of errors helps matching design features with usability principles such as consistency, predictability, observability, etc. Taxonomies, however, are limited in their diagnostic power and often give rise to double-classification problems. This is because many errors have multiple causes. Model-based analyses using walkthrough can help with more complex and subtle usability problems. One technique, based on cognitive complexity theory, matches the user's expected model of action and the system model implicit in the dialogue structure (see Figure 9.2). Two goal trees are created; one represents the user's model derived from protocol analysis or interviews; the other is derived from analysis of the command sequence in the product. The two trees are matched to bring out the incompatibilities and suggest changes to the system design.

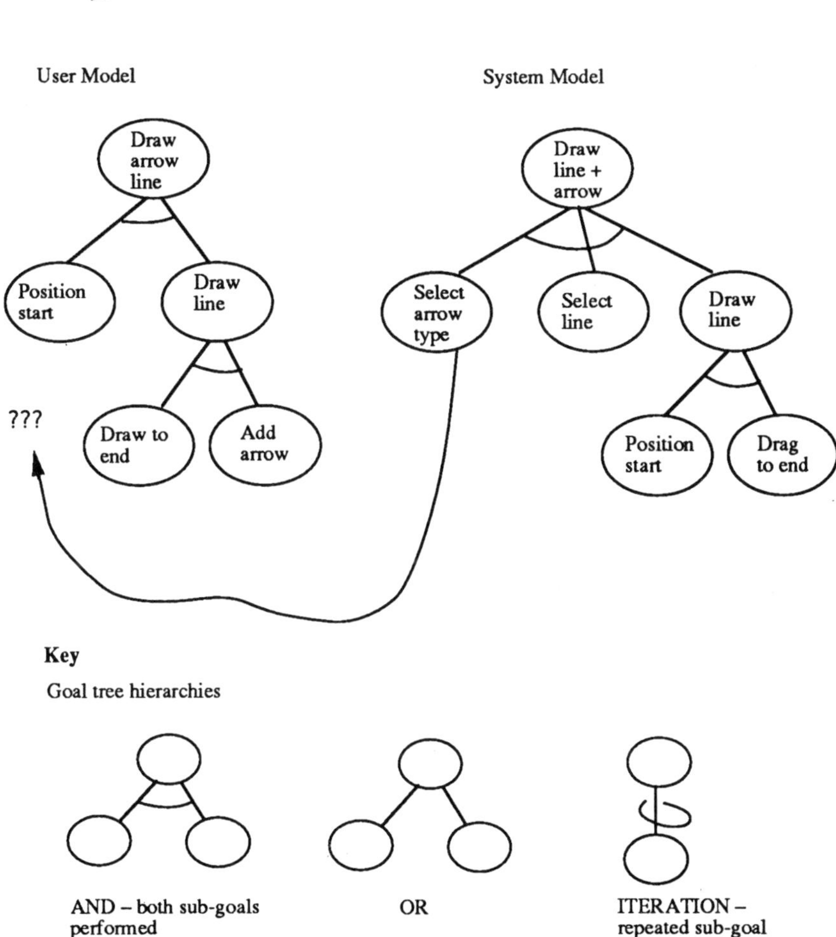

Figure 9.2 User and system models for drawing an arc with an arrow using MacDraw I system feature (from Sutcliffe and Springett, 1992).

Model-based walkthroughs use the cycle of interaction introduced in Chapter 6. The evaluator steps through the task, asking questions at each stage of interaction relating to metaphors, cues and prompts before a user action and then system feedback after the system action (see Figure 9.3). When errors are detected, further questions are triggered about the interpretability of the system state, presence of diagnostic information for the user and cues on how to repair the mistake.

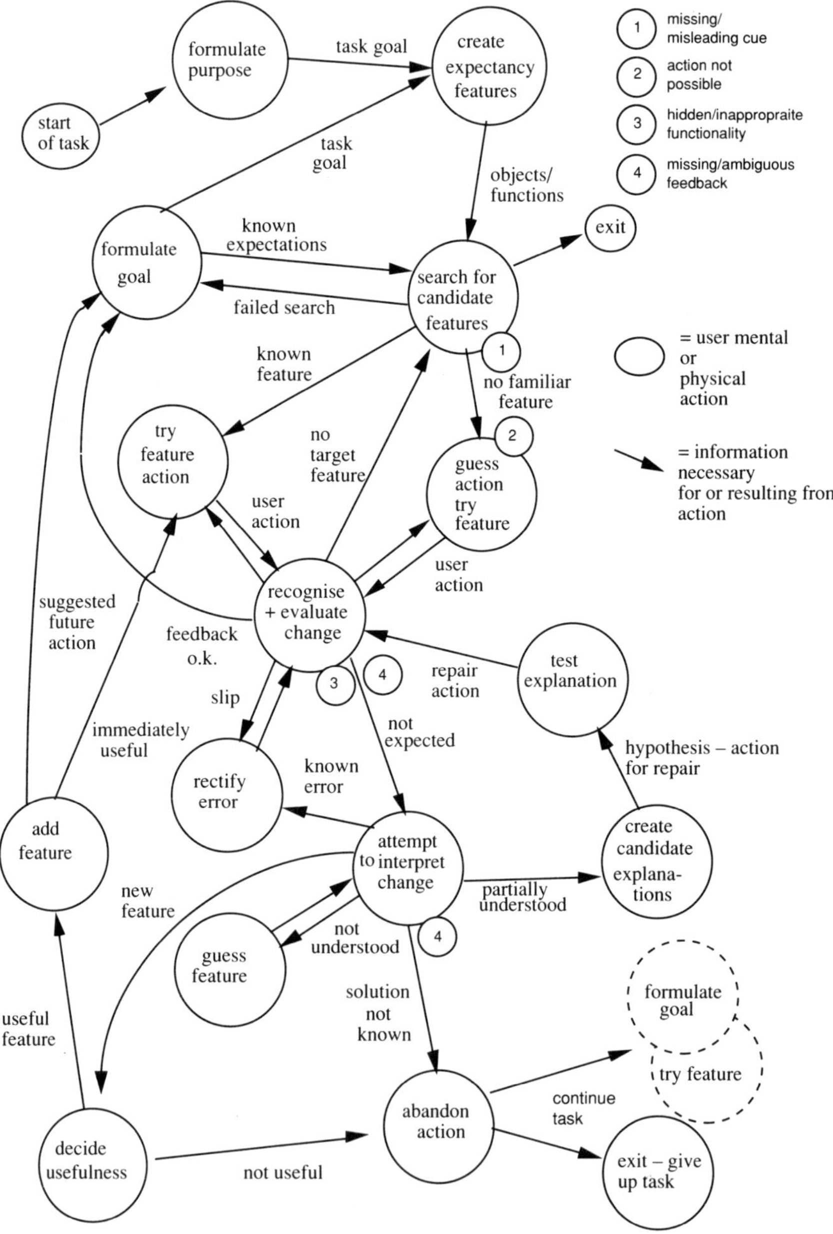

Figure 9.3 Model of direct manipulation interaction with possible error types (from Sutcliffe and Springett, 1992).

The above approaches to evaluation have assumed that a product or, at least, a prototype exists. However, sometimes it may be advantageous to evaluate a design before it is built.

9.3.4 Evaluating Specifications and Designs

Predictive evaluations of this kind apply a series of analytic metrics to assess either complexity of a design and, hence, its propensity for error, or estimated operation time. Complexity analysis techniques specify a dialogue in terms of a grammar and then analyse it for the number of words (i.e. commands) and rules (combinations of commands). The more words and rules a dialogue has, the more complex it is and the more difficult it may be to learn. Techniques in this class are the action grammar of Reisner (1984), Cognitive Complexity Theory (Kieras and Polson, 1985), which uses counts of rules and working memory variables for decisions, and Task Action Grammar (Payne and Green, 1986), which analyses complexity in generality/specificity as well as number of rules in the user's model. CCT and TAG can estimate the complexity of the knowledge which it is necessary for the user to learn but this may not always correlate well with errors in an actual design.

However, these techniques are useful when predicting transfer errors when users have to learn a new, yet similar product. The number of rules in common between the two products, the different rules and overlap/ambiguities between rules can be assessed to predict likely problems. Designers can then try to minimise transfer effects by incorporating cues to warn users of the differences between the products.

Time estimation techniques have been based on GOMS analysis. This breaks activity down into 'unit tasks', which are small atomic actions. The Model Human Processor (see Chapter 2) can be used with a set of idealised timing for each mental activity to estimate the time necessary for each unit task. This technique, known as the keystroke-level model, makes many assumptions, including error-free operation, and has not been widely used as an evaluation technique.

Heuristic evaluation is probably the most effective technique for early evaluation even though it is simple. This 'quick and dirty' technique uses a list of eight usability principles, yet it trapped 70% of the errors found by experts. Empirical studies of usability evaluations have demonstrated that 70–80% of the serious interface 'bugs' can be eliminated by quite simple techniques (Nielsen, 1993b). Although HCI experts do detect more problems, non-experts can find most problems even when equipped with simple checklists. Adding more experts or more evaluators demonstrates a law of diminishing returns, in the 80/20% tradition, i.e. most of the errors are found with modest effort. Experience suggests that 4–5 evaluators find most usability bugs. Even though all quality assurance costs money, there is no excuse for not employing these simple yet effective techniques.

9.4 Summary

The selection of recording techniques, approach and analysis techniques depends on the evaluator's objectives. While benchmark measures can give an overall impression of an interface's usability, finding out why an interface has usability problems is often more complicated. Evaluations, in conclusion, can be done simply to get an overall impression of how good an interface is, and observations can be inspected intuitively to diagnose problems; but teasing apart the reasons why an interface design is poor is more difficult.

Quality in HCI is a complex of utility and usability. Utility is related to system functionality and requirements analysis. Usability is a non-functional requirement for human performance in system operation. Good utility is delivered by accurate specification and creative design; this is assessed by prototype testing, simulation and functional validation. Usability is decomposed into effectiveness, learnability and memorability. These are assessed by metrics based on errors, task completion times and comprehension tests. Acceptability and user's satisfaction with a product covers both usability and utility.

Data collection can be by observation of users testing a product. Sessions may be videoed for subsequent analysis, or users may be asked to think out aloud to give explanations about problems. Monitoring techniques are less intrusive but miss out much context data, which can make interpretation of results more difficult. Questionnaires are essential for attitude data and useful for obtaining large data samples.

Evaluation can have two main motivations, to benchmark a product for quality assurance or to diagnose design problems. Benchmark evaluation starts by setting usability goals. Tests are then conducted with representative users to determine whether the goals have been attained. Diagnosis uses different techniques to focus on the reasons behind detected user problems. Error taxonomies, guidelines-checklists, walkthroughs and model-based analysis all help pinpoint errors and understanding of their causality in a design. The outcome of diagnostic evaluation is recommendation for design improvements. Early evaluation techniques assess specifications for complexity of rule sets and predicted interaction times. These techniques have not proved very useful; however, heuristic evaluation, employing a simple set of HCI principles, has been shown to be an effective technique for trapping HCI design errors.

Further Reading

Usability engineering (Nielsen, 1993b) covers usability concepts and different types of evaluation, with an emphasis on heuristic techniques. Checklist-type evaluation is described in detail by Ravden and Johnson (1989), while data collection and observational techniques are covered by Wright and Monk

(1989). Whitefield *et al.* (1991) give a useful framework for different types of evaluation.

Questions and Exercises

1. Assess the usability of a software product you are familiar with. Word processors or spreadsheet packages are good experimental material. Construct evaluation tasks and test the product following the procedure outlined in this chapter. You may concentrate on diagnostic or benchmark-type evaluation.

2. Discuss the concepts of usability and how these can be measured. Could you recommend any improvement in assessment of flexibility or adaptability of a product?

3. Can usability be assessed in absolute terms (i.e. $x\%$ for a product)? Critically examine what benchmark usability assessment means and how it should be interpreted.

4. How does utility relate to usability? Can utility of a product be assessed and, if so, how independent of usability will the assessment be?

5. Discuss the advantages and disadvantages of contextual evaluation and usability laboratories. Include a review of different data collection techniques in your answer and describe how these may be appropriate for contextual evaluation of lab-based evaluation.

10 Intelligent User Interfaces

In this chapter the application of intelligent processing to user interfaces is considered. Intelligence can be used for controlling interaction as in adaptive interfaces, or for making the system's response to the user more appropriate for co-operative interaction. Intelligence can be applied to support the design process, although this is still a research area in HCI. Another use is in intelligent help and explanation systems. As computer systems become more complex, the need for self-explanation becomes more pressing, while in knowledge-based systems, explanation facilities have been a standard design feature for many years. All explanation systems pose problems in dialogue control and this represents the main HCI challenge. They also demonstrate the problems inherent in trying to make user–system dialogues more natural by understanding questions in natural language and then trying to plan appropriate replies. Dialogue acts are reviewed as a means of delivering more sophisticated control beyond the user-action/system response cycle found in most dialogues.

The intelligent user interface introduces planning into interaction. Instead of the interface simply reacting to the user in a sequence of questions and answers, the system tries to look ahead and plan a series of interactions towards a goal. The goal, of course, is concerned with usability, be it adapting to the user, understanding their needs or providing more feedback by explanation. Planning also involves looking back into the dialogue history and using this information to choose an appropriate response. Finally, planning depends on more knowledge both of the user and of the application, in order first to analyse the context of interaction and then select future strategies. All this requires rules, planning algorithms and knowledge bases. This chapter does not cover the implementation issues of intelligent user interfaces (see Further Reading); instead, the objective is to investigate intelligent systems for their implications in design and dialogue control.

10.1 Explanation

Explanation started in response to a debugging problem in expert systems. It is often not clear why a conclusion is reached and explanation facilities were developed to help users and knowledge engineers understand the system's reasoning. The classic pioneer was MYCIN, an expert system (Clancey and Shortliffe, 1984) which diagnosed blood disorders. The system could explain its conclusions according to the rules which had been fired and their antecedents. Questions could be answered of the type:

- *How* a result was arrived at; this produced a trace of rule activation.
- *Why* a conclusion was reached; this listed the antecedents, the facts which trigger the IF (condition) part of the rule.

This, however, soon proved inadequate, as users wanted to ask questions about the reasoning strategy. Unfortunately, this knowledge was only possessed by the designer and once embedded in the structure of rules and variables it was lost. The next step in NEOMYCIN (Richter and Clancey, 1985) was to add that knowledge about knowledge (called meta-knowledge) to support explanation. This provided more sophisticated answers to why-type questions. A further development in the GUIDON programme was addition of meta-knowledge about the reason strategies employed and the knowledge types, and then visualising the rule trace execution in GUIDON-WATCH (Richter and Clancey, 1985).

Research in explanation facilities continues and as knowledge-based systems become more complex the challenges of explaining ever more sophisticated reasoning makes explanation a necessity.

Explanation, however, is not limited to expert systems. A wide variety of stand-alone and embedded uses exist, e.g.:

- *Co-operative advisory systems*: in these, explanation is the *raison d'ètre.* Advisory systems arise in many applications when knowledge rather than just information is required. For instance, in tourist information systems an answer to a question of what to do on a rainy day will only be available if the designer indexed the information for the question. Explanation-based advisory systems infer what information is appropriate.
- *Information services*: as part of information retrieval many libraries provide a question answering service. These use human intelligence at present; in the future machine-based explanation may be used.

Embedded applications may involve explanation of a design and information about the domain of an application:

- *Intelligent help systems*: these are related to explanation facilities, but also aim to provide appropriate information for the user's needs in a given context, i.e. the task he or she is carrying out in an application.
- *Explanation facilities*: these have been covered above, but it is worth noting that as the division between knowledge-based systems and standard information systems becomes blurred, explanation will become a standard 'help' facility.
- *Computer-based training*: when instructional programs advance beyond a simple scripted tutorial, explanation is necessary to answer questions about justification, etc. (e.g. why should I do it this way?).
- *Design critics*: in computer-based design environments, be they for soft-

ware design (CASE tools) or otherwise, explanation is necessary to point out what may be wrong in a design and how it may be improved.

This is just a small sample of the possible range of explanation systems. It does, however, beg the question, 'what is explanation'?

10.2 Explanation and Instruction

Ultimately explanation lies in the gap between data retrieval, i.e. simple provision of information, and teaching, i.e. purposeful, planned instruction with set learning objectives. Defining the boundaries accurately is difficult. Suffice it to say that explanation is concerned with the following issues:

- *Appropriate information.* The information that is delivered should fit the user's need. This raises the problem of understanding the need either as a direct question or by inferring that need from the user's action and context.
- *Effective delivery.* The explanation should be generated in a medium that makes it easy to comprehend. This involves user modelling to ensure the recipient does not get too much or too little information.
- *Problem solving.* Frequently the need will be expressed as a problem, so the generated explanation has to solve the problem by providing some information. This brings in the need to reason about the user's problem.

Explanation is therefore about added value beyond data retrieval, but it stops short of having a purposeful teaching plan. It is in the business of short-term instruction; learning may indeed be an objective, so explanation systems share many components with Intelligent Tutoring Systems (ITS).

10.2.1 Types of Explanation

The need for explanation is as diverse as the increasing spread of computer-based applications. However, explanations can be divided into categories according to the subject matter of what is to be explained. Many systems will, of course, have a mixture of these types:

- *Conceptual explanation.* Concepts are in themselves aggregations of facts which describe something about the world. For instance, the concept of a solar system consists of a complex of facts describing the sun, planets, orbit of the planets, laws of gravity to explain orbits, and so on. A conceptual model linking the facts and relationships is required as the knowledge base from which the explanation can be generated. Conceptual explanation can become complex, depending on the subject matter.

- *Causal explanation.* Causation implies a need to know how or why something happened. This type of explanation may be about natural systems, e.g. why chemical reactions occur involves knowledge of the chemicals and chemical laws to explain a reaction. Causal implications are about events and the reasons why events happen. This is often linked to concepts, e.g. what causes the planets to revolve around the sun requires knowledge of the laws of gravity and momentum.
- *Contrastive explanation.* In this case the need is to discover how or why something is different from a reference object, action or concept. Generating the answer may be simple if the difference is at the descriptive level, but it may be very complex at the conceptual level.
- *Task-based explanation.* Requests for tasks, procedures or responses to any how-to-do type question need task-based explanation. This may be simpler than causal and conceptual explanation as answer generation requires less reasoning. Procedures are step-by-step sequences of actions, as in the schema of Task Knowledge Structures (see Chapter 3). However, complexity can arise when questions refer to the task goals and objects involved.
- *Descriptive explanation.* This satisfies requests for information about objects and their relationships, and is the simplest type. Requests for attributes are close to information retrieval; however, explanation involving relationships, e.g. location, contents and time, are usually beyond standard database retrieval languages.

Taxonomies of explanation inevitably run into problems. Task-based explanations may be about human action or how a machine operates. Machine operation could be interpreted as causation if it is viewed from the effect produced. The categories, however, do give some view of the scope of explanation systems. Most systems to date are capable of descriptive and task-based explanation with limited capabilities for causal and contrastive explanation. Having considered, albeit briefly, what constitutes explanation, we now turn to the components found in explanation systems.

10.3 Conceptual Architecture for Explanation Systems

The system has first to acquire the user's request, then retrieve or construct the answer, and finally deliver it in an appropriate manner. In addition, the system has to maintain a coherent dialogue with the user, so that questions can be linked and followed up, and the conversation controlled by the user. Many of these issues are associated with natural language processing, so considerable research in explanation is motivated by natural language dialogues. Space precludes a comprehensive review of these problems.

The architecture of a 'typical' explanation system is summarised in Figure 10.1. This view does not reflect a design or implementation; instead it

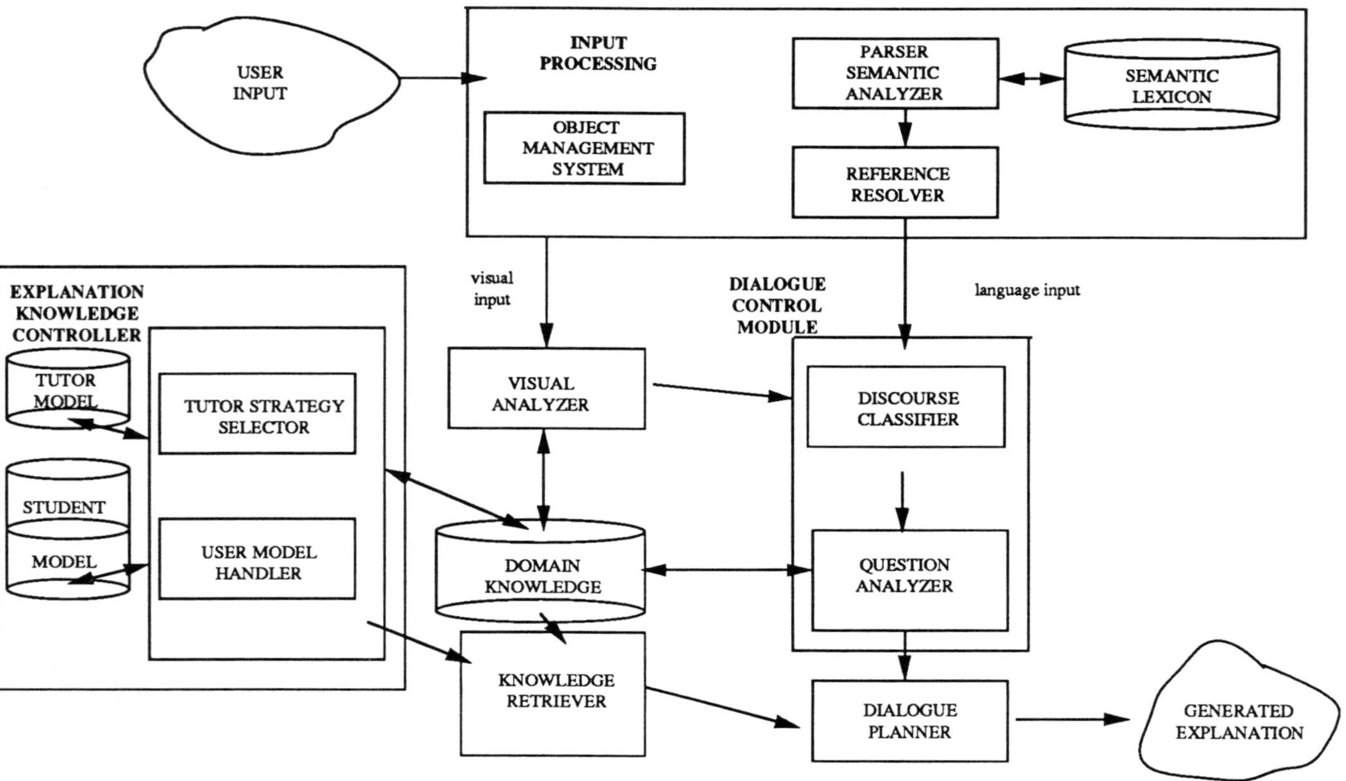

Figure 10.1 Architecture of an explanation system showing processing components and models (from IDEAL project).

summarises possible functional components. The design problems for each component are described in more detail below.

10.3.1 Question Analysis

Understanding users' needs in natural language is not easy. A common approach (see Maybury, 1990) is to use question taxonomies and map natural language input to a particular question type. Many taxonomies have been produced (see Gilbert, 1987; Maybury, 1990; Sarantinos and Johnson, 1991), leading to definitions such as:

- *Procedure*: 'how to do it' questions about tasks, action and operation, e.g. 'how do I address an electronic mail message?' Note that the answer to this question requires not only procedure of how to operate an e-mail system but also object-descriptive knowledge about e-mail addresses.
- *States*: 'what happens, or has happened' questions about the link between actions in procedures and the effect these have on objects and the world, e.g. 'what happens if I cancel a message?' The answer to this may be that it is deleted or that cancellation is not possible as it has already been transmitted. Sub-types in this category are about the consequence of action and the possibility of future states.
- *Time*: 'when, how long' questions about points in time and duration, and frequency, e.g. 'when does the next train leave for Manchester?' Again the answer may not be so easy to generate; it will depend in this case on whether the user is in, say, London or Bristol.
- *Location*: 'where' questions, that may have sub-types about pathways between objects, problems of proximity, adjacency, e.g. 'where is the station for Manchester?' The answer may require knowledge of where the user is now in order to issue appropriate directions, as well as knowledge that Manchester trains depart from Euston station in London.
- *Attributive*: 'what and which' questions, about object properties, e.g. 'What is the cost of a ticket from London to Manchester?' As well as requests for properties of objects such as colour, weight, size, value, etc., there are more complex sub-types such as composition, which require knowledge about sub-components of an object or possibly the materials from which it was constructed.
- *Contrastive and evaluative*: questions which all require some test of an object's properties, e.g. 'Is the train the quickest way of getting to Manchester?' Sub-type questions may imply the need to assess the similarity or difference between two objects, to evaluate an object's properties, or find out whether something is the same (equality).
- *Identity and category*: 'who' questions about people or 'what/which' questions about an instance of an object, e.g. 'what is the flight number for

the next plane to Manchester?' A further sub-type is to ask what set or category an object belongs to.
- *Justification*: 'why' questions implying an answer that explains the motivation and reason for action, e.g. 'why should I travel by plane?', which may generate the answer that it is quicker, although more expensive. Answering complex justification questions implies some analysis of a person's motivation and requires a sophisticated user model.

There are many permutations on question categories. Most taxonomies run into difficulties because there may be differences between the surface form of a question and the implied answer, e.g. 'Why is the order of the address important?', in an e-mail system The apparent question is a matter of justification for the address order, user-id, location, domain; however, further knowledge may be necessary if the context of the question related to the differences between addresses in the UK and elsewhere. In the latter case the UK is the wrong way round compared with the rest of the world; addresses start with the country and work inwards, e.g. me@uk.ac.city, whereas everyone else starts locally and works outwards, as me@mydept.myuniversity.uk. This sort of problem led to question and answer types with mapping rules between them. This partially solves the problem but there is no escape from the need to analyse the context in question analysis and answering using natural language. Not surprisingly, given the complexity of such an endeavour, many explanation systems take the easier way out by menus of question types such as fill-in templates; see Figure 10.2.

If free format language is being used, even recognising the appropriate question and answer types can be challenging. English and most other natural languages allow questions to be posed in different ways even though the intention is the same:

- Which way are messages read?
- How can I read my mail?
- Can I read messages?

These questions all refer to a procedure for reading electronic mail messages, although their syntactic form is different. Mapping to the answer type in this example is not too difficult, as they all require information about the procedure 'read' with the object 'mail' or 'messages'.

10.3.2 Answer Generation

Answers require domain knowledge, that is knowledge about the problem domain of the explanation system. That knowledge may be an expert system, or a database with an intelligent extraction process. The component holding information for answers is called the Domain Knowledge Base.

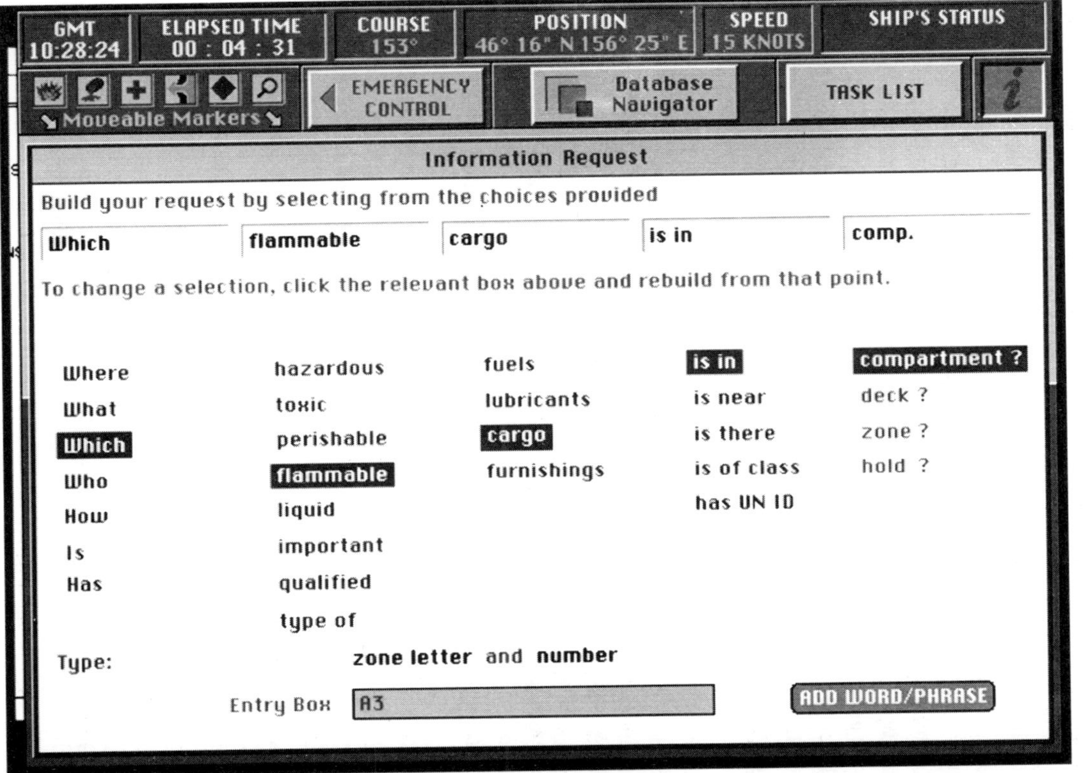

Figure 10.2 Question interface showing a menu-driven/template approach for formulating specific question types (What, Where, When, etc.) (from INTUITIVE project).

Constructing the answer, as can be guessed from the discussion of analysing the question, is not trivial. The easy approach is to use canned text, or pre-defined answers. This makes answer generation a simple matter of data retrieval, but it does not allow much flexibility, so the system appears to be unnatural. The next level of ambition is to compose answers from predesigned fragments or to fill in answer templates with details. This level requires composition rules for fragments of canned text and a customisation process. Even so, answers in the knowledge base have to be designed, which limits the system's flexibility to the designer's foresight in anticipating the user's questions. The third and final level of ambition is to generate the answers automatically at run-time by inference. As the answers come in a knowledge representation format, they have to be changed into something more palatable for users by natural language generation.

Answer generation by inference involves the complexity of knowledge-based systems themselves. Generally the scope of questions the system can answer is limited by three factors:

- The *domain knowledge*: the scope of any intelligent system depends on the depth of its knowledge, usually about a small part of the world.
- The *domain meta-knowledge*: how much the system knows about its own knowledge, strategies and reasoning abilities.
- The *inference engine:* the structure of the underlying KBS critically determines how it can explain phenomena. For instance, if case-based reasoning is employed, then typical examples can be generated, while abductive reasoning may support explanation about causality and states.

The state of the art in current systems is to generate answers with some flexibility for a restricted number of question types in a limited domain. Customising the answer is possible by user models, and some tailoring of answers to the preceding dialogue can be effected using a dialogue history (Cawsey, 1993). Domain knowledge and sophisticated answer generation belong more properly to the realm of artificial intelligence approaches to explanation. Further details can be found in Moore and Swartout (1989, 1991).

10.3.3 Planning Explanation Sessions

Some explanation systems have an instructional purpose and these approach the complexity of intelligent tutoring systems. The view of what an explanation is extends beyond a simple question and answer to a conversation directed towards a learning purpose. Three models are important for this endeavour:

- *Expert tutor model*: this contains strategies of how to explain and teach, for instance when to use examples, use of analogy, testing the student's knowledge. A simple strategy would be:

- Assess user's current knowledge.
- Explain background to the problem.
- Explain problem detail.
- Test user's understanding.
- Follow up with further explanation if necessary.

Tutor models can become lesson plans in ITS systems, and imply the need for a user model. Tutor models come in several types. Generic tutors have strategies for creating explanation sessions. More domain-specific versions have rules and tactics to dictate the explanation content, i.e. what domain knowledge should be delivered, and when, during a session. Finally, some tutors have knowledge about mistakes as well as good knowledge. These 'buggy' models can detect a user's mistakes and take remedial action.

- *User or student model*: this describes the user's current knowledge or at least the system's best guess about what this may be. Student models are used to influence tutoring plans. This may be done at global level by setting the sophistication of the explanation to 'novice' or 'expert' or, if the model holds a partial replica of the domain model, it can be used to plan what explanation content should be delivered next. In the latter case the system has to track the user's assimilation of knowledge. This can be tricky. If the system assumes that, having presented some facts, the user will have learned them, then it runs foul of misunderstanding. On the other hand, if the system rigorously quizzes the user after each explanation to ensure it knows how much the user knows, then it risks alienating the user by endless questions. There is no easy way out of this dilemma.

  User, or student models as they are known in ITSs, are either stereotype or overlaid. Stereotypes are non-updateable views of the type of user (e.g. novice, expert), whereas overlays allow updating so that the model reflects more accurately the user's progress during an explanation session. User models are updated by diagnostic modules which either ask the user questions to test their understanding, or track their interaction to assess performance in some task. In this way, error data can be used to decide what should be re-explained.

- *Domain model*: this holds subject matter to be explained; hence, is really the expert's knowledge of the domain. However, it is customary to separate the expert's strategies for delivering knowledge (i.e. instructional strategies) from the subject matter to be taught.

Domain knowledge, tutor and student models are the holy trinity components on which many an intelligent tutoring system has been based. Recently this conception has been questioned (Elsom-Cook, 1990) and more contextual or situational approaches have been proposed in which the user's understanding is promoted by guided discovery. For more on this debate and tutoring systems in general Wenger (1987), Self (1988) and Elsom-Cook (1990) will keep the interested well occupied.

Explanation systems have used many of the concepts drawn from the ITS field but the need for a long-range tutoring plan is less vital in explanation. Tutoring and user modelling tend to be realised as rules to control contextual responses. A good example is Cawsey's (1993) FUDGE system, which explained electrical components. This embedded response rules depending on the user actions, such as:

- If user makes a mistake, then re-explain topic with an example.
- If the user has already received explanation on the topic, try using an analogy.

Rules allow the system to generate a flexible response within a session and also allow the system to direct the overall course of an explanation towards a training goal. However, response requires some notion of the explanation dialogue.

10.3.4 Explanation Dialogues

The user interface component has to deal with several problems:

- Delivering the explanation content in an appropriate manner. This can be part of the multimedia presentation problem as described in Chapter 7. Selection rules are used to choose the most appropriate means of presenting knowledge of a certain type.
- Handling users' questions and interruptions, for clarification and cutting short an overelaborate explanation.
- Keeping track of the explanation at different levels. This involves managing the focus of a conversation which may be diverted. For example, during an explanation of sending an e-mail message, the user interrupts and asks a question about addresses. The system has to deal with the answer and then resume the planned explanation session where it left off.

Dialogue control for intelligent interaction becomes more complicated than just a sequence of user and system acts. The conversation has to be planned and controlled in a more sophisticated manner using dialogue acts and topic focus maintenance. These concepts are borrowed from linguistics and partially from sociological treatments of dialogue in conversation analysis. *Dialogue acts* are pragmatic-level units of language, corresponding to a whole sentence or just a phrase or single word. These are functional units of communication which achieve some goal and are derived from speech acts (Searle, 1969) defining the effect of communication as follows:

- *Locutory acts*: direct speech acts which convey meaning within the speech itself.
- *Illocutory acts*: indirect speech acts when the meaning has to be interpreted by reference to some context information.
- *Perlocutory acts*: when some request for action is made, e.g. a command.

Dialogue acts are useful concepts for planning and controlling more complex human–computer conversations. Each act has a definition and an effect clause describing the communicative function that the act should achieve.

A sample of dialogue acts for an explanation system follows:

- *Inform*. Giving information, transmission of facts by the explainer to the listener, e.g. 'your mail directory contains all the messages which have been sent to you'.
  Effect: information is acquired by the receiver who did not previously have the information.
- *Report*. An Inform which has an external, perceivable referent illustrating an action/event in the outside world, e.g. 'Ctrl-C has halted the process'.
  Effect: as for 'inform' except that the receiver is able to comprehend some event in the real world and relate this to information given verbally by the speaker.
- *Request*. Seeking information; usually direct questions with wh* markers (why, when, where, which, what, who) or verb inversion (can I ...?), although occasionally detected by prosody (voice tonality).
  Effect: the receiver understands that the speaker wants the receiver to pass the information to him/her.
- *Check*. Testing understanding; seeking clarification, or recapitulation or summarisation of the explanation. These are short phrases often prefixed by markers, e.g. 'So...when...' and are not syntactically interrogative apart from rhetorical questions 'So to send it's 's', isn't it ?'
  Effect: The receiver understands that the speaker wants the receiver to confirm their understanding of some previously communicated information.
- *Confirm*. Affirming a state of knowledge held by the listener to be true, e.g. 'Yeah', 'Right', 'Okay'. Direct confirms happen after questions (Requests) and Checks.
  Effect: In this case the speaker wants the receiver to understand that their belief states are the same.
- *Deny*. Negation of a proposition; communication that the facts just communicated are not held to be true; disagree; the converse of confirm.
  Effect: this is the opposite of confirm. In this case the speaker wants the receiver to understand that their belief states are not the same.

- *Continue.* Utterances which cannot be categorised as other acts but serve to maintain the smooth flow of conversation by conveying the listener's attention to the explainer, e.g. 'Yeah', 'yep', 'aha', 'okay'.
  Effect: The receiver is aware that the other party is attending and wishes to continue the dialogue.

Other acts are *Command* (someone to do some action), *Propose* (a course of action), and *Correct* (a misunderstanding).

The acts can be grouped for delivering explanation (Informs, Report); and illocutory–perlocutory acts associated with conversational control, testing understanding (Request, Check, Confirm, Deny, Correct); steering the general course of explanatory dialogues (Continue, Propose); and invoking action by the listener (Command).

Further acts can be defined for other types of conversation such as *Agree, Disagree, Support* (suggestion) in negotiation. Acts can then be combined into pairs called 'moves' and longer sequences or 'exchanges'. These can then be used for planning the system's response in a dialogue, i.e. if user act of type Check is detected, then respond by a Confirm/Deny or Inform as the situation warrants.

Dialogue acts can be used at two levels. The acts already described function to control conversations, but say little about the content of the dialogue. A second, deeper level of acts is derived from functional theories of language, such as Rhetorical Structure Theory (Mann and Thompson, 1988). This theory was designed as a means of planning text to achieve particular communicative effects, and has a set of dialogue components such as Motivate, Justify, Elaborate (detail), Enable (procedure), Condition and Result. In all, 22 components are defined in RST to describe how the context of a text can be structured to deliver the required information context or achieve the desired effect in the listener. RST components have been tailored as dialogue acts for planning in several explanations systems, e.g. Sarantinos and Johnson (1991), Maybury (1990) and Moore and Swartout (1989, 1991).

The planning utility in acts comes in regular associations between pairs of acts and even longer sequences. Conversation analysis (Sacks *et al.*, 1974) proposed that people take regular types of conversation turns, e.g. speaker 1 makes an assertion and speaker 2 either agrees or disagrees; speaker 1 suggests a course of action, speaker 2 agrees. These conversational adjacency pairs show regular patterns in human–human conversation. Although this research described the nature of interaction between people, it can be applied in user–computer dialogues. In explanation, the dialogue triplet (Inform-Respond-Clarify) was used by Cawsey to control exchanges between the user and the system.

For controlling explanation, the moves for the dialogue acts given above might be:

System act → *precedes* →	*User act*
Inform	Continue
Inform	Check (clarification follow-up)
Check	Confirm (system clarifies its understanding)
Propose	Agree (course of action)

User act → *precedes* →	*System act*
Request	Inform
Request	Check (question not clear)
Check	Confirm (user clarifies their belief)
Check	Deny (system lets user know their belief is not true)

Dialogue acts are combined with topic focus to keep track of an explanation. Topic focus can be the subject matter of the explanation itself, e.g. the objects and actions in procedural explanation such as sending and reading electronic mail, messages, files, folders and directories. Another focus is on the explanation goals held by the system. This allows the system to keep a trace of its past explanations and the reasoning behind them. The trace of a dialogue session is kept in a Dialogue (or Discourse) History. This holds all the user and system acts in sequence with details of the act contents. Dialogue histories are important for planning follow up questions, e.g. 'can you tell me more about networks?', and for tracing links between questions and topics already explained, e.g. 'how does saving a message differ from putting it in a folder?' Processing anaphora and ellipsis in natural language, such as 'tell me more about it', also makes use of dialogue histories to backtrack to find out what 'it' refers to in a previous question or reply.

Dialogue acts and topic focus can be used with user models to generate extended, co-operative answers. Many explanation systems provide a simple answer; however, the user may appreciate more background information; for instance, in a train-enquiry system:

> 'When is the next train to Cambridge?' may be answered by the simple statement that the next train is at 4.30, assuming the system knew the time was 4.00. A more co-operative answer could be generated if the system had knowledge that the user wanted detailed answers, and the topic was a general enquiry giving information that there is a regular service every hour, the journey lasts about 1 hour 10 minutes and the standard fare is £10.

Explanation systems have been developed for co-operative answering of follow-up questions, e.g. 'Huh?' indicating a misunderstood reply (Swartout, 1983; Moore and Swartout, 1991); and dialogue act planning has been used in several explanation systems to plan responses in appropriate media, depending on the communicative need and the domain knowledge to be delivered (Feiner and McKeown, 1990; Andre and Rist, 1990). Explanation remains a subject for considerable further research; current commercial applications are still limited to basic explanation facilities in expert systems.

10.4 Intelligent Help Systems

These share many of the problems and components of explanation systems, but there are subtle differences. Help systems have to diagnose what has gone wrong with interaction and then provide information to advise the user how to recover from the situation. Hence there is less emphasis on question answering, as help is either invoked directly by the user or indirectly by the system's detecting a mistake. Answer generation is more constrained by the task and operational nature of computer systems. Higher order causal and conceptual type explanations are not so necessary. Intelligent help systems have the further advantage that the system can track the user through the user-system dialogue. This allows easier updating of user models; however, inferring what a user needs from keystrokes is still a severe problem.

Intelligent help systems have a similar architecture to explanation systems but with some important differences:

- *Dialogue Manager*. The help system faces the same problem of conversation control. Direct user access by menus has to be interleaved with system initiative when a mistake is detected. The help repair conversation has to be integrated with the main user-system dialogue. Most help systems still use canned texts, with some template-based approaches. Ideally natural language generation should be available.
- *User Models*. These are vital in help systems for the generation of the appropriate response. Two models are maintained. First is a task model describing the user's goals, and the expected steps in the user-system dialogue to achieve each task goal. This model is therefore partly a model of the application held by the help system. It is used to track the user's dialogue and to make sure that help is context sensitive, i.e. the help text relates to the dialogue step in hand. Second there is the standard user model characterising the user's experience, where errors have been made, usage profile of commands, and so on. This information is used to tailor help responses, by adding more or less detail. More sophisticated systems can plan what sort of information to give an individual user and the most effective strategies for remediation, e.g. worked examples.

- *Diagnostic Module*. Intelligent help has to analyse the user's mistakes and try to come to the rescue. Diagnosis is attempting to infer the reason for an error which can occur at different levels, e.g.

  - *Lexical slips, typos and spelling mistakes*. These are simple to fix and present no problem. The system may even attempt to correct them automatically, e.g. mistyped commands.
  - *Syntactic errors*. These are commands typed in the wrong order or attempting to carry out illegal manipulation in a graphical user interface. Syntactic errors can be corrected by giving the user the correct template for the command.
  - *Semantic errors*. These occur when the user wants to carry out an action and is unable to do so to his or her satisfaction. Detecting these errors may be difficult as often nothing appears to be amiss.

  The diagnosis module has to track user interaction and attempt to guess when things are going wrong. A strong task model helps, but in general-purpose applications (e.g. graphics-drawing packages and word processors) this may not be present. Some detection can be driven from command sequences which are not completed, user escapes from sequences, undos and by counting illegal pointing actions in GUIs. These suggest that the user is trying to select the unselectable, but unfortunately the GUI does not usually respond, leaving the user with no explanation. Another strategy, borrowed from ITS, is to have 'buggy rules' in the system to detect typical errors. These have the form:

  If <error context> then suggest <reason for error, repair advice>

  The error context is taken from the events logged by the help systems and any error codes returned by the application. The diagnosis module has to decide when to intervene. When errors are detected this is not difficult, but getting system initiatives right for semantic-level errors is another of the HCI dilemmas. Too much intervention makes the system appear to be overbearing to the user; too little intervention means it fails in its purpose to help.

- *Remediation-repair Planner*. Having decided that something is wrong the intelligent help system has to plan the explanation to correct the problem. Diagnosis often requires inferring the link between the state of the computer system and user action. Contextual analysis can make the repair job easier. For instance, if the user's attempt to select an icon always happens after a certain action then this may be a problem of the system's not giving feedback that the action is complete, and the user therefore selecting the icon to try again.

Repair is not too difficult to plan for lexical and syntactic errors, although the system should explain the nature of the error to the user with a corrective action. Use of system-demonstrated examples is an effective technique. Repair of semantic-level errors is dependent on the wealth of the diagnostic information. Frequently, only the identity of the system function or command can be given. In this case the repair module has to plan a mini-explanation tutorial, by explaining the function, running the application to demonstrate an example or giving an analogy, etc. If more detailed diagnosis is available, then planning follows rules for procedural explanation and the repair points the user towards the necessary precondition for an action, the commands necessary for a goal, or the post-condition state of the system after a certain action.

Intelligent help systems are still an active area of research. So far they have made little impact on mainstream systems; however, as their close relative, diagnostic expert systems have been reasonably successful; intelligent help and explanation may become a standard part of future interface design. An excellent summary of one of the most influential projects in this area, EUROHELP, can be found in Breuker (1990).

10.5 Adaptive and Intelligent Interfaces

One of the central dilemmas of interface design is how to satisfy the conflicting demands of different users, in particular novices and experts. Novices require easy-to-use, supportive dialogues; experts, on the other hand, need quick, efficient dialogues with less support. However, with practice, most novices become experts. The choice is whether to adapt or not to adapt.

Adaptability in interfaces unfortunately implies change to some part of an interface design. Change offends the consistency principle and makes the user less sure of the interface, to say nothing of having to relearn parts of it as it changes. The quest to solve this problem led to the notion of adaptive interfaces. The problem is threefold:

- Assessing the user in order to determine when to change; the interface must monitor the user so it can determine that the novice is now an expert. This is the user-modelling problem.
- Adapting the dialogue so that it responds to changes in the users' needs.
- Making sure the quantity and type of change does not cause too much inconsistency in the interface design.

One simple approach to the first problem is to let users decide about their needs. Users are good judges of their skills; therefore, if an interface has a level switch built in to change the sophistication of the interface design, then users can elect when to switch the interface into expert mode. Unfortunately switches of style tend to create considerable inconsistency because a new dialogue style is suddenly presented to the user. Since the new style has to be learned, this can discourage people from changing levels.

In spite of this, adaptation by extending the system functionality, and hence the commands available at the interface, has been successfully demonstrated in the training-wheels approach (Carroll, 1990). The training-wheels metaphor comes from children's bicycles with steadying outrider wheels. Applied to interface design, the user is presented at first with functionality just sufficient to get the main tasks done (e.g. simple text entry and editing in word-processing). Complex functions are hidden until the user has mastered the basics, then the rest of the functionality is exposed in a layered approach. This form of adaptation may be controlled by the users themselves or semi-automatically by system monitoring.

If adaptation is not user driven then the problem is how to measure the user's abilities. This presents the same problems as any evaluation (see Chapter 9), compounded by the limitation that the interface can only collect data by system logging. The intelligent interface has to try and figure out how sophisticated a user is, based on simple measures such as error counts, command usage and task-completion time. Task operation, however, can be affected by mistakes at the lexical, syntactic or semantic level. A user may make a mistake in a command string either because of a simple syntactic error of mis-spelling a reserved word, or because of a syntactic error in word order, or a semantic error of entering a correct command for the wrong task or in the wrong context. Deciphering these possibilities requires subtle evaluation.

To make decisions about the user, the system has to have a model of the user. This model may be a general one in terms of user skill, driven from error rates and task completion time. Also included may be a model of how much a user knows about a system, determined by command usage statistics. As user exploration of the system increases, so the model assumes more knowledge, and this triggers the adaptive interface into providing the user with more facilities. The problem lies in trying to find the correct level of triggering and then the link between monitored data and inferences about the user. For instance, a user may use an advanced command once or twice out of curiosity but subsequently never use it. A frequency monitor may pick up the user's experimentation and decide, therefore, that the user has expertise.

Even when the interface has deduced how skilled its user is, the problem has not been solved. The next question is what part of the interface to change. Adaptation can be seen on a dimension of changing the application and ability of the application to change itself, i.e.:

- Change to the surface lexical features of the system, i.e. verbosity of prompts and cues.
- Adapting the dialogue syntax, so that the system provides a different way of doing the same thing. Change on interface look and feel is an example of this. Syntactically, styles vary; semantically they are the same. Systems could adapt to the user's preferences.
- Adapting to the user's task and way of working; this is a semantic level of change in which different ways of achieving the task are given. It runs the risk of confusing the user if the system's model is not made explicit.

Change of the dialogue style can present problems of consistency, although if different styles of task operation can be detected then it may be possible to match a user type to the task style; e.g. experts often take short cuts to complete a task, whereas novices will go through each step. This approach implies the system has a task model to match different levels of expertise.

A safer part of the interface to change is the support components. Messages, prompts and help screens can be very detailed, providing long explanations for novices or concise messages for expert users. Skilled users often ignore verbose messages in dialogues; consequently adaptive interfaces should be able to match the messaging to the users' abilities. This adaptation does not change the dialogue style, so there is little inconsistency in the change. Going beyond change to the interaction, applications can have varying degrees of adaptability:

- Configurable systems which allow change to the system to be made at design time. The customisation may in turn be at different levels:

  - *Lexical* change to menus, command names, prompts, etc. This can also be effective at the operating-system level, such as setting the mouse response, cursor blink rate, level of sound, etc.
  - *Syntactic* change either by choice of look and feel style, and basic behaviour of the system to a greater or lesser degree. Examples are setting the sort order in reports, or changing the format instructions by a word processor style sheet.
  - *Semantic* configuration of the dialogue; this necessitates some sort of programming by example so that the user can demonstrate how the task should be carried out and the system learn the sequence for future use. This level of configurability is rare.
  - *Functionality* configuration; some applications allow a pick and mix of functionality, so that users can configure a system to their tasks and level of complexity. This has to be achieved by careful control of module interfaces and system integration.

- Systems which change and adapt at run time. These adapt by monitoring the user and changing the interface behaviour and characteristics accord-

ingly. These systems can be considered able to learn, albeit in a primitive manner. Again, change may occur at different levels, but in practice most systems do not change the basic level of the system for fear of invoking inconsistency. Adaptation is effected by providing more, alternative ways of doing things.
- Systems which evolve and have the ability to change themselves by adding new components that were not part of the original design. True learning systems in artificial intelligence belong here. More prosaic examples may have the ability to decide how to change and then acquire new functionality by negotiation. Intelligent agents fall into this category, but as yet these are still research ideas.

A final variant in the adaptation story is to use common front-end systems. As legacy software (systems which were written years ago, but still work, and could be expensive to rewrite) becomes a more pressing problem, one solution is to change the user interface while keeping the back-end systems the same. In this way the user interface can be updated to GUI standard on old COBOL applications and adapted to modern user needs. Front-end systems can also be made semi-intelligent controllers which recognise different user input and then direct messages to one or more older legacy systems. The front-end system becomes a user client which communicates with servers holding the main transaction processing software. This requires a communications protocol between the user interface software and the back-end application.

Adaptation remains an issue of contention and is the subject of considerable research activity. How much adaptation is a good thing, and how well adaptation can be linked to the user's abilities, are problems still to be solved. However, adaptation through configurability has been a success and is now widely adopted in many systems through control panels, style sheets and preference lists. In conclusion, the received wisdom to date can be summarised as:

- Adapt to individual users and try to remain consistent for a single user.
- Make adaptation explicit so users are aware of the systems change, either by overt action, e.g. setting adaptation levels, or by giving feedback messages about changes made automatically.
- If changes are made automatically without feedback, they must be transparent to the user. The computer dialogue must change naturally and unobtrusively. This requires considerable intelligent processing and planning.
- Adapt by extending the interface and system functionality, rather than changing what is already familiar to the user.
- Retain consistency of look and feel.

In the future, adaptation may become to be seen as less of an issue of changing interfaces, and more like intelligent planning for co-operative dialogues. This may become more prevalent when natural-language interfaces reach maturity.

10.6 Summary

Use of intelligence in interaction is important for planning system responses with more sophistication. Applications in explanation systems are to control the dialogue using acts as planning units. Explanation systems have to deliver appropriate knowledge for a user's need. That need may be either explicit in a question or implicitly detected. Question and answer taxonomies can partially solve understanding user needs, but contextual analysis is necessary for a complete solution. Explanations are either based on preformed answers as canned text or generated by reasoning with a domain knowledge base. Customisation of answers is achieved by analysis of the original request and reference to the user-model holding properties of the user and their current knowledge state. Acquiring and updating user models presents a dilemma of accuracy and the problem of alienating users by asking too many questions for user-model updating.

Intelligent help systems share many properties with explanation systems. They are different because of the need to diagnose what has gone wrong in interaction. This may be directly detectable as errors or inferable for user actions indicating problems. Diagnosing user problems is difficult from low-level interaction data, and clarification dialogues may be necessary. Once a problem has been detected, a repair strategy is planned and advice given to the user to correct the error, or an explanation given to improve usage.

Adaptive user interfaces employ intelligence to model the user's activity, skills and knowledge, and then change the system to improve the fit of the user–system dialogue. Adaptation runs the risk of creating inconsistency, so choice of what to change is difficult. Few truly adaptive systems have been produced, although adaptation at design time by configuration has been more successful. Applications and interfaces can be configured at a variety of levels from surface-level syntax to the semantics of system operation and choice of functionality.

Further Reading

A good description of explanation systems research is contained in Cawsey (1993), while the best text to follow on intelligent help is Breuker (1990). Maybury (1993) contains a series of papers on explanation systems from a multimedia perspective. Further detail on adaptive user interfaces is covered in Edmonds (1992), with perspectives on intelligent user interfaces.

Questions and Exercises

1. Try to design an explanation system for your electronic mail system. What sort of domain knowledge will be necessary (see TKS in Chapter 3)? Describe the questions which may be asked of such a system and define the links from the question to the type of domain knowledge.

2. Record the questions people ask about a computer system. A good case study is the search system (online public access catalogue) in your library. Devise your taxonomy of question and answer types. How well do the questions recorded fit into the taxonomy? How many double and triple classifications are there for one question? Look at these questions to see what the effect of context is on answering.

3. How important are user models for the design of intelligent user interfaces. Discuss the role of user models and the problems inherent in updating them as interaction progresses.

4. Consider an application which gives you problems. How would you design a help system for this application? What should be considered in the design of context-sensitive help for the problems and how can intelligent help improve the quality of advice given (e.g. adapt the response to different people, explain reasons for problems, etc.)?

5. Discuss the role of dialogue acts in planning user system conversations. How can dialogue acts be used to control explanations and what are the problems in detecting user acts in graphical user interfaces and natural language input?

11 Perspectives in HCI: Future Developments and the Development Process

This chapter covers issues which relate to groups of people. First, there are people in the design process. How users are involved in design and how design itself can be managed are vital issues for introducing and applying human–computer interface design. HCI in the large concerns applications development as much as does software engineering, indeed more so, since the focus is on design of the whole system rather than just software. Methods for constructing and controlling the design process will be reviewed along with techniques for user-centred analysis and design. This area is related to Requirements Engineering, which is a growing field emerging from the software engineering community. The second theme is support for group interaction, usually referred to as Computer Supported Co-operative Work (CSCW). The problem in supporting and controlling interaction between several people is investigated, and this technology is itself involved in the design process of computer systems in Computer Aided Software Engineering (CASE) tools. The chapter ends with some thoughts on the prognosis of HCI as a technology and its impact on design methodology and systems engineering practice.

11.1 User-centred Design

It has already been emphasised that interface design is part of the system design process and should be integrated with current structured development methods. Unfortunately, system development methods have paid little attention to HCI or, so their critics would maintain, to the users themselves. A common theme within interface design is concern and involvement with users. A group of methods have been developed, partly within the HCI community and partly within the area of systems science, which aim to improve the human involvement in systems development. The following approaches all improve the user-centred nature of the design process:

- *User-participative design.* Users should be actively engaged with the process of design and should be assigned to the design team to share in decision making. This is intended to narrow the gap between computer specialists and computer users and to help eliminate errors in communication which result in poor requirements definitions. Critics point out that in practice 'user experts' get themselves elected on to design teams and become part of the system design community, thus perpetuating the user–specialist division.

Local experts can be recruited from the user community to act as semi-expert advisors on the system after training has been completed and the implementation team has departed. These individuals acquire sufficient technical knowledge to help others solve problems and act as trouble shooters. Local experts can increase commitment to the system as well as providing a human help system, although developers should beware of demanding too much from a single local expert. One of the best-known methods of participatory design is the ETHICS method of Mumford (1983), while further advice on designing the people side of the design process can be found in the Open Systems approach pioneered by Eason and Harker (1989).

- *User-centred design.* The system design should be driven by the needs of the users and not by functional processing requirements, hardware limitations, etc. All good methods of systems analysis should focus on the user's requirements. Emphasis on task analysis and design helps user-centred design; so too do prototyping, and usability evaluation. User-centred design is partly an attitude that sees users as customers and aims to deliver what they want. It is also good practice following the techniques, guidelines and methodical approach outlined in earlier chapters, although there is no one prescriptive method that can ensure user-centred design.

The main components of user-centred design are scenarios, storyboards, prototyping and usability evaluation, techniques already encountered in Chapter 8. Scenarios are invaluable in requirements analysis for showing users how the future will look and feel, and are an admirable way of eliciting feedback. However, scenarios can also be used to test out design ideas, and two levels of use are possible:

- *Scenarios in the small*: these are descriptions of a particular situation used to test out design techniques and methods. One classic HCI 'white rat' is the windows selection scenario. The user has two or more windows open on screen and has been working in one of them. An interruption occurs and the user's attention is diverted. When he/she returns to the screen, the intention is to work in a different window from the one originally being used. Unfortunately, typed input is directed to the old window and the user can't understand what has gone wrong. The design test is to cue which window is active in an effective yet unobtrusive manner.
- *Scenarios in the large*: these descriptions are of a prospective application; they sketch out the domain of use and how an application

will address a particular problem. Such scenarios are used in requirements analysis. A variant of this approach is to script a typical sequence of interaction, called a 'use case'. This illustrates the functionality of a product as well as giving some idea of how the interaction may occur. A variation of the scenarios theme is to use a human to simulate part of the system; this is called Wizard of Oz.

- *Wizard of Oz techniques.* The computer system is simulated by a human wizard who uses a computer to type in system replies and send them to the user's computer. The test users expect that they are operating a real system and are unaware of the human wizard. This technique is useful for testing prospective design but it is limited by the capacity and response time of the human wizard. These simulations are effective in testing knowledge-based systems when the human mimics the machine intelligence.

Scenarios require simulation and prototyping tools to be effective. Simulation tools generate the look and feel of a dialogue with limited functionality and a user-system provided by a scripting language. The application look and feel can be simulated before any functional prototype is built. Simulation packages grew out of authoring software for computer-based training of presentation scripting tools such as Macromind Director. These provide a drawing and screen painting facility to enable new designs to be rapidly developed with a programmable scripting language which control interaction as in the proposed application. After simulation, a wide variety of prototyping tools exist, ranging from hypertext to rapid interface building tools and programming languages with interface development libraries.

Finally, prototyping is not effective without evaluation. Thorough testing and improvement in the next cycle of design lead to an iterative life cycle for development.

- *Iterative design.* The concept of prototyping and cycles of refinement during design is frequently urged in the HCI literature. Early design stages are described as formative when the broad design features are specified and prototyped; the product then goes through stages of summative design in which details are added and improved upon. While prototyping works well when interface operation is not complicated and prototyping tools are available, it is more difficult for complex interface designs which stretch or exceed the resources of prototyping tools. In many cases it is essential to build a complete system to create the necessary interaction before judging a prototype. Also, prototyping can lead to poor specification in which problems are deliberately avoided with the excuse that the answers will be found during prototype trials.

Besides these general approaches there are HCI techniques for requirements analysis that help user-centred system definition: for instance, stakeholder analysis is important for assessing the impact of introducing technology and definition of requirements. Each approach undoubtedly has something to offer in improving systems and interface design. User-centred design can encourage better system operation as well as involving users within the design process.

11.2 Managing User-centred Development

To manage user-centred development implies that HCI design has first to be introduced into the organisation. Managers are often suspicious of new practices which will consume resources. To counter this problem the best way to start is by introducing HCI as a quality issue. Usability evaluations rapidly demonstrate problems with existing products. Evaluations can be conducted cheaply and quickly. They also bring user pull to bear on the process as, given the opportunity, users will soon voice their concerns over poor usability engineering.

Getting designers to respond is more difficult. If the organisation uses prototyping the job of persuasion is much easier, but the attitude change may be difficult in departments which champion waterfall life cycle oriented information systems. One solution is to set up small pilot projects which demonstrate user-centred design and prototyping; then user feedback (assuming the projects are successful!) can be used as evidence to justify the HCI approach.

Introduction of user-centred systems development raises three problems:

- Integration of HCI techniques into current system development methods used by the organisation. Structured methods such as SSADM and IE do not have 'slots' into which interface design can be fitted. To solve this problem, in-house methods have to be developed to customise structured methods by incorporating techniques, guidelines and models for HCI design. Some of the suggestions contained in this book can be used as a starting point.
- Computer support for the interface development process. HCI methods, in common with most software engineering methods, are cumbersome to use without software tool support. Diagrams are necessary to construct and verify models. Paper guidelines are difficult to apply, as there are many guidelines, and application rules are missing or inadequate. Designers do not know when or where to apply guidelines. A computer-based retrieval system could help by providing an index for context of use, but, unfortunately, current guidelines are still manuals on the shelf. Hypertext systems for computer-aided HCI engineering could be built at a modest cost.

- Education and training in HCI. This is now becoming part of the computer science curriculum (ACM, 1992), but most practising software developers will have little or no education in HCI. Training courses are necessary, but even without these, a start can be made by developing in-house procedures for user-centred design. Coupled with usability evaluation, this can increase the awareness and lead to further self-motivated training.

Successful introduction of user-centred design can be approached in two ways. First is by developing in-house style guides. The UI development environments are often accompanied by manufacturers' guidelines and style guides (e.g. CUA from IBM, Apple design guidelines). These can be adapted and expanded to suit local needs. Further advice can be given on the level and scope of guidelines, e.g. those applicable during task design, dialogue design, information presentation and display design. Another source of advice is ISO standard 9421, which gives copious guidelines for all aspects of the user interface. The main problem is that there is too much advice and developers cannot see the wood for the trees. Simplified in-house manuals can help.

Structured methods can be adapted to add HCI techniques, such as the models and notations for dialogue and presentation design described in Chapters 6 and 7. Guidelines can be grouped according to their applicability in the design process. Method-based guidance can improve the usability of guidelines by giving the agenda for their use. Many CASE tools provide configurable diagramming tools which can be adapted for HCI models. Standard software engineering models can be used directly, for instance data flow diagrams in task modelling, entity relationships for information models, entity life histories for dialogue structures; while bar charts are adaptable for planning presentations.

However, user-centred design is more than methods. The most important aspect is probably an attitude shift from developer-centric production of software to the user-centric approach. Adoption of prototyping where possible and iterative-development embedded usability testing is vital. Recruitment of users into the design teams and encouragement of user-led design are further managerial changes which can lead to an attitude of software development being a user service. The rewards for change need to be publicised as user satisfaction and product success stories.

11.3 Support for Group Interaction

Computer-supported co-operative work (CSCW) is a relatively new area which has grown out of HCI to establish an identity of its own. Co-operative work adds two dimensions to single person interaction:

- *The communication problem*: individuals within groups need to send messages and co-ordinate their activity.
- *Shared artefacts*: collaborative work involves building something together. The problem is controlling the development of the artefact so that work is achieved in an orderly fashion.

	synchronous	asynchronous
same location	meeting rooms	argumentation tools
distributed	video conferences	e-mail bulletin boards electronic conferences

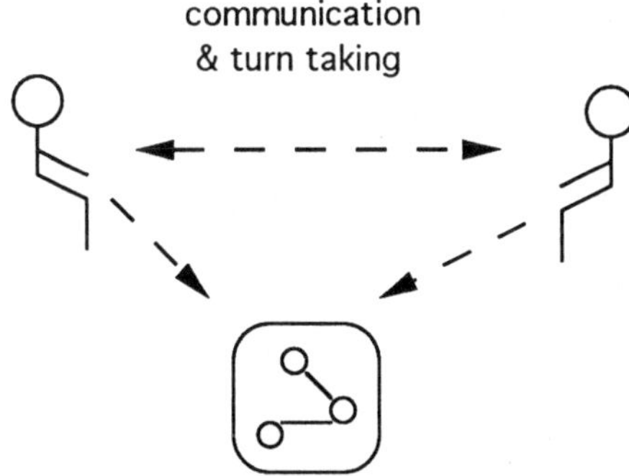

Figure 11.1 Computer-supported co-operative work: a framework for classifying different systems.

CSCW systems are classified according to how members of the group are distributed in location and how they interact in time (see Figure 11.1). Four possibilities emerge:

- *Common location, concurrent working.* The group share the same work space and collaborate together at the same time. Meetings and brainstorming sessions are the obvious examples of this sort of group working. Supporting this type of activity is often focused on the shared artefact or on recording the results of group discussion. In CASE tools a structured walkthrough of specifications is a group activity in this class. The shared artefact is specifications such as data flow, entity relationship, etc., diagrams. Design rationale in the gIBIS system (see Section 11.4) is another example where the arguments proposed by group members are recorded and worked on interactively.
- *Common location, asynchronous working.* Although the group works in the same place, they do so at different times. Support is again concerned with access to the shared artefact. The problem is to facilitate communication about what has been done so that the next individual can pick up where the last person left off. Version control in software development is an example of this class. Different software engineers collaborate on a common development, and CASE tools have to ensure that the first person signs off the artefact (i.e. a software module) before the next developer can access it. With asynchronous working, more support may be necessary for communication. Messages need to be passed between individuals to structure the work; for instance, a project manager may want to send messages for 'revise, explain, complete, approved' to a software developer.
- *Different location, concurrent working.* The individuals are geographically remote but collaborate at a preset time. Video conferencing systems and distributed meeting support are instances of this class. The problem becomes more complex when there is a shared artefact. The participants need to access the artefact which they are all working on. This may be solved by replicating the artefact at each site but this leads to a reconiliation problem when everyone has altered their version. Alternatively, one artefact is portrayed to each collaborator by telepresence. Access to the shared artefact can be negotiated by voice communication or actively supported by the computer software.
- *Different location, asynchronous working.* This category is not fundamentally different from the second class, because although the individuals are remote in this case, the main problem is the fact that they do not collaborate at the same time. Version control and communication protocols are required to co-ordinate group working. Electronic mail and messaging systems are typical examples of this type; however, shared artefacts can also be developed co-operatively.

CSCW systems have to solve problems of communication between participants, co-ordination of activity and access to the shared artefacts (see Figure 11.2 on p. 272). The baseline technology is network communications such as electronic mail, bulletin boards and structured messaging systems. On top of the communications, support for the following aspects should be developed:

- *Negotiation*: Structured exchange of views and rationalisation for discussion can be supported by either giving a means for common recording as in gIBIS, or more actively by using speech acts and discourse models to order the negotiation process. The computer co-ordinates exchanges between individuals by providing templates for various acts in the negotiation process, e.g. propose (issue), agree, disagree (position), refine (issue), etc.
- *Co-ordination*: This is based on analysis of the collaborative task. The computer structures work in light of a central master plan of the activity; for instance, in collaborative software development different parts of a specification have to be created, validated, then integrated, before being approved. The system can be used to apportion work tasks to different individuals, keep track of progress, and ensure orderly integration of the components of the collaboratively developed product.
- *Shared artefacts*: Control protocols are necessary to make sure two collaborators do not clash by trying to change the same thing at the same time. Access protocols are similar to those employed in distributed databases to gain access to a resource and then deny others access while updating it, e.g. request (access), commit, lock, unlock. Furthermore, the nature of change to the shared artefact has to be communicated to other group members, so updates need to be made explicit and tagged with authorship, so that everyone can see who has done what and where.

Current systems are still primarily research products, as the problems of co-ordination and control are being investigated. Some models enforce more centralised co-ordination by a strong task model, whereas others are more democratic and individuals can negotiate how the work is to be achieved.

11.3.1 Applications of CSCW

The first applications were in messaging and meeting co-ordination systems, which aimed to bring people together at the same time if not always in the same place. These systems do not have a shared artefact, and support is limited to facilitating the communication process between people. The most widespread example is electronic mail.

Electronic messaging systems

Electronic mail systems allow messages to be sent via computer networks all over the world. They are the electronic versions of post and employ metaphors from paper-based mail systems. Messages are addressed to the receiver using a shorthand code for the country and location, e.g.

a.person@dept.city.country

The address code is used by the e-mail network for routing between different national computer networks which are connected world wide as 'the Internet'. So, to send a message to the USA, I compose my message, which is sent to the United Kingdom's JANET (Joint Academic Network); this then passes the message on the appropriate part of the Internet, such as EDU (education) if I am sending a message to someone in a United States university, or COM (commerce) if the message's destination is in USA industry. The message can be copied to other receivers by filling in their address in the 'cc' field.

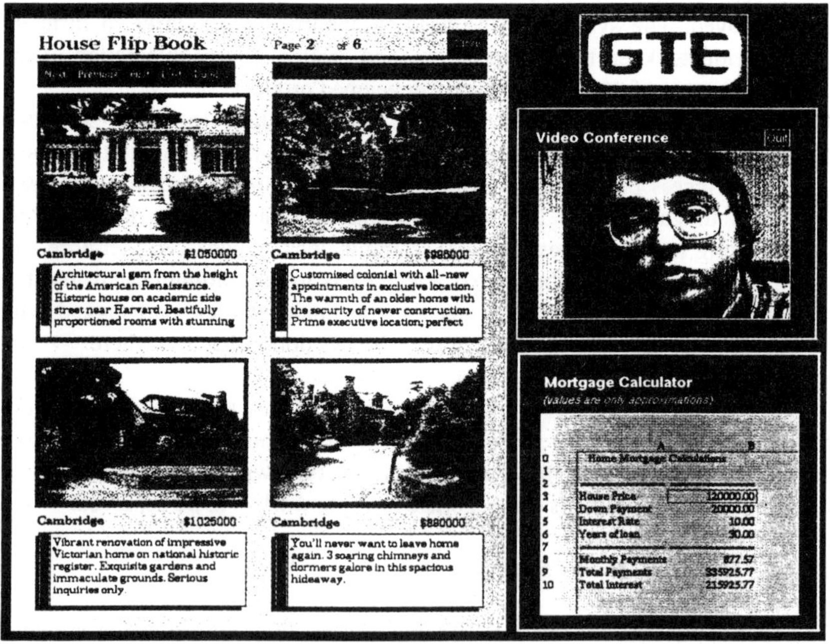

Figure 11.2 Example of a CSCW application.

On the receiving end messages are listed by their headers, which show their origin and some details of a title or subject. The problem with e-mail is that a large number of messages are broadcast to many people. While this is often helpful, it can lead to junk mail where you have to wade through dozens of unwanted messages to get at the one you want.

A solution to this is to structure communication by bulletin boards. These have to be actively accessed to read messages which are posted to them. Many networks run a series of bulletin boards which exchange information, and support debates and exchange of views on a variety of subjects. Messages are appended to the bulletin board as the debate proceeds. Often a moderator is appointed with special access privileges who can restructure the board by summarising arguments and posing new questions. Moderators may also be necessary to control opinions on controversial subjects.

Structured communication can be helped by use of filters to reduce the junk mail problem. The Information Lens (Malone *et al.*, 1987), used a set of user's defined views to accept only those message types defined in the user's filter. The next step beyond computer-mediated communication is support for recording the result.

Decision support systems

Group decision making involves communication and negotiation. A decision support model, such as a spreadsheet or simulation model, may also need to be accessed by several users.

Communication needs to be regulated, as turn taking is difficult when people are not in eye-to-eye contact. We use subtle cues to decide who goes next in a conversation, such as short silences to allow other people to jump in; the assumption that the speaker continues until signalling a finish; and gestural cues for negotiating turns. In distributed systems these cues are lost. Negotiation and decision making are about communication, so some way of helping turn taking is necessary. This can be partially achieved by video conferencing so the participants can at least see each other. Turn taking is still difficult because the slight delay in telecommunications voice transmission means that the silence gaps are not in the right place and people have difficulty in judging when to initiate a turn.

Structured decision support gives a means of negotiation according to a protocol of turns. This can be a model such as gIBIS to record the different positions, and a turn-taking control system which permits the participants to take orderly turns in the negotiation and decision making.

Collaborative design

Co-operative design environments are the most complex CSCW application because access to the shared artefact under design has to be supported; there is also the communication problem inherent in any CSCW application. The collaborating designers need to be able to see what each other is doing; hence, the term WYSIWIS, What You See Is What I See, has been added to the acronym library. Shared access is delivered either by video recording the interaction of each collaborator with a duplicated artefact, or by keeping one artefact and then giving each user access and manipulation controls. The problem is another version of turn taking. It has to be clear who is doing what to which bit of the shared design.

Shared artefact systems include collaborative authoring systems when individuals co-author documents, reports, academic papers, etc. Collaborative design systems are attracting considerable interest to support distributed design teams. For these systems co-working on a complex artefact can be supported by telepresence of each individual in a common design space. One approach, the video tunnel, projects a view to each participant of the shared design. Each person can see the others manipulating the object and group working progresses by negotiating who goes next. Although this technology has been tested in experimental systems, it still has a long way to go before effective commercial applications are possible.

In summary, CSCW involves task support, as with any system, but with the added dimension of communication. Domain analysis, to establish how people work together and communicate, is therefore important. CSCW has to support not only one person doing a job of work but also the communication process which people would normally use, as most CSCW is motivated by distribution of the group. Human communication becomes important, in particular how conversation turns are taken, the process of discourse for negotiation, and how protocols for access to shared objects evolve. No design method for CSCW has as yet been proposed, although the answer must lie in domain analysis for communication patterns and user roles, task analysis, with discourse analysis for user interaction by turn taking.

One important application for CSCW and a novel approach to supporting designer's reasoning is design rationale.

11.4 Design Rationales

Rationales are a means of preserving some of the history of a design. These techniques owe their heritage in part to work on argumentation models, of which IBIS (Issue Based Information System), developed into a graphical version gIBIS (Conklin and Begeman, 1988), is the best-known. This provided a means of modelling the negotiation history or a specification. An IBIS model has three components:

- *Issues*: these are the topics which have to be resolved to arrive at a specification. Issues are generally related to a problem statement.
- *Positions*: these are options which respond to the issue, and may be either solutions or a means of resolving the issue.
- *Arguments*: these support or refute a position. One position may have one or more arguments and arguments may support or detract from different positions.

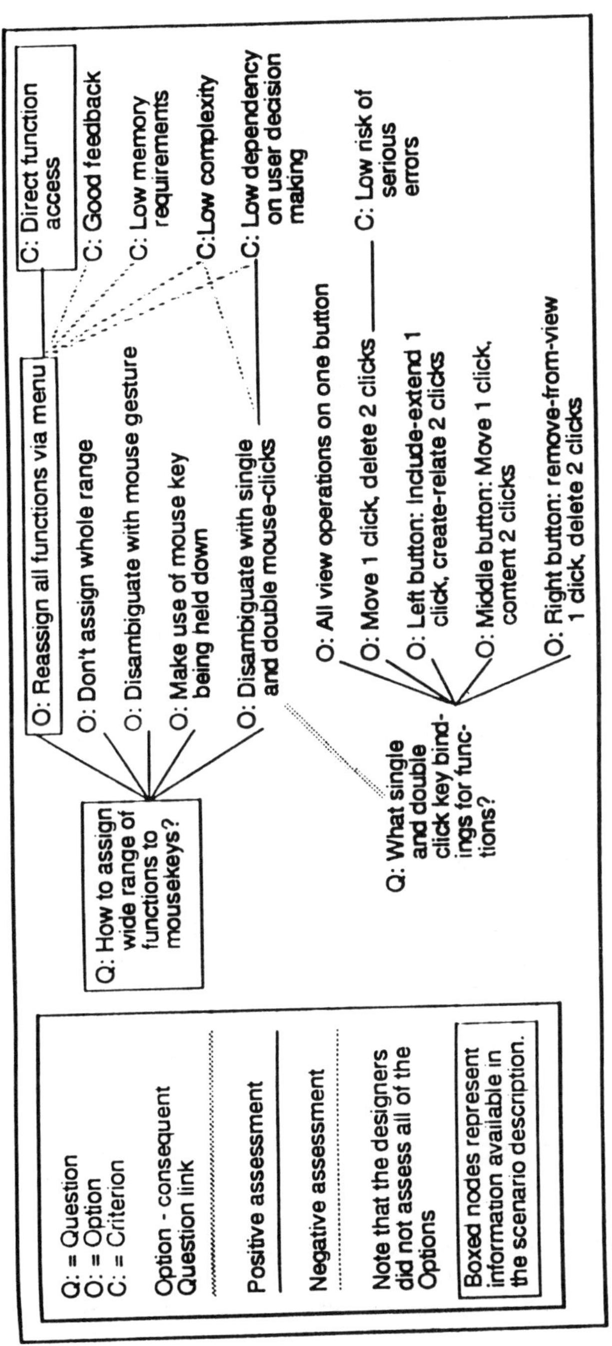

Figure 11.3 Argumentation modes: illustration of the QOC (Questions Options Criteria) approach to design rationale (MacLean et al., *1991).*

The model is hierarchical, so issues have nested sub-issues, and positions spawn questions as further issues to be resolved. In this way the history of a design debate can be recorded for subsequent re-use and as a means of communication within design groups.

Various authors have embellished the IBIS model by adding more relationship types between positions and arguments such as 'supports', 'inhibits', 'prohibits' and 'is precursor for'. These allow the interdependences between arguments to be described in more detail.

A development of the gIBIS tradition is the QOC (Questions Options Criteria) model of Maclean *et al.* (1991) for recording design rationale. This technique is used as a tool for thought about design and has the following components:

- *Questions*: these are issues which have to be resolved in a design, and act as the problem statement.
- *Options*: these describe design solutions to the problem statement in the question.
- *Criteria*: are the reasons for selecting different options and the implications of adopting certain options with their impact on the design.

QOC has been used to reason about design details and its use may be generalised to resolving issues early in the requirements analysis and specification stage; see Figure 11.3 on page 275.

Rationales provide a means of structured thought. When combined with scenarios, they promote awareness of the context of use and help, make design more user-centric, and, hence, constitute a useful addition to methods for software development. These techniques can improve usability; for instance, by using guidelines as criteria in QOC, the options can be selected to fit good HCI practice. However, user-centred techniques also improve utility by making requirements engineering more sensitive to user needs. Systematic study of the process and products of requirements analysis is emerging as a new subject area of requirements engineering. HCI has much to contribute, in techniques, notation and models for the refining of informal statements of what users want (i.e. their requirements for a new system) through to more precise descriptions and models of the new system expressed in the language of software developers.

11.5 Organisation Analysis and Business Process Design

HCI in the large is concerned with systems encompassing groups of people and organisations. Recently the new subject area business process re-engineering or redesign (BPR) has attracted considerable attention. This new area is still in the throes of formation, and it is worth questioning what HCI has to offer this developing area.

BPR is about radical change to business organisations. The motivation is to improve profitability, or often just to survive in the commercial marketplace given the ever-increasing competition from Japan and elsewhere. No definition exists, although the central idea is a radical rethink of how the business is carried out (Hammer and Champney, 1993). The essence of BPR can be summarised as change in three levels:

- Organisation change to structures in a business: typically decentralisation and down-sizing, i.e. cutting out layers of middle management.
- Change to activities: reorganising processes so the activities are more efficient and often more responsive to customers' needs.
- Change in attitude of the organisation, retraining and reorienting the way people think when they do their job. This can be a drive for quality, or for more customer orientation.

Many successful companies have carried out BPR to varying degrees: British Telecom, Xerox, Lucas, IBM, to name but a few. The approach to date has been to examine case studies of other successful BPR exercises, try to learn from experiences about the more efficient way to do things, and then introduce these ideas into the organisation. As BPR has much to do with people and their activities, it is germane to ask whether HCI has any techniques to help make BPR more systematic. The main relevant approaches are organisation analysis and socio-technical design.

11.5.1 Organisation Analysis

Few detailed HCI methods exist but modelling techniques have been proposed in the ORDIT project (Harker *et al.*, 1993). The ORDIT model is based on tasks and user roles. Organisation models have components for structures within organisations, user roles, groups of users, activities and tasks. Task activities are assigned to roles as responsibilities. Resources may also be modelled as well as the inputs (raw materials) and outputs (products). Using these modelling concepts, organisation analysis allows a picture of an organisation to be built up in terms of its structure and chain of control via role and responsibility relationships, activities and work groups who carry them out, and the products produced (see Figure 11.4). These models can be validated by simple tests such as tracing the links between roles and control structures to ensure autonomous organisations rather than centralised control, activities where no responsibility has been allocated, and so on.

Organisation analysis and modelling can be used to understand the current business before change is carried out. Activity paths can also be traced to ensure they are efficient and have the correct resource and operator roles assigned to them. Organisation models can also be found in the requirements engineering literature where they are more usually referred to as enterprise models (Mylopoulos *et al.*, 1992; Bubenko, 1993; F3, 1993).

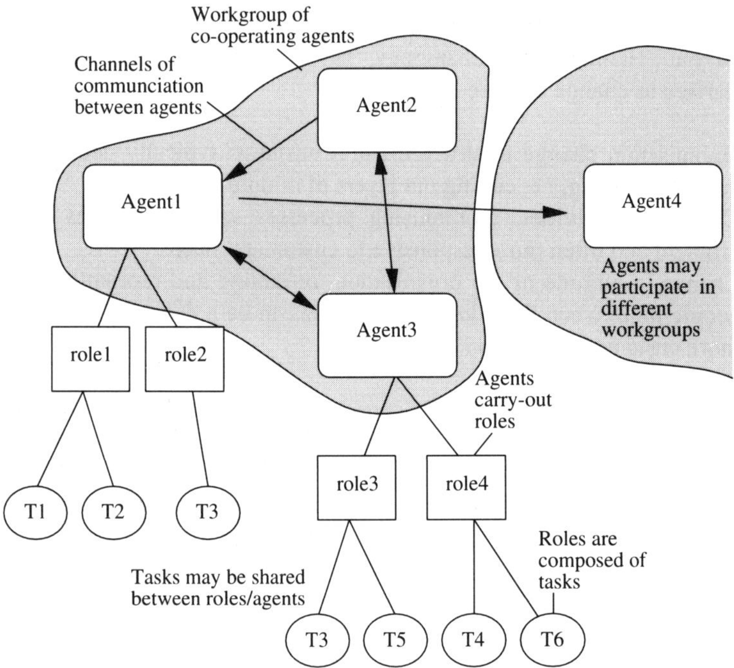

Figure 11.4 Organisational models: concepts and relationships.

11.5.2 Socio-technical Design

This school of thought approaches systems from a holistic viewpoint, in which the people part (socio-) complements the technical computer system. The analysis and modelling techniques are similar to organisation analysis; however, further guidance is devoted to defining the nature of technical systems and how this will support the overall system goals. A ladder of system categories proposed by Land and Kennedy MacGregor (1987) gives a 'tool for thought' about how business systems are constructed in terms of their control, organisation and ability to evolve with time. More flexible, decentralised systems are often better placed to respond to changing environments. These categories could be useful for BPR practitioners.

The other side of socio-technical design concerns how to use computer technology to support people's work at an organisational level for competitive advantage. In BPR simple computer systems are often the most effective, such as communications networks to allow information sharing. Quality control systems are important in manufacturing, while systems to support customer service are another important way of supporting BPR. In the future CSCW systems will allow more effective co-working. Technical systems frequently involve relationships between companies, and deploying technology to closely couple the relationship between suppliers and purchasers is a not uncommon strategy. By offering the suppliers computer systems for direct order processing, a purchasing company can get better and more prompt service for no extra cost. This also locks suppliers into a loyalty pack with the purchaser. A good example of using computer systems for competitive advantage is the travel industry, where the suppliers of holidays also supplied travel agents with computer systems for bookings, thereby ensuring they got the business.

11.6 HCI and the Future

Futurology is a risky business, but few authors can resist it. So my prognosis for HCI is that it will continue to develop and become integrated with mainstream software engineering; if not, it will wither and die. This may seem a severe view; however, as a subject which concerns itself with engineering-based design, it must be placed within the wider perspective of software design. So far HCI has had a poor track record of wheel reinvention in several areas, although to its credit it has produced innovative products and greatly influenced the design of software user interfaces. Design for usability is now becoming an essential quality issue for product success.

In the future HCI must develop methods and CASE tools that ensure more effective delivery of the considerable mass of advice, knowledge and guidelines. This can only be done when standard structured development methods take HCI seriously. There are already some encouraging signs in SSADM User Group (1993) and OOA (Coad and Yourdon, 1991). Structured development methods are rarely successful without CASE tools and the same applies to HCI. HCI should be embedded in CASE tools in several ways:

- As an agenda of issues which designers should address to create usable interfaces. These agendas will be the HCI contribution to the overall process model of development. Existing diagrammers and modelling tools could be easily adapted for task analysis, domain models and dialogue design, hence supporting a variety of HCI design techniques.
- In semi-intelligent tools to help designers use guidelines. So long as guidelines sit on designers' shelves in large manuals, most of them will never get used. But embedded design advice in a hypertext tool which produces context-sensitive advice for the design step in hand, and guidelines, may be used. The context could be driven from the design agenda.

- Usability evaluation tools to collect and analyse data, log user interaction and provide some semi-automatic interpretation, control evaluation sessions, and so on. Some tools have already been produced for this purpose (see DRUMS toolkit, from Esprit project MUSIC; Bevan *et al.*, 1994).

Computer-aided usability engineering will be one of the important means by which HCI may influence the design process and improve product quality in the future.

HCI in the large may well merge with the growing area of requirements engineering. Both are concerned with defining the necessary system functionality for users' needs, while HCI adds more emphasis on task and user-centred design. Rationales, scenarios, and prototype-led development are shared by both traditions. Again software support tools will be necessary to deliver ideas and techniques into effective practice, so this area should become another facet of CASE tools for user-centred systems engineering.

Human–computer dialogues will become more sophisticated and employ intelligent planning to make system responses more natural and appropriate for users. Human–computer communication may start to converge with human–human conversation by utilising linguistic techniques such as dialogue acts for control, with topic focus, dialogue histories and user models to generate more context-sensitive responses. This may allow user interface designers finally to realise the goal of separability, where the application supplies the content of what has to be communicated but the user interface plans how to say it. Indeed dialogue design may become redundant as the interface's response is controlled at run time rather than planned at design time.

The subject of intelligent dialogues raises the question of how such facilities may be delivered. This may lead to a convergence between HCI in the small and systems design, as user interfaces are composed of reusable agents rather than simple components as at present. Agents may fulfil various roles in guiding dialogues, such as monitoring users (i.e. user model agent), controlling conversation, planning presentation, and so on. The designer will no longer have to worry about low-level dialogue features, as the agents could incorporate rules for good design within them. In this way the standard recommendations of ISO 9241 may come off the shelf and into real software.

This leaves the question of what will be left for designers in such a scenario. Plenty, is the answer, since requirements, user, domain and task analysis will still be necessary to decide what should be designed and, at a high level, how the interface should operate. From then on design may be by high-level scripting languages to define the nature of task support. CASE tools, having subsumed UIDEs will match the definitions of task support to appropriate intelligent agents. HCI design should therefore converge with software design by reuse, in which libraries of user interface agents are composed into new interfaces. In spite of this, detailed design may still have its place, especially when interaction is critical. HCI has so far barely started to address the problems of safety critical interface design (see Hollnagel, 1993 for a review of progress to date).

Speech, natural language and multimedia will feature more prominently in future interfaces. While full natural language interfaces are probably some time away, restricted language is becoming more common. Speech-driven command languages and simple conversation interfaces in limited domains are just over the horizon. Speech-driven PC products will be the next generation, also providing full multimedia capabilities, so computer conversations can be multi-sensory. Multimedia will become a standard part of most software rather than restricted to educational applications as at present. Furthermore, multimedia services, combined with hypertext and networking, will give true momentum to the information revolution of electronic books, shared information spaces, and so on. One of the major new challenges for HCI will be to design systems to deal with this vast flood of information. The first signs of this research are emerging in 'sense making' (Russell *et al.*, 1993). Without application of user psychology to data retrieval interface design, we could all suffer from information overloading.

Design will also be necessary to tame emerging technologies of multimedia and virtual reality. We understand very little of the problems to be encountered with these technologies, as experience is only now being accumulated. Technology can always succeed when it is new because of the glamour factor, but to survive long term it must have a sound purpose based on thorough analysis of user needs. Only HCI design can provide such an analysis for future VR systems. New areas of task and domain analysis coupled with visualisation design may emerge. No doubt intelligent agents will become part of virtual environments. These agents may take on human roles as instructors, guides or adversaries and villains. The current generation of computer games which employ primitive virtual reality already have plenty of villainous characters. Design may then transcend dialogue towards drama and creative scripting of interactive stories.

Finally, I return to a more introspective theme. In Chapter 1 the nature of HCI as science, engineering and craft was reviewed. How will HCI progress? I suspect largely by the task–artefact cycle, which is a kind of engineering concentrating on iterative improvement and design reuse. Psychology and other findings from basic science will continue to be added to artefacts. Artefacts will become libraries of reusable components and agents for design in the future. Where does this leave methods? There is no fear of premature redundancy for this side of HCI because, as with any engineering discipline which reuses designs, and most do, understanding what to design in the first place is probably the most critical part. The appropriate agents/artefacts have to be selected to meet the requirements. Analysis and design methods will continue to be a necessary complement to artefact engineering for system usability for some time to come.

11.7 Summary

User-centred design methods aim to improve the involvement of users in the design process to give feedback, evaluate specifications and actually become designers themselves. Several methods have been proposed for participative design, of which ETHICS is the best-known. Introducing HCI in organisations is best initiated on quality issues. Usability evaluations bring immediate benefits which can be publicised. Methods and techniques can then be introduced by tailoring existing software engineering methods. Guidelines need guidance for use. This can be achieved by embedded when-to-use advice in methods, or by developing in-house style guides from *de facto* standards (e.g. CUA, Apple).

Scenarios help requirements analysis by creating a picture of how the system will be. Scenarios may be either small-scale or larger design mock-ups. Various techniques can be used to assess scenarios, such as walkthroughs with storyboards, simulations, Wizard of Oz techniques and prototypes. Rationales record the history of decision making during a design. Rationale models can be used to explore the possibilities for design as in the QOC model, or to structure negotiation about options as in gIBIS.

Co-operative work systems are a new area of HCI. Applications have been focused on communication support but more recently collaborative design has been researched. CSCW systems are classified according to the time and location of group collaboration. Distributed systems have to handle communication protocols between people for turn taking; asynchronous systems have to support version control and message passing. Shared artefact systems need to control who does what and WYSIWIS.

HCI in the future may converge with software engineering. CASE tools incorporating design guidelines and UI components will be necessary to deliver usable designs. Dialogues will become more sophisticated with intelligent planning. Multimedia, speech and natural language may merge as common features. Virtual reality and technology-led developments will still require design methods. HCI in the large may converge with requirements engineering to define what should be design, while information access interfaces represent a new challenge.

Further Reading

For this chapter and HCI as a whole there is plenty of literature. Three books have collected articles by leading HCI authors. The Handbook of Human–Computer Interaction (Hellander, 1988) is a collection of chapters targeted on specific HCI topics, although some material now requires updating. Readings in Human–Computer Interaction (Baeker and Buxton, 1987; second edition, 1994) collects significant papers by HCI authorities, while Preece *et al.* (1994)

contains a collection of interviews with leading HCI authors in a more general teaching text. Groupware and CSCW can be explored in more depth by consulting Greenberg (1991).

Questions and Exercises

1. Try a stakeholder analysis (see Section 3.1) for a collaborative authoring system. Imagine you are defining the requirements for a CSCW application to enable group work assignments to be collaboratively authored by students. The immediate users are yourselves but the system is also to be used on other courses. Create lists of functionality, and assess the impact of the system from the viewpoint of primary and secondary stakeholders. (Remember the staff who may want to access and assess group assignments!)

2. Carry out an outline design for the group assignment collaborative authoring system. How would you handle the problem of shared access? The system should allow asynchronous and concurrent working on text and diagrams, i.e. authoring reports which embed software engineering specifications and their diagrams.

3. Discuss the problems inherent in introducing HCI into an organisation which already has an existing system development method, such as SSADM. What strategies would you use to improve HCI practice?

4. How can user-centred design be encouraged? Discuss the effectiveness of prototyping and its relationship to other management action such as evaluation and user participation.

12 Case Study: Bank Deposit Forecasting System

12.1 Background

This case study is based on a real application implemented in a leading London bank. The actual implementation took place some years ago on a PC before GUIs were widespread. The interpretation of the HCI design is therefore slightly different from the original application, although details of the task and domain are the same.

First National Bank of Ruritania (FNBR) is interested in attracting money from very rich clients. As nearly every other bank has the same purpose, the FNBR offers its customers special rates if they place large sums of money on deposit for a set number of days, typically 30, 60 and 90 days. The FNBR then pools the money from several customers and places it on deposit with other banks at a higher interest rate than is obtainable for small sums. The FNBR makes money from the difference between the interest rate it pays to its customers and the rate it receives from other banks.

Unfortunately, some of the FNBR's customers have their own views about where their money should be placed and maintain a blacklist of banks which they consider not creditworthy. The FNBR undertakes, in the interest of good customer relations, not to place customers' money with banks on their personal blacklists. Therefore the art of successful money dealing becomes a question of placing the maximum amount on deposit in the bank with the most favourable interest rate within the constraints of individual customers.

The manager of Deposit Trading Operations has requested automation of the system to support the activity, known to the bankers as *fixed-term deposit dealing.*

12.2 Initial Analysis

Deposit recording

The terms of reference are to provide automated support for the deposit dealing and recording operations. The physical transfer of money is not within the brief.

The following narrative is a resumé of the analyst's first interview with personnel in the user department.

Two groups of people run this system: the dealers who decide where to place the money and the order clerks who make sure the paper work is carried out to record the deposit. From an interview with the chief order clerk we learn the details of the procedure.

When a dealer concludes a deal with another bank, he fills out a ticket which records the money deposited by customers, the currency value, rate of interest and the receiving bank. The ticket is passed to an order clerk, who checks the bank and customer IDs against a list, sense-checks the ticket and then raises a query with the dealer if necessary. The dealer amends the ticket as appropriate. When the order clerk is satisfied, he partitions out individual deposits by customer, calculates the interest due and raises a fixed-term deposit note for each customer's deposit. The deposit note is a two-part set: one part is sent to the bank's archives, the other is filed.

Next the order clerk raises a telex to move funds by interbank transfer. The telex is passed to the cables department and then the deposit is recorded: firstly to show each deposit by customer and by bank, and secondly, to add deposits to each customer's balance (if present) with the receiving bank.

At the beginning of each day old deposits mature, in other words the money which has been on deposit for the agreed amount of time is returned to the FNBR with interest. Matured deposits have to be removed from the ledgers at the start of each day's trading and the customer balances adjusted correspondingly.

Sometimes deposits do not run to their maturity date but are sold to other banks as *certificates of deposit*. In this case the FNBR places money with the other banks as a certificate of deposit which may be redeemed on any day according to the FNBR's wish. This enables money to be redeployed if more favourable market opportunities appear. Apart from the selling details, certificates of deposit are treated exactly as normal deposits. The decision whether to place money as a fixed-term deposit or a certificate of deposit is the responsibility of the head dealer; in practice, fixed-term deposits account for 90–95% of the deals.

When deposits are either sold or redeemed, the money is automatically returned to the FNBR. Checking that the correct amount is returned on time is the responsibility of the treasury department and is not within the scope of the study. In Trading Operations, the interest is calculated for matured deposits and entries are removed from deposit and balance ledgers before the beginning of each day's trading.

The dealing sub-system

In another interview one of the dealers describes his part of the system.

> New amounts of money arrive from customers, via the treasury department, at various times during the day. Money has to be deposited for a fixed duration (30, 60, 90 days). The funds received from customers are sorted in separate groups according to currency type and duration. These groups form potential deposits to be placed with another bank. For convenience the monies are batched into morning and afternoon sessions.
>
> Customers maintain blacklists of banks which impose either a credit limit which their balance with a particular bank must not exceed, or a complete ban on placing their money with a bank. Dealers forecast the effects of placing potential deposits by adding the new monies to customers' balances already held with other banks and then looking to see whether any of the customers' credit limits have been exceeded. If they have, the potential deposit is rejected. Otherwise the dealer adds the bank in question to a list of potential acceptable destination banks. When deposits for all the customers have been forecast, the dealer looks for banks which are common to all the individual customer lists. He then phones around these commonly acceptable banks to find out what interest rates are on offer for the amount of money available and then consults his own list of credit risk ratings. Generally the bank which offers the highest interest rate with the lowest credit risk is selected; however, the decision making is too complex to explain, and is part of the dealer's implicit expertise.
>
> Once he has made the decision the dealer confirms the deal by phone to the other bank and fills out a ticket, which he sends to the clerk to record the deposit. Telephone calls are recorded so any disputed deal can be investigated.

12.3 Requirements

Currently deposit trading has a batch system for recording deals and computer feeds for market information from Reuters and Telerate. Some technology has been provided to help dealers contact counter-parties (other banks) by telephone touch panels which automatically dial preset numbers. Each dealer has three VDU information displays which give his/her current traded position, the market rates for major currencies and outstanding transactions to be carried out. However, positions are usually out of date because of the time lag in entering new deals into the batch system.

The requirements have been set by the manager for the deposit trading operations. He has two head dealers answering to him, each with a team of dealers. The motivation for a new system is partly a push factor because of the increasing paper work burden of the current semi-manual system which also incur many errors from inaccurately recorded deals; and partly a pull factor for increasing dealing efficiency.

The requirements have been set as:

- To automate deal recording which currently uses a written ticket method.
- To help dealers achieve greater throughput with the forecasting system. This is to ensure client limits and the bank's risk criteria are not infringed, thereby reducing the number of erroneous deals.
- To improve the security and accuracy of the current system so more deals are processed without error.
- To improve information access for dealers so they can plan deals more effectively.
- To provide an audit trail so any transaction can be diagnosed if questions are asked subsequently.

Overall the requirements are for an improved information system which also helps control the current rather anarchic situation. The main business drivers are to reduce errors and costs of correction, and to increase throughput by increasing efficiency.

12.4 Stakeholders and User Characteristics

There are three main users of the system.

First are *dealers*, who negotiate deals and carry out the principal task of deposit trading. There are usually eight dealers per team responsible for deposit dealing in the bank. Their main problems are support for the time-consuming but boring part of recording deals, i.e. the process of writing out the tickets. Dealers are young and intelligent, although their formal qualifications vary from school GCSE passes to university degrees. Often the best dealers have few formal qualifications. The age range is currently 23 to 39 with a median of 30. Most dealers are male, all have had some computer experience in a casual manner and use technology such as phone touch panels, VDU displays, mobile phones and autopagers as part of their job. In spite of this, most dealers are suspicious of technology and particularly automation of their job. Even computer support of the more mundane aspects is viewed with suspicion. Dealers can be expected to become skilled users but are unlikely to have the time and patience to fully understand the system, so expert style usage is unlikely. Frequency of use is probably continuous once the system has been accepted. The main constraint that dealers face is time. Deals often have to be done quickly, which means they will not tolerate time-consuming operations.

The second stakeholder group is the *head dealers*. Head dealers set the strategy for dealing, advise dealers on appropriate opportunities and review the dealers' positions. Head dealers are also responsible for authorising all deals.

This is normally a routine task, but sometimes they may have to intervene and demand correction or cancellation of an erroneous or risky deal. One head dealer has eight dealers on his or her team. Head dealers are usually slightly older than dealers. Their main problem is checking what is going on in their group and keeping pace with developments in the market. Authorisation of deals could benefit from automated support. As head dealers are recruited from dealers, their qualifications are similar, although they will have a longer employment record with the bank, invariably 15–25 years. Some have considerable computer experience as users of word processors and spread sheet packages, although others have resisted technology and their knowledge of computers goes no further than their children's PC and automatic teller machines. They may be expected to become skilled users of the system in time, but the main constraint to be overcome is time to learn a new system and a lack of tolerance for new technology.

The final stakeholder group is the *clerks*, who run the administration and paper-based recording system. The clerks collect tickets from dealers and enter them into a batch computer system which generates the necessary financial transactions to fulfil the deal. The clerks also interact with the head dealer for authorisation and to clarify any minor problems with the dealers. The clerks feel threatened by the new system, as it may well automate a considerable part of their job, and redundancy is a real fear. There are four clerks for each dealing group. Most clerks are recruited straight from school with GCSE or A-level qualifications. Many aspire to become dealers, and becoming a clerk serves as an apprenticeship route to dealing. As clerks are younger, with ages from 17 up to 23, they are all computer-literate from experience at school. Some also have programming experience, although this is limited. Clerks operate the current batch recording system. They can be expected to become skilled users and some may progress to expert user status through their programming knowledge. The main problem with clerks is how the current system will help with their job without leaving them unemployed.

Secondary stakeholders are senior managers who wish to see an increase in the efficiency of the deposit dealing operation. To monitor and plan future developments senior managers require reports and online query facilities so they can track deposit dealing volumes and performance of individual dealers. Senior managers are also concerned with security of the new system to ensure no unauthorised deals are allowed.

12.5 Domain Analysis

The dealing room has two partitions, each of which houses one dealing team (see Figure 12.1). Four dealing desks are located on each side of the partition and the head dealer in charge of the team has a desk at one end of each partition. Each dealing section has overhead VDUs and LED displays carrying

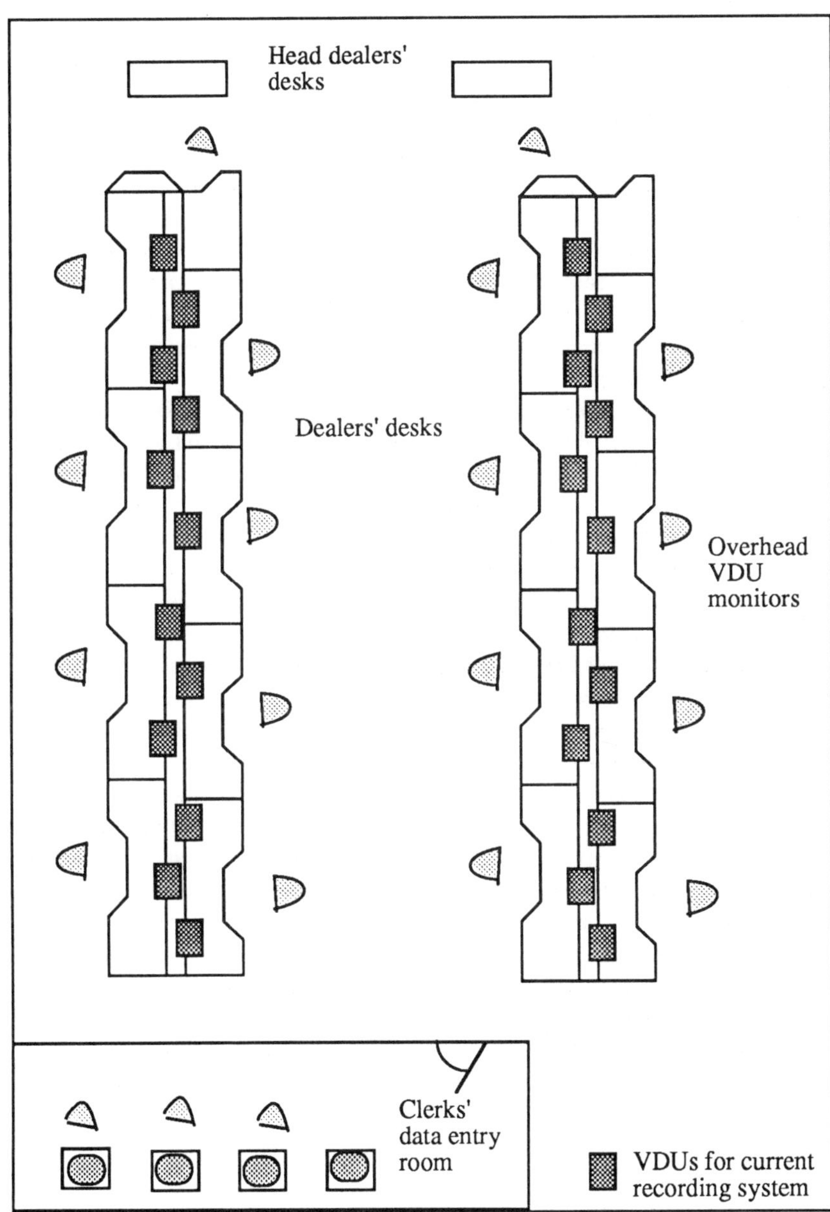

Figure 12.1 Layout of FNBR dealing room.

market information such as currency selling and buying rates, general stock market and bond indices, quotations for equities and gilts, and so on. Each dealer station has a three-sided desk (see Figure 12.2) with phone panels on right and left. These contain 24 keys coded for autodial numbers by reserved lines to frequently used counter-parties. Dealers' desks have 2–3 phone handsets and a jumble of notepads, pens, pencils, calculators, ash-trays, etc. Three VDU screens in the centre of the dealer's desk hold information on the current traded position, transactions outstanding and selected market information. The current traded position tends to be out of date because the batch system rarely keeps pace with transaction volumes. Dealers' telephones can be switched between incoming calls, outgoing calls and internal communication to the head dealers and colleagues. Most communication with other dealers is done by shouting; hence, the dealing room tends to be a noisy place.

The dealing room contains a back office area for the clerks. Beside each dealer there is a ticket bin into which each deal recorded on a ticket is put. Clerks take the tickets, and enter them, after verification from head dealers, into the batch system. The current computer system has dumb terminals connected to a mini computer. The terminals are located in a separate, adjoining room, where the clerks enter transactions in a batch.

The head dealer's desk, situated at one end of each set of dealing positions, gives an overview of dealing operations. Head dealers have VDU screens giving the same market information as the dealers and other screens showing the transactions which have been entered into the batch system. Enquiry screens can show total deals in a variety of formats, e.g. by dealers, currency and client deposits. Head dealers have telephone switch panels and their equipment is similar to other dealers', as they may, on occasion, also undertake some trading.

Informal communication between dealers is frequent. They talk to each other giving market information, interesting hints on possible strategies and deal offers phoned in from other banks. If a dealer does not want to undertake a particular transaction, he/she may offer it verbally to other colleagues usually on the same partition but also to the neighbours immediately behind them. When dealing is brisk, most communication has to be shouted to be heard. The head dealer also communicates strategies to other dealers and sometimes organises co-operation between two or more dealers to achieve a series of linked bilateral deals.

12.6 Task Analysis

Dealers' tasks

Figure 12.3 gives an overview of the dealing tasks.

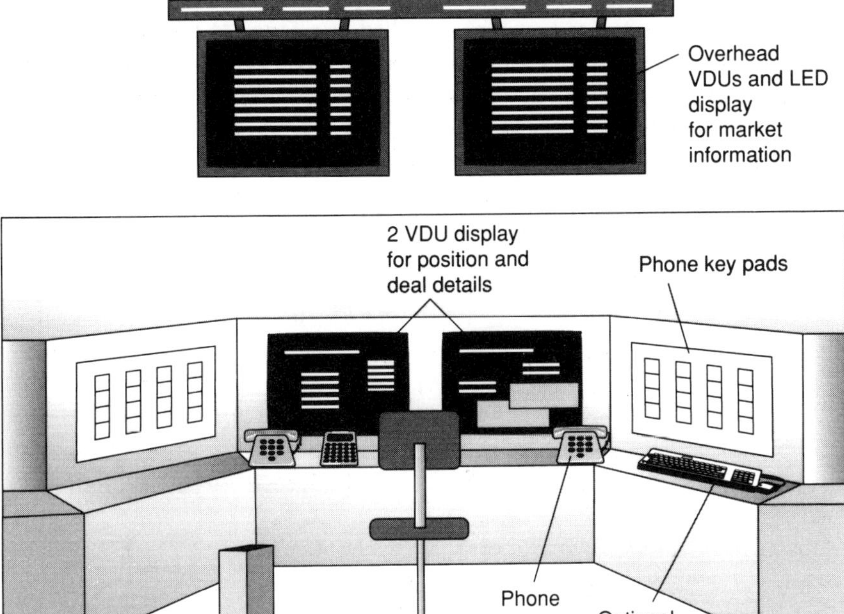

Figure 12.2 Schematic view of dealer's desk.

The dealer's main objective is to find the most favourable interest yield for the client's money. However, before this can be ascertained there are several preliminary checks which have to be undertaken. The essence of the task is to pool money from several clients to get the best interest rate, as more money attracts better rates. Unfortunately,this has to be achieved within each client's preferences and constraints about where and with whom they want their money to be placed. The first part of the task is summing all the clients' deposits by currency and duration. The individual clients deposits are added to their existing balances. The balances are then checked against the clients' limits for each possible counter-party to make sure that the clients' limits will be not infringed.

If the new deposit does not exceed the clients' limits,then all is well. However, if even one client's limit out of the batch is exceeded, then the summed money has to be split and the process retried. Once a favourable deal has been found which does not infringe any of the clients' limits, the dealer phones around for quotations. Usually 2/3 quotations are requested. Occasionally no favourable quotation is received, in which case the dealer contracts a broker to find a quote. When quotes are received, the yield is calculated, then another check is carried out to ensure the selected counter-parties do not infringe any of the bank's risk categories. If the counter-party is found to be on one of the risk files, then the deal has to be either cancelled or referred to the head dealer for further judgement. If one or more deals pass the risk check, they are evaluated for potential profit; then the chosen offer is confirmed verbally with the counter-party and recorded on a ticket which gives details of the amount, duration and conditions pertaining to the deposit.

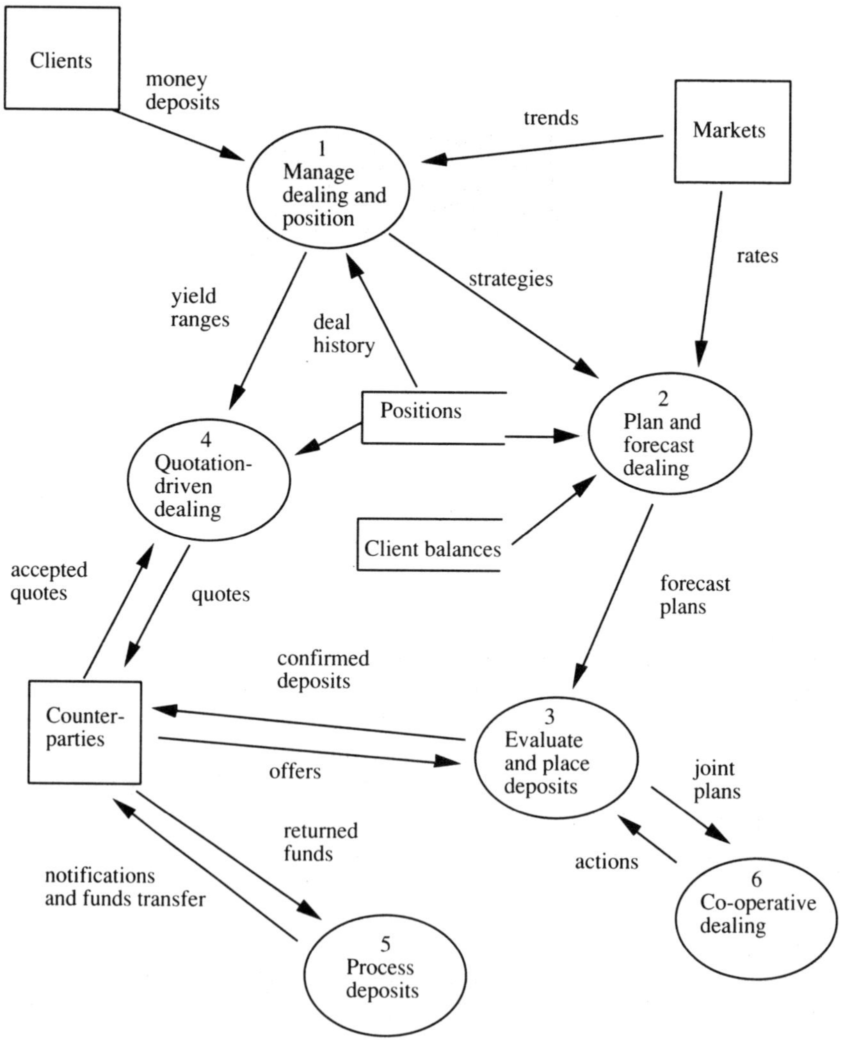

Figure 12.3 Overview of deposit dealing tasks.

Figure 12.4 is an expansion of the task analysis shown in the previous figure. Figure 12.5 gives an alternative view of the dealer's deposit trading tasks as a goal hierarchy diagram.

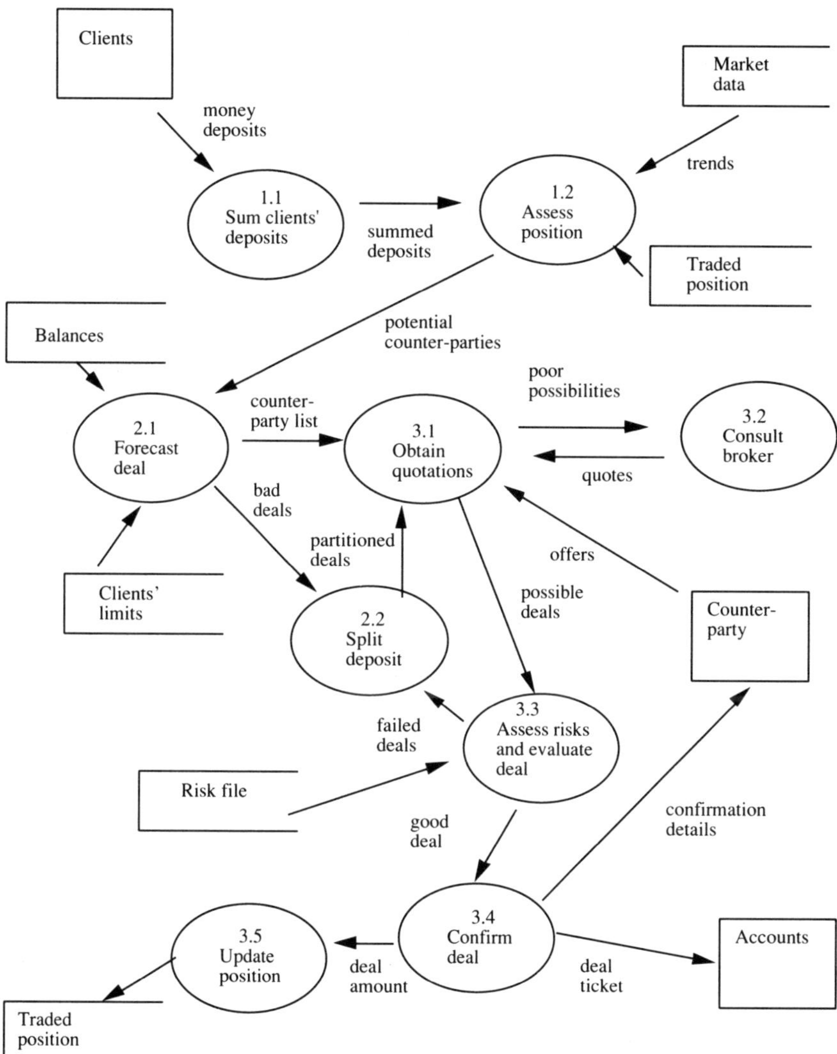

Figure 12.4 Task analysis diagram of deposit dealing system.

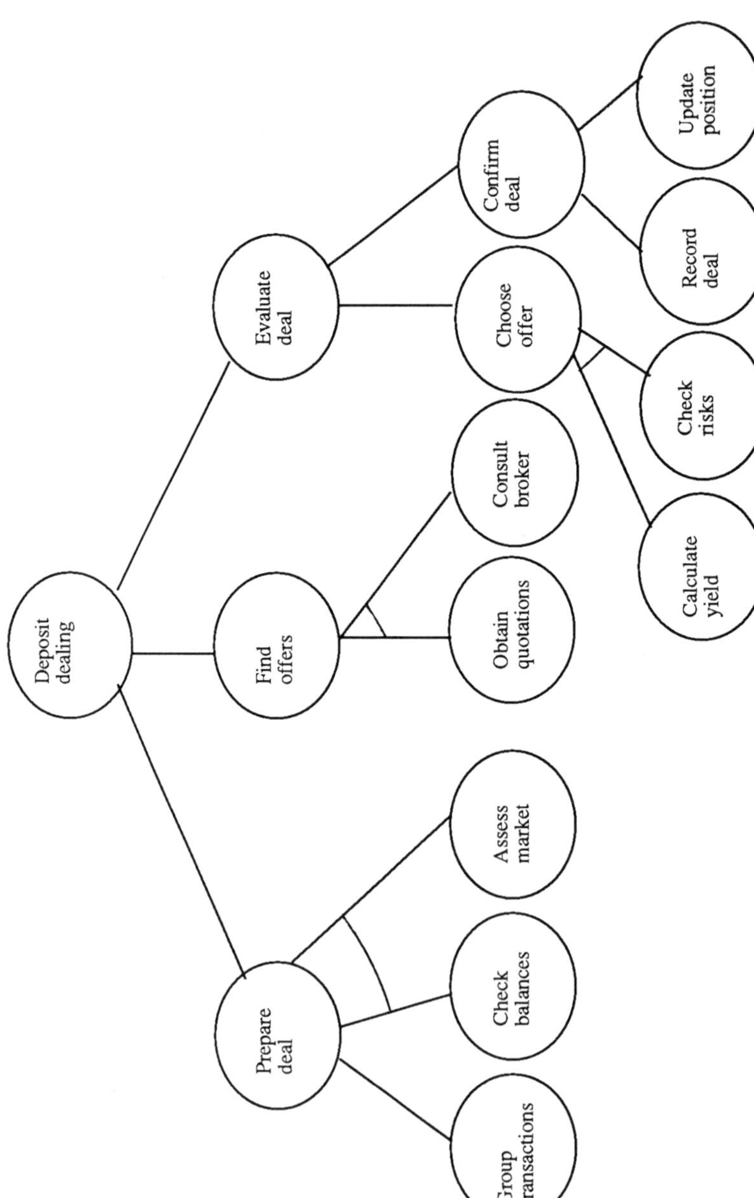

Figure 12.5 Goal hierarchy diagram of dealer's task: deposit trading.

As well as initiating deposits, dealers also receive phone calls from other banks requesting quotations for deposit trading. In this case the dealer either gives a quotation following the bank's current position, or refers the request to other dealers. If a deal is struck where the bank is taking the deposit, then the same authorisation procedures apply. The requesting counter-party is usually well known to the dealer, so there is no problem with risks, however, occasionally new counter-parties will request quotations and they have to be assessed for risk and referred to the head dealer for approval. If the deal is allowed, then a ticket is raised to record it. The task goal hierarchy for this task is illustrated in Figure 12.6.

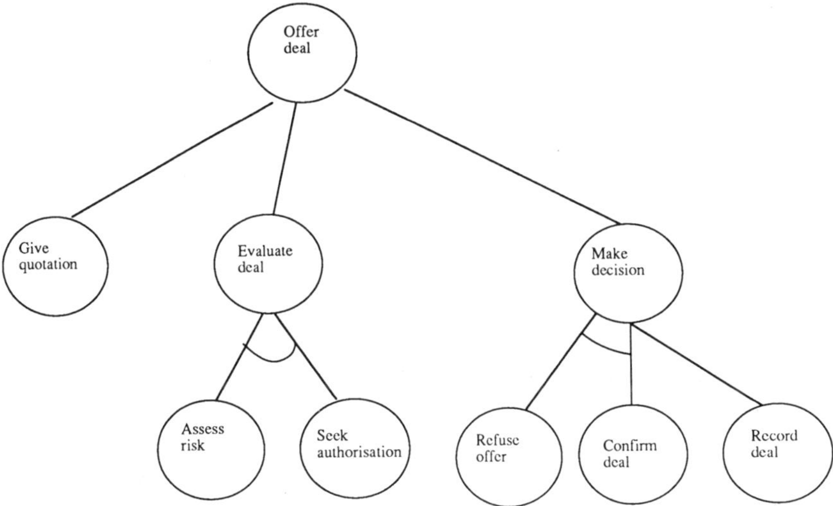

Figure 12.6 Goal hierarchy diagram of dealer's task: responding to quotation requests.

Besides initiating deals and giving quotations, dealers monitor the currency movements and quotations made by other banks for short- and medium-term deposits. They also check their own position and the clients' balances to see how close they are to limits by currency or with any particular counter-party. This information feeds into decisions on the strategic direction of dealing for the next batch of deposits. See Figure 12.7.

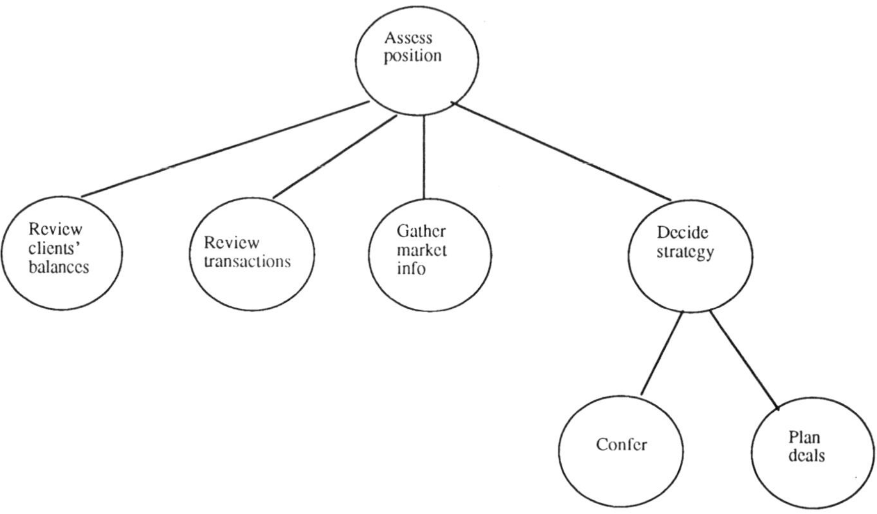

Figure 12.7 Goal hierarchy diagram of dealer's task: assessing position and market.

Head dealer's tasks

The head dealer's main task (see Figure 12.8) is monitoring and controlling the strategic direction of dealing to ensure the bank makes the most of market opportunities while not becoming exposed to risky contracts or transactions in any vulnerable currency. The aim is to maintain an even spread of deposits across currencies and counter-parties. This is achieved by monitoring markets, currency rates and quotations offered by other banks. The head dealer assesses this information together with the traded volumes and balances held by the bank. This enables him to make decisions about the strategic direction of dealing, although this is limited to an extent by clients' requests for deposits in specific currencies. The head dealer's decisions are communicated verbally to dealers and this often leads to further discussion and clarification of policy.

Authorisation of deals is the other principal sub-task. Although most deals have already been struck by the dealers, if the details obviously show gross errors, then the head dealer can renegotiate or cancel the deposit. This is rare, so most authorisations are routine. At the end of the day's trading the head dealer reviews each dealer's position to check for overexposures in particular currencies and gives advice for correction of adverse positions in the next day's trading. The bank's own position is reviewed by a conference of the head dealers with the deposit trading manager. This happens two or three times a week, and assesses the bank's performance, its service to clients and deposit trading with other counter-parties.

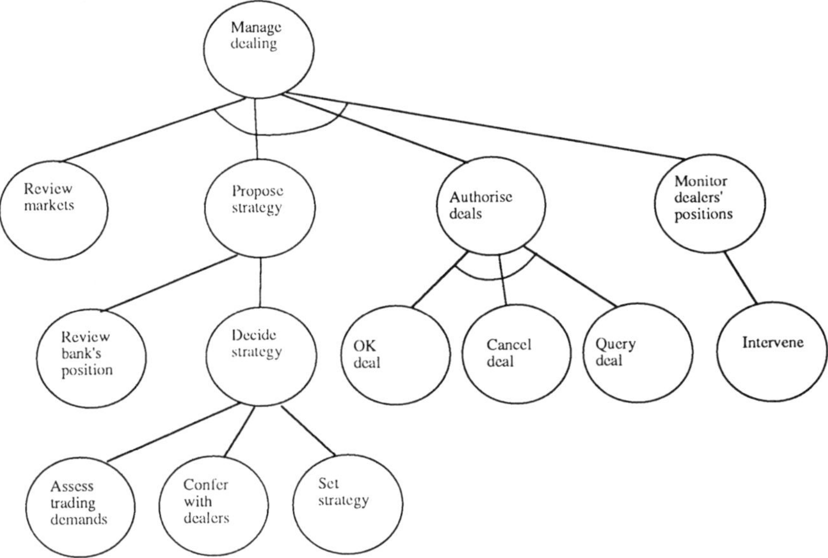

Figure 12.8 Goal hierarchy diagram of head dealer's task.

Clerks' tasks

Clerks first collect tickets and take them to the head dealer, who briefly checks the details and then authorises them. Any minor queries are noted on the ticket and the clerk has to resolve these with the dealer. Then tickets are entered into the batch recording system. Validation errors have to be corrected; then the deposit sent for processing, which raises an electronic inter-bank transfer of funds.

One day before deposits mature a notification is sent by the holding bank. Clerks acknowledge the note and then check that the money is received according to the original deal terms. The money is then partitioned into individual client portions and converted into the destination currency as necessary. The clerk then raises the necessary documentation to effect an inter-bank transfer to the client's account.

As well as these more formal tasks clerks run many ad hoc errands for dealers to check on clients' intentions, get information on counter-party activities, etc.

See Figure 12.9.

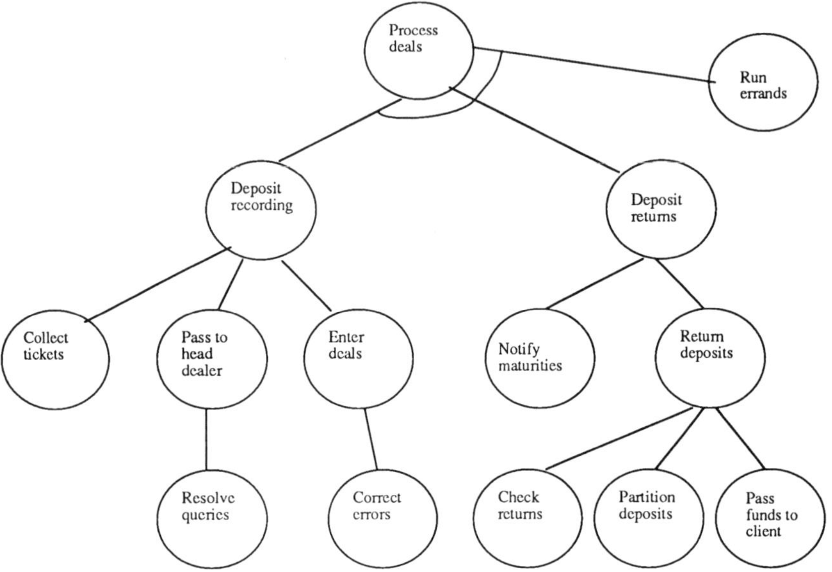

Figure 12.9 Goal hierarchy diagram of clerk's task.

12.6.1 Task-information Analysis

In the earlier part of their task, dealers need information to help deposit deal planning. First a list of the clients' new money placed with the bank is required to be summed by currency type. Once the currency types have been determined, a list of potential counter-parties which may be suitable for the required currency is needed. This information is generated by the 'check balances' goal, which needs input of the client's existing balances with any suitable counter-parties, and their limits for those counter-parties in order to check that limits will not be infringed by placing additional deposits.

The output from the check-balances is a list of suitable counter-parties who can be contacted for quotations by the dealer. On the occasion when brokers are contacted, just the currency and potential deposit value is required. For the choose-offer goal the potential yield has to be calculated from the rate quoted and deposit amount and this is weighed against the risks of dealing with the selected counter-parties. This enables the dealer to come to a decision; then information on the selected counter-party code, currency and amount are necessary for recording the deal on a ticket.

The end point of this analysis is the action-object list given on page 300.

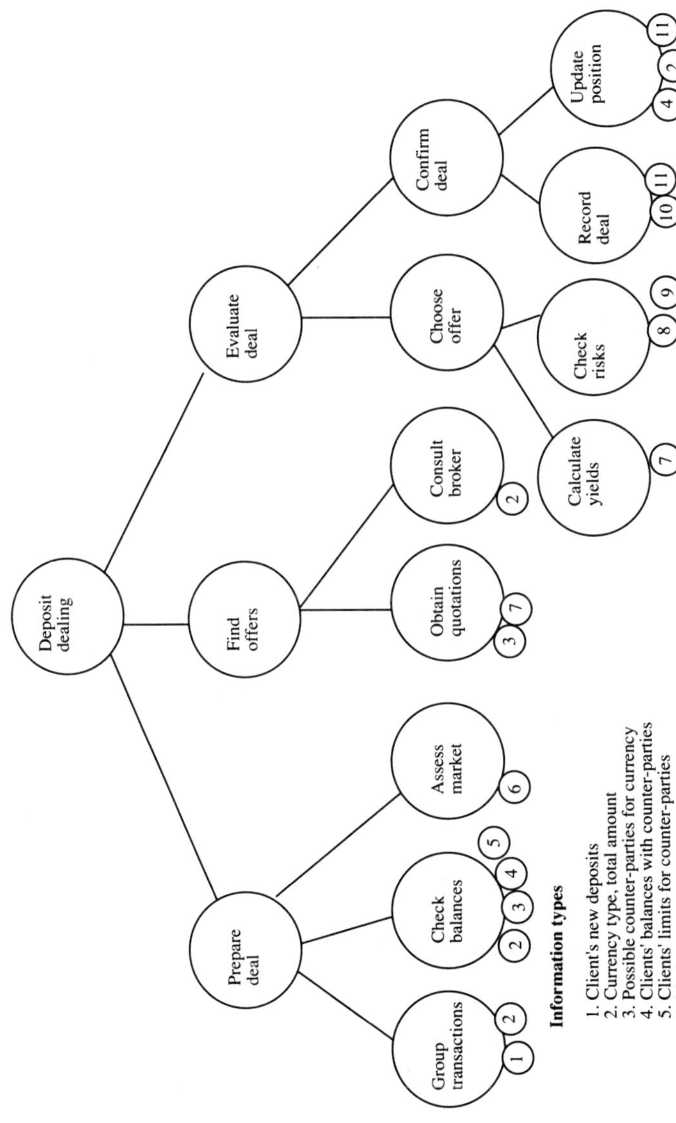

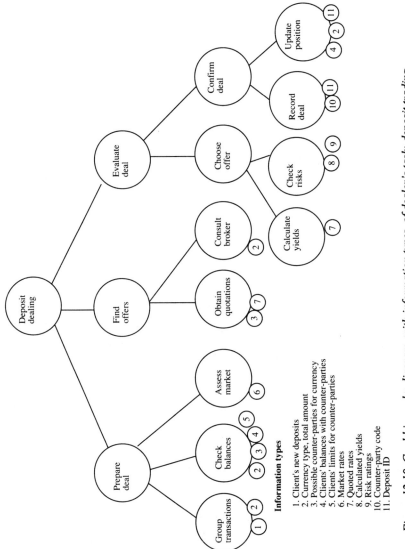

Figure 12.10 Goal hierarchy diagram, with information types, of dealer's task: deposit trading

Actions	*Objects (see Figure 12.10)*
Assess	Markets
Sum	Clients' deposits
Check	Balances
Forecast	Deposit
Obtain	Quotation
Consult	Broker
Calculate	Yield
Check	Risks
Choose	Deal
Record	Deal
Update	Position

In addition to the above objects, there are entities describing the counter-parties, other banks and clients; these are represented in the Entity Relationship Diagram (Figure 12.11).

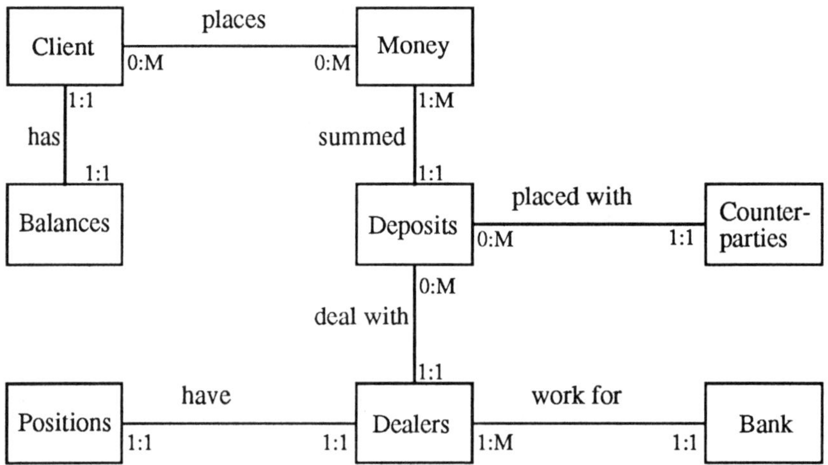

Figure 12.11 Entity relationship diagram: deposit trading.

12.6.2 Limitations of Task Analysis

The major discrepancy between the task models and actual activity is interleaving of tasks. In reality dealers handle several deals at once. They respond to offers from other counter-parties while planning deals of their own. They may also have more than one 'own initiated' deal in progress at once. One deal may be at the planning stage, while another is in the process of negotiation, while a third is being recorded.

Even within one task, some activities may be intermittent. For instance, assessing the market and gathering market information tends to be a nearly continuous activity. Dealers therefore multi-task, sampling information sources while they are carrying out dealing. Showing this concurrency on task models is difficult, as the notation is essentially sequential, although the DFD notation does give some hint about the interleaving of tasks.

A further limitation is in description of cognitive tasks. Choosing a deal requires considerable judgement and a complete understanding would require protocol analysis techniques. Likewise assess-markets and evaluate-position are judgement tasks which are unlikely to be automated given the initial terms of reference. Hence, the cognitive and communication type tasks are not analysed in detail.

12.7 Task Design

The first question is what automated support is necessary for the dealer's tasks. The central part of the dealer's job consists of judgement, and planning tasks. These are cognitive activities which would require extensive knowledge elicitation if they were to be automated as an expert system. As dealers' knowledge is often implicit and hard to formalise, this part of the system is not suitable for automation. The precursor activities to dealing, however, are suitable for automation. Summing the clients' deposits can be allocated to the computer. A data entry task will have to be added to the system to input the transactions. A display of summed transactions by currency, incorporating a client listing, can be provided to support the dealer's planning tasks. These steps are illustrated in Jackson diagrams showing the stages of aggregating client's monies, preparing the deal forecast, then making a deal (Figures 12.12, 12.13, 12.14 and 12.15).

Once the clients' potential deposits have been summed, the first check can be run to ensure that no limits will be infringed in future deals. This involves automated support for the forecast-deal task. The computer system can select the possible banks for future deposits in the required currency, then check the clients' current deposit balances against their limits for the selected banks. This eliminates invalid choices from the forecast list. As the dealer requires information on the consequent counter-parties' offered yield and risk rating to make a decision, this information needs to be displayed to support the 'decided-deal' task.

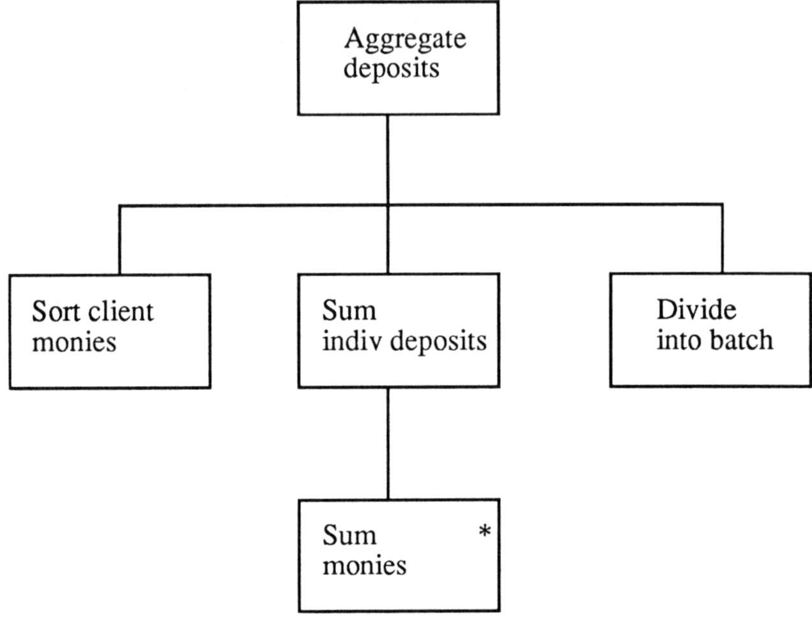

Figure 12.12 Jackson diagram showing task description for aggregating clients' money.

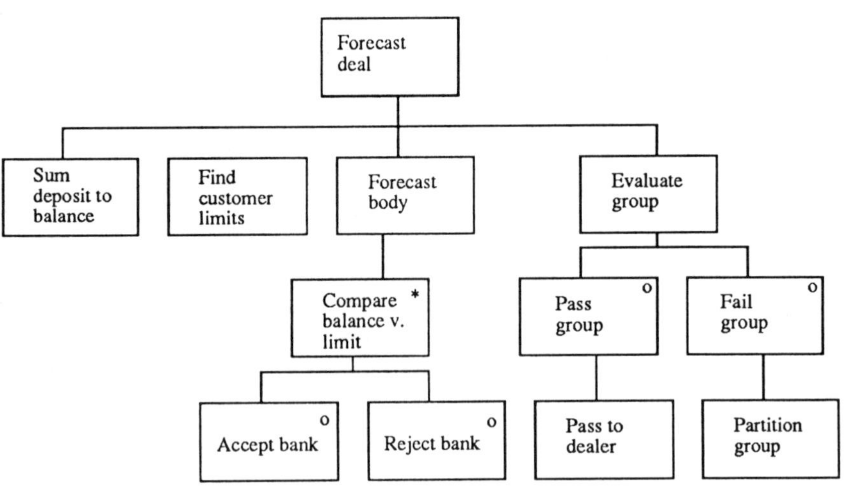

Figure 12.13 Jackson diagram showing task description for forecasting possible deals.

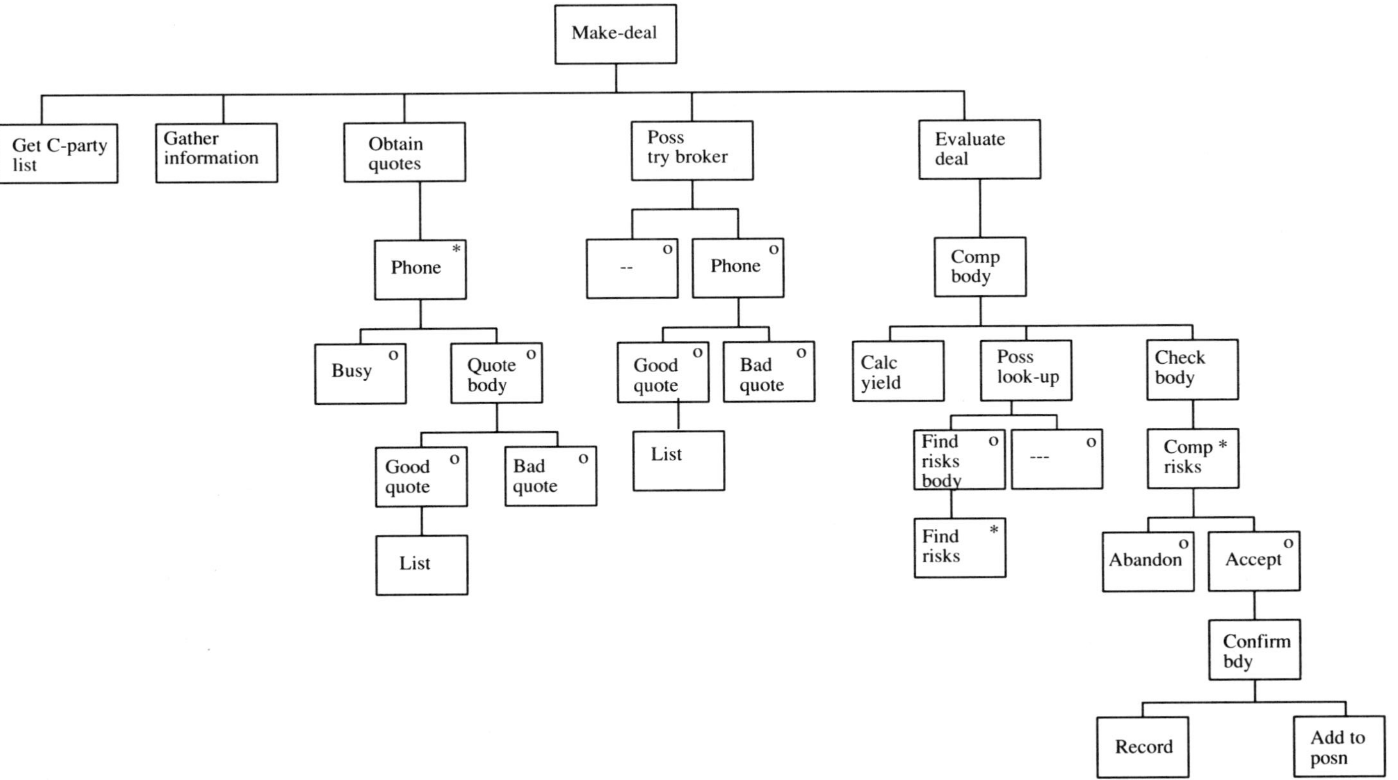

Figure 12.14 Jackson diagram of initial task description: Make-Deal.

If forecast fails, then the grouped pool of clients' transactions has to be split. This creates a separate task interaction path in which the dealer has to partition the client grouping to improve the chances of a successful forecast. This process could be automated by an algorithm which ranks the clients by severity of limits and then eliminates more awkward clients until a successful forecast is obtained. However, dealers frequently do not follow such strategies because it tends to result in one small deposit which attracts a poor interest rate, with a large deposit for the less stringent clients. To maximise profit overall it is better to have two moderately sized aggregates of money which attract good rates rather than one large aggregate and one small one. Consequently, dealers tend to split clients' money into more even groupings when forecasts fail. In the light of this, the task is designed for co-operative interaction in which the clients are listed by severity of limits for the dealer to choose where the group should be divided. The system then reforecasts the sub-groups.

Task allocation leads to partitioning of the task network; the task interaction diagram is shown in Figure 12.16. In the main part of the dealing sequence the computer supports the dealer's task by first providing a forecast list. This contains the counter-parties which have passed the limits check as input to the human task of choosing one or more counter-parties for quotations. This requires human judgement and tacit knowledge of other banks and financial institutions. This is part of the dealer's expertise and is not suitable for automation. Once the dealer has selected one of the counter-parties, obtaining quotations requires human communication, so this activity remains in the human task network. One or more counter-parties are contacted, depending on who is available (i.e. phones not engaged), and quotations are received. If the dealer gets one good quotation, he/she will not bother to obtain any more.

Evaluating a deal, which is composed of calculating yields and finding risks, could be partially automated but this is a difficult choice. The arithmetic involved for calculating yields is simple but dealers have little time for entering the necessary figures. Speech input may help (see Section 12.9) but this runs the risk of speech recognition errors. On balance it is considered worth while to provide automated support which is carefully designed to minimise the input actions. Even if dealers do not use the facility and fall back on their calculators or mental arithmetic, the cost of developing this task support is small. As most currency quotations vary by only one or two points from the official bank rate, a default can be supplied for each currency. The dealer therefore only has to enter one or two digits. The quoted rate and counter-party ID for risks could be input from keypads. Another possibility is to take the counter-party ID from the telephone panels dealers use for phoning.

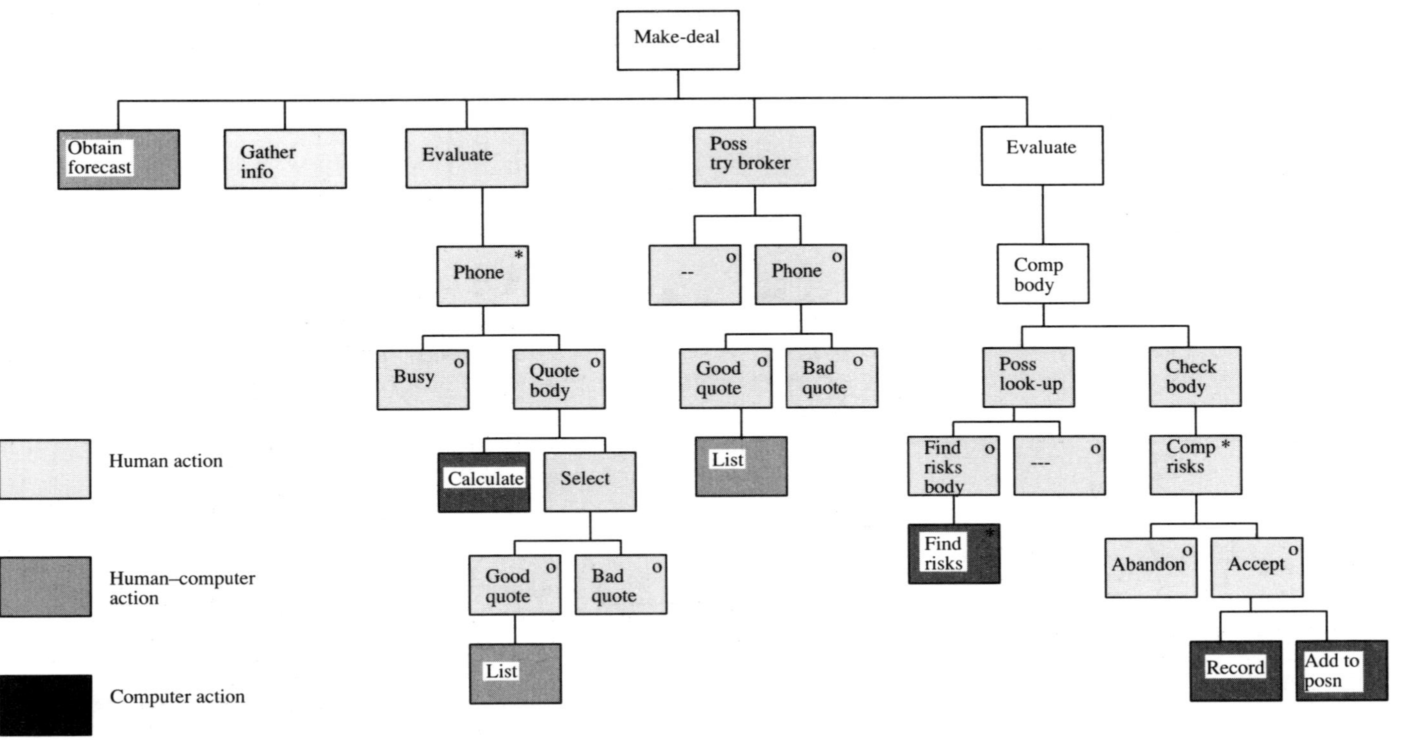

Figure 12.15 Jackson diagram of allocation of actions: Make-Deal task.

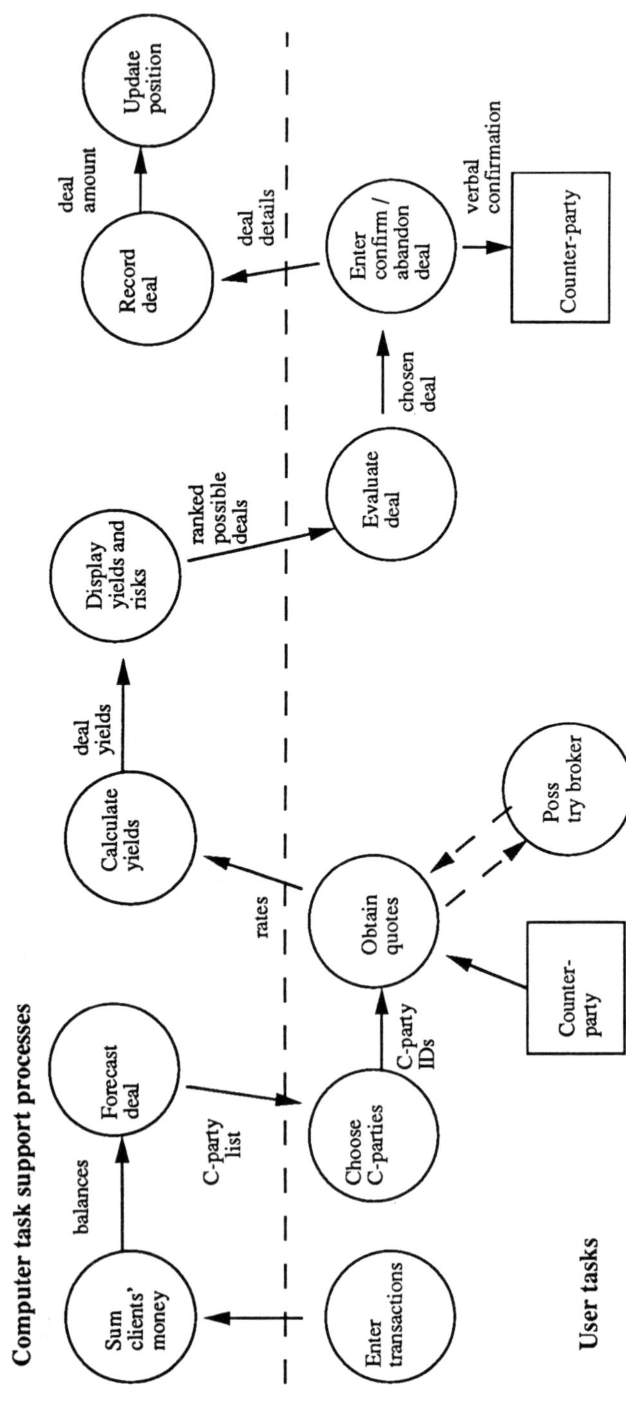

Figure 12.16 Task interaction diagram illustrating user and computer actions: in operational sequence with information flows for the Make-Deal task.

The next step of evaluating deals involves human judgement in a trade-off decision between the potential profit from the offered deals versus the risks of dealing with certain counter-parties and overexposure in some currencies. This task is therefore primarily for the user; however, some support may be possible by ranking the deals by potential yields with risk factors to allow easy comparison. This will only be needed if multiple offers need to be evaluated, so an optional display is developed. Recording the deal can be supported to link the dealer and the clerk's tasks. The final choice can then be selected by touch screen input. Rate data have already been captured in the 'calculate-yield' task.

In summary, the automated system for dealers is composed of the following interactive processes:

Sum clients' money	clients money aggregate list
Forecast deal	counter-party list with balances and limits by client
Re-forecast deal	counter-party list with clients' limits infringed
Choose C-party	counter-party list
Calculate yields	counter-part list ranked by offer
Find risks	yields and risks
Record deal	deal details, counter-party-ID, amount, date, yield, currency

12.8 Task and System Design

The domain analysis leads to consideration of how the interaction between users can be supported. The dealing system has elements of co-operative work, so is a CSCW system necessary or should a group decision support system be implemented? The main co-operative task is collaborative dealing, but this is heavily dependent on human communication and little support can be offered for this highly dynamic and variable co-operation. Dealing collaboration changes rapidly as dealers invent new ways of interacting with the market.

Less ambitious levels of support may be possible. A messaging system could be useful to support communication between head dealers and the dealers. Instructions for strategies and sign-off for deal authorisation could be handled by an e-mail facility. This has to be weighed against the danger that dealers may not notice electronic messages, or if attention-directing stimuli are over-used (e.g. warning sounds), then dealers may become annoyed by system interventions. A further problem is noise interference in an already noisy environment. As a result deal authorisation is not to be automated, as most deals are approved without problems; discrepancies can be handled informally, as in the current system. However, an e-mail facility is provided for head dealers to send messages on strategy and market direction. These can be read in quieter periods between peaks of dealing.

On the level of the technology interface, the main requirement is to minimise input effort. The following should be considered:

- *Standard keyboard and mouse/GUI screens*:. Dealers are unlikely to have the time and patience for GUI interaction and mice/keypads will only clutter up their desks, so this option is rejected for their system, although it is viable for the clerk support system.
- *Touch screen with limited numeric keypad.* This option seems to be promising so long as accurate responses for the touch screen technology can be guaranteed. User response could be by touch screen, data entry requiring a keypad for rates and currency amounts.
- *Speech technology* for computer command and data entry. This solution is ideal in theory, as it minimises effort, but the hazards are twofold. First is the error rate in speech recognition technology in a noisy environment. Good response times and lower error rates may be possible with speaker dependent systems. Second is switching between computer speech and speaking to colleagues. As dealers use speech extensively in their job, there is a danger of 'mode' type errors in forgetting who they are speaking to. Use of full natural language would be beyond the capacity of current commercial speech systems. In the light of these problems and the inconvenience of dealers wearing headsets and microphones, the speech technology option is rejected.

For the dealers, touch screens appear to be a suitable approach, in combination with a keypad for limited entry of numeric data. Specialised function keys may also be used to denote specific currencies, while codes for counter-parties can be taken from telephone keypads in the current interfaces. An optional keyboard and mouse are advisable for interaction with those parts of the system which are not time critical, such as queries on their positions, client balances, etc.

The head dealers and clerks will require standard keyboards for query processing and data entry.

12.9 Dialogue Design

The dialogue for part of the dealer's task is illustrated first using the Jackson diagram format shown in Figure 12.17. Elementary operations illustrated as mini-boxes specify the display and dialogue action detail. The dialogue and program structure follow the task structure found in Figures 12.14 and 12.16, apart from the Calculate-Yield action which has been placed earlier in the sequence where it is more appropriate. The yield is calculated as soon as rate information is entered by the dealer. A backtracking structure with two subtrees (Posit, Admit) has been used because unexpected events may occur at

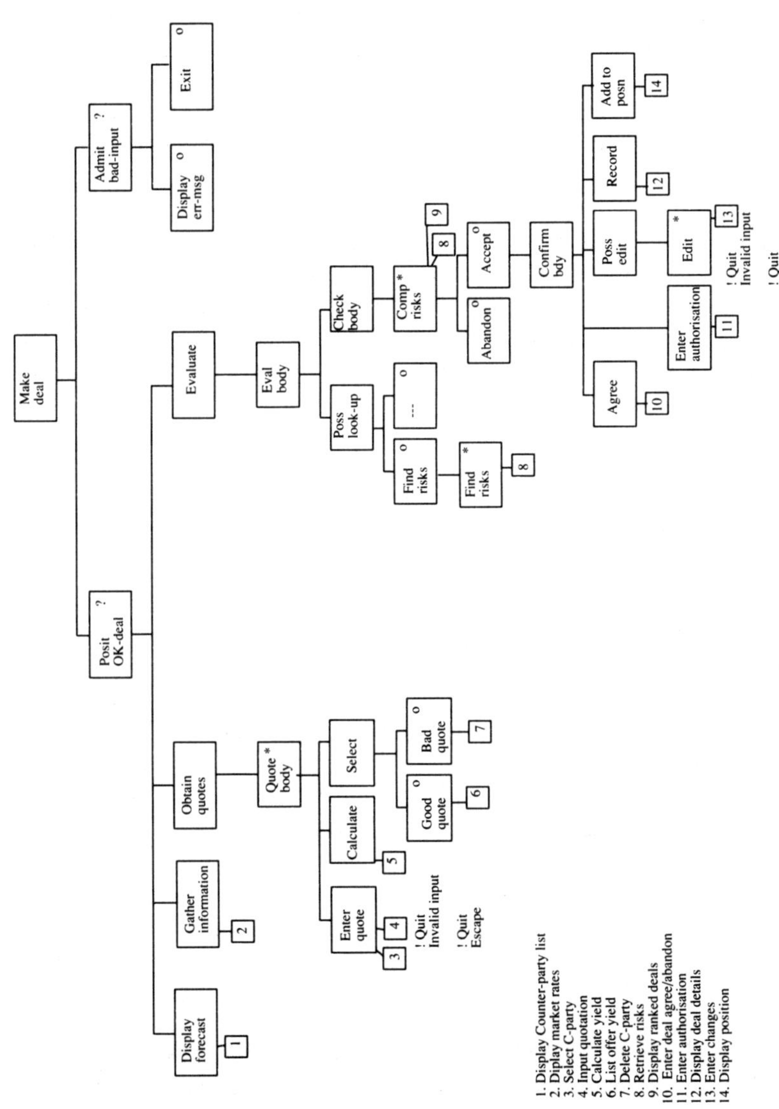

***Figure 12.17** Task support design with dialogue actions: Make-Deal. Illustrated in Jackson diagram format.*

several different steps during the dialogue. If the unexpected events, such as errors or escape commands, are given by the user, the sequence is switched to the error processing Admit branch. The normal sequence starts with displaying the counter-party list passed from the forecast process. Quotations can then be entered by the dealer; the system displays the calculated yield and allows the quotation to be kept or deleted. If required, risks may then be displayed; the quotations are shown in a ranked list for the dealer to choose the optimal one. One or none of the list may be selected. If one deal is chosen, then the details are filled in for recording. Editing facilities are provided in case the details are incorrect.

The same sequence is illustrated using a dialogue network diagram in Figure 12.18. This shows the same state transition sequence as the Jackson diagram, but adds a few extra details, such as the exit pathways to higher level menus, and individual error correction steps. The display of market information has been omitted from the dialogue network as this information has to be present throughout most of the dialogue sequence. Modelling such concurrency is not possible with dialogue network diagrams.

12.10 Presentation Design

Using the task information analysis and entity relationship data model, it appears that six information groupings will be required. The display bar chart (Figure 12.19) shows that, for the first part of the dialogue information, the customers' deposit, pooled deposit and market information are required. As market information is associated with a separate task, this will be displayed in a different area. Design of the information displays for 'partition-deposits' is more difficult. As the initial client grouping failed to find a counter-party to satisfy all limits, the dealer has to partition the client aggregations. To help this task a flexible information display is provided for decision support. The default display lists clients within the aggregate in order of their constraints on the suitable counter-parties (Figure 12.20). The clients that caused the forecast to fail are highlighted in red. Alternative ordering can be given, such as clients ranked by previous business volumes, value of current deposits or even flexibility with negotiated limits, should this information be available.

The next screen concerns quotations and evaluation of deals (Figure 12.21). The counter-parties' quotations, potential yield and risks are given, with the risk colour coded so that the dealer can easily scan the return *versus* potential risk. Following this screen the record-deal display uses the original paper deal ticket as a template (Figure 12.22). The counter-party code, deal value, currency, deposit duration, etc., are recorded.

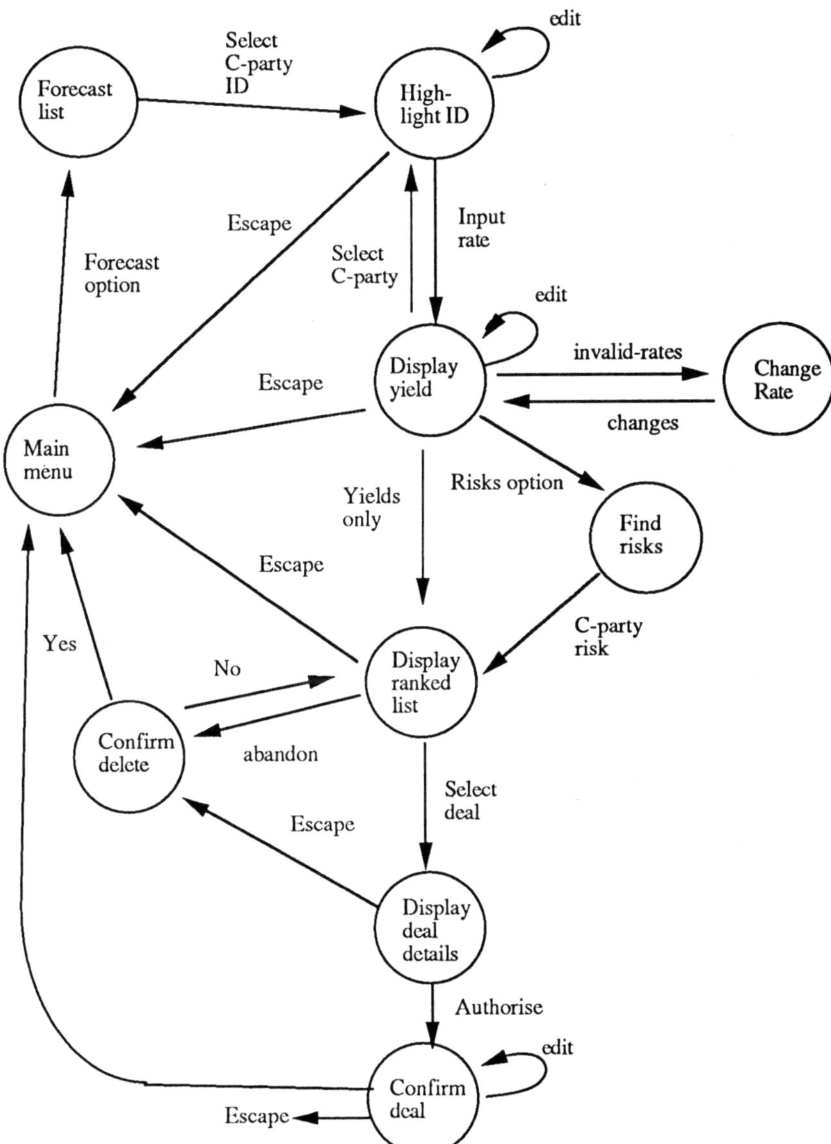

Figure 12.18 The same sequence (cf. Figure 12.7) using a dialogue network diagram.

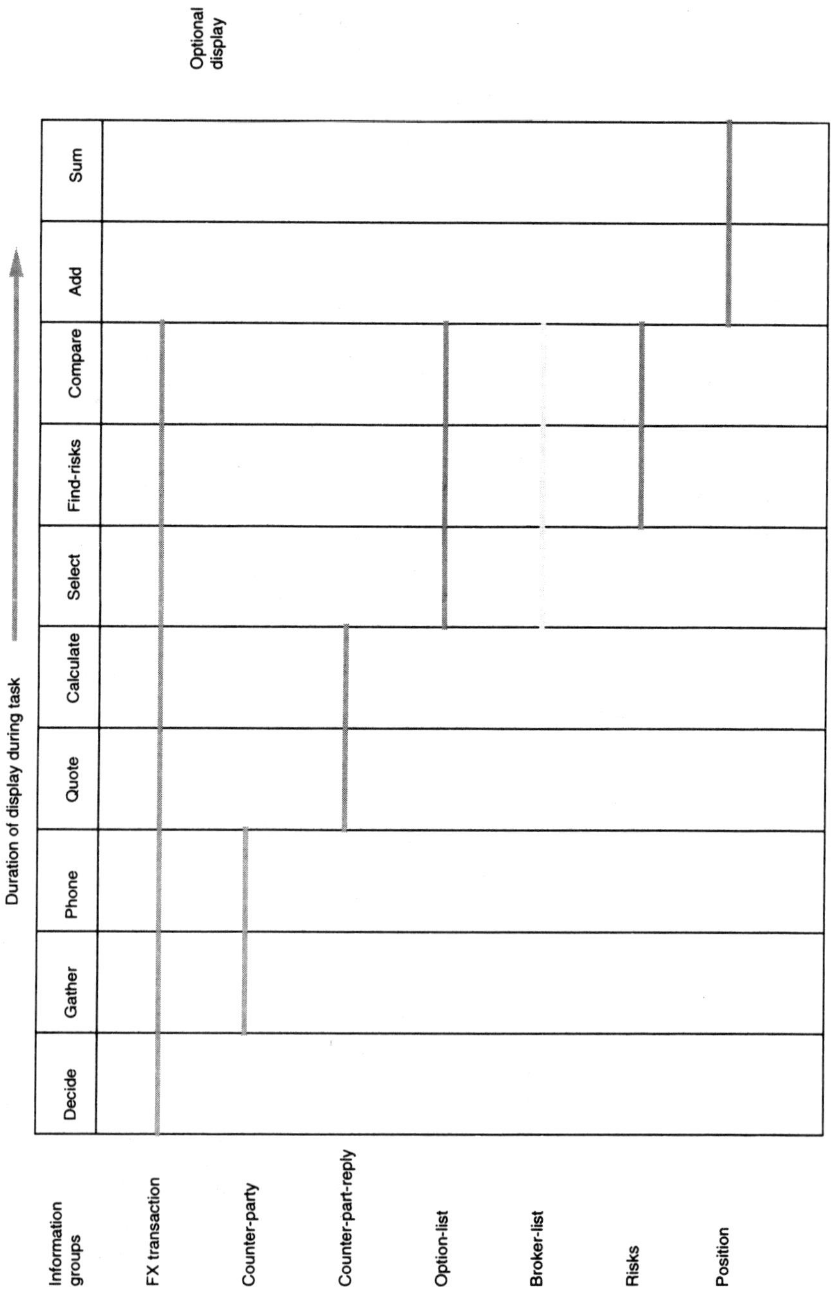

Optional display

Duration of display during task

Information groups	Decide	Gather	Phone	Quote	Calculate	Select	Find-risks	Compare	Add	Sum

FX transaction

Counter-party

Counter-part-reply

Option-list

Broker-list

Risks

Position

Figure 12.19 Bar chart showing inter-relationship of display duration of information and dialogue actions.

File Edit Forecast Record Position Other

Deposit Trading

Forecast Split: Batch AM: Group 2 | Transaction 94/1205

Client	Currency $	Limits		Balance
ZEN	200	CIT	500	650
		CMZ	500	120
		BCI	0	120
LON	120	DRZ	1000	700
		CMZ	500	450
		BCI	0	120
HLD	230	CIT	1000	440

Figure 12.20 *Screen showing forecast display; clients causing the forecast to fail are highlighted.*

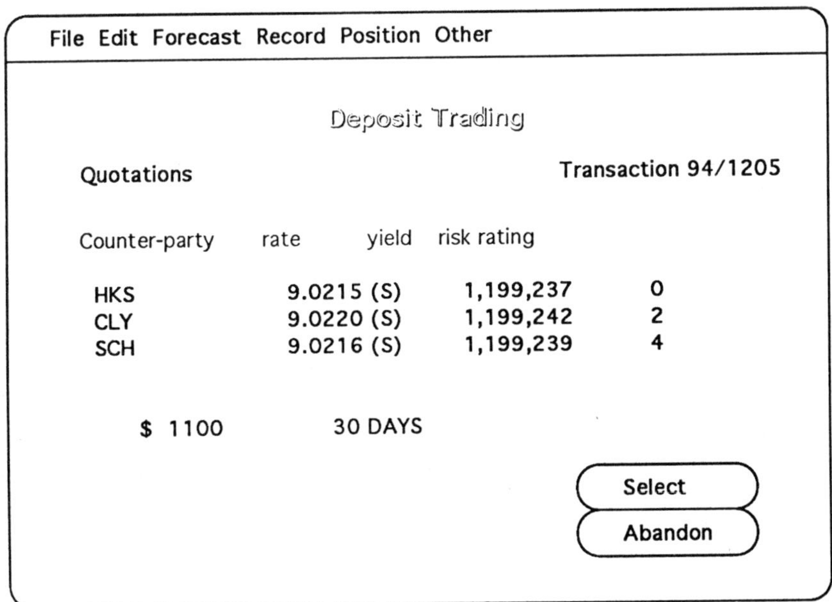

Figure 12.21 *Screen showing quotations and evaluation of deals.*

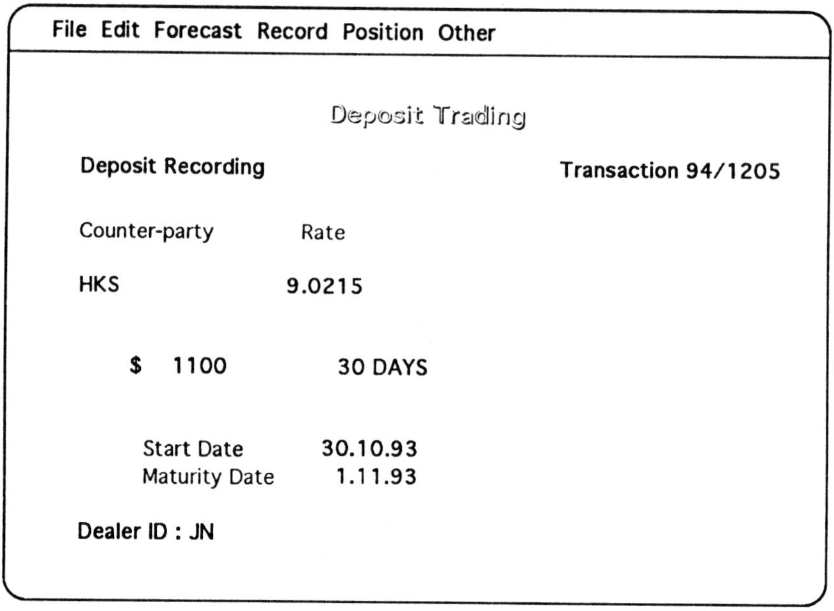

File Edit Forecast Record Position Other

Deposit Trading

Deposit Recording **Transaction 94/1205**

Counter-party Rate

HKS 9.0215

$ 1100 30 DAYS

Start Date 30.10.93
Maturity Date 1.11.93

Dealer ID : JN

Figure 12.22 Screen showing the Record-Deal display.

References

ACM (1992). ACM SIGCHI *Curricula for Human–Computer Interaction: Report of ACM Curriculum Development SIG*. ACM Press, Baltimore, MD.

Alexander, H. (1987). *Formally-based Tools and Techniques for Human–Computer Dialogues*. Ellis Horwood, Chichester.

Andre, E. and Rist, W. (1990). *Generating Illustrated Documents: A Plan Based Approach*. InfoJapan 90, Vol. 2, 163–170.

Annett, J. K. *et al.* (1971). *Task Analysis*. HMSO, London.

Apple Computers Inc. (1987). *Apple Human Interface Guidelines: The Apple Desktop Interface*. Apple Inc./Addison-Wesley, Cupertino, CA.

Baddeley, A. S. (1979). *Your Memory: A User's Guide*. Pelican, London.

Baeker, R. M. and Buxton, W. A. S. (Eds.) (1987). *Readings in Human–Computer Interaction: A Multidisciplinary Approach*. Morgan Kaufman, Los Altos, CA.

Bailey, R. W. (1982). *Human Performance Engineering: A Guide for System Designers*. Prentice-Hall, Englewood Cliffs, NJ.

Barnard, P. (1991). Bridging between Basic Theories and the Artefacts of Human–Computer Interaction. In Carroll, J. M. (Ed.), *Designing Interaction: Psychology at The Human–Computer Interface*. Cambridge University Press.

Barnard, P., Wilson, M. and Maclean, A. (1988). Approximate Modelling of Cognitive Activity with an Expert System: A Theory-based Strategy for Developing an Interactive Design Tool, *Computer Journal*, **31**(5), 445–456.

Bass, L. and Coutaz, J. (1991). *Developing Software for the User Interface*. Addison-Wesley, Reading, MA.

Belkin, N., Canter, L. and Rivers, R. (1985). Characterising User Navigation through Complex Data Structures, *Behaviour and Information Technology*, **4**(2), 93–102.

Bellotti, V. (1988). Implications of Current Design Practice for the Use of HCI Techniques. In Jones, D. M. and Winder, R. (Eds.), *People and Computers*, IV (HCI-88). Cambridge University Press, pp. 79–96.

Bevan, N. and Macleod M. (1994), Usability Measurement in Context. *Behaviour and Information Technology*, **13**(1–2), 132–145.

Breuker, J. A. (1990). *EUROHELP: Developing Intelligent Help Systems.* Report on Esprit project 280.

Brown, C. M. (1988). *Human–Computer Interface Design Guidelines*. Ablex, Norwood, NJ.

Bubenko, J. (1993). Extending the Scope of Information Modelling. In *Proceedings of The Fourth International Workshop on the Deductive Approach to Information Systems and Databases*, Lloret, Costa Brava, Research Report DSV 93-034, SISU, Stockholm.

Bush, V. (1945). As We May Think, *Atlantic Monthly*, **176**(1), 101–108. Reprinted in

Nyce and Kahn (1991).

Card, S. K., Moran, T.P. and Newell, A. (1983). *The Psychology of Human–Computer Interaction*. Lawrence Erlbaum Associates, Hillsdale, NJ.

Card, S. K., Robertson, G. and Mackinlay, J. (1991). The Information Visualiser: An Information Workspace. In Proceedings of CHI'91: *Human Factors in Computer Systems*. ACM Press, New York, pp. 181–188.

Carroll, J. M. (1989). Feeding the Interface Eaters. In Sutcliffe, A. G. and Macaulay, L. (Eds.), *People and Computers V*. Cambridge University Press, pp. 35–48.

Carroll, J. M. (1990). *The Nurnberg Funnel: Designing Minimalist Instruction for Practical Computer Skill.* MIT Press, Cambridge Mass.

Carroll, J. M. (Ed.) (1991). *Designing Interaction: Psychology at the Human–Computer Interface*. (Cambridge Series in Human–Computer Interaction.) Cambridge University Press.

Carroll, J. M., Kellogg, W. A. and Rosson, M. B. (1991). The Task–Artifact Cycle. In Carroll, J. M. (Ed.), *Designing Interaction: Psychology at the Human–Computer Interface*. Cambridge University Press, pp. 74–102.

Cawsey, A. (1993). *Explanation and Interaction: The Computer Generation of Explanatory Dialogues*. MIT Press/Bradford Books, Cambridge, Mass.

Checkland, P. (1981). *Systems Thinking, Systems Practice*, Wiley.

Christie, B. and Gardiner, M. M. (1987). *Applying Cognitive Psychology to User Interface Design*. Wiley, London.

Clancey, W. and Shortliffe, J. (1984). *Readings in Medical Artificial Intelligence: The First Decade*. Addison-Wesley, Reading, MA.

Coad, P. and Yourdon, E. (1991). *Object Oriented Analysis*. Yourdon Press, Englewood Cliffs, NJ.

Conklin, J. (1987). Hypertext: An Introduction and Survey, *IEEE Computer*, **20**(9), 17–41.

Conklin, J. and Begeman, M. L. (1988). A Hypertext Tool for Exploratory Policy Discussion, *ACM Transactions On Office Information Systems*, **6**(4), 140–151.

Coutaz, J. (1989). UIMS: Promises, Failures and Trends. In Sutcliffe, A. G. and Macaulay, L. (Eds.), *People and Computers V*. Cambridge University Press.

Damodaran, L., Simpson, A. and Wilson, P. (1980). *Designing Systems for People*. NCC Press/University of Loughborough.

De Marco, T. (1978). *Structured Systems Analysis and System Specification*. Yourdon Press, New York.

Dix, A. J. (1991). *Formal Methods for Interactive Systems*. Academic Press. London.

Dix, A. J. and Runciman, C. (1985). Abstract Models of Interactive Systems. In Johnson, P. and Cook, S. (Eds.), *People and Computers IV* (HCI-88), Cambridge University Press, pp. 13–22.

Eason, K. D. (1988). *Information Technology and Organisational Change*. Taylor and Francis, London.

Eason, K. D. and Harker, S. (1989). *An Open Systems Approach to Task Analysis*. HUSAT Research Centre, Loughborough University of Technology.

Edmonds, E. A. (Ed.) (1992). *The Separable User Interface*. Academic Press, London.

Elsom-Cook, M. (1990). Guided Discovery Tutoring. In Elsom-Cook, M. (Ed.), *Guided Discovery Tutoring*. Paul Chapman Publishing, London, pp. 3–23.

Ericsson, K. A. and Simon, H. A. (1985). *Protocol Analysis: Verbal Report As Data*. MIT Press, Cambridge, MA.

F3 (1993). *The F3 Reference Manual*. SISU, Box 1250, Kista, Sweden.

Feiner, S. and McKeown, K. R. (1990). Generating Coordinated Multimedia Explanations. In *Proceedings of 6th IEEE Conference on Artificial Intelligence Applications*. Santa Barbara, CA, pp. 290–296.

Fowler, C. *et al.* (1988). User Skills and Task Match (USTM): A Human Factors Based Methodology for Determining Product Requirements. In *Proceedings of the Fourth Alvey Conference*, Swansea.

Frisby, J. P. (1979). *Seeing: Illusion, Brain and Mind*. Oxford University Press.

Fry, D. B. (1977). *Homo Loquens*. Cambridge University Press.

Galer, M. (1987). *The Applied Ergonomics Handbook*. Butterworths, London.

Galitz, W. O. (1987). *Handbook of Screen Format Design*. 2nd edn. QED Publications, Wellesley, MA.

Gane, C. and Sarson T. (1979). *Structured Systems Analysis: Tools and Techniques*. Prentice-Hall, Englewood Cliffs, NJ.

Gentner, D. and Stevens, A. L. (1983). *Mental Models*. Lawrence Erlbaum Associates, Hillsdale, NJ.

Gibson, J. J. (1966). *The Senses Considered as Perceptual Systems*. Houghton Mifflin, Boston.

Gilbert, N. (1987). Question and Answer Types. In Moralee, D. S. (Ed.), *Research and Development in Expert Systems IV*, Cambridge University Press.

Glass, A. L., Holyoak, K. J. and Santa, J. L. (1979). *Cognition*. Addison-Wesley, Reading, MA.

Gould, J. D. (1987). How to Design Usable Systems. In Bullinger, H.-J. and Shackel, B. (Eds.), *Proceedings Interact 87*. North-Holland, Amsterdam.

Greenberg, S. (Ed.) (1991). *Computer-supported Cooperative Work and Groupware*. Academic Press, New York.

Hall, W. *et al.* (1992). Towards an Integrated Information Environment with Open Hypermedia. In *Proceedings of ECHT '92, 4th ACM Hypertext Conference*.

Hammer, M. and Champney, J. (1993). *Re-Engineering the Corporation: A Manifesto for Business Revolution*. Harper Collins, New York.

Harel, D. (1988). On Visual Formalisms, *Communications of the ACM*, **31**(5), 514–530.

Harker, S. D. P. and Eason, K. D. (Eds.) (1989). *The Application of Information Technology*. Taylor and Francis, London.

Harker, S. D. P. *et al.* (1993). The Change and Evolution of Requirements as a Challenge to the Practice of Software Engineering, *IEEE Symposium on Requirements Engineering*, RE '93, San Diego, CA, Jan. 4–6, pp. 266–272.

Harris, D. H. (1984). Human Factors Success Stories. In *Proceedings 28th Annual Meeting of the Human Factors Society*, pp. 1–5.

Harrison, M. D. and Barnard, P. (1993). On Defining Requirements for Interaction. In *Proceedings of IEEE International Symposium on Requirements Engineering*,

January 4–6, San Diego. IEEE Computer Society Press.

Harrison, M. D. and Thimbleby, H. W. (1985). Formalising Guidelines for the Design of Interactive Systems. In Johnson, P. and Cook, S. (Eds.), *People and Computers: Designing the Interface*. Cambridge University Press, pp. 161–171.

Harrison, M. D. and Thimbleby, H. W. (Eds.) (1990). *Formal Methods in Human–Computer Interaction*. Cambridge University Press.

Hellander, M. (Ed.) (1988). *Handbook of Human–Computer Interaction*. North-Holland, Amsterdam.

Hitch, G. J. (1987). Working Memory. In Christie, B. and Gardiner, M. M. (Eds.), *Applying Cognitive Psychology to User Interface Design*. Wiley, London.

Hix, D. and Hartson, H. R. (1993). *Developing User Interfaces: Ensuring Usability Through Product and Process*. John Wiley, New York.

Hollnagel, E. (1993). *Human Reliability Analysis: Context and Control*. Academic Press, London.

IBM (1991). *Systems Applications Architecture: Common User Access Guide to User Interface Design*. IBM.

ISO-9421 (1994). *Ergonomic Requirements for Office Work with Visual Display Terminals*. International Standards Organization.

Johnson, P. (1992). *Human–Computer Interaction: Psychology, Task Analysis and Software Engineering*. McGraw-Hill, London.

Johnson, P. *et al.* (1988). Task Related Knowledge Structures: Analysis, Modelling and Applications. In Jones, D. M. and Winder, R. (Eds.), *People and Computers: From Research to Implementation*. Cambridge University Press, pp. 35–62.

Johnson, P. *et al.* (1993). Beyond Hacking: A Model-based Approach to User Interface Development. In Alty, J. L. and Guest, S. (Eds.), *People and Computers, VIII* (HCI-93). Cambridge University Press.

Johnson-Laird, P. N. (1983). *Mental Models: Towards a Cognitive Science of Language, Inference and Consciousness*. Cambridge University Press.

Karat, C. (1990). Cost Benefit Analysis in Iterative Usability Testing. In Cockton, G. *et al.* (Eds.), *Proceedings of INTERACT-90*. IFIP/North-Holland, Amsterdam.

Kieras, D. E. and Polson, P. G. (1985). An Approach to the Formal Analysis of User Complexity, *International Journal of Man–Machine Studies*, **22**, 365–394.

Land, E. F. and Kennedy Macgregor, M. (1987). Information and Information Systems: Concepts and Perspective. In Galliers, R., *Information Analysis: Selected Readings*, Addison-Wesley.

Lewis, C. *et al.* (1990). Testing a Walkthrough Methodology for Theory-Based Design of Walk-up-and-use Interfaces. In Chew, J. R. and Whiteside, J. (Eds.), *Proceedings CHI-90*. ACM Press, pp. 235–241.

Lindsay, P. H. and Norman, D. A. (1977). *Human Information Processing: An Introduction to Psychology*. Academic Press, London.

Long, J. B. and Dowell, J. (1989). Conceptions of the Discipline of HCI: Craft, Applied Science and Engineering. In Sutcliffe, A. G. and Macaulay, L. (Eds.), *People and Computers V*. Cambridge University Press.

Longworth, G. and Nicholls, D. (1987). *The SSADM Manual*. NCC.

Luo, P., Szekely, P. and Neches, R. (1993). Management of Interface Design in HUMANOID. In *Proceedings of INTERCHI '93*. ACM/Addison-Wesley, Reading, MD, pp. 107–114.

Maclean, A. *et al.* (1991). Questions, Options and Criteria: Elements of Design Space Analysis, *Human–Computer Interaction*, **6**(3 & 4), 201–250.

Malone, T. W. *et al.* (1987). Semi-Structured Messages Are Surprisingly Useful for Computer Support Coordination, *ACM Transactions On Office Information Systems*, **5**(2), 115–131.

Mann, W. and Thompson, S. (1988). Rhetorical Structure Theory: Toward a Functional Theory of Text Organisation, *Text*, **6**(3), 243–281.

Marcus, A. (1992). *Graphic Design for Electronic Documents and User Interfaces*. ACM Press, New York.

Marr, D. (1982). *Vision*. Oxford University Press.

Martin, J. (1973). *Design of Man Computer Dialogues*. Prentice-Hall, Englewood Cliffs, NJ.

Maslow, A. H. (1987). *Motivation and Personality*. Harper and Row, New York.

Maybury, M. T. (1990). Custom Explanation: Exploiting User Models to Plan Multi-Sentential Text. In *Proceedings of Second International Workshop on User Modelling*, Hawaii.

Maybury, M. T. (1993). (Ed.), *Intelligent Multi Media Interfaces*. AAAI/MIT Press, Cambridge, Mass.

Mayhew, D. J. (1992). *Principles and Guidelines for Software User Interface Design*. Prentice-Hall, Englewood Cliffs, NJ.

Miller, G. A. (1956). The Magical Number Seven, Plus or Minus Two: Some Limits on Our Capacity to Process Information, *Psychological Review*, **63**(2), 81–97.

Moore, J. D. and Swartout, W. R. (1989). A Reactive Approach to Explanation. In *Proceedings of the Eleventh IJCAI*, Detroit, pp. 1504–1510.

Moore, J. D. and Swartout, W. R. (1991). A Reactive Approach to Explanation: Taking the User's Feedback into Account. In Paris, C. L., Swartout, W. R. and Mann, W. C. (Eds.), *Natural Language Generation in Artificial Intelligence and Computational Linguistics*. Kluwer, Dordrecht.

Mumford, E. (1983). *Designing Participatively*. Manchester Business School Publications.

Myers, B. A. (1991). *GARNET*. IEEE Software.

Myers, B. A. (1993). State of the Art in User Interface Software Tools. In Hartson, H. R. and Hix, D. (Eds.), *Advances in Human–Computer Interaction*. Ablex, Norwood, NJ, pp. 11–28.

Mylopoulos, J. *et al.* (1992). Representing and Using Non-functional Requirements: A Process-oriented Approach, *IEEE Transactions on Software Engineering*, **18**(6), 483–497.

Nelson, T. (1987). *Literary Machines*. OWL International.

Newell, A. and Simon, H. (1972). *Human Problem Solving*. Prentice-Hall, Englewood Cliffs, NJ.

Nielsen, J. (1990). Traditional Dialogue Design Applied to Modern User Interfaces,

Communications of the ACM, **33**, 109–118.

Nielsen, J. (1993a). *Hypertext and Hypermedia*. Academic Press, London.

Nielsen, J. (1993b). *Usability Engineering*. Academic Press, New York.

Nielsen, J. and Molich, R. (1990). Heuristic Evaluation of User Interfaces. In *Empowering People: CHI '90 Conference Proceedings*. ACM Press, New York.

Norman, D. A. (1986). Cognitive Engineering. In Norman, D. A. and Draper, S. W. (Eds.), *User Centered System Design: New Perspectives on Human–Computer Interaction*. Lawrence Erlbaum Associates, Hillsdale, NJ, pp. 31–61.

Norman, D. A. (1988). *The Psychology of Everyday Things*. Basic Books.

Nyce, J. M. and Kahn, P. (1991). *From Memex to Hypertext*. Academic Press, London.

Payne, S. J. and Green, T. R. G. (1986). Task Action Grammars: A Model of the Mental Representation of Task Languages, *Human–Computer Interaction*, **2**(2), pp. 93–133.

Preece, J. *et al.* (1994). *Human–Computer Interaction*. Addison-Wesley, Reading, MA.

Rasmussen (1986). Information Processing. In *Human–Computer Interaction: An Approach to Cognitive Engineering*. North-Holland, Amsterdam.

Ravden, S. and Johnson, G. (1989). *Evaluating Usability of Human–Computer Interfaces*. Ellis Horwood, New York.

Reason, J. (1990). *Human Error*. Cambridge University Press.

Reisner, P. (1984). Formal Grammar as a Tool for Analysing Ease of Use: Some Fundamental Concepts. In Thomas, J. C. and Schneider, M. L., *Human Factors in Computing Systems*. Ablex, Norwood, NJ.

Richter, M. H. and Clancey, W. J. (1985). GUIDON-WATCH: A Graphical Interface for Viewing a Knowledge-based System, *IEEE Computer Graphics and Applications*, **5**(1).

Rumelhart, D. E. and McClelland, J. H. (1987). *Parallel Distributed Processing*, Vols. 1 and 2. MIT Press, Cambridge, MA.

Russell D. M. *et al.* (1993). The Cost Structure of Sensemaking. In Ashlund, S. *et al.* (Eds.), *Proceedings of INTERCHI '93, Human Factor in Computing Systems*. ACM Press, pp. 269–274.

Sacks, H., Schlegoff, E. and Jefferson, G. (1974). A Simplest Systematics for the Organisation of Turn Taking for Conversation, *Language*, **50**, 696–735.

Sarantinos, E. and Johnson, P. (1991). Explanation Dialogues: Question Disambiguation and Test Generation. In *Proceedings of the Eleventh International Conference on Expert Systems and Their Applications*. Avignon.

Schank, R. C. (1982). Dynamic Memory: A Theory of Reminding and Learning. In *Computers and People*. Cambridge University Press.

Searle, J. R. (1969). Speech Acts: An Essay on Conversation. In Ellis, D. G. and. Donohue, W. A. (Eds.), *Contemporary Issues in Language and Discourse Processes*. Lawrence Erlbaum Associates, Hillsdale, NJ, pp. 7–19.

Self, J. A. (1988). Bypassing the Intractable Problem of Student Modelling. In *Proceedings of ITS-88*, June 1–3, Montreal, pp. 18–24.

Shackel, B. (1986). Ergonomics in Design for Usability. In Harrison, M. D. and Monk, A. F. (Eds.), *People and Computers: Designing for Usability*. Cambridge University

Press.

Shneiderman, B. (1981). Multi-party Grammars and Related Features for Defining Interactive Systems, *IEEE Transaction on Systems, Machines and Cybernetics*, **12**, 148–154.

Shneiderman, B. (1987). *Designing the User Interface: Strategies for Effective Human–Computer Interaction*. Addison-Wesley, New York.

Smith, S. and Mosier, J. N. (1986). *Design Guidelines for User–System Interface Software*. Mitre Corp., Bedford, MA.

SSADM User Group (1993). *SSADM and GUI Design: A Project Manager's Guide*. International SSADM User Group, 11 Burlings Lane, Knockholt, Kent TN14 7PB.

Stewart, T. (1991). *Directory of HCI Standards*. DTI/HMSO.

Sufrin, B. (1982). Formal Specification of a Display Editor, *Science of Computer Programming*, **1**, pp. 157–202.

Sutcliffe, A. G. and Springett, M. V. (1992). From User's Problems to Design Errors: Linking Evaluation to Improving Design Practice. In Monk, A. F., Diaper, D. and Harrison, M. D. (Eds.), *People and Computers VII*. Cambridge University Press.

Sutcliffe, A. G. and Wang, I. (1991). Integrating Human–Computer Interaction with Jackson System Development, *Computer Journal*, **34**(2), 132–142.

Swartout, W. (1983). XPLAIN: A System for Creating and Explaining Expert Consulting Programs, *Artifical Intelligence*, **21**, 285–325.

Thimbleby, H. W. (1990). *User Interface Design*. ACM Press/Addison-Wesley, New York.

Travis D. (1991). *Effective Colour Displays, Theory and Practice*. People and Computer Series. Academic Press, London.

Tufte, E. R. (1990). *Envisioning Information*. Graphics Press, Cheshire, Conn.

Tullis, T. S. (1986). Optimising the Usability of Computer Generated Displays. In Harrison, M. D. and Monk, A. F. (Eds.), *People and Computers: Designing for Usability*. Cambridge University Press.

Warren, R. M. and Warren, R. P. (1970). Auditory Illusions and Confusions, *Scientific American*, **223**, 30–36.

Waterworth, J. A. (1991). *Multimedia: Technology and Applications*. Ellis Horwood, New York.

Waterworth, J. A. (1992). *Multimedia Interaction with Computers: Human Factors Issues*. Ellis Horwood, New York.

Wenger, E. (1987). *Artificial Intelligence and Tutoring Sytems: Computational Approaches to the Communication of Knowledge*. Morgan-Kaufman, Los Altos, CA.

Whitefield, A., Wilson, F. and Dowell, J. (1991). A Framework for Human Factors Evaluation, *Behaviour and Information Technology*, **10**(1), 65–79.

Whiteside, J., Bennett, J. and Holzblatt, K. (1988). Usability Engineering: Our Experience and Evolution. In Hellander, M. (Ed.), *Handbook of Human–Computer Interaction*. North-Holland, Amsterdam, pp. 791–817.

Wright, P. and Monk, A. F. (1989). Evaluation for Design. In Sutcliffe, A. G. and Macaulay, L. (Eds.), *People and Computers V*. Cambridge University Press.

For those wishing to explore the literature further, the following journals and series of conference papers are well worth consulting:

Behaviour and Information Technology
Human–Computer Interaction
Interacting with Computers
International Journal of Human–Computer Studies (Formerly *International Journal of Man Machine Studies*)

CHI Series, *Proceedings of the ACM Conferences on Computer Human Interaction*, ACM Press, 1983–
HCI Series, *Proceedings of the BCS Conferences on Human–Computer Interaction*, Cambridge University Press, 1985–
INTERACT Series, *Proceedings of the IEEE/IFIP Conferences on Human–Computer Interaction*, North-Holland, Amsterdam, 1984–

Index